Life and Society
IN THE
Early Spanish Caribbean

Life and Society in the Early Spanish Caribbean

THE GREATER ANTILLES
1493–1550

Ida Altman

LOUISIANA STATE UNIVERSITY PRESS
BATON ROUGE

Published by Louisiana State University Press
lsupress.org

Copyright © 2021 by Louisiana State University Press
All rights reserved. Except in the case of brief quotations used in articles or reviews, no part of this publication may be reproduced or transmitted in any format or by any means without written permission of Louisiana State University Press.

DESIGNER: Michelle A. Neustrom
TYPEFACE: Arno Pro

The maps were created by Michael Waylen.

Cover illustration: Sketch of Santo Domingo by Juan Escalante de Mendoza, ca. 1570s, from his "Itinerario de navegación de las mares y tierras occidentales," MS in Museo Naval, Madrid.

LIBRARY OF CONGRESS CATALOGING-IN-PUBLICATION DATA
Names: Altman, Ida, author.
Title: Life and society in the early Spanish Caribbean : the Greater Antilles, 1493–1550 / Ida Altman.
Description: Baton Rouge : Louisiana State University Press, [2021] | Includes bibliographical references and index.
Identifiers: LCCN 2021000251 (print) | LCCN 2021000252 (ebook) | ISBN 978-0-8071-7597-2 (cloth) | ISBN 978-0-8071-7578-1 (paperback) | ISBN 978-0-8071-7618-4 (pdf) | ISBN 978-0-8071-7619-1 (epub)
Subjects: LCSH: Antilles, Greater—History—16th century. | Antilles, Greater—Ethnic relations. | Antilles, Greater—Social conditions. | Antilles, Greater—Relations—Spain. | Spain—Relations—Antilles, Greater. | Spain—Colonies—Antilles, Greater—Administration.
Classification: LCC F1741 .A46 2021 (print) | LCC F1741 (ebook) | DDC 972.9/02—dc23
LC record available at https://lccn.loc.gov/2021000251
LC ebook record available at https://lccn.loc.gov/2021000252

CONTENTS

PREFACE vii
TIMELINE OF THE EARLY SPANISH CARIBBEAN xi
MAPS xiii

Introduction 1
1. Creating a Spanish Caribbean 7
2. Death and Danger in the Islands 35
3. Government, Politics, and the Law 66
4. Church and Clergy 99
5. Transitions 132
6. Women and Family 161
Conclusion: Caribbean Connections 192

GLOSSARY 209
NOTES 215
BIBLIOGRAPHY 261
INDEX 273

PREFACE

My interest in the early Spanish Caribbean dates back many years. While doing doctoral work in history at Johns Hopkins University, I wrote a paper on Spanish society in Mexico City following the conquest. That research led me to wonder about not only the peninsular origins of the Spaniards who went to live in Mexico but also the connections between early society there and in the Caribbean, a topic that seemed surprisingly understudied; surely that history would have important implications for understanding subsequent developments in New Spain and elsewhere in Spanish America. That paper eventually became an article entitled "Spanish Society in Mexico City after the Conquest," published in the *Hispanic American Historical Review*. Notwithstanding its limitations, the article pointed to significant precedents for Mexican society in the Caribbean, noting, for example, "Squabbles between local and crown officials and the extensive involvement of all of them in the local economy (including trade in Indian slaves) . . . and the claims and presumptions of the Colóns and first conquerors all played a prominent part in ordering society in the Caribbean, as would similar factors in early Mexico and Peru" (445).

In 1990 I received funding from the National Endowment for the Humanities that allowed me to spend part of a summer doing research at the Archive of the Indies in Seville, which houses nearly all the extant documentation on the Spanish Caribbean in the first half of the sixteenth century. Although I used much of the material I found in one way or another, I did not pursue the research and indeed only returned to it, tentatively, when I received a yearlong grant from NEH in the mid-2000s. Although most of that fellowship period was devoted to another project, I also looked for sources on an Indigenous revolt led by the man known as Enriquillo, or Enrique, that took place in Hispaniola in the first third of the sixteenth century. The result was the 2007 publication of "The Revolt of Enriquillo and the Historiography of Early Spanish America," an article focused on his life and rebellion and their implications for our understanding of the early Spanish Caribbean and the rest of Spanish America.

That article probably has been read more than everything else I have published, most likely because of the human appeal of Enrique's story but perhaps also because we know so little about the time and place in which he lived. Writing about Enrique helped to convince me that the history of the Spanish Caribbean in the first half of the sixteenth century merited serious consideration. For many years it has received such attention from Hispanophone scholars, who have combed the archives for relevant material, transcribing and publishing many volumes of original documents—an enormous boon to scholarship. In more recent years, especially, these scholars have used this material to address the history of Spaniards' settlement of the Greater Antilles and the impact of their presence on the Indigenous peoples of the islands and the enslaved Africans whom Europeans brought to the Caribbean.

I am beholden to scholars such as Esteban Mira Caballos, Genaro Rodríguez Morel, Jalil Sued Badillo, and Francisco Moscoso for their studies of early institutional and socioeconomic development and the labor regimen that was imposed in the Greater Antilles, to Consuelo Varela for her research on Columbus and the period in which he was active, and to Juan Gil for his work on Columbus and the years that followed. Their extensive research in the archives greatly enriches this study. I discuss the historiography of the sixteenth-century Spanish Caribbean in my article "The Spanish Caribbean, 1492–1550" and in the introduction to *The Spanish Caribbean & the Atlantic World in the Long Sixteenth Century*, a book coedited with David Wheat. It is my hope that, among other things, the present book will help to familiarize an English-speaking audience with this important scholarship.

I have been most fortunate in the friends, colleagues, and students who have shared ideas, insights, and even their research and documents and encouraged me to bring this work to completion. First and foremost I thank David Wheat, who over the years has provided much-appreciated advice, insight, and reflections based on his own extensive research and scholarship, as well as documents, bibliography, and assurance that writing the book was worth the effort. (I hope that has proved true.) I am very grateful as well to James

Boyden, Shannon Lalor, Thiago Krause, and an anonymous reviewer who read the entire manuscript and provided thoughtful and valuable suggestions. I also thank the many people who over the years have helped me to clarify my thinking and aims in this research or have read and discussed parts of the manuscript. In no particular order, these include Sarah Cline, Kris Lane, Brian Hamm, Cacey Farnsworth, Nina Caputo, Oren Okhovat, Sara T. Nalle, Gabriel Aviles de Rocha, Stuart Schwartz, Matt Childs, Philip Morgan, Richard Kagan, and Franklin Knight. Many thanks to Judith Oppenheimer and Dan Hubbell for listening and responding kindly to my expressions of self-doubt. Paul Losch, former director of the University of Florida Latin American Library, was an unfailing source of support. I also thank Laurie Taylor, senior director for library technologies and digital strategies at the University of Florida, for incorporating into the Digital Library of the Caribbean the biographical file related to this book. I am very fortunate to have had Alisa Plant, director of LSU Press and dear friend, as my editor. I wish to thank as well the managing editor, Catherine Kadair, for her help and excellent work, and Michael Waylen for the maps.

I finished writing this book in early 2020 as the coronavirus pandemic was reaching the United States, bringing echoes of the devastating diseases that in the past ravaged, and in some places nearly obliterated, entire groups of people. In the first half of the sixteenth century the Greater Antilles was such a place. This book is dedicated to the memory of the Indigenous people of the early Spanish Caribbean, to the many victims of COVID-19, especially the heartbreakingly disproportionate numbers of Native Americans and people of color whose deaths in the United States were largely preventable, and to all the health care workers—doctors, nurses, technicians, orderlies, custodians—who gave their lives working to save them. It is dedicated as well to the memory of Richmond F. Brown.

TIMELINE OF THE EARLY SPANISH CARIBBEAN

October 1492	Europeans make landfall in the Bahamas
December 1492	The *Santa María* runs aground off the coast of Hispaniola
January 1493	Columbus departs Hispaniola, leaving behind thirty-nine Spaniards
November 1493	Columbus's second voyage reaches destroyed fort of La Navidad
December 1493	Site of La Isabela chosen on north coast of Hispaniola
1496	Founding of Santo Domingo
August 1500	Francisco de Bobadilla arrives in Hispaniola as governor
November 1500	Columbus and his brothers arrive back in Spain
April 1502	Frey Nicolás de Ovando arrives in Hispaniola as governor
June 1502	Fleet carrying Bobadilla wrecked in hurricane
January 1503	*Casa de la Contratación* established in Seville
June 1503–04	Columbus stranded on Jamaica
May 1506	Columbus dies in Valladolid
1508	Miguel de Pasamonte sent as treasurer-general of the Indies
	Spanish occupation of Puerto Rico
1509	Spanish occupation of Jamaica
July 1509	Don Diego Colón and doña María de Toledo arrive in Hispaniola

September 1509	Ovando returns to Spain
1510	Founding of Darién (Panama)
1511	Indigenous revolt begins in Puerto Rico
	Spanish occupation of Cuba
December 1511	Fray Antonio Montesino preaches famous sermon
1512	Promulgation of Laws of Burgos (amended 1513)
	Three appellate judges sent to Hispaniola
1514	*Repartimiento* reassigning remaining Indians of Hispaniola
1516	Hieronymites sent to Hispaniola
1518	First smallpox epidemic in the islands
	Hieronymites depart Hispaniola
1519	Beginning of revolt of Enriquillo (Enrique) in Hispaniola
	Creation of Real Audiencia of Santo Domingo
	Departure of Hernando Cortés expedition from Cuba to Mexico
1520	Departure of Pánfilo de Narváez from Cuba to Mexico
1521	Death of Juan Ponce de León
1524	Spanish crown creates the Council of the Indies
1526	Death of don Diego Colón
	Death of Lucas Vázquez de Ayllón
1533	Treaty signed with Enrique

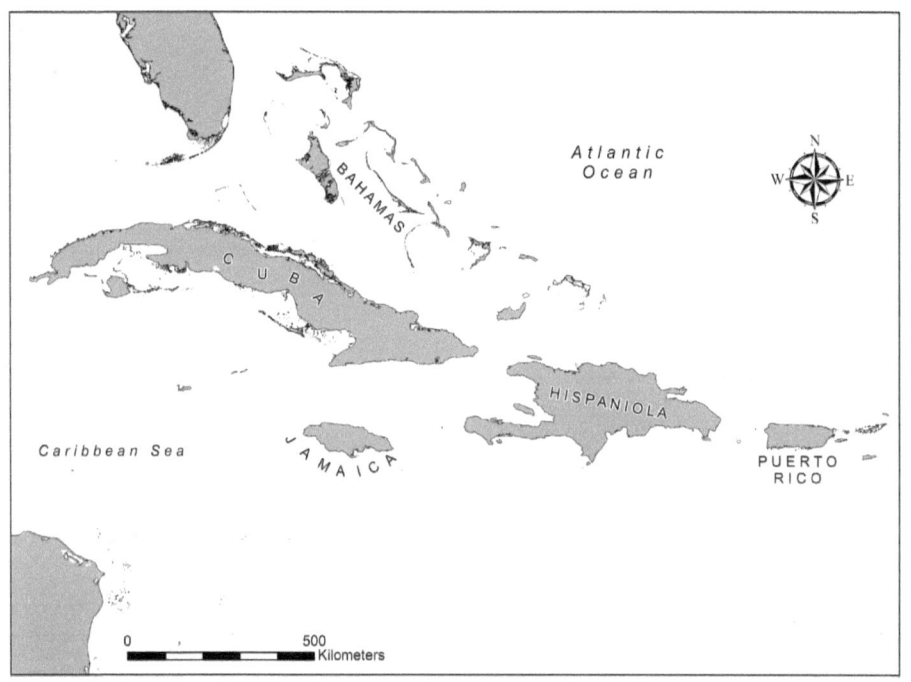

The Greater Antilles

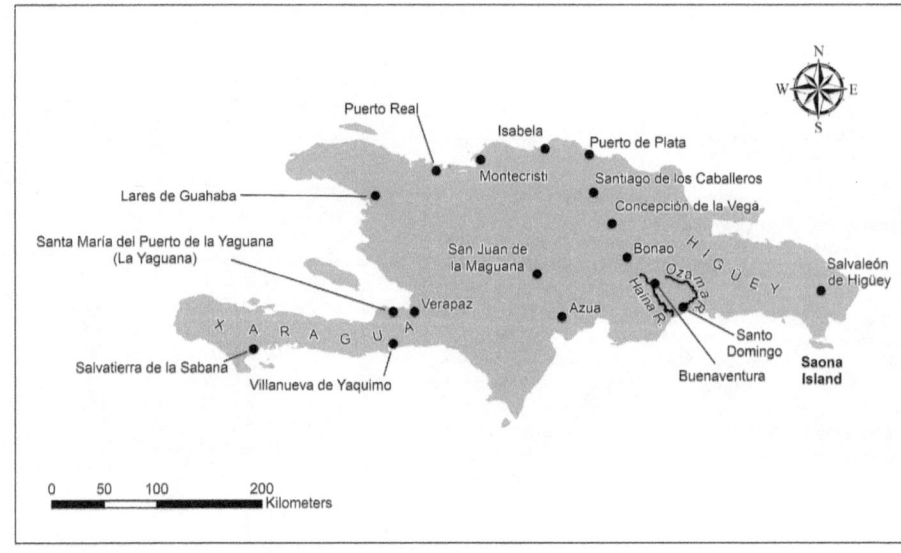

Hispaniola
(Hayti, La Española)

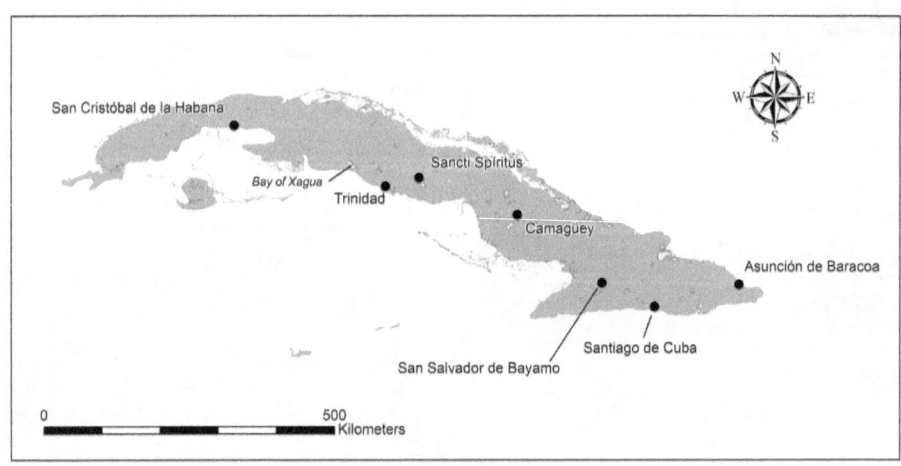

Cuba
(Isla Fernandina)

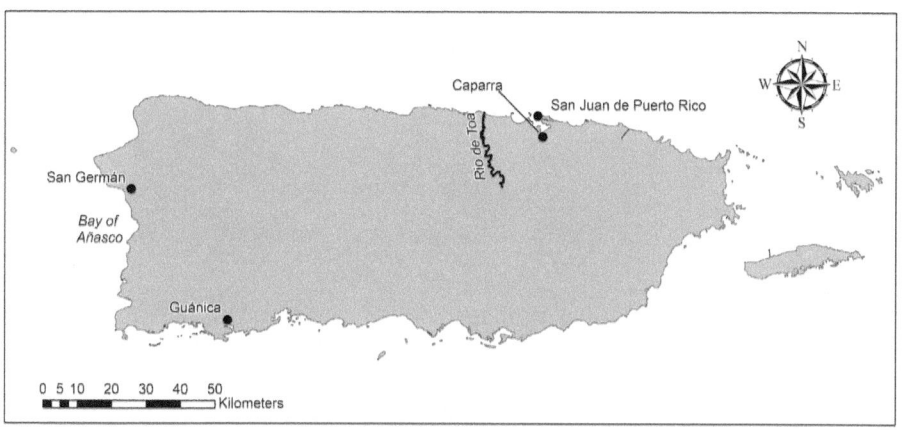

Puerto Rico
(Boriquen, San Juan)

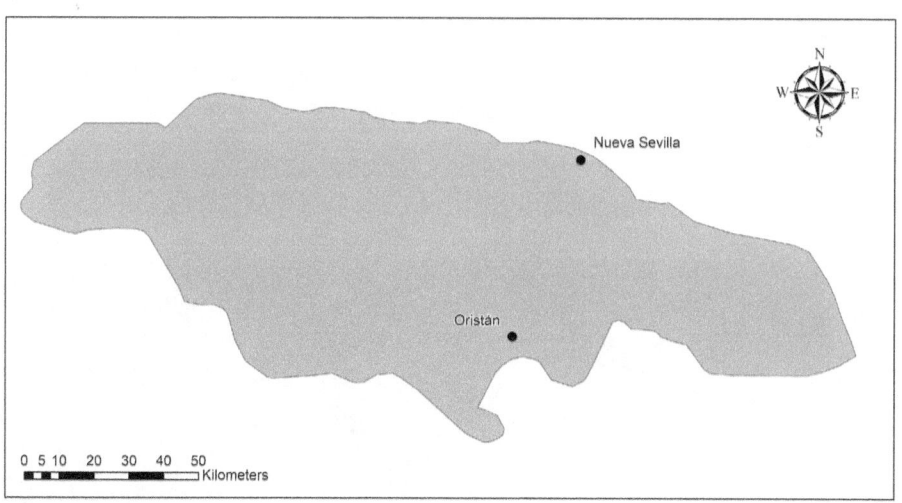

Jamaica

Life and Society
IN THE
Early Spanish Caribbean

Introduction

In the large islands of the northern Caribbean, Spaniards played a leading role in forging new societies that differed radically from the Indigenous ones that they largely replaced. Rooted in exploitation and violence, the socioeconomic systems that emerged following Columbus's first two voyages were profoundly unequal and coercive in nature. In the earliest years, in principle, only Europeans enjoyed freedom of movement and choice as they imposed their will and objectives on Indigenous residents of the Greater Antilles and on the Africans they brought to supplement their labor force, producing a range of unfree statuses that all functioned in much the same ways, even if legally they were distinct. Indians could be *encomienda* workers, permanent servants (*naborías*), or slaves, but in all cases they were subject to Spanish labor demands, strictures, and punishments, or to the threat of them, as were enslaved Blacks.

In reality, of course, the distinction between the European minority and a much larger unfree population never was as clear as it was in theory. From the earliest years, there were at least some free Blacks. Unknown but substantial numbers of Indians and Blacks rejected the coerced status to which they were consigned, by moving into remote areas or to other islands and resisting Spanish demands by whatever means possible. Spanish authorities experimented with the possibility of establishing "free" Indian communities. Probably of greatest importance in terms of blurring the dichotomy between a free white minority and unfree nonwhite majority, however, was the rapid emergence of a population of mixed Indigenous–African–European descent that was neither enslaved nor part of the quickly diminishing encomiendas. The growth of this group contributed both to an increasing socioeconomic complexity and to the survival of the societies of the Greater Antilles in the face of population loss, as Spaniards left the Caribbean to seek opportunities on the mainland and Indigenous populations nearly disappeared.

The central question this book addresses is what it was like to live in these societies that were forged in violence and structured by coercive relationships that affected nearly every aspect of daily life and enabled the establishment of an economy based on mining, commerce, and agriculture. To an extent, it has been possible to answer this question with regard to the Spanish minority. Official records, although largely administrative and financial in nature, nonetheless contain much detail about individual and collective experience, thanks in part to the existence of petitions to the crown—from private individuals (both men and women), officials, clergymen, town councils, and religious orders. Such petitions frequently included depositions (*probanzas* or *informaciones*) that contained biographical and other details about the petitioner, and often about associates and family members as well. Records that elsewhere have provided important insights into mundane activities, such as notarial documents and parish registers, do not exist for the period, making it difficult to trace lives and careers. Nonetheless, in some instances it has been possible to reconstruct a good deal about the experiences of Spaniards and other Europeans living in the Greater Antilles in the first half of the sixteenth century.

The same cannot be said for the lives of the Indians and Blacks. They appear in the records only at points of interaction with Europeans—and most of those interactions were unequal or coercive. An illustration of this may be seen in the Indigenous testimony taken in conjunction with efforts to create a "free" experimental Indigenous community in Cuba in 1530. In this rare instance in which Indians were summoned to testify, the signs of Spanish mediation and pressure are clear. Testimony was taken via a Spanish interpreter, who at times expressed his contempt for and distrust of the people with whom he dealt, and with only one exception, all the Indigenous witnesses were recorded as saying exactly the same thing. In the sole instance in which a witness deviated from the script, a correction quickly followed. The result, unfortunately, is that little more can be gleaned from the testimony than that functioning Indigenous communities with recognized leaders still existed near San Salvador de Bayamo at that time.[1]

Having to rely mainly on records that are sharply skewed toward Spanish institutions and people means that what can be learned about the experiences of non-Spaniards is largely indirect and contextual. The consequence of that reality, as will be seen throughout this book, is to relegate nonwhites to the shadows while Europeans emerge sharply, to all appearances exercising dominance with little challenge, although that appearance could be, and was, deceptive. Europeans at times struggled to maintain control and to ensure the compliance of the people they sought to dominate. Yet we know little of those struggles from the point of view of non-Europeans. To be sure, archaeological work focusing on contact and postcontact periods in the Caribbean has produced important evidence relating to the impact of Spanish encroachment on Indigenous communities and to the effect of interaction among Europeans, Indians, and Africans on material culture in villages and at the household level.[2] But individual lives and experiences, for the most part, remain elusive in both the historical and archaeological records.

The rebellion led by the *cacique* Enrique (also known as Enriquillo) ended in a treaty by which Spanish officials recognized the autonomy of his community, and this was a significant episode for several reasons—among them, of course, the unusual insight it affords into the life of an Indigenous individual.[3] But while Enrique's rebellion and its outcome remain an important symbol of courage and independence for people in the Dominican Republic, it should be pointed out that, although it was a unique story (for the period) of vindication and Indigenous success, there was a darker side to its outcome. In return for the freedom and autonomy of his community, Enrique accepted the continuing normality of a coercive regime, agreeing to surrender to authorities any escaped Black slaves who subsequently tried to join his community and to pursue any Indians who continued to resist in other parts of the island.[4] In this respect, as in others, Enrique's story encapsulates a reality that defined the big islands in those years: the continuing challenges that Spaniards faced in imposing and maintaining unfree labor systems, their creation of an institutional framework that had to incorporate Indians and Blacks in some fashion, and the presence of religious orders that worked and sometimes empathized with nonwhites (as a boy, Enrique had lived and studied at the Franciscan monastery at Verapaz) but in fact did little to ameliorate the conditions in which they lived and labored.

The implications of the opaqueness of the lives of the nonwhite majority in the first half of the sixteenth century are considerable, an insurmountable problem that skews not only the present study but also longer-term perceptions of the Caribbean as well. The inability to discuss Indians or Blacks as individuals or to explore their lives, as can be done for at least some Spaniards in the Greater Antilles, poses an enormous obstacle to achieving a full and balanced understanding of these societies. It also has affected how the Caribbean has been viewed and understood ever since. The rapid demise of much of the Indigenous population of the Greater Antilles seemingly has discouraged scholars from taking them into serious consideration, and Blacks often have been relegated to the role they played in furnishing labor for Spanish enterprises.[5] Nonetheless, the tendency of Indians and Blacks to move into spaces beyond the control of colonial authorities, and the rapid transformation of smaller towns, estates, and farms in the countryside into ethnically mixed communities, were crucial processes in forging the societies that would take hold and endure in the Caribbean, notwithstanding the peculiar notion that Indigenous mortality and the departures of many Spaniards from the Greater Antilles left these islands nearly empty in the second half of the sixteenth century.

This book is the result of my efforts to examine institutions and society in the four large islands of the Greater Antilles, addressing disease and the risks of living in the islands; government, politics, crime, and law; the relationship between the clergy and society, and the efforts made to evangelize Indians and Blacks; demographic change and the transition from an economy based on gold mining to one that was principally agricultural; and how the circumstances of life in the islands affected women and families. Each of these topics reflects, above all, the experiences of the Spaniards who lived in the islands, but they also can reveal aspects of how Indians and Blacks lived and of the interactions among all social groups.

Although the book offers nothing like a comprehensive or definitive history of the Greater Antilles in the period, my hope is that it provides a basis for understanding a vitally important and yet, until recently, inexplicably overlooked era and place. The explosion of research on the history of the Atlantic world in recent decades might have encouraged greater interest in the early Spanish Caribbean, but, with few exceptions, for many years it did not. Only recently has the Spanish Caribbean begun to figure more prominently in discussions of Atlantic history. The innovative scholarship of recent books such as David Wheat's *Atlantic Africa and the Spanish Caribbean, 1570–1640* and Pablo Gómez's *The Experiential Caribbean,* and of the contributors to Ida Altman and David Wheat's *The Spanish Caribbean & the Atlantic World in the Long Sixteenth Century,* has illuminated little-known but important aspects of the history of the early Spanish Caribbean. Such scholarship on the region and period not only challenges the long-held image of the region as an insignificant backwater but also realigns our understanding of early Spanish America in broader terms. Whereas the so-called core areas of central Mexico and the Andean region once claimed the attention of most historians of early Spanish America, while other regions were consigned to the periphery, in recent years the "fringes"—the Caribbean, above all—have emerged as far more dynamic in their own terms and as more vital to the larger colonial project than was previously understood.

Focus on the Spanish Caribbean in the late fifteenth century and first half of the sixteenth illuminates not only important developments in the Atlantic world and early Spanish America but also crucial transitions in Spain and the Spanish empire. While it was still in the process of consolidating dominion over the Canary Islands, in which members of the traditional Castilian nobility played an important role, the Spanish crown undertook a radical expansion of its territories, even as considerable changes were affecting the monarchy itself. Indeed, the acquisition and management of an overseas empire contributed directly to those changes.

Christopher Columbus undertook his voyages under the joint authority of Fernando and Isabel, but when Isabel died, in 1504, the throne passed to their daughter Juana and her husband Philip, who died in 1506. In 1508 Fernando was recognized as regent of Castile, serving as such until his death in early 1516, at which time Cardinal Jiménez de Cisneros again became regent, having served in that capacity briefly in 1506, after Philip died while Fernando was in Italy. The following year Charles of Ghent arrived in Spain to assume his Spanish grandparents' throne and reigned for three decades as king of Spain and Holy Roman Emperor Charles V, but before the middle of the century he was in the process of stepping down from the throne, and the future Philip II moved to the fore.

Each of these monarchical transitions had repercussions for government and society in the islands. Although Fernando and Isabel conceded broad powers to Columbus, they almost immediately began to curtail them. The trajectory of institutionalization in the Greater Antilles makes it clear that the crown intended to govern—and benefit from—the new territories as directly as possible, given the combined challenges posed by time and distance, not to mention the complicated issues raised by the existence of substantial populations in those territories of peoples who had not been Christianized. The result was a mosaic of royal policies that often were contradictory but that reflected a progression from the early perception of the Caribbean as existing mainly for the enrichment of the crown and a handful of favored elites to an acknowledgment that the untrammeled exploitation and abuse of Native peoples ultimately had undermined the colonial enterprise in the islands. If that realization, which found expression in the adoption of the New Laws of 1542, came much too late to prevent the devastation that befell the Indigenous peoples of the islands, at least it might have resulted in some moderation in the treatment of Indigenous groups elsewhere in the Americas.

The Spanish Caribbean in the first half of the sixteenth century, however, was far more than a failed testing ground for royal policies. If Atlantic islands such as the Canaries and Cabo Verde can be considered the earliest arena of the Atlantic world, then the Caribbean surely embodied its first full articulation. People from Europe, Africa, and the Americas clashed and interacted for the first time there, giving rise to new societies and unprecedented forms of interethnic relations. Trade networks based in the western Mediterranean and Atlantic islands rapidly extended to include the Caribbean, which soon began to ship sugar, hides, and therapeutic drugs, in addition to gold and pearls, to Europe. The hundreds, or more likely thousands, of Spaniards who poured into the islands in the first gold rush were joined by Portuguese merchants and settlers, Genoese and German merchants and financiers, French raiders, and a handful of English traders. Immigrants from the Iberian Peninsula included the descendants of Muslims and Jews, and Africans arrived in increasing numbers. My purpose here is to introduce readers to the new, dangerous, cruel, and complicated world that they created in the Caribbean.

1

Creating a Spanish Caribbean

When Europeans arrived in the Caribbean in October 1492, they found themselves moving around and through an archipelago of islands that formed a crescent some two thousand miles long, stretching almost from the tip of Florida to just off the northern coast of South America. The islands varied greatly in size, topography, climate, demography, ethnicity, and resources. Populations were substantial in the large islands of the northern Caribbean (Cuba, Hispaniola, Jamaica, and Puerto Rico), known today as the Greater Antilles, the principal focus of this study. The residents of these islands had complex forms of sociopolitical organization and practiced intensive agriculture. They took full advantage of the seas in which they fished and moved around with ease.

Accustomed to the arrival of migrants, raiders, and traders on their shores, the people who lived in the islands might not have found the appearance of Columbus's three ships as surprising as is often assumed. Judging by the first interactions that took place between Europeans and Indigenous islanders, the islanders were intrigued by the odd newcomers with their strange ships but not apparently alarmed. It must be emphasized, of course, that we know almost nothing about these encounters beyond the descriptions provided by Columbus.

Archaeological work has demonstrated that at the time of contact, the Caribbean was home to several groups speaking languages that probably were related but not always mutually intelligible. Starting around six thousand years ago, people began to arrive in the islands in waves. That movement continued for several thousand years, with the earliest migrants originating in Central America and later ones coming from the South American mainland.[1] Although Europeans quickly began to distinguish between the friendly people they encountered in the Greater Antilles and the more mobile groups of the smaller islands, whom they labeled "Caribs" and associated with cannibalism, the ethnolinguistic situation in the region was much more complicated than the simple distinction between friends or enemies would suggest, as probably at least some Europeans understood. Our understanding of the human map of the Caribbean at the time of Europeans' arrival and during the preceding centuries derives almost entirely from archaeological evidence, since European categories, as suggested, were more self-serving than accurate.[2]

The early emergence of this dichotomy in Europeans' categorization of the Native peoples of the region proved to be politically and ideologically useful, even if inaccurate, and contributed to how the newcomers constructed the region geopolitically as they worked to bring it under Spanish control. They sought to settle in the large islands, which had substantial Indigenous populations and indications of gold, but for some time they viewed other areas mainly as sources of captive labor. They considered the Bahamas, for example, to be "useless islands" (*islas inútiles*) because they lacked gold, and so they virtually emptied them of their inhabitants; many of the Lucayans, as the people of the Bahamas were known, ended up laboring for Spaniards in Hispaniola, Puerto Rico, or Cuba. Columbus very early began exporting Indigenous captives to be sold in Spain, and Europeans organized raids and *entradas* (expeditions) to the mainland, capturing large numbers of people to be used as auxiliaries or sold as slaves.[3]

The Spanish crown soon repudiated Columbus's decision to send Indigenous captives taken in early campaigns on Hispaniola to be sold as slaves in Spain, many for his own profit. Queen Isabel insisted that, as her vassals, the people of Hispaniola could not be enslaved. That decision, however, did not preclude the imposition of other forms of labor exploitation on the Indians of the Greater Antilles, and Spaniards found ways to justify taking captives who resisted Spanish domination and Christianization.

Although theories of "just war" long predated Iberian expansion to the Americas, in 1513 the Spanish crown adopted a formal proclamation called the *Requerimiento* (Requirement), which set out the terms by which Native Americans were "required" to recognize the legitimacy of the Roman Catholic church and the sovereignty of the Spanish crown as the protector of the church. Spaniards were to read this statement when they confronted potentially hostile Indigenous people. If their audience failed to comply, the Requirement gave Spaniards the legal basis to wage war on, and enslave, recalcitrant Natives.[4] By the time the Requerimiento was issued, Spaniards already had occupied all four of the big islands of the northern Caribbean, so it provided a legal ritual that justified what Spaniards had been doing almost from the outset.

Given that Europeans established themselves first in Hispaniola and from there moved on to the neighboring islands and nearby mainland, their initial contacts mainly were with Taíno peoples. Archaeologist William Keegan suggests that the term *Taíno* should not be understood as designating a single homogeneous group; rather, it incorporated a range of historical, socioeconomic, political, cultural, and linguistic patterns while also reflecting some shared practices.[5] These included sociopolitical organization in chiefdoms, or *cacicazgos*, some quite large and possibly incorporating a number of lesser chiefdoms; hierarchical organization within communities as well as among cacicazgos; the construction and grouping of houses according to social hierarchies and family and kinship ties; an emphasis on matrilineal descent and matrilocal residence; the practice of settled, varied, and in some places intensive forms of agriculture (irrigation, terracing, mounding), which included cultivation of yucca (both sweet and bitter, also known as cassava or manioc), maize, *aje* (a kind of sweet potato), fruit, and cotton; dependence on marine and riverine species for most of their animal protein; the construction and use of ball courts and plazas, some predating the Taíno; and sophisticated carving in wood and stone.

Notwithstanding such similarities, the islands of the Greater Antilles were differentiated from one another by geographic location in relation to other islands and the mainland; by the presence of distinctive groups; and by varying population numbers, topography, and mineral resources. For Europeans, these differences meant that, as they occupied the islands, they would confront— and perhaps create—on each a specific set of conditions that resulted in unique challenges or, possibly, advantages.[6] The proximity of Puerto Rico to the Leeward Islands, for example, made it something of a borderland between Taíno and Carib cultures, the result being that Caribs figured far more significantly in the early history of Spanish Puerto Rico than was the case in the other islands. The lack of gold in Jamaica meant that it would attract smaller numbers of potential settlers, while Hispaniola's large Indigenous population, numerous chiefdoms and communities, and substantial gold deposits ensured its institutional and economic primacy under Spanish rule. Indeed, Hispaniola remained the sole focus of Spanish colonizing activity for somewhat more than a decade and a half, which certainly contributed to its preeminence as well. On the other hand, the four islands had in common mountainous interiors that attracted Indians and Africans seeking to escape the Europeans and their demands, and abundant harbors that facilitated trade and movement throughout the region.

Columbus (Colón in Spanish) failed to encounter the wealthy trading societies he hoped to find by sailing west from Europe and reaching Asia. Instead, he and the people who went to the islands with and after him had to adjust their ambitions and expectations to the realities of the Caribbean milieu. They became accustomed, if not enthusiastically, to eating the *caçabi* (cassava) bread that local people produced by grating bitter yucca, squeezing out the poisonous juices, and drying it into flour, and they began to produce it commercially for export to other islands or to the mainland. They depended on large Indigenous-built dugout canoes to move around, and they used native materials and Native building styles (not to mention labor) to fashion houses for themselves and their slaves and servants. They learned about the therapeutic properties of local plants and trees and exported some brazilwood in the early years. Above all, they used the sea as a highway to connect the islands not only to one another and to the nearby mainland but also to the islands of the Atlantic—the Canaries, the Azores, and, later, São Tomé and Cabo Verde—and to the ports of Spain and Portugal.

Given the Caribbean's openness to anyone willing and able to cross the Atlantic, it is no surprise that Spaniards never maintained an exclusive presence in the region. Indeed, although Columbus sailed across the Atlantic on behalf of the Spanish crown, with crews drawn mostly from Andalucía in southern Spain, he was by origin Genoese. He had accrued mercantile experience in the eastern Mediterranean and Madeira and lived among the Italian community in Lisbon, eventually sailing to Guinea. He married a woman from an Italian family that had settled in Portugal in the late fourteenth century and thereby entered into the Portuguese nobility.[7] The commercial model that the Portuguese had developed along the coast of West Africa, and later in Asia, of establishing trade factories (*feitorias*) at defensible coastal locations, possibly influenced Columbus in some measure, although in Hispaniola he did not hesitate to order the construction of several inland forts to secure gold mining areas.

CREATING A SPANISH CARIBBEAN

From the outset, then, postcontact Caribbean society would be notably international. Italian merchants and Portuguese ships and settlers joined Spaniards in pursuing new economic opportunities in the islands, as did a small number of Englishmen.[8] The Caribbean became even more diverse as captive Africans were brought to the islands. German merchants became involved in the slave trade and obtained a concession from Charles V to settle Venezuela. They participated in the commerce of the large islands as well.[9]

Beginnings

Columbus and his party reached the Bahamas in October 1492. They sailed along some other islands but focused their attention on Hispaniola, where the cacique Guacanagarí welcomed them. On Christmas Eve, the *Santa María*, the largest of the three ships, ran aground near the present-day site of En Bas Saline (Haiti), on the island's northern coast.[10] Guacanagarí and his people helped the Europeans to salvage what they could from the ship and provided them with hospitality and shelter. Columbus had a fort built, which he named La Navidad, in part using timber salvaged from the ship and probably with the assistance of Guacanagarí's people. When he returned to Spain he left behind thirty-nine men under the leadership of a man named Rodrigo de Arana and a surgeon, Maestre Juan.[11]

Whether due to the men's bad behavior, a lack of food, or contention among the island's caciques over Guacanagarí's apparent alliance with the newcomers—probably all those factors played a part in the men's fate—none of the thirty-nine who stayed behind in Hispaniola survived to greet the approximately 1,200 people who participated in Columbus's second voyage, in 1493. The ships did not sail directly to Hispaniola but instead stopped at Guadaloupe and then Monserrat before reaching the site of the fort of La Navidad, where the Europeans discovered that the settlement had been destroyed. The ships then worked their way slowly along the north coast until Columbus chose the site that would become La Isabela, which archaeologist Kathleen Deagan has called the first medieval town in the Americas, at the mouth of the Río Bahabonico.

The ships' crews and passengers were exhausted from the extended voyage and soon began to sicken.[12] Supplies were scarce and arrived irregularly from Spain, so hunger afflicted nearly everyone from the start. Nonetheless, Columbus imposed a harsh work regimen on the men, most of whom were on salary, and refused to excuse them because of illness or starvation, pressing them not only to build the town but also to construct and man forts in the interior.[13] Hunger drove men to "rebel" by escaping into the interior, or to commit theft. Columbus responded to these acts with brutal punishments, which witnesses described in the inquiry (*pesquisa*) conducted by *comendador* Francisco de Bobadilla in 1500.[14]

Extensive archaeological work at La Isabela has shown that the town included a fortified tower, a storehouse, a church, a stone house for the admiral, a large open plaza, and earthen walls. Although the early abandonment of the site has fostered the notion that it was not viable, it did have some advantages, including proximity to good agricultural land. The Indigenous population in the area, however, was sparse, and most of the local inhabitants died or fled. Many Europeans left as well, returning to Spain, where they complained about the severe and arbitrary regime that Columbus, together with his brothers Diego and Bartolomé, who had arrived in 1494, had imposed. The decision to abandon La Isabela probably had more to do with its distance from sources of gold and substantial Indigenous communities than with a perception of failure. Under Columbus's brother, the *adelantado* Bartolomé Colón, the settlement moved to Santo Domingo, on the island's south coast. By 1498 La Isabela had been abandoned and was not resettled.[15]

Columbus had his allies and supporters, both at court in Spain and in Hispaniola, but there is little doubt that he was an incompetent leader and that his brothers were no better. His execution, before Bobadilla arrived, of three men who were directly connected to him reflects this failure of leadership. Those men were his *despensero* (steward), Pedro Gallego, who was hanged without trial, together with Columbus's *mayordomo,* both accused of selling bread from the warehouse; and the accountant Miguel Muliart, the husband of the admiral's sister-in-law, Briolanga Muñiz, sister of his first wife, with whom he enjoyed close relations. Muliart died under torture for having translated into *castellano* a letter that one of the friars had written in French to the Spanish monarchs. Columbus evidently did not want the letter to reach the sovereigns, at least not in a language that they could understand.[16]

Columbus's severity, and that of his brother Bartolomé (Diego seems mainly to have been occupied with administrative tasks), can be explained in some part by the daunting challenges they faced. They had to manage and discipline a disparate group of people forced to live and work in miserable circumstances while dealing with a large Indigenous population not yet under European control. Nonetheless, Columbus's reliance on force and brutality, his unwillingness to mitigate the difficulties the settlers faced (witnesses in the pesquisa said that he refused to distribute food stores, from which he hoped to make a profit),[17] and his frequent absences from Hispaniola as he continued his reconnaissance of the Caribbean weakened his authority and alienated potential settlers and clergy alike. Although many Spaniards might have found it difficult to accept as their leader a Genoese man with a maritime background, it is clear that Columbus's actions on the ground led to his downfall. With the rebellion of Francisco Roldán, who abandoned La Isabela and established himself with a number of other men in Xaraguá, Columbus himself became increasingly aware of his inability to control the situation in Hispaniola and he repeatedly wrote to the monarchs asking for competent officials, including a lawyer to serve as justice and someone to take charge of the royal treasury.[18]

Francisco de Bobadilla, comendador of the Order of Calatrava in Spain, arrived in Santo Domingo with two ships, late in August 1500, wielding a May 1499 appointment as governor with limited powers. The Reyes Católicos, Fernando and Isabel, also ordered Columbus to hand over to Bobadilla all forts, houses, ships, arms, horses, and cattle. Nineteen Indians, whom Columbus had sent to Spain the previous year and who had been freed, traveled to the island with Bobadilla.[19] Bobadilla arrested the three Colón brothers and dispatched them in chains to Spain, where they arrived in Cádiz in November. Although the monarchs pardoned Columbus and ordered that the properties that Bobadilla had confiscated be returned to him, he never again acted as viceroy of the Indies.[20]

Bobadilla, too, was soon dismissed, and in September 1501 the monarchs named frey Nicolás de Ovando, comendador of the Order of Alcántara, governor of the islands. He arrived in Santo Domingo in April 1502, accompanied by a huge fleet of thirty-two ships and an additional 1,200 potential settlers.[21] By the time Bobadilla was ready to depart for Spain, at the end of June, Columbus had returned to Hispaniola, but Ovando refused to allow him to enter Santo Domingo, to avoid an encounter between the two men. Ignoring warnings of an approaching storm, including one from Columbus himself, Ovando ordered the fleet to depart. The storm destroyed nearly two-thirds of the thirty-two ships; Bobadilla, Francisco Roldán, and the cacique Guarionex, who was being sent as prisoner to Castile, drowned, and some 200,000 castellanos of gold, half belonging to the crown, were lost.[22]

About a year later a strange episode that perhaps symbolized the passing of the Columbus era took place: the unexpectedly prolonged sojourn on Jamaica that marked the end of the admiral's career in the Indies. After losing all but two of his ships on his fourth voyage, he became stranded with his party on the island in June 1503.[23] The remaining ships were so waterlogged that they were unseaworthy by the time they reached Jamaica, an island Spaniards had barely visited before then. In July Columbus wrote to the king a lengthy, confusing letter that Carl O. Sauer characterizes as "hardly intelligible," describing the difficulties of the voyage.[24] Columbus gave the letter to Diego Méndez, his *criado* (retainer) and *escribano* (notary), whom he sent, along with a Genoese merchant named Bartolomé de Fisco, to try to reach Santo Domingo in two canoes, each carrying several other Spaniards and ten Indigenous rowers.

Las Casas described Méndez's grueling journey, during which some or most of the Indians died of thirst or illness. Méndez managed to reach Xaraguá in the fall of 1503, where he claimed to have witnessed Ovando's massacre of the caciques.[25] Using Columbus's rents in Hispaniola, he was able to purchase and supply a ship to send to Jamaica in May 1504. It arrived there the following month, meaning Columbus and the other Spaniards spent a year on Jamaica before being rescued. Having dispatched the rescue ship, Méndez traveled on to Spain to deliver Columbus's letter to the king.

In Hispaniola, governor Ovando had been disinclined to intervene. When he first learned of the admiral's situation, he sent a ship to Jamaica, instructing its captain, Diego de Escobar, not to land or retrieve the admiral but only to find out about the situation of the stranded party. According to Las Casas, Columbus suspected that Ovando only wanted to ascertain whether he was dead or alive. Escobar dropped off a letter from Ovando, together with a barrel of wine and a slab of bacon, provisions that were unlikely to last for long. When Columbus finally departed Jamaica at the end of June 1504 and reached Hispaniola, Ovando apparently treated him well and provided lodgings in his own house. The admiral then journeyed on to Spain, where he died in Valladolid on May 20, 1506.[26]

Despite the obvious importance of the first seven years of the nascent colony on Hispaniola, during which Columbus acted as viceroy, much remains obscure about this period. Little documentation from the 1490s generated on the island itself has survived. Some years ago, archivist Isabel Aguirre discovered a copy of Bobadilla's pesquisa, lost along with so much else in the shipwreck, in the Archivo General de Simancas.[27] Apart from that previously unknown source, scholars for the most part have relied on Columbus's letters and diaries, the extensive writings of Bartolomé de Las Casas, and the histories compiled by Peter Martyr and Gonzalo Fernández de Oviedo for their understanding of the period. Fernández de Oviedo did not go to the Indies until later, but he is careful to explain his principal sources for the early years in Hispaniola. They included Vicente Yáñez Pinzón, with whom he became friends in Spain; Juan de Rojas and Alonso de Valencia, who went to Hispaniola on Columbus's second voyage and remained on the island; and in particular Mosen Pedro Margarite, who was close to Fernando and Isabel and returned to Spain in 1494.[28] Later reports and testimony occasionally incorporate the recollections of people who were present in the early years, as some of the earliest arrivals in the islands stayed on and even thrived.

Establishing a Royal Colony

Ovando's term as governor of Hispaniola marked an important step toward the consolidation of royal authority and pacification of the island as well as the beginnings of expansion into other areas. His efforts to bring the entire island under royal control largely succeeded within two or three years after his arrival, at great cost to the Indigenous rulers and their people.[29] He pursued a dual approach, eliminating many caciques, especially the strongest among them, and granting Spaniards access to Indigenous labor in the form of *repartimientos* (from *repartir*, "to distribute"), a practice that had been adopted informally during the Columbus years. The recipient of a repartimiento had the right to use the labor of a specified group, usually a cacique and his people, on a rotating basis. Over time, official use of the word *encomienda* to refer to these grants became common, although for many years, in the islands and elsewhere in Spanish America, *repartimiento* and *encomienda* were synonymous terms.[30]

The institutionalization of the encomienda system had momentous consequences for Hispaniola and later for the other islands and territories where it was introduced. For Spaniards, it immediately created a society of haves and have-nots, as a minority of wealthy and well-connected individuals obtained access to substantial amounts of essentially free labor while the majority enjoyed no such advantage.³¹ During the early years in Hispaniola, the length of time that a repartimiento grant lasted varied. Initially, it seems to have been intended to be short term, although it is not clear to what extent that limitation was observed. Already by the time of Diego Colón's governorship (starting in 1510), some heirs were being allowed to succeed to encomiendas. During the time that the encomienda was important and viable in the islands, newly arrived officials often reassigned grants, usually to their own relatives, friends, and political allies, alienating previous holders and giving rise to a great deal of resentment and conflict. Awarding encomiendas to people at court who never spent any time in the Indies further heightened resentments and the class divide.

The imposition of encomiendas opened the door to systematic exploitation of Indians, for whom the only alternatives were flight or death.³² Although in principle Indians were supposed to continue to live in their own communities and cultivate their own subsistence crops, Spaniards often ignored or subverted these restrictions. Both men and women could be sent to work in gold mines for months at a time, disrupting family life and agricultural cycles, and the miserable conditions in which they labored contributed to high mortality rates. In response to protests from members of the religious orders, especially the Dominicans, about the abuse of Indians and the conditions in which they worked, the crown issued the Laws of Burgos in 1512 (amended the following year). The laws were intended to ameliorate those conditions, provide some protections for Indigenous women, and ensure the provision of religious instruction. Coming soon thereafter, however, the Repartimiento of 1514, in which officials attempted to regularize assignments of labor in Hispaniola, reflected how drastically the numbers of potential laborers had decreased during the first two decades of Spanish rule.³³

The arrival in late 1516 of a group of three Hieronymites, charged by regent Cardinal Jiménez de Cisneros with investigating the operation of the encomienda system and making recommendations for change, marked another phase of attempted reform. Although they succeeded in mostly eliminating absentee holders of repartimientos (other than the crown), other reforms, such as the effort to create "free" communities that would operate outside the encomienda system (although under Spanish supervision), failed.³⁴ As Indigenous populations plummeted, authorities tried to ensure the continuing viability of repartimientos by relocating people, further severely disrupting

Indigenous society, undermining the integrity of Native communities, and contributing to rising mortality rates. In all likelihood, within two decades following the establishment of European control, Indigenous populations on each of the islands had decreased to perhaps a quarter or less of their numbers at the time of contact.[35]

Over the years of Ovando's term as governor, King Fernando became increasingly unhappy with him, as Ovando clashed with people who had strong connections to the royal court. In one such conflict Cristóbal de Tapia brought a suit regarding land he had lost when, at Ovando's orders, Santo Domingo was relocated from the eastern to the western side of the Ozama River; the move meant that Tapia forfeited some income-producing property he owned. Formerly, the two men had been on excellent terms—Ovando dined with Tapia and his wife, apparently a rare sign of favor, and even was godfather to their children. Tapia, however, bitterly resented Ovando's decision to appoint his nephew Diego López de Salcedo (or Saucedo) as *alcaide* (warden) of Santo Domingo's *fortaleza* (fort or fortress), which had been constructed under Tapia's supervision. Tapia was supposed to receive the title of alcaide, but Ovando apparently was dissatisfied with how the fort was built and instead named him *veedor de fundición* (overseer of smelting) in Concepción de la Vega. In 1508 the crown ordered that Cristóbal's brother Francisco de Tapia be invested as the new alcaide. Ovando, however, not only ignored the order but also incarcerated both brothers and took away their repartimientos de indios. On learning of this, the king immediately ordered their release and confirmed Francisco's appointment as alcaide, although in the interim royal treasurer Miguel de Pasamonte served as warden.[36]

The details of this conflict are known because records of the suit survived, but there were other complaints lodged against Ovando as well. As Esteban Mira Caballos's study of his political regime demonstrates, Ovando heavily favored his closest associates, creating an elite with strong ties to his home region of Extremadura, whom he appointed to offices in Hispaniola's towns.[37] Extremeños who accompanied Ovando to the island in 1502 and would play prominent roles in the Caribbean and elsewhere in Spanish America included Francisco Pizarro, Hernando de Soto, Francisco de Orellana, and Pedro de Alvarado. The extremeños were known as *los garrovillas*, after the town in Extremadura with which Ovando was associated (though he actually was born in Las Brozas). Ovando awarded the biggest repartimientos to his favorites.[38]

He also amassed a fortune for himself, owning fifteen stone houses that he had built in Santo Domingo as well as others in Concepción de la Vega and Buenaventura (an early mining town), together with large herds of cattle and extensive agricultural holdings.[39]

Even as the king was becoming disenchanted with Ovando, he found himself under pressure to recognize Columbus's son, don Diego Colón, as governor. Columbus had been frustrated in his plans to bring Diego to Hispaniola during his tenure there as viceroy; instead, the young don Diego had remained at court, where he served as page to Prince Juan. Notwithstanding his presence at court, a much more important factor in the king's decision to send him to Hispaniola as governor was Diego's marriage to doña María de Toledo, the daughter of don Hernando de Toledo and niece of don Fadrique de Toledo, the Duque de Alba. The brothers were Fernando's first cousins, and the Duke of Alba enjoyed a good deal of influence over the king. The king had hoped to dispense with the claims of the Colón family to political office in the Indies altogether, but his powerful cousins persuaded him to send Diego Colón to Hispaniola instead.[40]

Don Diego and doña María departed Sanlúcar de Barrameda on June 3, 1509, reaching Santo Domingo on July 9 with nine ships and a large entourage that included Diego's half brother Hernando, his uncles Diego and Bartolomé, his former tutor, Jerónimo de Agüero, and his uncle by marriage, Francisco de Garay.[41] The second admiral soon sent his half brother Hernando, who was eighteen years old at the time, back to Spain to pursue his studies, since he was "inclined toward the sciences and to having many books."[42] Colón also made the surprising decision to name the youthful Hernando captain general of the fleet in which Ovando traveled, meaning the governor found himself under the authority of an inexperienced teenager for the duration of the voyage. Las Casas commented that "it did not seem well even to those who were fondest of the admiral."[43] Ovando departed in September 1509 and died soon after he returned to Spain.

In the absence of the alcaide (Diego López de Salcedo), Diego Colón and his wife took possession of the fortress as their temporary lodgings upon arriving in Santo Domingo, subsequently taking up residence in Francisco de Garay's house until they could build one of their own. At the time Ovando was forty leagues from Santo Domingo, in Santiago de los Caballeros, where he apparently liked to spend part of each year "for the health and gaiety of the pueblo."[44] Days of festivities followed the arrival of Colón and his wife and entourage, though this was soon marred by a devastating hurricane, at the end of July. The hurricane destroyed most of the buildings on the island, along with the fleet in which the admiral had arrived, including his ship the *San Jorge*, which Las Casas described as "very large and very beautiful" and which still contained hundreds of *quintales* of biscuit yet to be unloaded.[45]

King Fernando made other important appointments in those years that signaled his continuing commitment to strengthening royal control in the Caribbean, notwithstanding the reestablishment of the Colóns on the island and royal recognition of don Diego's claims to authority. In 1508 he sent Miguel de Pasamonte, who had served as ambassador to France and England and secretary to Fernando's second wife, Germaine de Foix, as treasurer-general of the Indies. Pasamonte served the crown with unwavering loyalty until his death in 1535 and for a few years was the most powerful man in Hispaniola. Luis Arranz refers to the "continual concentration of power in the treasurer to the detriment of other officials, above all the Admiral."[46] After Pasamonte, no other treasurer would enjoy such comprehensive power, as subsequently the crown named treasurers for each island.

In 1512, the king sent three appellate judges to the island, along with a royal *fiscal* (prosecutor) and other officials, establishing the basis for the future *audiencia*, or high court, and further undercutting Diego Colón's authority, although the judges were charged only with hearing appeals from local magistrates.[47] The three judges were Juan Ortiz de Matienzo, Marcelo de Villalobos, and Lucas Vázquez de Ayllón, who previously had served as *alcalde mayor* of Concepción de la Vega under Ovando, who generously awarded him a repartimiento of four hundred Indians. Ayllón left the island with Ovando in 1509 and spent part of the intervening years earning a law degree in Valladolid. The fiscal was Sancho Velázquez.[48]

The audiencia as such came into existence in 1519 after the Hieronymites left Hispaniola. Colón returned from a visit to Spain in 1520 and in subsequent years found himself in nearly constant conflict with the audiencia judges. Charles V officially reprimanded him in 1523 for overstepping his powers in a number of respects and recalled him to Spain. He hoped to return to Hispaniola, where his family had remained, but fell ill and died near Toledo in 1526.[49] His body was taken to Seville and buried alongside his father at the monasterio de las Cuevas, or La Cartuja. His son Luis would succeed him as the third admiral. The year that Colón died the king elevated the audiencia of Santo Domingo to the status of *real chancillería*, making it comparable to the tribunals of Granada and Valladolid. Although it still mainly functioned as an appellate court, the audiencia's president was to act as governor of Hispaniola.[50]

The Colón family did not disappear from the islands. After her husband's death, doña María traveled to Spain with her two youngest children (daughter doña Isabel and son don Diego), leaving her eldest daughter, doña Felipa, and sons don Luis and don Cristóbal in Santo Domingo. In Castile, her son Diego followed in his father's footsteps and became a page to Prince Philip at court, and daughter Isabel married the Count of Gelves. Given Luis's youth (he was only six years old when his father died), Charles V was under no pressure to concede any significant political authority to him. He made him Duque de Veragua and Marqués de Jamaica, earmarking for him a generous annual stipend of 10,000 ducados situated in the rents of Hispaniola, as well as naming him to the post of *alguacil mayor* (chief constable) for the island, which gave him a vote and precedence in Santo Domingo's city council, and confirming his title of admiral.[51]

Settling in the Caribbean

By 1520 Spaniards had expanded their efforts well beyond Hispaniola. Ovando sent Juan Ponce de León, who together with Juan de Esquivel had pacified the southeastern end of the island and founded Salvaleón de Higüey, to initiate the occupation of Puerto Rico in 1508. Esquivel occupied Jamaica starting in 1509, with Pánfilo de Narváez acting as second-in-command. Diego Velázquez, who went to Hispaniola with Columbus in 1493 and conquered the western end of the island, where he founded Salvatierra de la Sabana, organized his expedition to conquer Cuba in 1511. Narváez, who had left Jamaica, joined him, as did Bartolomé de Las Casas, whose experience of the brutal occupation of Cuba would convince him of the immorality of Spaniards' treatment of the Indians.

During the same years, Spaniards established a foothold in Panama and what they would call Tierra Firme (the northern coast of South America). In 1510 Darién (Panama) became the first permanent settlement on the mainland. Velázquez remained in Cuba as lieutenant governor until his death, while Colón appointed Francisco de Garay lieutenant governor of Jamaica in 1514.[52] Juan Ponce de León, conqueror of Puerto Rico, soon found himself denied the governorship of the island as the result of a conflict between the king and Diego Colón, who had anticipated exercising authority there and had appointed his own officials. In compensation, the king awarded Ponce license to conquer Bimini and La Florida, with the title of adelantado.

One of the most important events of the early years in Hispaniola was the decision to move the core of the new colony from La Isabela in the north to Santo Domingo on the south coast. Miguel Díaz de Aux usually receives credit for having found the site and recognizing its potential as both a port and a base for gold mining operations. Fernández de Oviedo claims that Miguel Díaz fled south from La Isabela with several other men after stabbing one of Bartolomé Colón's criados. In the area of what became Santo Domingo, Díaz supposedly met and formed a relationship with an Indigenous woman known to him as Catalina, with whom he had two children. She ostensibly told Díaz of the existence of gold in the area. He decided to return to La Isabela to inform the adelantado, who, because the stabbing victim had recovered, pardoned Díaz and agreed to travel to see the site. Subsequently, two ships sailed from La Isabela with most of the people who remained there. They settled along the Ozama River on the opposite side from where Catalina and her people lived. Fernández de Oviedo, who later lived for twenty years in Santo Domingo, underscored the advantages of this move, noting that once the colonists established themselves there, "everyone was restored by the abundance and fertility of the land, and they recovered [their] health."[53]

Founding cities and towns provided the template for the development of an Iberian-style society in the islands of the northern Caribbean. The ideals of urban living and municipal self-government that Spaniards brought with them to the Indies meant that they would devote considerable effort to establishing towns to serve as centers for institutions, economic enterprises, and civil society. The two largest islands, Hispaniola and Cuba, not surprisingly, had the most towns, while the smaller islands of Puerto Rico and Jamaica each had only two. Nearly all the towns created in Hispaniola by the end of the first half of the sixteenth century came into existence during the Columbus and Ovando years, meaning that by the time Spaniards began to occupy the other islands of the Greater Antilles, an urban network already had begun to take shape in Hispaniola. Although both documentary and archaeological evidence suggests that Spanish towns usually were located in proximity to Indigenous communities, specific descriptions of the relationship between the new and existing foundations are lacking for the Greater Antilles.[54]

The new urban creations often were unstable. Because of the haste with which the locations for new towns frequently were chosen, their sites sometimes shifted. Some early towns soon shrank in size or importance, and others did not survive. As noted, La Isabela was abandoned in favor of Santo Domingo, which itself moved across the river. Concepción de la Vega, which Columbus founded in 1495 and anticipated would be one of the island's major cities because of its location near substantial gold mines, experienced an early building boom, but by the 1520s it had lost much of its population as revenues from gold mining declined. The early mining town of Buenaventura disappeared, as did Lares de Guahaba.[55] In Puerto Rico, after about a decade, Spaniards abandoned the island's first town, Caparra, which not only suffered damage from fire during the Indigenous revolt on the island but also, and probably more importantly, occupied an unhealthy site,[56] while San Germán, on the western end of the island (which itself had replaced the earlier settlement of Sotomayor, which was destroyed in the revolt), eventually had to be moved inland. In Cuba, Santiago, on the south coast, soon eclipsed Baracoa, the town at the eastern end of the island that had been expected to be the capital, but by 1550 Santiago itself had begun to yield to the growing importance of Havana. Havana moved from the south to the north coast, and Puerto del Príncipe moved to central Camagüey, both within a few years of their founding.[57] Jamaica's main town moved from the north to the south, but not until the 1530s.

Even the early names of towns could be tenuous. Compostela in Hispaniola quickly gave way to Azua, and Santa María del Puerto de la Yaguana was shortened to La Yaguana. In Cuba, Baracoa eventually prevailed over Asunción, as did Bayamo over San Salvador. The prevalence of Indigenous names was not universal, however. Cotuy in Hispaniola also became known as La Mejorada, although during this period neither name entirely displaced the other.[58]

Establishing towns meant there was a sustained demand for experts in construction trades as well as for necessary materials, although in most places locally available resources (such as wood and thatch) and building techniques predominated for many years. Fernández de Oviedo described with considerable pride the house he had built in Darién, suggesting that notwithstanding the nearly exclusive use of indigenous materials, it was in no way inferior to European styles: "It had nothing but wood and canes and thatch and some nails, and it cost me more than one thousand five hundred pesos of good gold; in which a prince could lodge, with rooms above and below, and a beautiful orchard with many oranges and other trees, over the bank of a lovely river that passes through that city."[59] It is very likely that Spaniards living in Hispaniola and the other islands had similar houses built, although Juan Ponce de Leon imported bricks and tile from Spain to build his house in Caparra.[60] By 1528 there was a tile works (*tejar*) near the river in Santo Domingo that originally belonged to Francisco de Garay.[61]

The demand for masons and stonecutters mostly existed in larger towns such as Santo Domingo, Concepción de la Vega, and, to a lesser extent, San Juan. Some tradesmen were recruited in Spain for building projects in the islands. Master stonecutters who went to work on the construction of churches in Hispaniola in 1510 earned 100 pesos a year, while journeymen earned a daily wage of 280 maravedís. Mira Caballos has identified a *morisco* named Juan Ravé, a stonecutter, who worked on the Torre del Homenaje (part of Santo Domingo's fort) in 1506 and 1507.[62]

Indians and Blacks, not imported tradesmen, would have performed the bulk of the menial labor for construction projects and most likely were responsible for a growing share of the skilled work as well. Local officials sometimes required the holders of repartimientos to provide a specified number of Indian workers for public works. Several caciques and one cacica from the region of Xaraguá, presumably with their people, participated in the construction of Santo Domingo's fort between 1506 and 1507 and were said to be very skilled in masonry. In Jamaica the cacique and his people who built the fort at Nueva Sevilla were considered to be so expert "in making lime and brick and in building" that they were asked to build the church as well.[63]

In addition to the stone houses that some *vecinos* started to build in Santo Domingo, construction of the fortaleza and House of Trade also got under way during Ovando's term as governor. When Diego Colón and his wife arrived in Santo Domingo he described the fort as having "a tower and one long room within it, and a room and chamber and kitchen. For this country it's good, but if there were [a need to] fight, it couldn't be defended for many days." Indeed, the sea had hollowed out much of the rock on which it was situated, so that "with the smallest earthquake it won't be secure, and if they attack with gunpowder it would be done in two hours."[64] Over the ensuing decades, the fort constantly needed repair and expansion. During the years that he lived in the fortress as alcaide, Gonzalo Fernández de Oviedo regularly lobbied the crown and its Council of the Indies (Consejo de Indias) to invest more money in strengthening, staffing, and arming the fortress.[65]

Plans for the construction of the Casa de la Contratación (House of Trade) dated to 1503. In 1509 the king sent a *cédula* (ordinance) to Diego Colón, saying that the design for the building was overly ambitious and should be scaled back in line with its actual function: it was to be subordinate to the Casa de la Contratación in Seville and would deal only with the commerce of Hispaniola. In 1511 the Council of the Indies instructed that the appellate judges should be given space in the Casa to conduct their audiences, but apparently there was lodging only for the factor.[66] The city at this time also lacked a cathedral. In his report of 1509, Diego Colón wrote to the crown that Santo Domingo had a church "of thatch, very small, in which on holy day[s] only half the pueblo can fit, and it has no space to expand, nor [for] a cemetery." He urged the king to purchase additional lots for construction.[67]

In 1518 Puerto Rico's treasurer, Andrés de Haro, complained that "there's no fort or house of trade or foundry made of stone" on the island.[68] As late as 1532, stonecutter Diego de Arroyo informed the king that "it was notorious the necessity that there is in that island of masons and carpenters for buildings of stone and masonry in the said island for its vecinos, apart from the [public] works that we are ordered to build in the city of Puerto Rico and the town of San Germán." Arroyo was commissioned to take charge of "said works" (unspecified), for which he would receive free passage for himself and his wife, children, criados, and household as well as three or four tradesmen.[69] The House of Trade as originally built in San Juan had lodgings only on the ground floor, which "because of the land's humidity is very sickly." The king authorized building a second story, where the treasurer and accountant could live and books could be stored.[70]

In the late 1530s, however, the city was struggling to maintain its infrastructure. Two stone causeways that connected San Juan to the rest of the island were constantly battered by the sea and always in need of repair. A fountain "where all the pueblo comes" had been knocked over and needed fixing, roads that led to the mines needed clearing, and the city lacked a butcher shop, jail, or town hall. Prisoners escaped for lack of a jail, people could not reach the mines to collect gold, and the city suffered from a shortage of supplies because of the dangerous state of the causeways.[71] All the towns in the islands faced problems in maintaining roads, fountains, and public buildings, but San Juan's site created particular challenges.

Other than in Santo Domingo, efforts to convince Spanish vecinos to build houses of stone made slow progress, and construction lagged even in Santo Domingo. In 1528 the oidor Licenciado Espinosa complained about the lack of "casas principales" in the city and how difficult and expensive it was to build them.[72] By 1530 San Juan had the following buildings of stone: the royal house, which included lodgings for the treasurer and accountant and served as the customhouse and foundry; a two-story hospital that had been reduced to ruins in a storm; the bishop's two-story residence; the cathedral; and three private residences, one with two stories that was shared by two vecinos. In addition, there were thirty houses built of wood with tiled roofs and another twenty thatched houses. The church, merchants, and *cofradía de Nuestra Señora*, a lay brotherhood, owned thirty to thirty-five *tiendas*, small wood and tile buildings that were homes to merchants and other people or were rented out as shops. In contrast, San Germán had no stone buildings, although it had a church with adobe walls and a tiled roof.[73]

At some time, officials in San Juan had declared that anyone who built a wooden house with a tile roof that had at least five people living in it would be assigned a gold mine. Although this plan met with some success, in 1537 the king advised that in order to have access to gold mines, vecinos instead should be required to build stone houses.[74] Not everyone agreed that stone houses were desirable, however, given the Caribbean climate. In Santiago de Cuba in 1540 Bernaldino de Quesada complained that stone houses were very humid and caused illness. He contended that "houses of tile and boards . . . cost as much as if they were stone" and compared them to similar houses built in the Basque country of Vizcaya and Guipúzcoa.[75] In some places, sandy ground literally could not support stone structures.[76]

In what must have been a flight of fancy, Bishop Alessandro Geraldini, newly arrived in Santo Domingo in 1522, wrote that the city's "buildings are tall and beautiful like those of Italy; the port itself spacious [enough] for all the ships of Europe; the streets long and straight in such fashion that not even those of Florence can be compared to them." He took the city's vecinos to task, however, for not yet having built a proper cathedral: "It pains me that my pueblo should have put so much effort into their private houses which would provide them a brief home and would not have had the least consideration for building the church, where they will have eternal welcome."[77]

Fernández de Oviedo noted that the arrival of Diego Colón and his wife, doña María, with their entourages, gave rise to a more aristocratic society in the city, as hidalgos and prominent men began to marry Spanish women or to bring their wives from Spain, "and so this city has grown into such a beautiful republic, which is something for which to give God many thanks."[78] He admired the city's physical beauty, citing the "beautiful streets and very well ordered and wide," and noted that the houses along the river "are close to the ships as in Naples, or Rome on the Tiber, or Seville and Triana on the Guadalquivir."[79] Notwithstanding the difficulties of finding materials, expertise, labor, and funding for construction projects, Santo Domingo, with its gardens, orchards, and views of the harbor, eventually became a source of pride for at least some residents.

A report from 1523 listing properties belonging to the city reflects its commercial development. The city owned an inn, the Venta de la Fuente de la Palma, located a couple of leagues away, although another inn had fallen down. There was a butcher shop built of stone, with "arcades that serve as stores around it" in the upper plaza and sites for five ironsmiths' shops. Near the house of Francisco de Garay was a fountain. The city had purchased the "casas del cabildo y carcel" from Antonio Maldonado for 1,500 pesos. The city also owned two boats, one on the Haina River and the other in the port, presumably used to ferry passengers and goods.[80] By the 1550s the city owned a kiln and Black slaves to make lime.[81]

Economic considerations—facilitating commerce or providing access to mining areas—to a great extent dictated the location and character of towns in the early Spanish Caribbean. The constant movement of people and goods among the islands, to and from the mainland, and back and forth across the Atlantic guaranteed that from the outset ports would be busy and diverse. Although the leading port towns—Santo Domingo, San Juan, and Santiago de Cuba—have received most attention from scholars, smaller ports were important in transportation and in intra- and interisland trade. In western Hispaniola, for example, La Yaguana played an important role in internal trade and was the closest port to Cuba, offering easy passage to Santiago. San Germán, in Puerto Rico, often was the first stop for ships arriving from Spain and the Canaries, preferred over San Juan by some shipmasters because it was an "open" port.[82] In contrast to most of Spanish America, where ports generally remained secondary to cities in the interior, port towns to a great extent defined the Spanish Caribbean, not only controlling and funneling trade and the movement of people but also acting as centers for institutions of church and government and for the formation of Spanish society.

Moving to the Islands

During the first decade, the movement of people from Europe to the islands included some large expeditions, such as Columbus's second voyage of 1493 and Ovando's fleet of 1502.[83] Las Casas felt that Ovando "had brought more people than he could support (and this was one of the main causes that have devastated these Indies . . . allowing too many people to come from Spain)."[84] The two men holding royal appointments as *veedor* (inspector) and *marcador* (assayer, brander) who traveled with Ovando, for example, each received license to bring eight criados if their wives accompanied them. The king sent a member of the royal household, Alvar Pérez de Meneses, to catch falcons and send them back to him.[85] Only a few years later, Ovando himself became alarmed about the influx of migrants to Hispaniola and, to the consternation of the king, urged that departures from Spain, even of working people, be minimized. He apparently worried that a large group of emigrants who departed from Seville in 1506, a time of high mortality in Spain itself, might bring new contagion to the Indigenous people of Hispaniola.[86] The arrivals continued, and don Diego Colón and his wife both traveled with substantial entourages.

The majority of emigrants most likely undertook their transatlantic journeys on a private basis, which does not preclude, of course, their traveling as part of the entourages of officials or other prominent men, or with family members or friends. For the most part the Spanish crown eschewed the practice that other countries followed of using their overseas colonies as dumping grounds for undesirables, instead attempting to prevent the emigration to the Indies of people deemed unacceptable because of race or religion and regulating departures through a cumbersome system of licensing.[87]

In the early years, however, those policies and procedures were still embryonic. Fernández de Oviedo reports, for example, that in the 1490s, when many people were returning to Castile, Columbus sent three ships from the Canaries carrying "three hundred men convicted and exiled to this island. . . . They were the reason this country didn't depopulate."[88] In one instance preserved in the records, the Reyes Católicos commuted the death sentence that had been imposed on Sebastián de Ocampo into an order of permanent exile in Hispaniola, on October 2, 1501.[89] Evidence from the pesquisa conducted by Bobadilla around that time suggests that prostitutes went to Hispaniola as early as Columbus's second voyage. Instructions to Alonso Velez de Mendoza, a vecino of Moguer, who undertook to recruit fifty vecinos to take to Hispaniola with

Ovando, however, did include the stipulation that "exiles, Moors [and] Jews" should not be permitted to live in the new settlement they were to establish.[90]

The movement to the islands from Spain was preponderantly male, consisting mostly of single young men or married men who left their wives and families behind, but it was not uncommon that women accompanied their spouses, joined them later, or even migrated on their own.[91] The organizers of a 1497 voyage hoped to include at least thirty women in their projected total of 330 passengers, although it is unlikely that they recruited anywhere near that number. When Vélez de Mendoza contracted to transport fifty emigrants to Hispaniola, the crown stipulated that at least ten of them should be married men with their households.[92] The king also instructed Ovando that in any division of lands or Indians, married men should receive grants that were one-third larger than those of single men. Married men traveling with their wives also were eligible for additional concessions in the form of tax exemptions and permission to bring larger numbers of criados with them. There is no evidence, however, that these policies were consistently followed, especially with regard to the distribution of Indians in repartimientos.[93]

As early as 1501 the crown proposed an ambitious colonization scheme to convey European married couples and families to the Indies. The monarchs made a contract with Luis de Arriaga to recruit and take two hundred or more married men, with their wives and households, to Hispaniola for the purpose of settling four towns of fifty vecinos each. In the event, Arriaga sent seventy-three married men with their wives and families, a substantial group of settlers, if far below the target number.[94]

In July 1511 a letter from the king to Diego Colón addressed the need to encourage people to go to Hispaniola by publicizing throughout Spain that gold mines had been found there. He directed Colón to make inquiries regarding the possibility of recruiting emigrants in *"las montañas* and Guipuzcoa, that there are many people and little on which to live, in order to solicit working people to go to the said lands in those parts." The king ordered officials of the Casa de la Contratación not to prevent people from leaving Seville for the Indies, so that as many working people as possible would go.[95]

In September 1520 Licenciado Figueroa wrote to the crown that a group of "thirty-seven households of *labradores* [farmers]" from Antequera sent by the king had fallen ill on arrival. Some of the women and children had died, even though the officials had done what they could to help them. Two months later many remained ill, having been settled in a town five leagues from Santo Domingo. In Figueroa's opinion, the effort to recruit families barely justified the expense, whereas he thought there would be no difficulty at all in finding plenty of willing young men who would make the journey for nothing more than the price of passage and food for the voyage.[96] Ten years later, however, the crown once again was promoting the recruitment of labradores to the Caribbean, the warden of Santo Domingo's jail, Cristóbal Pérez, having offered to take some of them with him to Hispaniola. The king instructed the officials of Seville's House of Trade to receive the married farmers "with much care, love, and good treatment" while they awaited passage and to provide them with whatever they would need in the way of plants and equipment.[97]

Movement among the islands, Spain, and the Canaries was constant. Notwithstanding the discomforts and even dangers of the Atlantic crossing, some people, especially merchants and officials of church and government, made the journey repeatedly. The timing and trajectory of any given individual's decision to depart for the Caribbean reflected a range of factors, including sources of information (letters and personal communications), the decisions and circumstances of family members and other relatives, the choice of destination, and any business or employment opportunities that might arise.[98] Often, some of the same considerations informed a decision to return to Spain.

The First Generations

Each wave of migration to the islands yielded a core of long-term vecinos who, by virtue of longevity and connections, would play influential roles over the course of many years, even as migrants continued to arrive and, often, subsequently depart for other destinations. Some of the earliest arrivals remained in Hispaniola. Cristóbal de Santa Clara, an early treasurer of Hispaniola, and Antonio de Villasante, who married an Indigenous woman and received a monopoly on the export of balsam, arrived in the 1490s and stayed. Others moved on, such as Francisco Manuel de Lando, who arrived at some point in the 1490s, spent ten years in Hispaniola, then moved to Puerto Rico, where he remained, serving for several years as lieutenant governor of the island.

Men who arrived in the 1490s and left Hispaniola in search of other opportunities included Diego de Alvarado, who went with Columbus in 1493 and in the 1520s joined his brothers Pedro and Jorge in Mexico, and Juan Suárez de

Peralta, the brother-in-law of Hernando Cortés. He went to Hispaniola with Ovando in 1502 and then on to Cuba and later to Mexico.[99] A number of early leaders, including Diego Velázquez, Juan Ponce de León, Pánfilo de Narváez, and Francisco de Garay, spent some or even most of their careers outside Hispaniola. In contrast, many people who arrived with Ovando and remained in the Indies stayed in Hispaniola, including such prominent men as Álvaro Bravo, Gonzalo de Guzmán, Pedro Gallego, Juan Mosquera, Licenciado Cristóbal Serrano, and Alonso Martel, all of whom were still living there in the 1530s and 1540s. Witnesses in a 1520 deposition included Juan Dello, vecino of La Buenaventura, who had been in Hispaniola around eighteen years; Hernando Gorjón, vecino of Azua, eighteen years (he remained until his death in 1546); Alonso Hernández Galisteo, vecino of Salvatierra de la Sabana, thirteen or fourteen years; Francisco Orejón, vecino of Concepción de la Vega, eighteen years; Juan de Loredo, vecino of Bonao, twelve years; Juan de Villoria, vecino and regidor of Concepción, eleven years; Cristóbal de Ávalos, vecino of Santa María del Puerto (La Yaguana), thirteen or fourteen years; and Francisco de Vallejo, vecino of Santo Domingo, seventeen years.[100]

A number of men who arrived after Ovando also enjoyed long careers in the Caribbean. In 1560 Lope de Bardecí was over sixty years old and had been living in Hispaniola for forty-nine years. In 1512, Manuel de Rojas went to Cuba, where he served twice as lieutenant governor. He probably died there in the 1550s, although he went to Peru in the 1540s to visit his brother and then was unable to leave for some time because of the turmoil caused by the Gonzalo Pizarro rebellion. In a 1532 deposition prepared by Diego Alonso in Santiago de Cuba, he stated that he had been there for more than twenty years; witness Pedro de Valverde had known Diego Alonso and his brother Hernando for fifteen or sixteen years, as had Francisco Pozuelo.[101] Diego de Cuéllar, who arrived in Puerto Rico with don Cristóbal de Sotomayor and a group from Valladolid and Ávila and was seriously wounded in the Indigenous revolt, stated in 1528 that he had been living there for eighteen or twenty years; witnesses in his deposition of 1528 included Francisco de Consuegra, Pedro de Mata, Gil de Cabanillas, Lucas Calderón, and Martín Hernández, all of whom had arrived in Puerto Rico with don Cristóbal de Sotomayor and had been there ever since. In 1532 Pedro de Hojacastro had been in Puerto Rico for twenty-one years. Hernando de Lepe, who had lived in Puerto Rico for twenty-two years and probably went to Hispaniola with Ovando, returned to Puerto Rico from

Spain in 1534 with a large entourage of family members, including a brother and his family, and lived there until his death a few years later.[102] In 1542, Gonzalo de Santa Olalla had been living in the Indies for thirty-five years, the first six in Hispaniola followed by twenty-nine or thirty years in San Juan. In Jamaica, too, a core of longtime vecinos formed, including Bernardino de Calderón, Francisco de Bejarano, Cristóbal de Castro, and Antonio de Burguillos, all of whom, in 1524, had been on the island fifteen or sixteen years.[103] In contrast to the picture of early island populations that were constantly in flux, stable cores of population formed in all the big islands.

Longevity in the islands in itself did not ensure socioeconomic success. Far more important were advantageous connections and favorable timing, which could provide access to Indigenous labor, mining claims, or financial wherewithal, all of which played a major role in determining who would stay and who would return to Spain or move on to other destinations in the Indies. Those who enjoyed these advantages were much more likely to remain and prosper than those who did not. Yet, as some people discovered, privilege and favorable circumstances were not guarantors of long-term success. Sometimes men's ambitions exceeded their luck. The career of Lucas Vázquez de Ayllón, who served first as alcalde mayor of Concepción de la Vega and subsequently as royal appeals judge and then oidor of the audiencia, in many ways exemplifies both the promise and the pitfalls of forging a career and the basis for a family fortune in a volatile and unpredictable milieu.

Ayllón belonged to a distinguished family of Toledo, where his father, Juan de Ayllón, known as "el bueno," had been regidor and was brother to Pero Álvarez de Ayllón, a knight of the Order of Santiago, who had served the Reyes Católicos in Naples as a cavalry captain. In 1504 Lucas Vázquez went to Hispaniola, where Ovando appointed him alcalde mayor and awarded him a repartimiento in Concepción de la Vega. He became involved in mining and agriculture in the northern part of the island and forged an alliance with the Manzorro-Becerra clan, marrying Ana Becerra, the daughter of Licenciado Francisco Becerra, the leading entrepreneur and regidor of the town of Santiago de los Caballeros.

Ayllón received a repartimiento of two hundred Indians in Santiago in 1514. With his in-laws, who included the early-arriving Rodrigo Manzorro, he became an active participant in the Indigenous slave trade, especially in the Bahamas. He was one of Hispaniola's earliest investors in sugar production, before 1518 forming a partnership with Francisco de Ceballos to build an *ingenio*,[104] and he owned properties in and around Santo Domingo. He and his in-laws belonged to the political faction closely connected to the crown, headed by treasurer Pasamonte.

Information brought back from slaving voyages that touched on Florida led to a fateful turn in Ayllón's career. Favorable reports of a land on the Atlantic coast that slavers called Chicora encouraged him to petition the crown for a contract to conquer the area, which he received in June 1523. He sent Pedro de Quejo to reconnoiter the coast in 1525, after which he organized an expedition of some six hundred people and five or six ships at his own expense.[105] The attempt to establish a colony met with disaster, and Lucas Vázquez died in Florida in October 1526.[106]

The abrupt end to the career of a wealthy and politically powerful man with years of experience in the islands left his family some 15,000 pesos in debt. Lope de Bardecí testified that Ayllón's widow sold her house in Santo Domingo and went to live with her children in Puerto Plata, where they owned half of the sugar mill, although several years later she regained the house because the purchaser failed to make the payments. Ayllón's son Pero Vázquez married doña Juana de Pasamonte, the daughter of treasurer Esteban de Pasamonte, nephew and heir of Miguel de Pasamonte. Notwithstanding their distinguished parentage, in 1560 Pero Vázquez claimed that they "suffered necessity because of having little means or property."[107]

Ayllón's misadventure echoed that of other prominent men who left the islands for the mainland: Ponce de León died in 1521 after his second unsuccessful attempt to land on the Florida coast; Rodrigo de Bastidas died at the hands of fellow Spaniards in Santa Marta in 1526; and Pánfilo de Narváez and Hernando de Soto died in the course of expeditions to the present-day southeastern United States, in 1528 and 1542, respectively. As so many discovered, starting with Columbus himself, in these years the Caribbean offered few guarantees of wealth or stability.

Some Thoughts on Indians and Africans

Beginning in 1493 a new society began to take shape in the Greater Antilles. The available documentation, for the most part, sheds only indirect light on the experience of the Indians of the islands after Europeans arrived in the Caribbean, or of the Africans the newcomers brought to augment their workforce. Indigenous communities did not disappear, but they quickly came under ever-increasing stress from Spanish military campaigns, demands for gold, imposition of a new labor regime, and attempts to reduce the numbers of communities following population loss due to disease, flight, and Spanish recruitment of Indians for entradas to other islands or the mainland. These "reductions" inevitably entailed relocating people, often at some distance from their own territory, in greater proximity to Spanish towns or enterprises, and aggregating groups that hitherto had been separate. References to Indigenous communities in the Greater Antilles are scattered throughout the records but lack descriptions of their size, physical appearance, or even exact location.

Archaeological work that focuses on the contact (or early postcontact) period has shown that Europeans' impact was limited in the earliest years; there is little indication of significant changes in the Indians' material culture in their own communities.[108] Given that they came into increasing contact with Spaniards with the imposition of repartimientos, which usually required Indians to spend months living and working outside of their communities at mines or on agricultural estates, the eschewing of European goods or foods could be viewed as a choice—that is, they became familiar with European material culture but did not necessarily prefer it to their own.

Over time, however, as Spaniards imposed a coercive labor regimen and certain Christian practices (such as those relating to burial or marriage), that situation changed.[109] Las Casas's description of the famous rebel Enrique's community in the Bahoruco mentions roosters whose tongues were cut out so they would not crow and thus alert patrols to their location. Feral hogs that spread throughout the interior became part of their diet; both poultry and swine were European introductions. Yet, as Roberto Valcárcel Rojas argues, archaeological evidence suggests that some Indigenous communities continued to limit the impact of European influences or at least to manage them in ways that were relatively familiar.[110] Enrique's leadership of his community and efforts to ensure its welfare and survival suggest exactly such a strategy.[111] Floris W. M. Fleehner, however, points out that "growing power imbalances could have jeopardized indigenous self-determination with respect to the adoption and use of foreign material culture."[112]

Destined to be attached to European owners and enterprises, the Africans who were brought to the islands, in principle, lacked communities or networks of kin when they arrived. Nonetheless, many Blacks moved away from Spanish society and attained autonomy in mountainous and relatively remote areas, as did many Indians, and constituted their own communities.[113] Even with the enormous and rapid reduction in Indigenous populations, Europeans remained a minority everywhere in the islands. Although they dominated the towns, the countryside became (or remained) to a great extent the province of non-Europeans and people of mixed ancestry. That dichotomy changed little over time, and arguably continues in the present day.

2

Death and Danger in the Islands

Danger and death marked the Spanish enterprise in the islands, affecting all socioeconomic and ethnic groups. The *Santa María* ran aground near where the Spanish town of Puerto Real later would be established, on the north shore of Hispaniola, and though there was no loss of life, the ship's destruction meant that Columbus left behind a substantial contingent of men when he departed for Castile. On returning to the island in late 1493 he discovered that not one of the men who had stayed had survived to welcome them back. Fernández de Oviedo wrote that, among the group of mariners left behind, "few or none . . . had the capacity to do what the Admiral wanted, which was to know how to behave or conduct themselves among the Indians and learn their language and customs." Instead, according to what the Indigenous interpreter Diego Colón claimed to discover, the Europeans "did many bad things and took the women and daughters and everything they had."[1] Apparently in response, the Indians withheld supplies from the men, who starved as a consequence. Very possibly, however, the men's unrestrained behavior was only partially responsible for their fate; island politics probably played a part, as the relationship Guacanagarí formed with Columbus could have been viewed by other caciques as an alliance and a bid for power that threatened to disrupt existing political hierarchies. By killing the Europeans, rival caciques might have sought to undercut Guacanagarí's seeming advantage.

Given the multiple dangers that affected life in the early Spanish Caribbean—disease, famine, hurricanes, fires, conflicts with Indians and Africans, raids by French corsairs and Caribs—the destruction of the fort and men at La Navidad seems a fitting start to the Europeans' colonizing venture. Europeans encountered hazards and challenges in the Caribbean that structured life and expectations for all groups. Officials worried about defense and constantly sought royal funds to build, maintain, and staff fortifications and equip them with arms and munitions; hurricanes, fires, and insects forced the recurrent reconstruction of buildings and towns and damaged or destroyed lives, rural property, crops, and livestock; the sites of some new towns were so unhealthy that children failed to thrive; Indians committed suicide rather than live under the new order Europeans sought to impose; epidemics destroyed the labor force Spaniards needed to sustain their economic enterprises; Africans sometimes arrived in the islands already ill or succumbed thereafter to the dangerous conditions of work in gold mines or sugar estates; and rural areas were vulnerable to attack.

Responding to Disease and Health Needs

The robust Fernández de Oviedo, who lived to nearly eighty and enjoyed a long and active career in the Indies, commented matter-of-factly, "This country doesn't allow anyone to avoid being tested by diseases when they are newly arrived."[2] Epidemic diseases and their demographic impact in many ways shaped the early history of the Spanish Caribbean.[3] New diseases introduced as the result of European contact devastated Indigenous populations and caused extremely high mortality, although it should be pointed out that Indigenous populations were dropping precipitously even before the first documented epidemic, in 1518. The Americas had not been free of disease prior to the arrival of Europeans. Fernández de Oviedo discussed the spread of *buhas* in Europe after people returned from the islands, writing, "Here it is very common among the Indians, and they know how to treat [it] and have many excellent herbs and trees and plants appropriate for this and other illnesses."[4]

After contact, disease and poor health not only ravaged Native islanders but also affected Europeans and Africans, who likewise suffered illness and high mortality, if usually not at the catastrophic levels experienced by Indians.[5] Passengers who crossed the Atlantic, both enslaved and free, were at times already sick, or they became ill upon reaching the Caribbean. Indeed, illness struck at the very outset of European settlement. Just days after Columbus and the people who accompanied him on his second voyage landed on the north coast of Hispaniola in late November 1493, nearly all the passengers began to sicken from a disease apparently carried by the very domestic animals they brought with them to the islands: swine flu.[6] Influenza quickly spread from

Europeans to Indians, with devastating effects. Columbus himself fell ill. The physician Diego Álvarez Chanca did what he could to help the sick and dying, and he and Columbus remained convinced of the healthful nature of the island, although they were unable to provide an explanation for the outbreak.[7]

Thus, the first outbreak of disease in the postcontact Caribbean affected both Europeans and Indians, although with much more devastating consequences for the latter. According to Fernández de Oviedo, many people who returned to Castile from the islands in the 1490s "were ill and poor and of such bad color that they seemed dead [and as a result] they greatly defamed this land and the Indies, and people couldn't be found who wanted to come to them."[8] That general perception probably did not last long. Historian Juan Gil points out that by 1506 substantial numbers of passengers were willing to pay their own way to the Caribbean, suggesting that by this time "Hispaniola had ceased to be an inhospitable place."[9]

Spaniards in the Caribbean were well aware of shortcomings in medical care and of the unhealthy conditions that contributed to high mortality rates. Responses to health challenges were individual and private, on the one hand, and public and institutional on the other. The church (mainly bishops and religious orders) as well as royal and local officials tried to respond to medical needs.[10] When frey Nicolás de Ovando went to Hispaniola in 1502 as royal governor, the large group that accompanied him included a physician, Dr. Ponce; his brother, a surgeon, Alfonso Ponce; and a pharmacist, Ordóñez, each of them accompanied by a "mozo" (probably an assistant or apprentice).[11]

The inevitable concentration in the islands' most populous towns of both medical professionals and institutions dedicated to providing medical care, however, meant that access to treatment by a professional practitioner was limited, although whether such care as physicians could offer had any real efficacy is doubtful. Historian Esteban Mira Caballos points out that despite the continuing presence of physicians in Santo Domingo from the earliest years following contact, these practitioners, including physicians who received a salary from the royal treasury or municipal funds, were for the most part noted for neither their skill nor the consistency of their commitment to treating patients.[12]

Despite the limited results of royal and ecclesiastical efforts to ensure the availability of some kind of medical care, however, the need was generally understood to be urgent. In his instructions to don Diego Colón in 1509, King

Fernando mentioned hospitals in Buenaventura and Concepción de la Vega in Hispaniola and told the admiral to give them each 200 pesos. The king also asked if more hospitals were needed, noting, "I am informed that the majority of people who go from here become sick on arriving to the said island [Hispaniola]."[13] The king was concerned with the medical needs of Europeans, a bias that characterized Spanish health care efforts during this period.

As in Castile, towns tried to address the problem of providing care for those in need (again, this mainly meant people who belonged to Spanish society) by employing medical practitioners who would agree to treat those who could not afford to pay. This was in keeping with Spanish tradition, as municipalities often retained physicians on salary to treat indigent patients. In 1541 the royal accountant Álvaro Caballero, acting as Santo Domingo's representative at the royal court, informed the king that the city "had great necessity of having a physician who will reside in it, to treat the sick who are there as well as those in all of the island, because its villages are small and they have no doctors and they come to the city every day to be treated." He claimed that because the city's resources (*propios*) were minimal, it could not pay the salary of a doctor, "and for that reason none wants to live in it." He went on to note that there was a well-educated physician named Juan de Ibar in Santo Domingo who might be willing to fill the position, if funds from the royal treasury could be used to pay him an annual salary of 15,000 maravedís for five years.[14] The salary was minuscule, a good deal less than the city had been able to afford in earlier and more prosperous years, when salaries for physicians—and even a surgeon—ranged from 30,000 to 60,000 maravedís annually.[15] In 1529, when the lieutenant governor of Cuba, Gonzalo de Guzmán, asked for funds from the royal treasury to hire a physician in Santiago, the response was negative.[16]

In Puerto Rico in 1519 medical practitioners were limited to a barber, Maestre Juan, and a pharmacist.[17] Even after physicians appeared on the island, the situation resembled that of Hispaniola, with professional practitioners confined to San Juan. In 1536 Gaspar de Bruselas, a vecino of San Germán on the western end of the island, prepared a petition requesting permission to move to San Juan with six Indians in his service because the town lacked a physician, pharmacist, or medications. Two physicians in San Juan, Dr. Juan Carrera and Dr. Diego de Formicedo, testified in his deposition. According to Formicedo, who had treated him, Bruselas suffered from pleurisy. In his deposition, Bruselas noted that San Germán had only fifteen or twenty vecinos and could not afford to retain a physician on salary. In requesting that he be allowed to move to San Juan with his Indigenous servants (possibly slaves), he explained that the journey of some thirty leagues between the towns over rough terrain posed a grave risk to his health and even to his life. Witnesses upheld his claim, pointing out that there were no accommodations along the route for a man in Bruselas's condition and that he was "lame in his feet and hands."[18]

Another group of professional practitioners in the islands were pharmacists (*boticarios*). Pharmacist Francisco de Zamora went to Hispaniola in 1506, but he was not the first member of his trade to reach the island. The same year Sevillian pharmacist Juan Bernal shipped medicines along with other merchandise to be sold in Hispaniola.[19] Like physicians, pharmacists were required to hold licenses to practice; also like physicians, they mostly lived and worked in the larger towns, where they would be more likely to earn a decent living. Gregorio Navarro, who in 1543 was a vecino of Puerto Rico, worked as a pharmacist and was considered to be "very competent and capable in said trade" but had no license. He declared that he could not afford to go to Spain to be examined, so it was agreed that physicians on the island could administer the examination.[20]

Early hospitals were small, lacked resources, and probably were not much more reliable sources of treatment than were medical professionals. Governor Nicolás de Ovando founded the first hospital in the Caribbean, San Nicolás de Bari, in Santo Domingo in 1503.[21] In 1519 a stone building replaced the original thatched structure, but the hospital still was very small, equipped with only six beds.[22] Hospitals founded by bishops were supposed to be supported by tithes, but these often proved insufficient. In 1533, for example, a royal order instructed that the tithes intended for the hospital in Santiago in Cuba be provided because "the poor in the said hospital are being harmed and are not being treated as they should be."[23] In the 1530s, Havana's vecinos complained that they alone supported the town's church and hospital, both built of thatch, in which many of the "sick poor" died. They requested royal funds to build a new hospital of stone and in 1538 were promised the proceeds from *penas de cámara* (fines for certain crimes) for the next ten years for the purpose.[24]

In the first half of the sixteenth century there also was at least one private initiative to found a hospital, part of the ambitious plans made by wealthy sugar planter Hernando Gorjón, who earmarked most of his fortune to establish a *colegio* and chapel in Santo Domingo. Gorjón planned to donate his large estate upon his death to found the colegio and a hospital for the poor in Santo Domingo.[25] Francisco de Tapia, who served as alcaide of the port city's fortaleza in the 1520s and early 1530s, made a substantial donation of 3,000 pounds of sugar to the hospital of San Nicolás in his will.[26]

Official, ecclesiastical, and even private efforts to establish and maintain hospitals and attract or retain physicians, surgeons, and pharmacists did not address the problems posed by practitioners whose abilities and qualifications often were dubious,[27] nor did they provide a solution to the overall shortage of facilities and practitioners outside the main towns. Probably the most numerous medical practitioners among Spaniards were barbers, or barber-surgeons. Because of the shortage of medical professionals, people inevitably relied on unlicensed practitioners, whose practical skills in setting bones or treating wounds were most likely much in demand, especially in mines, on sugar estates, or in towns where major construction projects were under way. In 1537, for example, Gonzalo de Moya, a clergyman in Santo Domingo, presented a deposition in which he stated that his father, Luis de Moya, was the master builder (*alarife*) in charge of the construction of the city's cathedral and also was skilled in setting broken bones, an apt sideline for a man whose trade no doubt produced a good number of injuries. For these services, Moya accepted whatever someone was willing to pay.[28]

Nonpractitioners also concerned themselves with the provision of medicines. In 1537 doña Juana de Villasante stated that she wanted to return to Puerto Rico from Spain to take over the sugar estate she had inherited from her father, Blas de Villasante, near San Germán, and she asked to be allowed to retain the Indians he had held in encomienda. One of the arguments she made in support of her request emphasized the importance of sugar in preparing pharmaceuticals. She noted that there was no pharmacist in San Germán and thus the ingenio played an important role because it could provide "the sugar necessary for medicines and other things," as well as carpenters, blacksmiths, and other artisans, who also were lacking in the town.[29]

A number of plants that were thought to have therapeutic properties, such as balsam and canafistula, grew in the islands.[30] Certainly, the islands' Native inhabitants were well acquainted with and relied upon a range of plants for treating wounds, broken bones, and diseases like syphilis. Fernández de Oviedo described how the fleshy leaves of a plant called *espinoso* could be crushed to make a paste that, when applied to a linen cloth wrapped around the affected limb, would heal broken bones.[31] Indeed, for all groups living in the islands—Spaniards, Indians, Africans, and their descendants—the use of plants and their derivatives probably was the most common form of medical treatment and the area of medical practice in which, over time, the highest degree of convergence and mutual influence among different groups prevailed.[32]

In the countryside, where one would not expect to find any professional medical practitioners, the *estancieros* (managers or foremen) or owners of rural estates "bleed and make ointments and treat the wounds of Indians and slaves," although they were prohibited from treating people who did not belong to or serve them.[33] On an individual basis, disabled or sick Spaniards relied on the services of Indian or Black servants or slaves to care for them. A man named Pero de Ochoa, a vecino of Seville who had no feet, traveled several times between Seville and Cuba because he could not make a living in Spain, although the nature of the business that took him to and from Cuba is not known. He had purchased a Black slave to help him. When he got to Cuba in 1541, officials seized the slave and sold him for thirty *ducados* because Ochoa had failed to obtain a license to bring him. Ochoa appealed the ruling against him on the basis of his poverty and disability.[34]

In 1533 Bartolomé Sánchez Borrego, a vecino of Santiago, testified that he was very ill and more than seventy years old. He claimed to have been one of the first conquerors and settlers of Cuba. A woman named Juana, a native of Cuba, lived with and cared for him. When oidor Licenciado Juan de Vadillo conducted the residencia of the island's officials, he took Juana away from Sánchez Borrego, accusing him of keeping her as his mistress, but (according to Sánchez) did not allow Sánchez the opportunity to explain or defend himself. Sánchez pointed out that, given his age and illnesses, he hardly was likely to be consorting with a mistress. He protested not only Juana's removal from his house but also the bad treatment he claimed she had received at the hands of the people in Santiago with whom she was placed. Sánchez said that he planned to free her in his will and to leave her 100 castellanos with which to marry when he died.[35] In contrast, Guillermo de Buesos was so poor that he had no one in his home to look after him. He was a vecino of the small town of Trinidad in Cuba, and in 1534 was seventy years old, with no wife, children, retainers, Indians, or slaves. Old, ill, and alone, he depended on neighbors, who fed him and probably assisted him in other ways as well.[36]

Possibly such informal networks of care provided a safety net of sorts for the impoverished, elderly, and ill, but precisely because they were informal, there is little concrete evidence of their existence. In the Iberian world, cofradías often were sources of charity and provided some forms of aid for their members, but it is not clear whether these lay religious organizations took shape outside the largest towns, such as Santo Domingo and San Juan, during the first half of the sixteenth century. Thus, charity often depended on individual initiative.

In 1544 Pedro Vaca, a canon in the cathedral of Concepción de la Vega, said that he had become impoverished during his twelve years there because he spent everything he had helping travelers and the poor and providing them with food and money. One witness stated that Vaca's house "had become an inn for the poor" and pointed out that, in contrast, all the other clergy who held benefices in Concepción de la Vega were rich.[37] This statement suggests that such charitable commitment was not the norm. Vaca in effect established an almshouse for the poor that probably much resembled the hospitals of the time.

Among Spaniards, a not uncommon response to illness was to return to Spain. The wealthy Hispaniola-based merchant Rodrigo Manzorro took his daughter, doña Elvira Manzorro, to Spain around 1518 "to instruct her in the matters of our holy faith." Born on the island, she most likely was his daughter by an Indigenous woman. While they were in Spain, Manzorro died and doña Elvira married Francisco de Barrionuevo, another prominent figure in the early Caribbean, who was a successful entrepreneur in the pearl trade and had invested in Indigenous slave raiding expeditions. They returned together to Hispaniola, but in 1527 Barrionuevo decided to take his wife to his hometown of Soria, in north central Spain, to recuperate from an illness. She died there, thousands of miles from her home.[38]

While it may seem counterintuitive that people would undertake the sometimes difficult and always uncomfortable transatlantic voyage rather than pursue the (admittedly limited) treatment options available in the islands, many Spaniards made this choice for themselves or their family members. At times, though, other considerations likely motivated these requests for permission to return because of illness, especially those made by royal officials. Baltasar de Castro, the royal factor in Puerto Rico, asked for permission to go to Spain in 1535 to be treated for a "certain illness,"[39] and in 1539 the island's treasurer, Juan de Castellanos, sought permission to take his wife, doña Ana Pimentel, back to Castile and her *naturaleza.* He claimed that "the doctors that there are in said island say that if she doesn't go to those kingdoms to be treated she won't recover." Permission was granted, if he could find someone who would serve as treasurer in his stead.[40] In October 1536 the dean of the cathedral of Santiago de Cuba, Bachiller Diego López, said he had been ill, bedridden, and unable to get up for more than fifteen months, only having arrived there in 1534. He declared that "in this island there's no doctor or pharmacist and he can't be treated and he thinks he'll die if he can't leave to be treated." Somewhat confusingly, he claimed to have been advised to leave by a physician.[41] He received permission to return to Castile.

Not everyone associated Castile with good health. In 1534 Cuban lieutenant governor Manuel de Rojas acted on a royal order to determine why some married men were living in Cuba without their spouses and to require them either to return to Spain or to send for their wives to join them. He questioned a man named Cristóbal Verdejo, who was living in Santiago. Verdejo had been in Cuba for fourteen or fifteen years, while his wife, Ana Rodríguez, remained in the bishopric of Cartagena in southeastern Spain. He explained that he had been ill for some time but that if he went back to Spain, "he would experience even greater illness or he would die because *this country is healthier* than where he had lived" (emphasis mine). He testified that his son was on his way to Cuba and that he would arrange to bring his wife soon.[42]

In another case, a man named Andrés García said that he had been living in Cuba for fifteen or sixteen years while his wife stayed in Seville. Soon after he arrived in the island, he had gotten sick and his wife asked him to return, which he was unable to do. When he subsequently wrote to her, the "messengers" to whom he had entrusted his letter failed to find her "because of the hunger and pestilence in Seville." Receiving no reply, he assumed that she had died in the epidemic. Although he later found out that she was alive, and sent money for her passage to Cuba, she refused to make the journey unless he came for her.[43] His situation, like that of Cristóbal Verdejo, is a reminder that Spain itself could present significant challenges to health and well-being during this period. In the same inquiry, Rodrigo Alonso testified that he had sent money to his wife for her passage to Cuba but she was unable to make the trip because their son was too ill.[44]

Although no other group in the islands came close to experiencing the overall levels of mortality that devastated Indigenous populations, the omnipresence of illness and the knowledge that little could be done to treat it or to prevent its spread, together with the challenges posed by the Caribbean climate, meant that health issues often were at the forefront of Europeans' concerns. They perceived certain places as unhealthy and "sickly," probably justifiably. An early example of a site abandoned because of health concerns was Caparra, the first settlement established in Puerto Rico, in 1509, where Juan Ponce de León had a stone house built. Fernández de Oviedo wrote at some length about the site, which he described as "unhealthy and sickly, because it was between woods and swamps, and the water was brown, and children couldn't grow" but instead suffered more and more until they died. The adults, too—at least "all the Christian people"—were "pale and sick." The site posed other problems, and in 1521 it was abandoned. The town moved to what would be the site of San Juan. Although it proved difficult to supply with water, firewood, and fodder for horses, the new location of San Juan was "very healthy." In contrast, he argued that moving Santo Domingo from one side of the Ozama River to the other actually placed it in a less healthful situation and made access to good drinking water more difficult.[45]

In 1533 the vecinos of the gold mining town of La Mejorada (Cotuy) contrasted it with the nearby mining towns of Buenaventura and Bonao. At the time, La Mejorada was flourishing, while the other two towns had lost nearly all of their residents. The vecinos of La Mejorada claimed that "in the said towns of Buenaventura and Bonao, children could not be raised and multiply because of [their] being sickly places, and if some were born there they grew up sickly and potbellied and finally they died." Juan Sánchez de Honçaje testified that he had lived in La Mejorada for seventeen years and had many children; "the people who live here live very healthily," he claimed. The town's notary, Antonio Rodríguez, testified that he had children who were thirteen, seven, and three years old and that "they have grown up healthy and very well and I see that all the children born in this pueblo are." He went on to comment that in all the other pueblos he had visited, he hardly saw any children or, if there was a child, "it was sick and potbellied."[46] "Potbellied" suggests malnutrition, but the witnesses did not offer any explanation for why the children were sickly.

Although Fernández de Oviedo declared Jamaica to be "very healthy country,"[47] in 1534 the island's treasurer, Pedro de Mazuelo, petitioned the king for permission to relocate the town of Nueva Sevilla because of the unhealthiness of its site. He claimed that most of the town's eighty vecinos had died "of illnesses and pestilences" caused by its location and that people could not raise children because they died very young. Mazuelo said that only twenty vecinos remained and that the former eighty had "never had even one healthy day" because of the pueblo's site. It was "near the port, and between the port and town there are swamps and estuaries, and the breeze from the sea" passed over them, bringing "mal olor." Of the many children who had been born there, perhaps ten had survived, the rest dying at five or six months. He and others wanted to move the town to the southern coast of the island, which he argued was far healthier.[48]

In 1544 clergyman Bachiller Juan Díaz prepared a deposition and petition detailing his reasons for wanting to leave his benefice in Salvaleón de Higüey in eastern Hispaniola. Before arriving in the Caribbean, he had served in the Canaries as a vicar, working with the Holy Office and in other positions. After several years, he left Salvaleón to live in Santo Domingo because the town was far from Santo Domingo and suffered "a lack of social exchange [*conversación*] and dearth of supplies and because the land is very sickly."[49] Because there was little bread or wine, these commodities were excessively expensive. Díaz contended that the land itself was "*doliente*" (sickly) and that everyone who went there to live became ill. Witness Arias Vuelta confirmed Díaz's complaints, testifying that when he went to live in Salvaleón, he had fallen ill to the point of death and was forced to return to Santo Domingo.

Island residents did not only deem certain sites unhealthy. In 1540 Bernaldino de Quesada wrote a complaint to the king on behalf of the vecinos of Santiago de Cuba:

> Houses of stone are very humid if air and sun don't enter, and of the vecinos who live and have lived in them, many are dead . . . as has been seen from experience, that Gonzalo de Guzmán and his wife, almost within a year that they lived in . . . a stone house, they died, and it's public and well known to all the vecinos that the great humidity of the . . . houses caused it. . . . [In] this city of Santiago, more than three-quarters of the houses . . . are made of tile and walls of board. . . . They are better to live in and inhabit . . . than the stone ones.[50]

Pablo Gómez has shown that in the second half of the sixteenth century, on both an institutional and a private basis, Europeans over time attempted with some success to deal with the enormous problems posed by disease and climate by ensuring the availability of medical practitioners, establishing hospitals, and moving away from sites that they thought were unhealthy. In the first half of the century, however, such efforts often proved partial, inadequate, or tardy. Nearly all "professional" medical practitioners lived and worked in the largest towns—Santo Domingo and, to a lesser extent, San Juan. Spaniards were much aware of disease and mortality among their Indian and African slaves and servants, but there is little evidence to suggest how they addressed these issues. Domestic slaves and servants might have received medical attention because of their presence in Spanish households, but contemporary documents are mostly silent as to what if any measures were taken to care for workers on estates or in mines.

Health and the Conditions of Labor

Although they were preoccupied with their own challenges of dealing with illness and finding or providing adequate treatment, Spaniards in the Greater Antilles were well aware of the situation of the Indians and Africans with whom they lived. With few exceptions, their concerns about the mortality and morbidity that affected their encomienda workers, servants, and slaves were not (or not mainly) humanitarian but hinged instead on their anxieties about maintaining a productive workforce, an ever-growing problem as disease, forced relocation, and flight took a huge toll on the Indigenous population and, at times, on Spaniards' Black slaves as well.

Efforts to "reduce" the diminishing and scattered Indigenous population and create more centralized communities most likely accelerated the spread of disease, in addition to taking people away from their traditional lands and disrupting agricultural cycles. Enslaved Indian captives brought to the Greater Antilles from the Bahamas, Central America, Mexico, and Tierra Firme arrived traumatized, exhausted, and sometimes starving, sick, or suffering from injuries. In their weakened state, they probably succumbed rapidly to the new pathogens introduced by Europeans and Africans. At least some Spaniards drew a connection between the Indians' inability to embrace Christianity and their physical debility. According to the early treasurer of Puerto Rico, Andrés de Haro, despite efforts to treat the Indians well, "they decrease every day because they are [as] incapable in the things of the faith [as] they are in regard to their health and [are] of very weak constitution."[51]

While scholarly discussion of demographic change mainly has focused on calculating population numbers at contact in order to gauge the extent and rate of subsequent population loss, the impact of disease and mortality on specific communities, or even on individuals, can be obscured by the attention paid to larger trends. Records relating to the hacienda de Toa, in Puerto Rico, provide rare insight into the downward spiral of Indigenous population loss at the micro level. Located in the northern part of the island, near San Juan, the hacienda of the Ribera de Toa underwent several changes of administration over the course of a couple of decades. Founded by Juan Ponce de León and originally owned by the crown, it subsequently (and briefly) became an "experimental" community (*experiencia*) in which the Indians theoretically were free, although they lived under Spanish supervision. It was then (also briefly) an encomienda, assigned to Puerto Rico's treasurer Blas de Villasante, and finally an estate, rented by Diego Muriel, who previously had served as the hacienda's mayordomo and who married the cacica doña María at the urging of the bishop of Santo Domingo.[52]

Some of the people who lived and labored at the hacienda de Toa had been relocated to that area. The hacienda became home to an aggregated community, suggesting that population loss already had started to occur, perhaps due, at least in part, to the violent revolt that engulfed much of the island starting in 1510.[53] The first recorded smallpox epidemic took place in Hispaniola in 1518 and 1519 and probably affected Puerto Rico as well. Muriel's wife, doña María, succeeded to the position of cacica at the death of her uncle, Caguas, probably around 1520. Why she became ruler in preference to her brother Juan Comerio is not known, as Juan was alive during the 1520s.[54]

After the hacienda was assigned to Blas de Villasante in encomienda, Muriel traveled to Spain to ask that he be allowed to rent it from the crown, along with the Indians attached to it, citing his "*amor*" (love) for the Indians. The king agreed to the arrangement. Villasante prepared an inventory before handing the hacienda back to Muriel in 1528. That year and the following one, three lists of the people who remained at the hacienda were compiled. Muriel claimed that when Caguas died, there had been three hundred people, although not nearly that many remained when he left for Spain. He returned to find only thirty-nine men and women, and he alleged that twenty-seven others had died during Villasante's brief administration.[55]

Most notable in these inventories was the apparent disappearance of young men, some of whom probably had fled, and the breakdown of family structure. In December 1528 there were seventeen married couples, including doña

María's brother Juan Comerio and his wife, Catalina. Three of the couples were called "viejos." In April 1529 there remained at Toa only four married couples: Juan Comerio and Catalina; Francisco and Elvira, described as very old and ill; Francisco Aramana and Isabel, both old; and Diego and Catalina, also both old. Most of the other members of the diminished group were elderly women. Juan, who was blind in both eyes, had lost his wife, Elvira; a man named Juan (or Juanico) morisco [sic] was ill. Muriel stated that because so many of the Indians were sick or injured, he "wanted to take them and send them somewhere else, where they would be healthier and better protected."[56]

Testimony elicited at Muriel's behest emphasized Villasante's harsh work regimen, which contrasted with Muriel's ostensibly milder treatment. Four men from the community testified that Villasante forced them to work straight through the day with no break, supervised by estancieros and "another Christian," who pressured them to work faster, called them dogs, and occasionally beat them with a staff. When they finished their day's labor, they were forced to work into the night to make bread from the yucca they had harvested. Six adults were required to work in the mine located on the estate, including Juan Comerio and his wife. Three women and a man died there and were replaced by others. The Indigenous witnesses also mentioned their unhealthy living conditions, a complaint underscored by several Spanish witnesses, who attested to the poor state of the Indians' *bohíos* (houses) and their location in a site that was described as humid and sickly.

By 1530 the Indians living at the hacienda de Toa had all but disappeared. A hurricane in July 1529 caused widespread destruction on the island and killed many of Muriel's sheep, and, over the next two years, epidemics brought more devastation to Puerto Rico.[57] In 1536 Muriel prepared another información regarding his debts to the crown, in which he sought relief from repayment because, not surprisingly, he was unable to make the hacienda solvent and could not pay the rent he owed. At that time there remained only eight or nine Indians at Toa.[58]

This dismal history suggests some of the differential impact of specific labor requirements (particularly in mining) on different cohorts within the Indigenous group (men, women, children, and the elderly). Given that, when Villasante took control of the hacienda and its people in 1527, the community already had shrunk by around 80 percent in a decade and a half,[59] Muriel's claim that Villasante's harsh work regimen and inadequate care were mainly responsible for the continuing high mortality was tenuous. Yet both he and the Spanish and Indigenous witnesses who testified believed that poor treatment and an immoderate work regimen had an impact on the welfare of the Indians. These ideas had become part of an ongoing discussion of Spanish–Indigenous relations that extended well beyond the clergy and the crown into the larger community.

Spaniards used the need to protect the welfare of the Indians as a pretext to argue for the retention of their encomiendas. In 1527, for example, fray Pedro Mejía, provincial of the Franciscan order in Hispaniola and royal judge appointed to deal with matters relating to the Indians, said that the audiencia had released the Indians who had belonged to the encomienda of Licenciado Pero Vásquez. He argued that they should be returned to Vásquez, "because I am informed and it is well known that the said Licenciado Pero Vásquez has treated and treats the Indians very well ... and also because I've been told and I'm very certain that if the Indians were removed and taken away from where they are at present, which is their country and place of origin [naturaleza], they would die, especially being so few."[60] In 1534, in Puerto Rico, Juan de Villasante, in the name of the widow and daughter of Blas de Villasante (probably his brother), argued that the Indians who had been assigned to the ingenio near San Germán that was now held by them "are in their own place of origin where they were born and raised, and now if they were to be removed they would die and the properties would be lost."[61]

The decision about how to deal with the Indians who had been taken away from Francisco de Agüero in Cuba in 1533 suggests that in cases where repartimiento assignments were contested, the Indians most likely would suffer as a result. Agüero had argued that whoever had been reassigned "his" Indians might treat them poorly, either because they did not expect to retain them or in order to cause Agüero harm, the result of which could be that by the time a final determination was made in the case, most of the Indians would have died. A petition from Ana de Bazan, vecina of Santiago, regarding a similar case, used virtually identical language to argue the potential harm that could befall the Indians of her encomienda.[62]

These arguments had precedents. A few of the men who testified in the Interrogatorio Jeronimiano, the survey conducted in 1517 by the Hieronymites who went to Hispaniola and were charged with making certain reforms on the island, had warned of the dangers of moving Indians away from their lands, although not necessarily because of the risk of exposure to disease.[63] Juan Mosquera, who arrived with Ovando in 1502, warned that if people were forced to leave their lands, they might commit suicide, "as other times they have done for less important reasons." Mosquera also testified that because of the repeated reassignment of Indians in repartimientos, "the country has received much damage . . . because of the Indians who were moved, many have died and been poorly treated."[64] Lucas Vázquez de Ayllón was emphatic that people should not be moved from their own communities and lands, echoing Mosquera in arguing that they would be likely to kill themselves or run off.[65] Worries on the part of Spaniards that Indians were taking their own lives were common enough that suicide, along with disease, should be viewed as a serious health risk for the Indigenous population in this period.[66]

Other witnesses argued the opposite and insisted that the Indians should be brought to live in closer proximity to Spaniards. Antón de Villasante, who probably went to Hispaniola with Columbus in 1493, learned an Indigenous language from his wife. He was adamant that the Indians should not be left to live on their own.[67] Indeed, Licenciado Serrano, who went to the island with Columbus in 1493, suggested that moving the Indians closer to the haciendas where they labored would allow them to avoid the rigors of traveling back and forth and having to leave their families behind.[68] Ultimately, all the arguments were self-serving; most of the men whose opinions were solicited were encomenderos who did not want to lose their workforce. Yet they had lived in Hispaniola for quite a few years, and their opinions—however skewed by self-interest—in some measure reflected an understanding derived from personal observation of the circumstances that contributed to the illness and mortality that had engulfed the islands' peoples. Perhaps they did not fully grasp the health consequences of breaking up and moving communities or parts of them, disrupting agricultural cycles, and forcing people into contact with strangers, whether European, African, or Indigenous. In retrospect, however, it is clear that those actions accelerated the spread of disease and exacerbated its impact.

Although it is generally assumed that growing numbers of Africans were brought to the islands to redress labor shortages, in part, because they had greater resistance to the diseases that were killing the Indians, they were not immune to illness or injury. In 1533 doña Theodora de Castellón said she was unable to sell the Black slaves who had belonged to her father to pay off some of his debts "because they are ill and unable to serve other than in the said ingenio."[69] The next heir to the ingenio near San Germán (Puerto Rico), Juana de Villasante, said in 1540 that twenty of the ingenio's Black slaves had died.[70] Two years later, Gonzalo de Santa Olalla, a longtime resident of Puerto Rico, testified that more than fifty Black slaves he had purchased for the ingenio he was building near San Juan had died and needed to be replaced.[71] Given that they probably had not been in Puerto Rico for very long, it is possible that the slaves arrived already ill. That might have been true for others, as well. Officials worried about reports of *"pestilencia"* in Cabo Verde and at times tried to prevent slaves from being brought from that source, although not very successfully.[72]

Black slaves also might have died as a result of the frequently dangerous conditions involved in building and maintaining sugar mills. Hernán López, a Portuguese vecino of Santo Domingo, testified that in the 1530s, when he helped to build the irrigation works that brought water from more than a mile away to the sugar mill established by Diego Caballero, longtime secretary of the audiencia, "many Blacks died" during the construction.[73] In the mid-1530s a vecino of Santo Domingo named Pedro Sarmiento complained that Black slaves who belonged to him had been removed from his custody because of debts that he owed and had been rented out to work on ingenios and irrigation works, where they were likely to be forced to perform "excessive labor, in which the said Blacks could die." Some were working on ingenios twenty or thirty leagues away, so he was unable to visit to check on their situation. He also mentioned that six or seven slaves who remained in his house were ill. Two women cared for them, possibly Black slaves as well.[74] Sarmiento had purchased twenty-two slaves and an estancia north of Santo Domingo, jointly with Esteban Basiniana (who subsequently ceded rights in the property to Sarmiento), from the Genoese merchant Esteban Justiniano. He claimed that all twenty-two slaves were sick, lame, or otherwise unable to work; four died several days after the purchase. He said he spent 200 pesos in trying to care for them. He argued that the estancia itself was nearly worthless and that he had been deceived in the sale of both the land and the slaves. He had paid 1,300 pesos and claimed they were worth no more than 550.[75]

Although they tried to prevent the entry into the islands of Africans from places rumored to be experiencing epidemics, as far as is known, Spaniards did not impose quarantines during outbreaks of disease in the Caribbean, even though in Spain at the time such measures were known to be effective in containing or at least slowing the spread of illness.[76] Very likely, the scale and rapid dissemination of diseases, together with ignorance of their causes, kept Spaniards from making systematic efforts to separate the healthy from the ill. Even though they relied on Indigenous labor, the callous attitudes toward the Indians held by many Europeans, some of whom believed that the diseases disproportionately affecting Indians represented divine retribution for the Indians' sinful nature,[77] reflected an indifference to their suffering that is in accord with our understanding of early Spanish–Indigenous relations in the islands.

Defending the Greater Antilles

Along with health challenges, people living in the Greater Antilles, especially in port towns and coastal settlements, faced danger from sporadic external attacks by raiders. During this period the threat was mainly from French corsairs and, to a lesser extent (and mainly in Puerto Rico), Caribs. The same factors that made the Greater Antilles so vital to the Spanish enterprise in the Indies—their strategic position on the sea-lanes, their numerous and accessible harbors, their capacity to provision ships, even their human capital—made them attractive targets for outsiders. The result was constant preoccupation with defensive needs, and the varied responses included building and maintaining fortifications at the principal ports of Santo Domingo and San Juan (and later Havana), requiring Spanish men to own arms and to be available for militia service, and sometimes moving towns like San Germán in Puerto Rico and Trinidad in Cuba some distance inland to place them out of the range of shipborne artillery.

In 1538 the king instructed Hernando de Soto, the newly appointed governor of Cuba, who had been charged with the construction of fortifications for Havana, to include in the plans a "citadel where the vecinos of the said Havana can gather."[78] In the early 1540s plans were made to place a heavy chain to span the Ozama River from the fortress to the other shore and to erect a wall to surround Santo Domingo, for which authorities requested from the crown "sixty Blacks" to work on construction.[79] The king agreed to provide forty Black slaves and 4,000 pesos for the wall, along with a third of the royally owned cattle on the island (presumably to be sold to raise additional funds), and promised to send "a man experienced in these things" to direct the project.[80]

Because royal funds and the occasional shipment of arms, or even the material to construct boats, never sufficed to meet all the islands' defensive needs, private and local initiatives were of considerable importance.[81] As had been true from the time of Columbus and the earliest settlement of the islands, the crown expected ambitious individuals and private investors to organize and underwrite defense. The actions of Pero Martín de Agramonte, a regidor of the port town of Santa María del Puerto de la Yaguana in Hispaniola, show how one individual and community dealt with their external and internal defensive needs.

In May 1559 Juan Ochoa de la Vega, the general representative (*personero*) of La Yaguana, prepared a petition directed to Licenciado Cepeda, the president of the audiencia in Santo Domingo, asking that Pero Martín de Agramonte be reappointed to serve as captain, a position he had filled very successfully in the past. A year earlier, the *cabildo*, or some members of it, rather than recognizing Pero Martín's accomplishments and apparent popularity, had conferred the post on another man, Francisco Machado. Machado was brother to one of the regidores and compadre to one *alcalde*, his "great friend," while the other alcalde owed him money. Juan Ochoa contended that the decision had been made in secret, in the absence of the other regidores, and then sent to the audiencia.[82]

Ochoa's deposition described Pero Martín de Agramonte as a long-standing vecino, honorable, rich, and "genial to all." Thirteen years previously, in 1546, he had been appointed by the crown and audiencia to serve as captain in a campaign against "the Blacks in this island who are rebelling, robbing, and killing Christians and burning and destroying the towns of this island in which the said rebel Blacks are wreaking great destruction, [so that Hispaniola] was at the point of being lost, and among the towns that were burned and devastated was San Juan de la Maguana."[83] In response, Pero Martín had organized a company of thirty Spaniards, "trusted Blacks" (*negros de confianza*), and porters, who went to San Juan de la Maguana, which they found abandoned and recently burned. Three "Christians," probably mestizos, had been killed there.[84]

Martín and his men pursued the "rebel" Blacks, some hundred fighting men, killing many and capturing forty or fifty while the others escaped. Among those captured was their interpreter (*lengua*), who told them that the women, children, elderly, and ill had been left in a secret place, together with some men to guard them. The men who escaped Pero Martín's attack were in such poor straits that, for a while at least, they ceased marauding. Pero Martín de Agramonte was only one of several Spaniards who participated in these campaigns.

Several years later, in 1551, Pero Martín once again organized a campaign, this time against French raiders. A party of corsairs was reported to have landed at Yaquimo. Martín traveled overland with some other Spaniards and managed to capture twenty-three Frenchmen, with their boat, taking them back to La Yaguana. The Spaniards burned the boat and sent the prisoners on to the audiencia after Pero Martín considerately provided them with food and drink.

Unfortunately for the people of La Yaguana, this did not end their troubles with French invaders, more of whom arrived two years later, in March 1553, in a squadron of eleven ships. A heavily armed landing party looted and burned the town, which according to one report they occupied for a month. Witnesses testified that Martín was one of the last to remain there. Occupied with the town's defense, he failed to protect his own family and hacienda adequately and suffered substantial damage to his property. The French took his wife, doña Catalina de Sandoval, hostage and held her, along with an Indian woman (probably a slave) and two servants, on their ships for more than two weeks. They demanded an impossible ransom of 10,000 pesos but eventually agreed to 1,500 pesos.[85] One of the town's regidores, Baltasar Moreno, pointed out that had Martín deployed his carts and slaves to ensure the safety of his own home and family, rather than in defense of the town, his losses would have been minimal.[86]

Witnesses emphasized that Martín's wealth and generosity, together with his ingenio's proximity to town ("a matter of three shots of a crossbow"), were key to his success as captain. His ingenio afforded a full view of the sea and of any ships that might arrive, making him the town's premier guardian. He maintained arms and munitions and a *casa poblada* as well as a lookout on the mountain whence there was an unobstructed view of the sea. Fellow regidor Diego de Castro testified that Martín owned more property than the three other wealthiest vecinos of the town combined, as well as the town's finest house. His ingenio was located just a quarter league from La Yaguana and, according to one witness, could be seen from anywhere in the pueblo. Although the bells in the town's church were small, they could be heard clearly at the ingenio, so the townspeople could summon Martín readily if he was on his estate. La Yaguana's mayordomo and chief constable, Alonso Morales, testified that, in addition to the arms and artillery that Martín maintained, he also had seven or eight Spaniards in his service. Morales claimed that Martín's popularity in the pueblo was such that "if there were a vote, he would not lack even four vecinos," who supported him because, according to witness Baltasar Moreno, "the pueblo has much love for him."[87]

In the 1540s La Yaguana's vecinos numbered twenty or fewer. After off-and-on discussions of fortifying the town, officials in Santo Domingo had concluded that its geographic situation made it all but impossible to defend, "because the port is open on the coast of the sea, which is said to go on for three or four leagues, and in all of them the enemies can safely land and come to the pueblo to burn it. . . . If fortifications were built, it would only serve for the enemies to fortify themselves in it."[88] With treasury funds for public works always scarce in any case,[89] the vecinos of La Yaguana had to depend on their own resources—or those of their wealthiest vecino—for defense. Relying on private resources for defense was not unusual, and wealthy landowners often took the initiative, no doubt with an eye to protecting their own properties as well as the surrounding area.

In Puerto Rico, for example, Blas de Villasante proposed building a *casa fuerte*, a fort or strong house, at his ingenio "in order to keep arms and artillery for the security of the ingenio and of its district and the seacoast, and defend against and attack the French enemy if they were to come at some time to the said island, and the Blacks if they want to rebel, as at some time they have tried." The queen granted him permission in 1531.[90] In 1538 Diego Caballero proposed building a tower and casa fuerte of stone at his ingenio on the Nigua River, four leagues from Santo Domingo, near the coast. He promised to maintain a considerable store of arms and munitions (including fifty lances, two dozen shields, six crossbows, and more). In return, Caballero requested that the tenancy of the fort be granted to him and his descendants, with a salary of 150,000 maravedís a year, a sum that also would cover the salaries of four people who would serve there.[91] It is not known whether the king agreed to this proposal.

Attacks by the French were commonplace, but their frequency rendered them no less destructive.[92] Although the quick response of a ship captain to an attempted attack on Santiago de Cuba in 1537 spared the town from damage, the same French ships went on to attack and loot Havana.[93] Such attacks devastated individual lives as well as towns. In July 1555 French corsairs again attacked Havana, where they captured Juan de Lovera, the alcaide of the fortress, robbing him and his wife, doña Aldonza Maldonado, of most of their valuables. In order to pay a ransom of 2,100 pesos de oro for her husband's release, doña Aldonza had to sell six Black slaves as well as jewelry and some clothing she had managed to keep, which had been part of her dowry. The couple was left destitute. By 1558 doña Aldonza was a widow, described as "poor and wretched," dependent on others for food and lodging, and accompanied by only an "old Black woman and her daughter." Lovera and his wife were not the only ones to suffer losses, of course. Regidor Antonio de la Torre said that the French stole much of his property and burned his home along with much of the rest of the town.[94]

The main towns organized militias for defense, a practice formalized by a royal cédula issued in October 1540 mandating the organization of militia companies that were supposed to drill every four months and requiring vecinos to maintain arms.[95] A muster conducted in Santo Domingo in 1530, possibly in response to the arrival of French corsairs, provides a detailed account of vecinos' arms, together with any horses they owned and men who were in their service. As would be expected, wealthy men, including officials, presented the largest number and variety of arms and had the most men in their service. Diego Caballero, longtime secretary of the audiencia and the owner of two ingenios, presented four lances, four pickaxes, two shields, three daggers, seven or eight swords, and four horsemen, and reported another "eight or ten Spaniards in his house and his properties and ingenios and other Spaniards, among whom fifteen could come on horseback."[96] Luis Fernández stated that he had "some Christians who work in the ingenio" as well as a shield, sword, and lance.

The secular clergy were not exempt; a canon of the cathedral presented a lance and two swords and the sacristan a sword, while another canon declared two lances and two swords and the services of "a Christian." The dean had "three Christians in his house and in his haciendas four, [and has] two horses with their saddles and two swords." The longtime porter for the audiencia, Pedro de Vidaguren, owned a horse and saddle, two kinds of lances, a dagger, two swords, and a small shield. The *virreina* doña María de Toledo's household could provide "nineteen Christians, twenty crossbows, and a cart of pikes, fifteen muskets, two horses, two small cannons, and fourteen shields."[97]

A typical vecino, of course, owned only a sword and perhaps a shield. In 1541 a similar muster took place in San Juan in Puerto Rico. The list was not organized by place of residence, as in Santo Domingo; instead, the men were grouped according to whether or not they had horses.[98] The possession of arms did not necessarily mean, however, that all these men also had fighting skills or were willing to employ them when summoned.

Confronting Resistance

The occupation of the Greater Antilles by Europeans entailed substantial violence. Conflict with the Native people of Hispaniola was ongoing by the mid-1490s, and as was discussed in chapter 1, soon after his arrival in 1502 royal governor frey Nicolás de Ovando initiated a successful series of military campaigns aimed at suppressing the most powerful remaining caciques. As late as 1512 the king worried that if colonists in the Indies built strong houses (casas fuertes) of stone, Indians could seize them. He instructed that stone should be used only for the foundation and three feet of the walls; above that, colonists should erect earthen walls (*tapias de tierra*) and brick buttresses.[99] Although by 1512 such a threat no longer existed in Hispaniola, Spaniards' attempt to settle on Puerto Rico not long before that time had set off an Indigenous uprising that resulted in the deaths of probably half the Spaniards on the island and lasted, in one form or another, until around 1517.[100]

Perhaps because of the extensive violence of those years, subsequent conflicts in Puerto Rico, at least with Indians, mainly involved external raids and attacks. In 1520 Baltasar de Castro described a substantial raid in which some 150 "men of war" in five canoes disembarked at the Humacao River and attacked some estancias. They killed a total of thirteen Spaniards and at least the same number of Indian women, burned houses, captured a fishing boat on the coast, and carried off four Natives of the island.[101]

Hispaniola and Cuba experienced decades of turmoil in the countryside, resulting from determined resistance on the part of both Indians and Blacks who evaded Spanish control. In response, Spanish officials dispatched armed patrols, or *cuadrillas*, consisting of Spaniards, together with Indian and Black slaves and servants, in pursuit of the people they called *indios y negros alzados*, or *cimarrones*.[102] Outside of the largest towns, disorder and defiance on the part of Indians and Blacks presented at least as great a threat to Spanish residents as did external attacks.

Some of these conflicts became substantial confrontations, as suggested by the description of Pero Martín de Agramonte's role in dealing with the large force of Blacks that attacked San Juan de la Maguana. What is usually considered the first revolt of enslaved Africans in Hispaniola started on the rural estate of the second admiral don Diego Colón, in late 1521, with twenty of his slaves, most of them ostensibly Wolofs ("Gelofes"). The uprising spread rapidly and grew in strength to perhaps forty people. According to Fernández de Oviedo, they headed toward the town of Azua and reached a cattle estate owned by Melchor de Castro, the *escribano de minas,* some nine leagues from Santo Domingo, where they killed a mason, took a Black and a dozen Indian slaves captive, and robbed the estate. From there they went to the ingenio of the oidor Licenciado Alonso de Zuazo, where there were around 120 slaves whom the rebels hoped to recruit. With some horsemen and men on foot sent by Colón, Castro led an attack that killed six Blacks. Castro suffered a serious wound to his left arm. Subsequently, some of the other rebels were killed or apprehended.[103]

The inconclusive end of this revolt, much like the uprising in San Juan de la Maguana twenty-five years later, suggests why disorder and unease continued to trouble the countryside. Very seldom did these confrontations result in the definitive suppression of rebel groups. In this and other ways the best-known revolt of the period, that of Enrique, or Enriquillo, in Hispaniola, was unusual, even unique, in its outcome. After some fourteen years of fruitless and expensive patrols and failed efforts to negotiate with Enrique, Spanish officials finally persuaded him to resume negotiations. He agreed to a treaty that recognized the independence of his community, which received lands near Azua, where they settled.[104] By the time of the treaty (1533), Enrique's community numbered several hundred people living in the Bahoruco mountains and included mestizos and Blacks. Under its terms Enrique agreed to help pursue and return to Spanish authorities any future runaways or "rebels." The similarity between the terms of this treaty and the treaties that Spaniards subsequently would make with Black maroon communities is striking.

Financing and staffing patrols in the countryside was a burden on local resources. In 1529 the audiencia estimated that they had spent 25,000 pesos on the "war" with Enrique, only one-quarter of which came from the royal treasury.[105] In 1532 Santo Domingo's cabildo noted that some vecinos complained that ingenio owners had failed to contribute their fair share to the costs. Not surprisingly, given that some of the councilmen themselves owned ingenios, they insisted that they had in fact "contributed more than anyone else" and that each ingenio owner "had provided at his cost ... a Spaniard and a trustworthy

Black who has a wife and children and an Indian," occasionally for five or six months at a time.[106]

If the resolution of Enrique's lengthy revolt was unique in the fraught history of Spanish–Indian interactions in the Caribbean, in some ways its outcome did not differ all that much from the outcome of other episodes. During the years of Enrique's rebellion—1519 to 1533—there were other maroons, both Indian and Black, in the countryside, and Enrique's agreement to the treaty did not end the endemic violence. In 1527 a witness in La Mejorada testified that a man named Hernandillo "el tuerto" (the one-eyed) was "well known for being cruel and better armed than Enriquillo, because it is said publicly that the damage that Enriquillo did, he did on the advice of Hernandillo." Bachiller Álvaro de Castro credited Pedro Romero—who subsequently played a key role in the negotiations with Enrique—for finding Hernandillo in the mountains, killing his companions, and later capturing him and bringing him to justice.[107]

Oidor Dr. Infante wrote to the king in February 1532 that in an incident near Puerto Real, the wife of a Spaniard, along with two children and fourteen enslaved Indian men and women, had died, and that the Indians belonging to the Spaniard had helped to fight off the attack. In May of the same year, he reported that a cuadrilla of eight Spaniards had been formed in each of four towns (San Juan de la Maguana, La Yaguana, Puerto Real, and Cotuy). He added that there was no need for patrols to protect the sugar ingenios because each "has sufficient population to defend itself against the cimarrones, because it has at least one hundred people, between Spaniards and Blacks."[108]

Although it is likely that the various "rebel" groups were aware of one another and maintained some contact, there is no solid evidence that they were part of a single, larger movement. Indeed, the fact that similar activity on the part of Indians and Blacks continued unabated after Enrique signed the treaty suggests that many people did not recognize him as their leader or consider themselves part of his community.[109] Historian Gabriel de Avilez Rocha suggests that "over the 1520s and early 1530s, they [Enriquillo's people] and hundreds of other settlers of Native, African, and mixed heritage established a sprawling constellation of autonomous communities" in the interior.[110]

Officials invoked the memory of Enriquillo long after the treaty had been concluded. Licenciado Cerrato wrote to the king in 1544 complaining about the "many *ladino* slaves born in the country, because this is a bad nation of people, very daring and badly inclined, and that from experience it's been seen that all those ... who became their captains have been and are ladinos ... and this also was seen in the business with Enriquillo."¹¹¹ Indeed, Enrique's reputation quickly spread beyond Hispaniola. Cuba's lieutenant governor, Manuel de Rojas, worried that Enrique had crossed to Cuba and made common cause with Indigenous rebels there. In a deposition he prepared in 1533 Rojas stated that "it's notorious how in past times this island has been very troubled by *indios cimarrones* who have done many killings of Spaniards and Indians and other robberies and damages in different parts of the country and ... for the remedy of which many times at my own cost I have organized *cuadrillas de gente*."¹¹²

Rojas also wrote that one Indigenous leader, named Guama, had been in rebellion for more than ten years. Rojas sent an armed patrol of Spaniards, Blacks, and Indians under the command of Diego Barba which attacked Guama's settlement, killing or apprehending most of the people. Some people who were being held captive there said that there were signs that Enriquillo, "el de Española," had come to Cuba—they had seen several canoes that they thought belonged to him—and that Guama either had been advised of or was hoping for his arrival. That hope (or fear) failed to materialize, and Barba returned from his mission with twenty-two prisoners.¹¹³

Over the years, Rojas equipped several patrols at his own expense, at times borrowing money in order to pay the participants. A witness named Andrés García stated that Rojas "gave *cacona* [goods given in compensation] abundantly to the Indians and Blacks such that all of them were left happy and willing to go on patrol again."¹¹⁴ Rodrigo Alonso testified that in the raid in which he participated, Spaniards received in compensation 3.5 pesos per month, together with any slaves they took.¹¹⁵ In a lengthy letter to the king, in 1532, Rojas criticized the efforts of his predecessor, Gonzalo de Guzmán, accusing him of "a certain negligence in addressing the issue of the rebel Indians." Guzmán simply instructed the councils of the various towns to organize and equip patrols to "wage war," rather than traveling personally to the areas most affected. Guzmán collected funds from the towns by imposing an excise tax (*sisa*) to acquire arms that he then distributed, but according to Rojas, this effort left the vecinos "unhappy and saying that the said Gonzalo de Guzmán had more desire to return home to this city [Santiago] than to concern himself with the things of war."¹¹⁶

In another wave of violence around the same time, Indians burned the town of Puerto del Príncipe. Vasco Porcallo de Figueroa fended off attacks in the area of Trinidad and Sancti Spíritus, as Rojas himself did in San Salvador (Bayamo), where he owned property, at his own expense. Only when there was trouble near Santiago did Guzmán involve himself directly.[117]

Conflicts with the island's Indians continued in Cuba in the 1530s. Rojas reported the presence of "ciertos esclavos indios alzados" (some rebel Indian slaves) near Santiago in 1534, and their kidnapping of a married woman in the city.[118] In February 1539 the king responded to a report from the town council of Santiago that explained that the fall in the amount of gold smelted mainly was due to "an uprising by certain Indians against the Spaniards and peaceful Indians in which they killed eight Spaniards and forty peaceful Indians."[119] Given that the attack occurred during the period in which Cuba's governor, Hernando de Soto, had left his wife, doña Isabel de Bobadilla, to serve as acting governor while he led his expedition to Florida, it is possible that the Indians saw an opportunity to challenge Spanish control in the absence of a strong authority on the island.[120] In August 1539 Guzmán wrote to the king complaining that Soto had left the island vulnerable by recruiting men like Vasco Porcallo and others for his expedition. He mentioned that in the previous two years more than twenty-five Spaniards had died in the province of Santiago alone due to conflict with the Indians.[121]

Violence on the part of Blacks in the countryside was equally intractable and in some ways more complicated, since Black slaves were valuable property. In October 1533 the king wrote to the audiencia, saying that Francisco Dean, in the name of the town of San Salvador, had complained that Blacks were going around armed, entering Indian pueblos, robbing them, and taking their women and doing other damage. He alleged that local authorities were unable to send patrols out after them because most or all of these Black slaves belonged to the governor and other officials and "principal people" and thus operated with impunity.[122] At the end of 1533 Rojas wrote to the king that "four Black slaves among those who work in the mines have rebelled" and that he had sent two patrols to deal with them, one of which engaged the men, who died in the fighting. Their heads were brought to San Salvador and placed on pikes, which Rojas felt served as an effective warning to other potential rebels.[123]

In 1536 Gonzalo de Guzmán explained to the king that even before there were so many Blacks in Cuba, they had established "*una hermandad de arca*" for the island's security, to which everyone who owned slaves contributed. They used the fund to pay people to pursue runaways. When Licenciado Juan de Vadillo went to Cuba to conduct his residencia, he discontinued the practice. Guzmán argued that because the numbers of slaves had increased considerably, they should reinstate it, calling it "a very necessary thing, because even though there might be ten rebel Blacks, there's no one who will go after them voluntarily if he's not paid and given food and arms and other things."[124] A royal order reinstated the collection of funds from slave owners.

In Hispaniola, as well, problems with maroons in the countryside were endemic. In 1543 oidor Licenciado Juan López Cerrato wrote to the king that "ciertas cuadrillas" (certain gangs) of Blacks had killed some Christians in the sierras de Santiago and in the mountain range that extended up to Montecristi on the northern coast.[125] Melchor de Castro wrote to the king in April 1544 that the potential threat from maroon Blacks had affected gold mining, as people were afraid to enter the mining areas.[126] In a letter of the same month, Cerrato wrote:

> In this island there are many rebel Blacks in such quantity that the vecinos of la Vega [Concepción] and Puerto de Plata or Santiago don't dare leave their homes to visit their estates except in patrols and that the miners sleep eight by eight with their lances in their hands for fear of the said Blacks. . . . They injured a Christian and carried off a Black man and Black woman from Francisco de Ávila, and on the road from La Yaguana near San Juan de la Maguana many Blacks are around and they have killed and every day kill Christians. . . . The Blacks are people in need of great punishment and suppression because if they sense in their owners . . . any fear or that they don't dare to command them, they have no respect for them.[127]

Even at this relatively late date, there still were Indians in Hispaniola who also continued to defy Spanish authority. Cerrato sent a cacique named García Hernández in pursuit of another cacique and his people in the mountains. In contrast to Castro's report, however, in the same year (1544) he wrote that the situation with Black cimarrones had improved, and he went on to say that of one hundred Blacks who flee to the mountains, "ninety-nine [do so] because of bad treatment and cruelties done to them by their owners and overseers, and this is clearly seen, because not one man who treats his slaves well" had his slaves escape.[128]

Worries about Blacks in Puerto Rico were somewhat different than in Hispaniola. According to Juan de Castellanos, a longtime resident of the island who represented the city of San Juan at court in 1534, "In the said island of San Juan [Puerto Rico], there are few Christian Spaniards and many Blacks, for which reason the said island is in much danger that the said Blacks will rebel . . . because of their being . . . very good friends of the Carib Indians of the nearby islands."[129] Many residents believed that Wolof slaves were the principal culprits in "the uprising of the Blacks and deaths of Christians" and asked the king to ban them from the island, as they incited others "who are peaceful and from other lands and of good habits."[130] Like Cuba, Puerto Rico had what they called an *arca de los negros* to finance patrols to capture escaped slaves.[131] Notwithstanding their worries about potential violence from Black slaves, however, vecinos of the island requested that the stipulation that there must be one Spaniard for every three Blacks in a work gang be modified to one for every five instead, suggesting that worries about controlling slaves might have been exaggerated.[132]

A Hazardous Existence

The hazards of living in the islands during this period perhaps did not greatly exceed the norm for contemporary early modern societies, but the combination of external and internal threats, together with the impact of disease and environmental forces, could make life seem precarious. Then as now hurricanes in the Caribbean frequently, if unpredictably, caused substantial damage in both towns and countryside. Fernández de Oviedo described three destructive hurricanes in 1508 and 1509, optimistically (and erroneously) declaring that the threat had been eliminated for good by ridding Hispaniola of the devil. He credited the *mariscal* Pero Gallego for having established the first sanctuary of stone for the *Santo Sacramento* in the Franciscan monastery in Santo Domingo. He believed that the presence of the Holy Sacrament in the city's churches and monasteries had brought an end to hurricanes, although in fact they continued to visit the islands regularly.[133]

In 1527, for example, García de Aguilar referred to the damage from a hurricane in the previous year that "carried off all his property and cattle." The ingenio near San Germán (Puerto Rico) that doña Theodora de Castellón inherited from her father suffered major damage from three hurricanes in 1530, which destroyed most of the fields of cane as well as the building that housed the sugar refinery and other property, where some one hundred people lived. Damages were estimated to exceed 4,000 pesos.[134] Garcí Troche provided a particularly graphic description of the damage from the hurricane that struck Puerto Rico on July 28, 1530. At the time, he and his family were at their hacienda on the Ribera de Toa, where the wind knocked over all the bohíos and the river flooded the fields. Many ships in the port were driven onto land, where they were smashed to pieces.[135] The destruction on the island was so widespread that in 1531 San Juan's town council asked the king to declare a two-year moratorium on the repayment of debts owed by vecinos.[136] In 1532 Cuban lieutenant governor Manuel de Rojas also blamed the "storms and hurricanes that destroy haciendas and [cause] other tribulations and uneasiness" on the lack of a *sagrario* (sanctuary), where the holy sacrament could be kept, in any of the island's churches.[137]

Given that during this period the majority of buildings were constructed of highly perishable materials—wood and thatch—fire also wrought considerable destruction. While Benito de Astorga was building his sugar estate in Hispaniola, for example, fire destroyed not only all of the wood that was to be used to build the ingenio but also a number of carts, thirty huts in which slaves were housed, and two other lodgings, along with other items, including cut wood, and a field of cane, sparing only a couple of small shacks and a kitchen.[138] The city of Santiago in Cuba burned in the 1530s, and French raiders burned down San Germán in Puerto Rico three times. No earthquakes were recorded for this period, although a devastating one struck Hispaniola on December 2, 1562. Santiago de los Caballeros experienced the most direct hit, but the destruction of Concepción de la Vega was extensive, "not leaving a single house standing." In Santo Domingo it destroyed the Mercedarian church and partially damaged the Franciscan monastery and the Dominican church.[139]

Insects could damage crops and make certain places nearly uninhabitable. Stinging ants descended on Puerto Rico and Hispaniola in 1518 and 1519, destroying many fruit trees. The infestation eventually subsided, although whether this was the result of processions and prayers seeking saintly intervention cannot be known. Although indigenous crops such as yucca and sweet potatoes were relatively resistant to pests, the tendency of Europeans to introduce monocropping was very likely responsible for increasing problems with insects over time. The proliferation of fruit trees in places like Santo Domingo itself could have been a contributing factor to infestations.[140]

If hurricanes, insects, and fires were mostly natural disasters—fire frequently could be used as another means of waging war—humans were entirely responsible for militarizing the early Spanish Caribbean. Spaniards not only conducted brutal military campaigns in the islands of the Greater Antilles but also deployed considerable manpower and resources in seeking out and fighting groups of autonomous Indians and Blacks in the countryside. They also carried out their personal and political feuds in both urban and rural areas, as will be discussed further in chapter 3. Nearly every European man or household owned arms, but Europeans also put arms into the hands of Indians and Blacks whom they considered to be "docile" or "trusted" (*mansos* or *de confianza*), so that they could assist in campaigns to pacify the countryside or, again, in personal vendettas. In effect, Europeans "weaponized" the very people they sought to control.

3

Government, Politics, and the Law

As would be true wherever Spaniards encountered substantial Indigenous populations in the Americas, finding peoples who practiced agriculture and lived in societies with recognized rulers and forms of sociopolitical organization proved crucial to how Spaniards organized everything, from their economic enterprises to choosing sites for towns to the imposition of laws and institutions. They first began to figure out how to do this in the Caribbean. The extension of Spanish control over new lands and peoples of differing religion, language, and customs had significant precedents in the centuries-long Reconquista of the Iberian Peninsula and the protracted and often strongly resisted conquest and settlement of the Canary Islands.[1] As we saw in chapter 1, however, the occupation of the large islands of the Caribbean and the subsequent expansion of Spanish dominion to the mainland presented new and unanticipated challenges to government, oversight, and control.

Not least of these challenges was the multiethnic composition of the overseas enterprise. Spaniards had to figure out how to deal with the varied peoples Indigenous to the places where they intended to live, and they also brought Africans to the islands, introducing additional ethnic groups that would have to be integrated into the new order. The result, in the early years, was a good deal of experimentation and inconsistent, often contradictory, policies and behavior on the part of the crown, the clergy, and the officials and settlers on the ground.

The disorder and inevitably provisional character of the early years of settlement, in which Columbus and his relatives and retainers clashed with would-be rivals and to some extent with the crown itself, while at the same time fighting with and attempting to subdue local groups, challenged royal efforts to construct a system of government and administration. The crown aspired to secure new sources of revenue while of necessity accommodating the ambitions of individuals who actually were on the scene, directing and participating in the enterprises that would produce the wealth to which all aspired. At the heart of—and complicating—many of the issues related to the establishment of Spanish claims to authority were questions about how to deal with the islands' Native inhabitants and who should benefit from their labor. As the discussion in chapter 1 suggests, the broad powers and privileges granted to Columbus by royal concession before he ever crossed the Atlantic delayed the establishment of royal institutions and hence, to some extent, the implementation of royal policy in Hispaniola following Columbus's first two voyages.

In the early years the intense, even obsessive, interest of Fernando and his officials at court in the wealth to be reaped from the islands made the king as much a contender for control over local affairs as were rival factions of Europeans, one aligned with Columbus and his family and the other more closely tied to the crown.[2] By the middle of the second decade of the sixteenth century the supporters of the crown, whom Manuel Giménez Fernández calls the "clan pasamontista" and which Miguel de Pasamonte himself referred to as the "*servidores*," dominated most of Hispaniola's towns and included the appellate judges (Ayllón, Villalobos, and Matienzo), royal officials, and a number of merchants and other wealthy men.[3]

The king's interest in the islands translated into a stream of ordinances and regulations directed toward officials on the scene. These touched every aspect of life, from marriage between Spaniards and Indians and desired gender balances in groups of African slaves to colonization schemes, taxation, and how often and where gold would be smelted and registered.[4] The constant royal intervention in local affairs entailed inconsistencies and contradictions that suggest the newness of the circumstances encountered in the Caribbean as well as the complications that arose not only from the crown's efforts to maximize the benefits to be gained from the islands but also from royal officials' determination to profit from the enterprise on an individual basis as well. Like other settlers, officials in the islands received repartimientos that entitled them to use Indian labor in their mines and agricultural lands, and royal officials in Spain itself also held such grants in absentia. Probably the most effective reform accomplished by the Hieronymite commission during its brief tenure was to reduce the number of encomiendas held by people who had never set foot on the islands.[5]

The encomienda system as established in the Greater Antilles represented a significant institutional innovation. In Castile, encomiendas were grants of jurisdiction made in the lands of the military orders. The encomiendas created in the Caribbean and subsequently elsewhere in the Indies bore only a distant relationship to their peninsular counterpart. Although it served a similar function of rewarding people for their services to the king (in practice, often meaning those who possessed favorable connections to the crown and its court), the Spanish American encomienda, unlike its Spanish predecessor, did not concede jurisdiction over "vassals" but rather over access to labor. Recipients of these awards readily embraced the new title, *encomendero*, that the grant conferred, but they did not enjoy anything like the privileges of a *comendador* of a military order or of a noble who exercised lordship over a town and its district in Castile.

Encomenderos often exceeded the limited prerogatives that they could legally exercise over "their" Indians, but the encomienda was not a concession of jurisdiction, nor did it represent a devolution of judicial or governing authority; the encomendero, in principle at least, did not have the power to govern or to exercise judicial powers. Thus, the crown stopped well short of creating a new noble class in the Indies and avoided vesting political authority in ambitious and independent individuals who were not directly accountable to it. In the early years the encomienda was an important vehicle for interaction between Spaniards and Indians, and it provided the recipients with a significant (if ephemeral) concession of royal largesse; it did so, however, in a form quite distinct from that of its peninsular counterpart.

The crown not only prevented the emergence of a new noble group in the Caribbean but also stymied the formation of Spanish–Indigenous chiefdoms in the Greater Antilles.[6] Spanish–Indian marriages were discouraged in the early years, and royal ordinances explicitly stated that Spanish men who married Indigenous women would have no rights to the lands or people attached to their in-laws and kin. As the existing chiefly group—and the Indigenous population as a whole—shrank in size and the number of women rulers increased, the marriage of Spaniards to so-called cacicas began to have greater appeal because of the possibilities it offered for expanding Spanish control over people and territory. The 1516 instructions to the three Hieronymites encouraged Spaniards to marry cacicas or the daughters of caciques because that way a Spaniard "will become cacique and will be regarded and obeyed as such."[7]

If on the one hand the crown circumscribed the prerogatives of the encomenderos, on the other it barely recognized the sovereignty of the islands' Indigenous rulers, though it made some limited concessions to the authority that caciques exercised over their own people, presumably hoping to use them as intermediaries. Perhaps drawing on Spanish experience in the Canaries, Ovando attempted to incorporate two or three of the Native chiefs into the new order by making them encomenderos, with results that were far from satisfactory from the Spanish point of view.[8] In only one instance did royal officials negotiate with an Indigenous group in Hispaniola that had defied Spanish authority for many years (from 1519 to 1533). Enriquillo (or Enrique), discussed in chapter 2, was kin to Anacaona and Behecchio, highly placed members of the former cacique group, and he eventually gained official recognition of his autonomy and that of his followers.[9]

The treaty made with Enrique did not have broader implications for the sovereignty of Indigenous peoples in the Caribbean; it did, however, have repercussions for the third group that by then was living in the region in some numbers: Black slaves. Africans were present in the islands from the earliest years, most commonly employed in skilled and semiskilled occupations—at first construction and gold mining, then later the many tasks related to the creation of sugar estates and cultivating and refining sugarcane. As such, they were invaluable participants in the establishment of European enterprises and society, but they proved far from easy for Spanish authorities to control. While the revolt that began on the estate of don Diego Colón at the end of 1521 (discussed in chapter 2) generally is considered to have been the first revolt of African slaves on Hispaniola, slaves had been escaping, and sometimes making common cause with Indians who also had fled Spanish control, for quite some time before that.[10]

Although Spaniards were extremely reluctant to negotiate with Indigenous groups, they were more willing to come to terms with Africans who defied the colonial order. In Hispaniola they at times negotiated and made agreements with the leaders of bands of rebel slaves.[11] Treaties concluded with groups of fugitive Black slaves elsewhere in the Indies closely followed the model set by the 1533 agreement with Enriquillo. Under the terms of that pact, he and his people gained the rights to their own community and lands and received certain goods, in return for which they agreed to seek out and apprehend other rebels and to turn over to Spanish authorities any fugitive slaves who tried to join them.

Government and politics in the islands, therefore, had to take into account the self-imposed need to control Indians and Blacks and to ensure the availability of their labor. This perceived need was both a matter of safety and of profitability, as the new colonies could not survive unless they could become self-sustaining. The church, too, played a part in the effort to incorporate Indians and, to a lesser extent, Africans, into the new colonial order. While the clergy sometimes buttressed royal policy and at other times sought to modify it, they for the most part did not oppose the fundamental goals of bringing Indians and Africans into Christian society and making them productive subjects of the crown. They directed their criticisms toward the methods used by officials and encomenderos to achieve these objectives but not toward the ends themselves. The role of the church and clergy in the islands is discussed more fully in chapter 4.

In the Caribbean the crown had little choice but to rely on men who gained prominence by virtue of their participation in the often violent imposition of Spanish rule and the early development of economic enterprises. Although they sometimes received official titles from the crown, as Columbus had, such men almost always invested their own fortunes or went into debt to others in order to conduct campaigns of conquest and occupation. Not surprisingly they expected generous rewards in the form of offices and grants of land and Indians in return.

Not all officials emerged from the local scene, of course. The king continued to send men from Spain to serve in a range of offices. But in the early years, especially, the distinctions between local and royal officials—and indeed among officials, encomenderos, and entrepreneurs—could be difficult to discern, as they all were doing much the same things. Common business interests, marital ties and strategies, and kinship networks blurred the lines between royal and local interests and elites.

From a pragmatic point of view this blurring had the advantage of encouraging and facilitating collaboration among the crown, officials, and nascent elites in the Indies. Although friction and factionalism characterized the politics of the early Caribbean, these did not reflect clear lines of contention between local and royal concerns. Indeed contention among various parties allowed the king and his officials to work toward safeguarding royal interests while retaining the support of at least some of the local actors involved. Whether in the early years the resulting system of government, characterized as it was by ineffective enforcement of royal ordinances and a high level of factionalism, was the most efficient model achievable is debatable. Its very contentiousness left the crown considerable latitude to impose its will, but at the same time political feuds, corruption, and even criminal behavior on the part of officials undermined the effective functioning of laws and institutions.

Structure of Government

The institutions of government introduced in the Greater Antilles drew on Iberian models but did not strictly duplicate them. The audiencia only became fully functional in the 1520s. After the death of Diego Colón, there was no viceroy, but in any case the audiencia often had circumvented him and reported and responded directly to the king and the Council of the Indies. Santo Domingo's high court, the first established in the Americas, was modeled on the audiencias of Valladolid and Granada.[12] In 1544, for example, a royal cédula stipulated that the hours during which the audiencia conducted business should be the same as in Valladolid and Granada, but it allowed that, because the weather in Hispaniola varied little throughout the year, they could convene at whatever time in the morning they preferred, as long as they conducted business for three hours. Two years later, the oidores received instructions to carry staffs of office (*varas*), as did the oidores in New Spain.[13]

Hispaniola's audiencia, however, took on functions that the appellate courts in Castile did not perform. Oidores, for example, were expected to oversee the periodic smelting of gold and to conduct visits of inspection to towns and mines. They often were also charged with conducting *residencias* of other officials, especially of lieutenant governors.[14] In addition to the oidores, the audiencia had other officials attached to it, including a prosecutor, secretary, and porter. Oidores earned a decent annual salary of 1,000 ducados but almost invariably also owned income-producing properties and invested in commercial enterprises that could generate a good deal of additional wealth.[15]

The crown sent other royal officials to the Caribbean as well. Each island had a treasurer and (usually) an accountant (*contador*), a factor, and an inspector (*veedor*), all of whom were concerned in one way or another with collecting royal revenues and accounting for expenditures. This proliferation of offices led to some overlap in function and to friction among officials and institutions. Lieutenant governor Manuel de Rojas, for example, recommended that in Cuba the accountant should also serve as inspector of smelting and the treasurer as factor, arguing that "not having more than two officials, with the said moderation there won't be so many passions and unrest."[16] Other royal officials included *alcaides* (wardens) for the fortresses of the main towns, an *alguacil mayor* (chief constable) for each island, and officials who oversaw mining and smelting operations and revenues (an *escribano de minas* and a *fundidor*, or smelter). Each island had a lieutenant governor. These men usually emerged from the local milieu, which often was true of royal officials as well. A major difference between them, however, was that, notwithstanding the considerable authority they wielded and the duties they exercised, the lieutenant governors did not receive salaries, whereas other royal officials did.

Municipal government, consisting of *regidores* (councilmen) and *alcaldes* (magistrates), resembled its Iberian counterpart but with some significant differences. In the towns that had royal officials, these men almost invariably received appointments as regidores as well, tying local government closely to the crown. Although, as in Castile, regidores in the islands usually elected alcaldes annually, the king often appointed regidores who served for indefinite terms. In a letter of March 1528 the representatives of Cuba's towns complained to the king of the "great harm" that resulted from having the royal officials serve as regidores for life, and they pleaded for an end to the practice of appointing *regidores perpétuos*.[17] As would be true elsewhere in the Indies, from the outset the crown took advantage of the opportunity to impose a proprietorial form of municipal council on many towns in the islands, eliminating rotation in office and the annual elections still held in municipalities in central Castile.[18]

Vecinos of the towns did elect representatives, or *procuradores*, on an annual basis. In 1537 the married vecinos of San Juan claimed that they, rather than the regidores, should have the right to elect the city's representative (*personero*). The personero attended meetings of the cabildo as the representative of "all the people [*pueblo*], to oppose anything that is against their best interests [*utilidad*]." The vecinos should elect him, they argued, to avoid his following "the will and opinion of the said regidores ... [for] the good and vitality of the said city."[19] Regidores received little remuneration. In 1539, the king wrote to the president and audiencia regarding a request from Santo Domingo's regidores that, given the burden of their duties, they should be paid a salary and each should receive "one hundred bushels of salt for his house and two dozen chickens [*capones*]."[20]

Cabildos appointed other municipal officials, such as jailers and people who oversaw markets. In 1537 Santo Domingo's cabildo asked the king to allow the *fiel ejecutor* to carry a staff of office, "as do all the other public inspectors in all Your Majesty's kingdoms and dominions."[21] The city employed two *almotacenes* (inspectors of weights and measures), who functioned under the supervision of the fiel ejecutor and were responsible not only for weighing items but also for cleaning streets; they carried short staffs because they collected fines and enforced municipal ordinances.[22]

Municipal councils typically had the prerogative to distribute urban lots and agricultural land, but in Santo Domingo in 1519 the crown revoked these privileges and assigned them instead to the audiencia and royal officials, alleging irregularities in the allotment of properties.[23] In 1530, however, Juan García Caballero declared that in the more than twenty-three years he had lived in Santo Domingo, "he had always seen and heard it said that the cabildo and regimiento of this city has given and distributed lots and lands and other things to the vecinos of this city . . . and they build and have sold them and done with them what they want as with their own property."[24] Most vecinos, in other words, continued to view this as a municipal, not a royal, prerogative. In 1532 the cabildo once again asked the crown to authorize the cabildos of all the island's towns and cities to distribute land, water, and lots "as until now they have done."[25]

Santo Domingo's cabildo concerned itself with other matters as well, as reflected in a letter of 1532 to Charles V in which they praised Gonzalo Fernández de Oviedo's efforts to "write about the things of these parts and speculate about her secrets" and asked the king to order him to continue work on his *Crónica General y Natural Historia de estas Indias y Reinos*.[26] Two years later the council made a fervent plea for royal support to complete the construction of a Mercedarian church "because this church has Mother of God as its name."[27]

The cabildo does not seem to have exercised oversight of trades. A farrier named Gonzalo Moreno had been living in Hispaniola and working in his trade for twelve years when, in 1539, some recently arrived farriers demanded to see the title certifying that he had been examined in their trade. Moreno admitted that he no longer had it and claimed (no doubt correctly) that they only wanted cause him problems and that it was not financially feasible for him to travel back to court to be examined. He asked to be examined in Hispaniola by two farriers, "the most able that there are," and if he demonstrated his competence, that they be allowed to give him the license.[28]

The structure of government that took shape in the Greater Antilles in many ways mirrored that of Castile, but the extension of political offices and institutions across the Atlantic did not result in their complete replication.[29] The practice of sending royal representatives, or *corregidores*, to preside over town councils, which had expanded under Fernando and Isabel, did not extend to the islands during this period, and alcaldes mayores initially were named only for Concepción de la Vega and Santo Domingo in Hispaniola, and later for Havana, during the absentee governorship of Hernando de Soto.[30] The crown might have decided that placing its own officials on the cabildos of the main towns would be a sufficient check on their activities and that as a result there was no need for a royal representative to preside. The decision to appoint lieutenant governors to exercise authority in Cuba, Puerto Rico, and Jamaica introduced a form of territorial government that did not exist in Castile, which essentially consisted of a patchwork of the jurisdictions of its many municipalities.[31]

These differences did not go unnoticed in the Greater Antilles, of course. Manuel de Rojas noted in a letter to the king that it would be preferable that royal officials not serve as regidores or hold encomiendas.[32] In the smaller towns, however, the traditional means of choosing local officials seems to have persisted. During his visit to Cuba's towns in 1533, Rojas discovered that Trinidad had no regidores or alcalde. He summoned the vecinos, who voted to elect two regidores and then an alcalde.[33]

Iberian urban traditions were of fundamental importance to the Spaniards who settled in the islands. Vecinos of the town of Sancti Spíritus surely had in mind Castile's tradition of municipal self-government when, in the spring of 1521, they elected a procurador and declared themselves a commune on the model of the *comuneros* of central Castile. They had their Indians erect a gallows and pillory, traditional symbols of justice and municipal autonomy. They were acting in opposition to a new distribution of repartimientos. In a brief but bloody clash, the local justice, Vasco Porcallo de Figueroa, suppressed the protest.[34]

Challenges and Complaints

Contemporary records are filled with bitter complaints and criticisms lodged against (and among) governing officials. Grievances often reflected personal antagonisms and rivalries; in many instances they stemmed from corruption, incompetence, the flouting of norms, and even criminal behavior. Judge Licenciado Figueroa described the bishop Geraldini as being totally useless and having "no more comprehension than a child."[35] In 1532 the bishop of Cuba excommunicated Licenciado Juan de Vadillo, who had conducted the residencia of the island's officials, because he had ordered an arrest to which, clearly, the bishop objected.[36] Bishop Fuenmayor complained that the oidores of the audiencia met in their houses and made their judgments "according to their inclination [*pasión*]. Every day, they make new laws."[37] There were similar complaints, in 1541, that oidor Licenciado Cervantes held audiencias in his home, a practice the crown strictly prohibited.[38] In a letter of June 1550, canon Juan Tarifeño explained to the king that people, merchants in particular, who had dealings with the oidores would send presents of clothing and jewelry to their wives.[39]

Such pretensions on the part of upper-class women in the Caribbean were nothing new. Enrique Otte refers to the "excessive social ambition" of doña Isabel de Manrique, the wife of early oidor Marcelo Villalobos. Doña Isabel belonged to a high-ranking noble family and "maintained, or hoped to maintain, a small court in Santo Domingo, although lacking the economic means to do so."[40] Unfortunately, her husband was in debt when he arrived in Hispaniola and never seems to have emerged from that state.

When the influential longtime secretary of the audiencia, Diego Caballero, died in 1554, Gonzalo Fernández de Oviedo declared that at last Santo Domingo "had been freed from tyranny, that he controlled everything." According to Fernández de Oviedo, the presence of audiencia secretary Diego Caballero on the cabildo meant that the city council was unable to move forward on anything that the audiencia did not approve.[41] Likely motivated by resentment of the privileges and power of the oidores, in 1532 Santo Domingo's cabildo asked the king to limit their terms to no more than three years.[42]

Yet, despite antagonism between the cabildo and audiencia, the two could close ranks in solidarity—which, given the ties between them, is hardly surprising. In defending two oidores against what they considered to be unfounded accusations brought against them in 1550, the cabildo pointed to "the banquets and fiestas that the said *licenciados* [oidores] and their wives have had with some from the cabildo and other gentlemen and principal persons of this city and their wives.... Since the royal audiencia was established here there has been in it a president and judges of considerable quality... who have never failed to communicate with principal people and to be the *compadres* and godfathers of all of them and be present at their weddings and funerals."[43]

The audiencia judges, however, did insist on their privileges. Churches in Santo Domingo lacked seating, and the audiencia judges claimed that they alone had the right to sit in church. The crown agreed that the president could bring a chair and the oidores a bench on which they could sit, which could be placed near to the president's chair, "which is in the most preeminent place." Other "honorable citizens of that city," however, also could bring benches so they could sit to hear mass. The judges also lorded it over less prominent officials. When they visited the jail, the oidores made the alcaldes ordinarios remain standing, with their hats in their hands, "for which reason many people avoid being alcaldes, given the treatment" that they received. The king insisted that the alcaldes ordinarios should be treated courteously and that during the oidores' visits to the jail they should all sit down together to chat.[44]

Charges of irregularities and incompetence in office were common, and the king ordered cabildo officials in San Juan to hold their sessions in the town hall, "not in your homes and in the streets."[45] In the 1530s Manuel de Rojas complained to the king that the manner of electing alcaldes ordinarios in Cuba's towns, in which everyone voted, resulted in the election of "the vecino of least ability and who is least deserving," because such a person would secure votes from among the "vulgar people" (*gente baja*). As a result, in his view, honorable, long-standing vecinos were being excluded from office. Gonzalo de Guzmán described the electoral process, in which the vecinos nominated two people, the regidores two, and the lieutenant governor one, and then the names were placed in a bucket. In his experience, however, "the common people [*el común*] always choose the tailor and butcher and other similar people." Both he and Rojas asked the king to reinstate the practice by which the regidores elected alcaldes.[46] In 1536, when Guzmán again was lieutenant governor of Cuba, the king wrote saying that he agreed with him that it would be good if Santiago's alcaldes ordinarios knew how to read and write.[47]

Notwithstanding allegations of incompetence leveled against many officials, the changing circumstances of life in the islands presented many challenges to government. In 1541, for example, Álvaro Caballero, who was at court representing Santo Domingo and Hispaniola's other towns, described the problems that officials of the small towns experienced when they had to travel long distances to bring judicial cases to the audiencia in Santo Domingo, for which reason it was difficult to find people to serve as alcaldes or alguaciles. He also pointed out that although towns like Buenaventura had depopulated completely, there were farms and ingenios in the countryside with substantial populations that the judicial system was not serving. He suggested that magistrates travel through these areas to identify criminal or civil cases that could be brought before the audiencia or Santo Domingo's alcaldes ordinarios. Caballero also argued the need for an *alcalde de mesta,* or magistrate of a stock raisers' association, because of the island's large herds of cattle, which the king said should be discussed further among the cattle owners and Santo Domingo's officials, and the election of an *alcalde de hermandad,* which the king approved.[48] Presumably the alcalde of the hermandad, as in Spain, would be responsible for policing disorder and criminal activity in the countryside.

The isolation of many communities posed serious problems of oversight, especially on a large island like Cuba, where the distances between towns were substantial. Witnesses in Trinidad, in a deposition prepared by Vasco Porcallo de Figueroa in November 1521, affirmed that before Porcallo became *teniente de justicia,* the local alcaldes mistreated people with impunity, knowing that there was no superior authority within many leagues of the town.[49] In 1529 the town council of Santiago wrote to the king to bring a complaint against the two "*visitadores generales*" that Lieutenant Governor Guzmán and Bishop Ramírez had employed, alleging that they were "people in whom the qualities that are necessary do not concur." One of the inspectors went to Puerto del Príncipe and, without presenting his authorization to the town's cabildo, started to exercise his office and clashed with the cabildo. Guzmán sent his notary to investigate the situation, paying him a salary of 1,000 maravedís a day and paying four other men half a castellano each a day. They arrested the alcaldes, two regidores, and several other people, removing their Indians and sequestering their goods, "by which they remain lost and destroyed." The same visitors went to Baracoa, where again they refused to present their authorization, the result of which was another confrontation. One night they forced themselves into the alcalde's home and in his presence attempted to rape his wife.[50]

Towns found it difficult to address the problems of maintaining infrastructure and services because they lacked the funds. In 1528 the representatives of Cuba's towns complained that they had no propios (municipal properties). Santiago possessed very little in the way of propios because some houses on the plaza that it had owned were lost when the town was burned. None of the island's other towns owned any property at all. As a result, whenever they needed funds, they had to levy a special tax on the vecinos in all the towns.[51] The crown conceded to Puerto Rico 50 pesos annually from the profits of the estates on Mona Island for ten years, beginning in 1528, to be used for the construction of roads and bridges on the island. In 1533, however, local officials had not received the funds in two years.[52] In 1534 Santo Domingo's cabildo obtained royal permission to build a bridge, both to serve as an aqueduct to bring water to the city and to allow people, carts, and livestock to cross the river. The city council had to request the audiencia's permission to impose a special tax, but the funds would be sufficient only to initiate the project. They asked the crown to provide additional funding, with a concession of three thousand head of cattle and two houses the Hieronymites had owned.[53]

Government in the islands often suffered from the absenteeism of officials, which was frequent and in some cases chronic. Pedro de Paz, Cuba's contador in the 1520s, asked permission to go to Seville in late 1529 for reasons of poor health. He received a license to go to Spain for sixteen months and then regularly requested extensions up until his death in 1537.[54] In April 1547 the crown urged Bishop Fuenmayor, who at the time also was president of the audiencia, to return to Hispaniola, pointing out, "Your absence creates a great lack in it [his bishopric] and the service of God our Lord and the good of the vecinos."[55] Many officials who received permission to go to Castile seemed reluctant to return to the Caribbean, and when they were sent to Spain on official business they did not always attend to the issues that ostensibly motivated their visits. In 1530 a man named Sancho del Castillo complained to the king that the cabildo and governor of San Juan, "without license or authority," collected 400 pesos from the vecinos to send Juan de Castellanos to court to deal with a dispute regarding the collection of the tithe on gold in the island. Instead, Castillo alleged, Castellanos had spent the time dealing with his own affairs.[56]

There also were instances in which officials were unable to exercise their duties. A man named Juan de Orihuela held a royal appointment as visitor of ships in Santo Domingo. As such, he was supposed to inspect ships arriving and leaving the port. In a deposition presented in 1520 before the alcalde mayor of Santo Domingo, Licenciado García de Montalban, and the *justicia mayor*, Licenciado Rodrigo de Figueroa, Orihuela claimed that royal officials, among them treasurer Miguel de Pasamonte, would not allow him to conduct inspections. The witnesses, who had been in Hispaniola for anywhere from five to eighteen years, unanimously testified that they had never seen or heard of anyone who inspected ships to see whether they are "good to sail or not or if they have adequate arms and necessary supplies."[57]

Conflict and Corruption

Conflicts between officials and the perception of officials as corrupt also could generate turmoil and bad feeling. Oidor Licenciado Cervantes, who was in Puerto Rico in 1540 as *juez de cuentas* (judicial auditor), talked about the unease that existed on the island, especially in the city of San Juan, "being as they are people so turbulent and disrespectful of the service of the king."[58] A bitter conflict over land and grazing rights erupted in Puerto Rico in the early 1540s; some of these tensions probably had begun to surface while Cervantes was on the island.[59]

During the years that Francisco Manuel de Lando was in office, the island might have been less troubled. He became lieutenant governor of Puerto Rico in 1530, after serving as alguacil mayor for eight years, and he seems to have handled the island's affairs judiciously.[60] When Licenciado Lucas Vázquez de Ayllón conducted a residencia of officials on the island, he did not bring any charges against Lando for his term as alguacil mayor, nor did Licenciado Antonio de la Gama, when he conducted a second residencia. Witnesses noted that Lando frequently conducted visits of inspection of the island. Notary Alonso de Cáceres said he had never heard a complaint about Lando, whom he described as pleasant and courteous to everyone; he was known to help people with their debts and to reconcile parties who wanted to sue each other or who were otherwise at odds. Like other lieutenant governors, he received no salary. Longtime resident Diego de Cuéllar, who in 1534 was alcalde in San Juan, noted that Lando's conscientious exercise of his office meant that he seldom had time to see to his own properties, which had suffered from neglect as a result.

Society and politics in the island seem to have become considerably more fractious in the years following Lando's term in office. In 1551 a vecino of San Juan named Pedro de Salvatierra lodged a bitter complaint about the conduct in office of three men who had formed close ties through marriage. One of them, Alonso Pérez Martel, was appointed treasurer by the new governor, Luis de Vallejo, to replace Juan de Castellanos following the latter's death. The governor asked for and received permission to marry Alonso Pérez's daughter.

Alonso Pérez was a regidor and married to the sister of Juan Ponce, a regidor and the alcaide of San Juan's fort. Ponce was the grandson of Juan Ponce de León and was married to the sister of Luis Pérez de Lugo, the contador. Luis Pérez de Lugo, married to Alonso Pérez's sister, was the third member of this closely interconnected political triumvirate. All three owned sugar ingenios by this time.

Salvatierra alleged that these rich and powerful men were able to intimidate the other regidores into following their will because they had the support of the governor—"teniendo de su parte y bando al dicho governador."[61] He argued that they used their influence and position to further their own agenda, which included securing an indefinite appointment for Vallejo as governor. Salvatierra claimed that Alonso Pérez Martel owed the royal treasury more than 2,000 castellanos, which should have been placed in the royal chest but instead had been given to Martel to cover his expenses to travel to Spain to ask for the office of treasurer; the implication was that he used some of the money to redress his own financial difficulties. The cabildo named him procurador general so that he could go to court to "ask certain things" from the king. Salvatierra concluded his charges by stating that both within the cabildo and in the city more generally these allied officials had done as they pleased for more than six years. He maintained that Alonso Pérez Martel was poor and that all his possessions were worth no more than the 10,000 pesos that his wife doña Leonor had brought to the marriage as her dowry. He called Pérez Martel a "restless man" who had fomented trouble in the city and was "very prejudicial to the republic." Witnesses thought that by holding the office of treasurer, Pérez Martel most likely would improve his financial situation. It is worth noting that most of the witnesses were younger men in their twenties and thirties who might have chafed at their exclusion from access to Puerto Rico's more lucrative economic opportunities.

In Cuba, controversy and criticism for many years swirled around Gonzalo de Guzmán, who twice served as the island's lieutenant governor as well as in other offices, as did Manuel de Rojas. The conqueror and first lieutenant governor of Cuba, Diego Velázquez, died in 1524, soon after which Manuel de Rojas took office. In 1526 Guzmán became lieutenant governor and remained in office until Licenciado Juan de Vadillo arrived in November 1531 to conduct the residencia of his term. The residencia lasted until the beginning of March 1532, when Vadillo again appointed Rojas, who served as lieutenant governor until Guzmán resumed the post, from March 1535 until May 1537.[62] Both Rojas and Guzmán were related to Velázquez, although they do not seem to have had close kinship ties to each other.

Historian Irene Wright has called the period from Velázquez's death through Hernando de Soto's governorship (during most of which he was away from the island) "a time of stagnation ebullient with bitter personal quarrels."[63] Guzmán intervened in the annual election of a procurador in Santiago, insisting on conducting it in his house, even though the king twice instructed him not to do so.[64] In 1529 he managed to have Juan Barba elected procurador, although the cabildo refused to accept him.[65] He also made his relative Juan Pérez, who was a minor and living in his house, regidor. The cabildo objected that they had been forced to accept Pérez although he was underage. They claimed he did only Guzmán's bidding.[66]

Manuel de Rojas saw Guzmán as the primary instigator of the factionalism that had taken hold in the island, writing that after Guzmán became lieutenant governor, "The [royal] officials had many prejudices and passions, from the outset of his term as governor, and those grew steadily and reached the point of set enmities, and especially after bishop don fray Miguel Ramírez and the treasurer Lope Hurtado arrived in the island, and this was because of the friendship that the said bishop and governor had between them."[67]

The arrival of Licenciado Vadillo to initiate the residencia of Guzmán in some ways made matters worse. Vadillo arrived at the time of the annual smelting of gold in Santiago, when people from all over the island converged on the town. According to Rojas, Vadillo "showed himself partial to some and hateful to others," although on the whole he seems to have aligned himself with the royal officials.[68] Rojas, too, had traveled to Santiago from his home in Bayamo, and when he was confronted with the political chaos in the city, he tried with some success to "put them at peace."

Underlying the political factionalism was resentment of Guzmán's assignments of repartimientos.[69] Following the death of treasurer Pedro Núñez de Guzmán, the lieutenant governor had assigned his repartimiento not to his successor, Lope Hurtado, as Hurtado anticipated and the king had promised, but to the widow of Pedro Núñez, doña Catalina de Agüero, whom Gonzalo de Guzmán married. Vadillo ordered the repartimiento reassigned to Hurtado.[70] The contador Pedro de Paz claimed that Guzmán had mistreated him, confiscating the Indian slaves he had working in gold mines for no other reason than to "satisfy [his] anger and passions."[71] Guzmán also had reassigned an encomienda that Rojas had received from Diego Velázquez, "maliciously and because of envy and bad will," and had done the same to others.[72] Rojas, then, was not a disinterested party when he criticized Guzmán. Guzmán's actions, however, were anything but subtle. Ostensibly he lobbied the procuradores of the other towns to write to the king on his behalf, asking that he be reinstated as governor, but in fact he dictated the letters to be sent.[73]

The extremely bad feelings between Hurtado and Guzmán and his allies culminated in Hurtado's arrest in 1537 on the orders of don Diego López, the dean of the cathedral of Santiago, and sequestration of his property. López's men entered Hurtado's house, forced his servants out, and took from his wife the key to the chests and desk, from which they removed and carried off accounts, books, and documents relating to the treasury. They also robbed them of jewelry and other valuable items worth more than 3,000 castellanos and tore up and burned documents. Hurtado went to Spain, where he presented a criminal complaint against Guzmán and a number of other men, including one of Guzmán's criados and the husband of one of his criadas.[74] When Hurtado planned to return to Cuba in February 1540, he asked for (and obtained) a royal license permitting him to maintain an escort of two armed Blacks, because there were people on the island who wanted to hurt or kill him.[75]

Crime and Violence

As this discussion suggests, the line between politics and crime often was narrow to nonexistent. The islands could be violent and dangerous places, and personal feuds that resulted in injuries and deaths were not uncommon, nor were crimes such as rape and theft. Most Spanish men had ready access to arms; they also could call on their friends, relatives, retainers, servants, or slaves to do their bidding in settling scores. Government and church officials not infrequently became involved in feuds and acts of vengeance or covered for those who did. In 1533, for example, Gonzalo de Guzmán complained to the king that an alcalde of Santiago, Juan Barba, had failed to arrest a vecino named Juan Enríquez, whom Guzmán accused of "treacherously" killing his brother, Pedro de Guzmán, when he had the opportunity to do so.[76] Criminal activity might have increased when officials were perceived as lax and partial, but in some instances, especially in remote areas, officials themselves were the perpetrators, as seen in the case of the visitor-inspectors that Guzmán hired.

Crimes that involved powerful people were difficult to adjudicate, meaning such people often acted with impunity, notwithstanding the presence of witnesses. The influential Bachiller Álvaro de Castro had a reputation for violent behavior. During his lengthy career in Hispaniola, he held several important ecclesiastical positions, including that of dean and canon of the cathedral of Concepción de la Vega and treasurer and *arcediano* (archdeacon) of the cathedral of Santo Domingo. He also pursued an active economic life, owning cattle estates and becoming involved in silver mining and retail sales. Witnesses in a lengthy *proceso* (judicial case) conducted against him in 1532 mentioned that Castro had owned a shop in Concepción de la Vega in partnership with a relative and that he avoided paying taxes on goods and cloth imported from Castile by claiming that the items were intended for clergymen.[77]

A number of people spoke out against Castro, many of them fellow clerics. Diego Sánchez testified that he "has treated many of his Spanish criados angrily, cutting and whipping them with his own hands because they asked for their salaries and [payment for] services they had done for him, and ordering his Blacks to cut their beards," a grave humiliation. Sánchez probably was referring to an incident involving a man named Alonso Martín, who had worked for Castro. Martín obtained a judgment against Castro for back pay that Castro owed him. Martín had left Concepción de la Vega and was operating an inn on the road to Santiago, where Castro appeared one day on horseback. Castro dismounted and immediately attacked his former criado, stabbing him several times, according to Cristóbal de Deza, also a canon in Concepción de la Vega. Deza claimed to have known Castro for twenty-four years in Hispaniola and in Castile and had heard the details of the incident directly from Martín, who showed him his wounds.[78]

Castro's predilection for violent confrontations emerged in another incident, when an enslaved Black woman belonging to royal accountant Alonso de Ávila, who was staying at Castro's house in Concepción de la Vega, went to get water from a stream near an enclosure belonging to Alonso Román. She claimed that one of Román's criados attacked her. The following evening, Castro took with him two or three Black slaves, who beat the criado while Castro cut or attempted to cut off his beard. The criado was Alonso Rodríguez, who claimed that when he had warned the woman away from the sheep enclosure he was guarding, she attacked him with a knife, at which point he struck her. Rodríguez offered a dramatic and possibly exaggerated account of what happened next. According to him, Castro arrived at Rodríguez's bohío with eight or nine Blacks, who dragged him outside by the hair as Castro yelled, "Here, here, dogs, kill him for me!" The Blacks were holding him by the testicles when a couple of other men intervened.

After Rodríguez complained to the alcalde mayor of Concepción, Temiño de Velasco, Velasco sent an alguacil to arrest the Black men at the mines of Cibao. Failing to find them, he arrested Castro's criado Juan de Gamarra, who was in charge. Hearing of the arrest, Castro armed himself and went to the plaza to free Gamarra, but Gamarra already had been released.[79] Witnesses also accused Castro of trying to kill then-alcalde mayor Velasco in 1520 with a crossbow. *Maestrescuela* Antonio Marques was there and managed to cut the string of the crossbow with his sword, saving Velasco's life.[80] Whether this attempted assassination was related to the incident with Alonso Rodríguez is not clear.

Álvaro de Castro was not the only prominent man in the islands to be accused of crimes. In the late 1530s Gaspar Troche, the son-in-law of Juan Ponce de León, became involved in a violent conflict with regidor Pedro de Espinosa. Troche arrived in Puerto Rico in 1515, married doña María Ponce de León, and served as regidor, alcalde, and alguacil mayor in San Juan. The alcalde Alonso de Molina accused Troche of having sent his Black slave Roque to beat Espinosa with a rod on October 8, 1538, following which Roque took refuge in a monastery in the city. Troche responded that Espinosa had tried to stab him and had ordered one of his criados to kill him. He alleged that Espinosa would have killed him had not others who were present intervened. He claimed that the island's lieutenant governor, Francisco Manuel de Lando, tried to bring a case against Espinosa but had been unable to do so because Espinosa was a well-connected regidor, "una persona favorecida." Troche also mentioned an earlier episode, in which Espinosa ostensibly had attacked him with a dagger and attempted to wrest away his staff of office.

Troche apparently decided that the best hope of making his case was to appeal directly to the king, so he stowed away on a ship heading to Spain. Notwithstanding the evidence that Troche offered in August 1539 to clear his name, he received a sentence of six years' exile from the island and a fine of 70 pesos. In 1540 he was back in Puerto Rico and asked to be allowed to delay his exile for two years to settle his affairs on the island. It appears that, in the end, the term of exile was reduced to a year and a half. Whether he actually left the island for that period of time is not known.[81]

An attack on don Diego Alvarez Osorio, the *chantre* of Tierra Firme, near the plaza of Santo Domingo on the night of March 15, 1523, featured a notable trio of prominent young men: Esteban de Pasamonte, nephew of treasurer Miguel de Pasamonte and himself treasurer of Hispaniola; Francisco de Tapia, the alcaide of the fortress; and Rodrigo de Bastidas *el mozo* (the younger), nephew of the founder of Santa Marta, Rodrigo de Bastidas. A man named Cristóbal Navarro accompanied Alvarez Osorio. Francisco de Tapia dealt Navarro an enormous blow to the head with a double-handed sword. Navarro collapsed in the street and died a few days later. The chantre himself avoided serious injury until someone's sword lopped off parts of the fingers of one hand. Bastidas escaped to Yucatan, where he died three years later. Pasamonte and Tapia seem to have avoided any serious consequences for the death of Navarro, even though three years later Navarro's father, Hernando de Baeza, obtained a royal directive to the audiencia to bring the perpetrators to justice, which he himself took to Hispaniola.[82]

Such confrontations involving prominent men surely arose from political or personal tensions and rivalries, but the actual causes seldom emerge clearly in the documents. On the evening of May 25, 1540, the fiscal of the audiencia, Licenciado Frías, was attacked and wounded at the door of his home, apparently at the behest of Licenciado Castañeda, who was arrested. Castañeda denied any involvement in the crime, but two of his criados were questioned and tortured. One confessed but subsequently retracted, and the other said nothing even after "twelve jars of water" had been administered.[83]

Violence that involved non-Spaniards might have been as common, or even more common, but probably left even fewer traces in existing records. In 1541, for example, a vecino of San Germán named García de Matienzo stated that he had lived fifteen or sixteen years in Puerto Rico. Seven years prior, he had had "cierto enojo" (an argument or angry confrontation) with an Indian named Diego, who was the servant of Blas de Villasante. Matienzo wounded Diego and the man subsequently died. Matienzo never faced charges for the death, although clearly authorities were aware of the crime, as Matienzo sought a pardon so that he could return to live in Puerto Rico with his wife and family.[84]

It is possible that violence against Indians and Blacks did not attract much official attention, and violent acts committed against enslaved people might have been settled mainly as property crimes. Hernán López portugués, a vecino of Santo Domingo, got into an argument with an enslaved Black named

Francisco Maco and killed him with a blow from a lance. The slave's owner, doña Leonor de Acebedo, denounced López to the audiencia, which sequestered his goods. Doña Leonor and her children must have settled the case, as they signed a letter of pardon.[85]

Such extrajudicial settlements normally consisted of agreements by the aggrieved parties to issue pardons in exchange for compensation, usually monetary. The agreement that followed the death of Pero Gutiérrez at the hands of Pedro de Salazar, a notary in Santo Domingo, took a surprising turn.[86] The facts of the incident, which occurred on November 13, 1540, were clear enough, although the reasons behind it are not. That evening, Gutiérrez went to Salazar's house at the behest of another notary for whom he worked, Francisco de Trejo, to speak to a man named Nicolás López, also a notary, who had dined at Salazar's house.[87] López testified that Gutiérrez arrived with a sword in his hand, suggesting that he anticipated trouble. As they spoke, Salazar appeared, angry that Gutiérrez had entered his house without permission, because Salazar had told him repeatedly not to do so. Salazar approached with a drawn sword and shield and attacked, wounding Gutiérrez in the head. Gutiérrez ran down the steps and out of the house, crying out that he had been killed.[88] A number of neighbors heard the commotion and Gutiérrez's shouts. Salazar's Black slave Bartolomé said that his master struck Gutiérrez only once, but he was not sworn in as a witness.

Two days after the incident, Pero Gutiérrez, mortally wounded but still alive, made a statement from his deathbed before the alcalde Juan Mosquera and notary Alonso de Llerena in which he pardoned Salazar. He said that when Salazar asked why Gutiérrez had entered the house when Salazar had forbidden him to do so, Gutiérrez had replied that he would enter as frequently as he liked. At that point, Salazar, "moved by passion," attacked. Given that he expected to die, Gutiérrez said that he wished to pardon Salazar for both the wound and his likely death, "so that God our Lord would pardon him when he left this world." He stated explicitly that the pardon was also on behalf of his siblings and all his relatives within the fourth degree. Gutiérrez was under the age of twenty-five but over eighteen; he was Francisco de Trejo's criado and probably training with him to be a notary.

Salazar escaped from the jail in Santo Domingo, hoping to gain asylum in the cathedral, which the cathedral dignitaries allowed, although it was controversial. There was disagreement among officials as to whether Salazar actually reached what properly could be considered part of the cathedral before he was apprehended—or rather knocked to the ground—by the alcaide of the jail, Bernabé Ramírez, and an Indian guard named China. Oddly, Francisco de Trejo also helped to apprehend him, perhaps worried that he might be blamed for his criado's escape.[89]

Salazar subsequently traveled to Spain to seek out Gutiérrez's relatives in Sanlúcar and Seville, with the intention of confirming the dead man's pardon with his extended family (his parents were no longer living). The terms of the pardon were unusual. The parties agreed that Salazar would marry his victim's sister, Beatriz Gutiérrez, providing a dowry consisting of "goods in certain quantity and certain maravedís" not specified in the version of the agreement that survives. The dowry was confirmed before a notary in Seville, Alonso de Cazalla, on May 5, 1542, together with the statement of pardon.[90]

Salazar's new in-laws were well-to-do professionals. His wife's sister Juana was married to Bachiller Francisco de Alfaro, a surgeon; her uncle Juan de Bolaños was escribano of the cabildo of Sanlúcar; and another relative was a clergyman in Seville. The wealthy mariscal Diego Caballero, who had been a prominent figure in Santo Domingo before returning permanently to Seville, knew Salazar and Gutiérrez's parents and claimed that he played a key role in reconciling Salazar with Gutiérrez's relatives, with the result that there "was between them much peace, as between relatives and friends."[91] Salazar most likely returned to Santo Domingo with his wife.

Apart from its unexpected outcome, the case is a reminder of the omnipresence of arms in the hands of Spanish men, which heightened the likelihood that rivalries and resentments would lead to bloodshed. Although most violence that took place within Spanish society probably involved no more than a few individuals, in the episode mentioned earlier, in which the vecinos of Sancti Spíritus in Cuba formed a commune, two parties of armed Spaniards clashed with one another. Vasco Porcallo de Figueroa, who was teniente de justicia for Sancti Spíritus and Trinidad, mustered a group of men in Trinidad who engaged in an armed confrontation with the comuneros, who were arrested. The episode came to a swift end with no deaths, although there were some serious injuries. Prior to its conclusion, angry vecinos had pursued the regidor Juan de Oliva, throwing rocks at him and calling him a "treacherous sodomite" because he refused to join the commune.[92]

It is impossible to judge the frequency of violent crime or whether crimes involving prominent Spaniards as perpetrators or victims were more likely to enter into the documentary record than were acts of violence among the lower classes or non-Spaniards. On the evening of June 15, 1542, two men in disguise sought out and killed a man named Alonso Sánchez in the house that belonged to the oidor Licenciado Juan de Vadillo. Sánchez, presumably a servant himself, was dining with other servants and slaves. The two men who attacked him were brothers and the criados of the bishop and president of the audiencia, Fuenmayor. Like Pedro de Salazar, they took refuge in the cathedral.[93] In this case, too, the repercussions for the attackers are unknown.

The residencia that Licenciado Antonio de la Gama conducted of the term in office of Licenciado Sancho Velázquez, the *justicia mayor* of Puerto Rico in 1519 and 1520, included many charges of corruption, partiality, misconduct, and failure to respond adequately to criminal activity, especially when it involved his friends.[94] Alonso de Cea, for example, alleged that the factor of a relative of the treasurer Andrés de Haro, a close associate of Velázquez, had stabbed a merchant and that Velázquez had done nothing. Witnesses recounted two incidents in which Haro had sent his criados to rural establishments to administer punishments; when informed about this, Velázquez again failed to act. In one incident, Haro's criados went to the estancia of Cristóbal Maldonado and hanged one of his dogs, which they alleged were attacking Haro's cattle that had been destroying the estancia's fields. In another instance, Velázquez placed the surgeon Maestre Juan under house arrest when he was apprehended entering the house of Juan de Molina with a sword and shield to kill him, but "because he was so much his friend and ally, and because he treated everyone in the said Licenciado's house without payment," he was freed with no penalties.[95] In a secret inquiry conducted in San Germán by authority of Licenciado Alonso de Zuazo, a vecino named Martín Garcés testified that Velázquez had freed from jail in San Germán "un indio, capitán" accused of killing "dos cristianos" and that after he was freed he had killed a regidor named Ribadeneira and three other men, "hasta cinco o seis cristianos" (as many as five or six Christians).[96]

As seen in the case of Bachiller Álvaro de Castro, the relative isolation of rural estates or inns left people vulnerable to violence, whether at the hands of Black or Indian cimarrones, rogue officials, or resentful neighbors. One especially ugly episode that emerged in the residencia of Velázquez involved the severe beating of a young man named Francisco Ximón at Velázquez's instigation. Ximón testified in San Germán in October 1519 that about eight months before, while he was living with the fundidor Jerónimo de Bruselas, he had left Bruselas's estancia to go to one belonging to Andrés de Haro to get bread. He ran into Velázquez, who was traveling to San Germán for the *fundición* (smelting), who asked if he would take some corn and sweet potatoes to the town, which Ximón agreed to do. They stopped at the nearby estancia of Vasco Troche and, while Ximón was in a bohío, Velázquez ordered his miner, Andrés Caballero, and a muleteer named Olmedo, who also worked for him, to seize Ximón. They bound his arms and legs, hanged him by the feet, and Velázquez personally, together with his Black slave, administered fifty lashes with a halter. Velázquez then swore all the witnesses to silence in the matter.

Several men asked Ximón not to bring any charges against Velázquez, including Vasco Troche, who promised him 10 pesos de oro, which he seems to have received in a combination of clothing and money. The explanation for the beating was that Ximón had encountered and given directions to a man named Juan de Levas, who ostensibly had taken an Indian woman belonging to Velázquez. Velázquez denied the beating and claimed that he only ordered Ximón stripped and threatened in order to discover the truth of his activities with Juan de Leva, whom he accused of "every day committing many excesses and crimes."[97]

A quite different sort of criminal activity, one in which the island's officials were well positioned to participate, was financial fraud. Evidence of fraudulent accounting by Ovando's first and much-favored treasurer, Cristóbal de Santa Clara, was uncovered years after he stepped down from office, in 1507. The charming and convivial Santa Clara made free use of royal funds, which he was able to do in part because he had unrestrained access to them, given that the use of an *arca de tres llaves* had not yet been implemented.[98] Although Ovando took no action with regard to Santa Clara's lavish spending on himself and on others, the accountant Cristóbal de Cuéllar, who was close to the Reyes Católicos and not to Ovando, informed the king. Santa Clara did not suffer any grave consequences and lived in Santo Domingo into the 1530s.[99] His son Luis de Santa Clara succeeded to his regimiento after his death.[100]

The trade in Indigenous captives gave rise to numerous instances of fraud. The three Hieronymite governors tried to prohibit the traffic in slaves on the coast of Tierra Firme, but it proved impossible to enforce the restriction, especially as the royal justice Alonso de Zuazo was himself an active participant in the trade. As judge of the residencia, he had accused the three appellate judges (Lucas Vázquez de Ayllón, Juan Ortiz de Matienzo, and Marcelo de Villalobos) of participating in the trade but then became involved himself, authorizing the traffic in June 1518 and issuing fraudulent licenses to close friends and associates such as Diego Caballero, Juan Mosquera, and Rodrigo de Bastidas. Rodrigo de Figueroa upheld Zuazo's policy. Although he ordered that Indians not be brought from Tierra Firme "against their will," according to Mira Caballos at least fifty-four slaving expeditions took place in 1519 and 1520, most of them organized by vecinos of Hispaniola and San Juan.[101]

In 1538 Gaspar de Astudillo, who held the offices of veedor de fundiciones, veedor of the audiencia, and regidor, wrote at length to the king regarding the audit that he had conducted of treasury accounts after the new treasurer, Alonso de la Torre, arrived in Hispaniola in 1536.[102] He uncovered evidence that members of the wealthy and influential Caballero family, along with other merchants, had been involved in smuggling unregistered Black slaves into Hispaniola for some years.[103] Astudillo wrote, "There appear many departures and large numbers of Blacks that came without Your Majesty's license, by many and different persons, merchants and some vecinos."[104] In the year 1526 alone, more than six hundred enslaved Blacks had arrived without a license. The brothers Diego and Alonso Caballero, together with their nephew, the contador Álvaro Caballero, seem to have been the principal organizers of the scheme, although they were not the only ones responsible for smuggling slaves. Stating that he had not come to the island "to disinter dead people, and there was no reason to inquire into it," Alonso de la Torre sided with Álvaro Caballero and resisted Astudillo's efforts to uncover the facts of the case.[105]

Astudillo himself had long been entangled in legal difficulties, including a lengthy lawsuit with Fernández de Oviedo dating to 1525. In October 1538 the cabildo wrote to the king, denouncing Astudillo as "a boisterous and scandalous man." More specifically, around that time Astudillo faced charges of fraud relating to nonpayment of taxes on gold.[106] It should be noted, however, that the regidores of the cabildo included Álvaro Caballero and Alonso de la Torre, who obviously had good reason to undercut Astudillo's credibility with the crown. Indeed, Astudillo's conflicts with the cabildo were long-standing, perhaps stemming to some degree from his ties to the audiencia.

Some fraud was more personal. In 1534 Juan de Castellanos claimed that when he went to court in 1528 as Puerto Rico's procurador, he left his properties in the care of Ángelo Álvarez de Astorga. In the course of four years Ángelo de Astorga stole or sold from Castellanos's estate cassava bread; maize; 240 head of cattle, together with some horses and mares; slaves; and other items, including a boat that he used to carry off much of his plunder. Castellanos estimated his total losses at around 8,000 ducados.[107] Although Castellanos was able to obtain an order for the perpetrator's arrest, the defrauding of heirs and creditors in Spain, who frequently failed to receive funds owed to them by the executors, administrators, or acquaintances or partners of their deceased relatives or debtors, was more insidious and often went unresolved. If the funds that should have been forwarded to heirs remained in the hands of unscrupulous parties in the islands, it could be all but impossible to recover them, unless one traveled there oneself, sent a representative, or found someone on the scene willing to intervene.[108]

In all fairness, though, it is likely that many people who spent time in the islands died intestate, especially those who were more transient, meaning that funds—*bienes de difuntos*—could accumulate and local authorities had no means of identifying or finding appropriate heirs.[109] In 1550, however, canon Juan Tarifeño alleged that some of the oidores of the audiencia who brought their sisters-in-law to be married in the island would choose for their potential spouses "alcaldes and inspectors and executors of some orphans and other things where they could steal so as to pay them a dowry with what they stole."[110]

Law and the Multiethnic Society

The blurring of lines between political and personal feuds, the use of political office for personal and familial advancement and gain, the formation of political cliques to promote mutual interests, and the difficulty of holding officials accountable for crimes and infractions all characterized government and politics in the early Spanish Caribbean, even as they do in many countries today. Yet, fractious and violent as they often were, these were not lawless societies. Residencias provided regular opportunities for grievances to be aired, corruption addressed, and wrongs righted. People constantly petitioned the crown and freely expressed their opinions about everything from how officials and clergymen conducted themselves to what should be done to promote the welfare of the islands.[111] If anything, the stream of ordinances that flowed from the crown to the Caribbean suggests that, far from being "unlawed," these new societies came close to drowning under the weight of innumerable laws and regulations—which might have been the case if they all had been observed and implemented, which assuredly they were not.[112]

The novelty of life and conditions in the Caribbean, particularly in terms of the challenges of dealing with a multiethnic society, meant that issues and situations arose for which there were no clear legal precedents. From the very outset, Spaniards' relations with the Indians raised questions of law and ethics that were not easily answered. The Laws of Burgos (1512), a response of sorts to the strident criticisms made by Dominicans in Hispaniola about the impact of the encomienda system on the Indians, represented a first attempt to regulate the conditions in which Indians lived and worked. Many provisions concerned Christianization and maintaining Christian observance among the Indians. Others attempted to establish standards for the provision of food and clothing, which in effect the Indians purchased, as their compensation of one gold peso per year was to be provided in the form of goods, usually clothing.

The amendment to the laws, issued in July 1513, required that within two years all Indigenous men and women must be clad. Although the laws regulated some conditions of labor—Indian women who were more than four months pregnant or nursing, for example, were exempted from mine work—they also mandated that encomenderos have at least one-third of their people working in gold mines at all times. Indians were to work for five months in the mines, followed by a period of forty days during which they were not to be required to work other than for their own subsistence.

The laws, then, reflected the crown's attempt to reconcile its prodigious interest in the revenues to be gained from mining gold with the demands of officials and settlers and moderate concern for the Indians' welfare and religious life. If the results seem strange from a modern perspective, at least some contemporaries found them contradictory and inadequate as well. Las Casas devoted several chapters of his history to a thorough critique and condemnation of the laws.[113]

Almost exactly thirty years later Charles V promulgated the New Laws, further amending and limiting the privileges enjoyed by encomenderos and placing restrictions on certain kinds of labor. Encomienda Indians, for example, were not to be used as bearers (a common practice in New Spain). Indeed, encomenderos lost access to all virtually unpaid labor and in the future were to receive only tribute. The New Laws also prohibited any future enslavement of Indians (although the practice continued, in some places, through the eighteenth century) and mandated the freeing of Indians already enslaved.

Given the almost complete collapse of the encomienda system in the islands and the drastic reduction in Indigenous populations that had taken place in the fifty years since Europeans had arrived, the impact of the New Laws in the Greater Antilles would be nothing like the consequences occasioned by their introduction in New Spain or Peru, although there was resistance and their application in the islands was delayed. In 1549, however, the oidores of the audiencia reported that the majority of Indians were free to go where they wished. The real impact of the laws was on slaveholders. In 1545 the audiencia estimated that there were some five thousand Indian slaves in Hispaniola. In Cuba there were an estimated 900 Indians still in encomiendas, and 730 Indian slaves in 1544.[114]

In July 1543 Bachiller Álvaro de Castro, arcediano of Santo Domingo's cathedral, received orders stating that the emperor, "by a chapter of the ordinances now recently [made] . . . for the good government of the Indies and treatment of its natives, ordered that the Indians that at present are alive in that island and the islands of San Juan [Puerto Rico] and Cuba, for now and for as long as it is his will, should not be bothered with tribute or other royal or personal services. . . . For the good account that we have of your person, life, and customs, we have agreed to charge you with the care of the Indians of that island."[115]

If Castro's well-documented episodes of violent and decidedly unchristian behavior seem at odds with the king's assessment of his character, he in any case died before he exercised any functions related to this charge. A vecino of Santo Domingo, Juan de Betanzos, was sent to Puerto Rico to oversee the implementation of the laws there. He reported to the juez de residencia Licenciado Cerrato in September 1544 that he had been engaged "in the liberty of the Indians of that island," a job he characterized as laborious, although he provided no detail as to what he had done in the performance of his duties or if any Indian slaves actually obtained their freedom.[116] Cerrato wrote to the king in April 1545 that one hundred people had been set free, but he found that determining an individual's status in the absence of any documentation was nearly impossible. Even as he and other officials were at work, two ships arrived from La Margarita and Cubagua with more than 250 Indians who had been branded, ostensibly before the slavers learned of the new legislation.[117]

As Cerrato was expressing his frustration, further clarification of the mandate to free slaves arrived, stipulating that enslaved women of any age and boys under the age of fourteen should be freed. Not surprisingly, given that almost from the time they had begun to occupy the islands Spaniards had claimed the right to control the peoples of the Caribbean and to use their labor, the additional instructions from Prince Philip qualified the conditions of "liberty." Indians who had been freed would "be placed with masters whom they will serve, who will treat them well and teach and catechize them in the things of the Catholic faith and will pay them the salary that seems fair . . . and they won't go around idle and for which reason are lost."[118] Unfortunately, the records provide little more indication of the laws' impact. In 1547 Dr. Montaño, the dean of Santo Domingo's cathedral, wrote to the crown that the audiencia had done nothing to implement them.[119]

In the Greater Antilles the New Laws had their greatest consequences for Spaniards who still held enslaved Indians, who continued to arrive in the islands as slavers pursued their activities elsewhere. In July 1543 the king wrote to the audiencia that he had information that "in the provinces of Venezuela and the province and Gulf of Paria and islands of Cubagua and La Margarita, many persons have taken Indians native to said islands and provinces and taken them to sell and sold them in the islands of Hispaniola and San Juan [Puerto Rico] and other places." They were to be freed and returned to their places of origin (naturalezas), at the cost of whoever was responsible for their captivity.[120] In 1556 the governor of Cuba, Diego de Mazariegos, estimated that around two hundred Indigenous slaves remained on the island because the royal order to return them to their homelands was not enforced. He argued that they had intermarried with Natives of the island and should not be separated from their spouses and families.[121]

Residents of Hispaniola were required to provide documentation of how the people they held in bondage had been enslaved and purchased.[122] The audiencia ordered slave owners to bring their slaves before them to be examined, but almost immediately the process of determining whether Indians had been enslaved legally broke down, as slave owners argued that if their slaves' faces were marked with the royal brand, that should suffice to demonstrate their legal right of ownership. The crown insisted, however, that the burden of proof lay with the owners, not with the Indians.[123]

Representing the city of Santo Domingo, Gonzalo Fernández de Oviedo and captain Alonso de le Peña argued that removing Indian slaves from owners who had cared for them and instructed them in the holy faith would cause them harm and that they were likely to become thieves or "bad women." They also expressed concern that if the slaves were freed, they might become the victims of unscrupulous men who would take them wherever they liked, to sell in the Azores or elsewhere.[124] In October 1546 the cabildo asked that the Indian slaves "that had been taken from the vecinos" be returned to them, claiming that the Indians "have returned to their vices and abominations, it being a pity to see them wander around lost and dying in the montes and woods."[125]

People also protested a provision of the New Laws that mandated that "Berber slaves and free people who descend from Moors newly converted" should be sent back to Spain, arguing that there probably were no more than one hundred such people living in the islands and that they had done no harm whatsoever. Those who were there had arrived legally and now were married with children, and those who were free were masons and carpenters or worked at "other trades very beneficial to the land's population." Officials asked that they be allowed to remain.[126]

The laws pertaining to the growing numbers of African and African-descended slaves mainly aimed to regulate their movements and behavior and to punish infractions. Ordinances issued by the audiencia in 1528 affecting "all the slaves, Black and white" specified punishments for running away that varied in severity depending on the length of absence, whether a slave returned voluntarily, and how many times previously he or she had been absent. Slaves were not to bear arms other than a knife, if it were necessary for their occupation.[127] The perceived need to control slaves far outweighed concerns about their living conditions, although officials acknowledged that some problems arose from the bad treatment that slaves might experience, from receiving insufficient food and drink to excessive punishment. Slaves were to receive adequate provisions and were not to be required to work on Sundays and holidays.[128]

In the early years, the question of whether slave status was permanent and how enslaved persons might achieve their freedom did not have a consistent answer. In Puerto Rico in 1511, for example, it was proposed that if a Black slave served his master for fifteen years without running off, he should gain his freedom, as should a slave who collected 15 *marcos de oro*.[129] The king seems (temporarily) to have been swayed by this argument. In 1526 he directed officials in

Cuba that Black slaves who "do not rebel nor run away and are willing to work and serve their owners more willingly ... it would be good that after serving a certain time and each giving his owner up to 20 marks of gold at the minimum, or higher depending on what you think ... that the women and children of those who are married should become free."[130] Although there is no evidence that any slaves achieved freedom for themselves or their families in this fashion, there continued to be uncertainty as to whether slaves who married could expect to be freed.[131] In 1527, however, Charles V clarified his policy on slave marriage, stating that while it would be beneficial to encourage slaves to marry, because having wives and children would be a source of happiness for them, they nonetheless would remain enslaved.[132]

Other ordinances mandated that equal numbers of African men and women be brought to the islands, although this changed to a more realistic stipulation that at least one-third of slaves imported should be women. Apart from his concern about slave marriages, Charles V showed little inclination to ensure humane treatment for slaves under the law. In 1533 he responded to the petition of two vecinos of Cuba who had been prohibited from putting chains on their slaves, directing the island's lieutenant governor to allow them to punish their slaves in this fashion.[133]

When Gonzalo de Guzmán and Sancho Seco conducted their visit of estancias near Santiago in 1537, they found that the conditions for all workers, Indian and African alike, varied a good deal. Blacks on the estancia of Diego Alonso claimed that their owner had ordered that they be well fed but that the estanciero, Francisco Escudero, withheld food meant for them and in general mistreated and beat them.[134] In contrast, two Cuban Indians, five Black men, two Black women, and "cuatro negritos" on the estancia of Juan Carmañes said that he fed them well, and Juan Barba's workers also said they were well fed and treated. On the estancia of treasurer Lope Hurtado and his wife, Leonor de Medina, however, both Indians and Blacks complained that they received little to eat, and what they did get was mainly yucca and sweet potatoes. The Blacks also claimed that if they worked on Sundays or holidays, it was to try to acquire some clothing, as they were nearly naked. In 1544 Licenciado Cerrato informed Prince Philip that slave owners were forcing their slaves to work "on Sundays and holidays like the other days that are for work, without making any difference from one day to the other," which the prince thought set a very poor example.[135]

Conditions for slaves, then, varied a good deal. Although most of the Indians and Blacks on the estancias near Santiago said that they received adequate food and in general were treated well, there is no way to know if their responses were freely given. In any case the variation in their responses suggests that, at least in Cuba, ordinances regulating the distribution of food and clothing were not always observed.

A number of factors complicated government, politics, and the formulation and imposition of law in the early Spanish Caribbean: the distance from the metropolis, which slowed communications and to some extent was matched by the challenges of travel and communication among locales in the Caribbean; the sometimes competing responsibilities and aspirations of royal and local officials, and the overlap among them, represented by the presence of royal officials on municipal cabildos; the devolution of authority, if not jurisdiction, over Indians through the encomienda; the presence of royal officials whose duties sometimes intersected with (or were overshadowed by) their economic interests; and the strong connections established between particular families and political offices. That pattern, of course, began with the Colón family. Treasurer Miguel de Pasamonte was succeeded by his nephew Esteban and then briefly by a cousin.

The extended Caballero family exemplified the benefits of combining office holding with mercantile activity. Two men named Diego Caballero were prominent in Santo Domingo. It can be difficult to distinguish between them, especially because they were kin and engaged in business together. Diego Caballero "de la Rosa" was the longtime secretary of the audiencia and briefly served as contador. The other, Diego Caballero "de la Cazalla," held the position of contador in Hispaniola. He passed the position first to his nephew Hernando Caballero, son of his brother Alonso.

When Hernando died, in 1529, the secretary Diego Caballero briefly served as contador, then the position went to another nephew, Álvaro Caballero, who also was appointed alcaide of the fort at La Yaguana, with an annual salary of 250,000 maravedís.[136] His uncle Diego Caballero de la Cazalla renounced his regimiento in Santo Domingo in Álvaro's favor. This Diego Caballero, together with his brother Alonso, was active in the slave trade. He eventually returned permanently to Seville, where he founded a famous chapel in the cathedral, with a painting of himself with his son and his brother Alonso. Diego Caballero de la Rosa, the influential secretary of the audiencia who owned two sugar estates near Santo Domingo, remained in Hispaniola.[137] The many activities and responsibilities that secretary of the audiencia Diego Caballero documented in his información of 1535 show him to have been a capable and hardworking bureaucrat and servant of the crown, but almost certainly he too was involved in some of the fraudulent activities of his Caballero kin.

In this era, nearly all officials in the islands were immigrants. Below the level of the audiencia judges, who usually aspired to move on to other positions, however, many or even most officials remained in the islands. They married there or brought their wives to join them, raised their families, and became extensively involved in the Caribbean economy of commerce, slave raiding, gold mining, agriculture, and cattle raising. The possibilities for personal advancement and enrichment that came with office holding and through kinship and marital relations with other prominent residents of the islands were numerous, and whether many (if any) officials resisted the temptation to take advantage of those opportunities is impossible to say.

4

Church and Clergy

As was true throughout the Iberian world, the church and its clergy, both secular and regular, were enmeshed in early Spanish Caribbean society. Members of the clergy worked to bring the Indigenous people of the islands and African slaves into the Catholic church and provided most of the schooling for both Spanish and Indigenous children. Although the mendicant orders traditionally are associated with conversion campaigns in the Indies, the secular clergy were not only important in Spanish society but also engaged with Indians. The Franciscans and Dominicans were present and active in the islands from an early time, as were the Mercedarians on a smaller scale.[1] Hispaniola, Puerto Rico, and Cuba each had a bishop and cathedral, while Jamaica had an *abad* attached to the bishopric of Cuba.[2]

Bishops and cathedral dignitaries typically enjoyed reasonably high social status and influence and not infrequently became actively involved in politics and government. Perhaps the most notable expression of that connection was the concurrent exercise of the position of bishop of Santo Domingo and Concepción de la Vega and of president of the audiencia, first by Sebastián Ramírez de Fuenleal (1528–1530), who left Hispaniola to take up the position of president of New Spain's second audiencia, and then by don Alonso de Fuenmayor, who served as bishop and president and then, in 1546, became the first archbishop of Santo Domingo.

The crown's appointment of two clergymen to hold both the highest ecclesiastical and the highest governmental positions in Santo Domingo may reflect some residual influence of its earlier decision to send three members of the Order of St. Jerome (Hieronymites) to Hispaniola to act as governing authorities, in 1516.[3] The conflation of ecclesiastical and political office may have been a product, in part, of the perceived challenges of simultaneously imposing political authority and Christianity on these turbulent societies. What follows is a consideration of the activities and influence of the clergy; the relations between the ecclesiastical establishment and Spaniards, Indians, and Blacks; and the construction and establishment of monasteries, churches, schools, and a convent for women.

Evangelization

Fernando and Isabel received the title of Reyes Católicos from the pope in recognition of their victory over the last Muslim kingdom in southern Spain, Granada, in 1492. With the title came the power of patronage over the church in the newly opened territories of the Indies. One might assume, given the timing, that evangelization of the Americas' Indigenous peoples would receive high priority in the early Spanish Caribbean. Yet despite his confidence that the people he encountered in the Greater Antilles would be receptive to Christianity, Columbus made only minimal efforts to convert the Indians, although members of the regular orders were present from the outset. In 1511 King Fernando wrote to don Diego Colón that "the conversion of the Indians is the foremost basis of the conquest and the one to which attention principally should be paid."[4] Throughout the period considered here, however, evangelization in the islands was improvisational and eclectic, carried out (if at all) with varying levels of enthusiasm and intensity by members of the regular orders, secular clergy, lay Spanish men and women, and Indigenous converts.

Notwithstanding his strong religiosity, Columbus severely restricted the clergy's latitude to baptize Hispaniola's Indians. He maintained these restrictions even for Spaniards whose Indigenous wives were pregnant. It is possible that his reservations about baptism hinged on the question of whether it was acceptable to baptize people who had not yet received adequate instruction in Christian prayer and doctrine, but the more likely explanation for his reluctance was that he hoped to profit from sending Indians to Spain to be sold as slaves.[5]

Two Franciscan lay brothers, fray Juan de la Deule and fray Juan de Tisin, accompanied Columbus on his second voyage, in 1493.[6] They worked with Hieronymite Ramón Pané to attract converts and teach the catechism, baptizing Guatícabanú, a man from the northern part of the island who, as their first convert, took the Christian name Juan Mateo.[7] Deule and Tisin soon returned to Spain, hoping to convince the crown to send priests, and several Franciscans went with them to Hispaniola when they returned with Bobadilla in 1500. That same year, three other Franciscans traveled to the island, reporting soon after their arrival that they had baptized three thousand souls—"after due instruction it is to be hoped," in the words of Franciscan historian Antonine Tibesar.[8] If true, these early Franciscans would have been extraordinarily active and successful, capable of communicating effectively with the Indians and fortunate enough to find large numbers of willing converts.

Those assumptions may be questioned. Lauren MacDonald's perceptive discussion of Pané's experiences and conversion efforts strongly suggests that the friars encountered considerable resistance and substantial challenges to their conversion efforts.[9] The king wrote to Diego Colón in 1511 that, with the exception of the boys being brought up by the friars, the Indians of Hispaniola were Christian in name only.[10] The violence that occurred in the course of Spanish efforts to occupy the islands surely had an impact on evangelization as well. Juan de Tisin traveled to Cuba, where, according to Diego Velázquez, by 1514 he had "baptized all the people that until now have been secured"—in other words, conquered.[11] The meaning of a mass baptism in those circumstances is questionable; it might have been tantamount to forced conversion, and about as effective. Juan de Esquivel reported to the king about the many people in Jamaica who had converted "and the good Christians that they are." Fernando went so far as to suggest that the taking of Indigenous slaves would be a means to convert them: "Indians should be brought from the islands where there is no gold to Hispaniola to serve the Christians, be instructed in the faith, and separated from their vices and idolatry."[12]

The arrival of seventeen Franciscans led by fray Alonso de Espinal, as part of the group that accompanied governor frey Nicolás de Ovando, marked the real beginning of the establishment of the Franciscan Order in Hispaniola. In 1503 they started construction on a church and residence. The crown charged the Franciscans with responsibility for instructing caciques' sons who were thirteen years old or younger in the Christian faith, reading, and writing, and it agreed to pay the salary of Bachiller Suárez to teach them *gramática*.[13] Apart from the few sons of caciques whom the Franciscans instructed, Las Casas otherwise was unimpressed by the evangelization efforts made during Ovando's governorship; he seems to have viewed the Franciscans as well intentioned but clueless.[14]

The Laws of Burgos of 1512 included the requirement that at least one son of each cacique should be educated by the friars. The year after the laws were issued, the Franciscans received twenty grammar books and ten volumes of gospels and homilies, along with classroom supplies.[15] In Hispaniola they eventually established monasteries in Concepción de la Vega, Verapaz, Buenaventura, and La Mejorada (Cotuy). Enrique, who in 1519 led his people into the mountains of Bahoruco and out of the reach of Spanish control, lived for some part of his life and was educated at the Franciscan monastery and school at Verapaz.

Members of the Dominican Order arrived in Hispaniola in 1510 with fray Domingo de Mendoza, brother to fray García de Loaysa, who subsequently became confessor to Carlos V, archbishop of Seville and later president of the Council of Indies. Fray Pedro de Córdoba, whom Las Casas called a "devout and excellent preacher," was vicar. The other two Dominicans were fray Antonio Montesino (or Montesinos) and fray Bernardo de Santo Domingo. A vecino of Santo Domingo named Pedro de Lumbreras provided them with a bohío at one end of a corral he owned.[16]

The Dominicans' somewhat later arrival in Hispaniola probably accounts for their horrified reaction when they learned of the cruelty and abuse the Indians had suffered at the hands of the Spaniards. Franciscans, after all, had been present on the island from the earliest years; perhaps they accepted that violence and destruction were the price to be paid for the opportunity to bring the Indians to Christianity. The Dominicans might have known little about conditions on the island before they arrived, and they soon resolved to take action. On December 21, 1511, fray Antonio Montesino delivered his famous sermon condemning Spaniards for their mistreatment and exploitation of the Indians. In the days leading up to the sermon, Dominicans visited don Diego Colón and all the royal officials in their homes to secure their promise to attend. As Las Casas suggests, had these men known what to expect, they probably would have stayed home.[17]

Following Montesino's unprecedented and scathing sermon, outraged officials complained to the vicar of the order, fray Pedro de Córdoba, pointing out that by condemning the encomienda, Montesino was preaching against an institution that the crown itself had authorized—and from which, of course, it was benefiting considerably. Both the Franciscan fray Alonso del Espinal and Montesino traveled to court, separately, to argue their cases, and the king convened a group of theologians and jurists to deliberate on the dispute.[18] The result was the promulgation of the Laws of Burgos at the end of December 1512, followed by an amendment issued in July 1513 in response to criticisms that the laws did little to mitigate the situation of the Indians.

One member of the royal council who participated in these deliberations was Dr. Juan López de Palacios Rubios, whom Las Casas considered to be someone who "favored" the Indians and was a person "of virtue." He also was author of the Requerimiento, adopted around the same time, which ostensibly provided Spaniards a legal basis to wage war on and enslave people who refused to accept the sovereignty of their church and crown.[19] Although the Franciscans might have been in closer contact with the Indians of Hispaniola than were the Dominicans, the latter were primarily responsible for instigating the first serious effort to restrain the rampant exploitation of the Indigenous people of the Caribbean, even if the results—the Laws of Burgos—had little impact. As members of the so-called Order of Preachers, they also might have been the first on the island to preach to the Indians via interpreters. Whether any of the Dominicans acquired sufficient knowledge of an Indigenous language to deliver sermons without the aid of an interpreter is not known. Such proficiency would have taken some time to achieve, and the rapid reduction of island populations might have acted as a disincentive to devoting time and effort to learning another language.[20] Members of the Mercedarian order arrived in Hispaniola soon after the Dominicans.

In all likelihood the monastery schools that were established for the education of Indigenous boys were the most successful vehicles for Christianization, even if they were limited in their overall impact. Not only did they produce some converts to Christianity—Enriquillo apparently remained a practicing Christian during his years of rebellion, and after negotiating a peace treaty with Spanish officials, he asked for a priest to baptize the children who had been born in his community—but also at least some of the students learned Spanish well enough to serve as interpreters. In 1516 the Hieronymites in Hispaniola ordered some of the ladino students educated by the Franciscans to accompany priests who were heading to Tierra Firme in order to act as their interpreters.[21] In 1528 the canon Benito Muñoz, in the name of the cabildo of Santo Domingo's cathedral, asked that four Indian boys "from the pueblo of which fray Remigio of the order of San Francisco" has charge be assigned to serve as altar boys. Muñoz specifically sought permission to teach two boys "to be good readers and singers of plainsong and of organ [sic]."[22]

In addition to the monastery schools, the crown also stipulated that every church should provide instruction. Governor Ovando mandated that Indian children meet twice a day to learn the catechism, but little came of this early initiative.[23] In 1530 the queen instructed bishop and audiencia president Sebastián Ramírez de Fuenleal to use a house purchased by the Hieronymites as a school, the rent from which was earmarked to pay the priests who were to be in charge of the Indians and to educate "los hijos de los naturales" (the children of the Natives).[24] Although the monastery schools targeted boys, in 1533 the Council of the Indies advised that Indian girls should be taught at convents for women, although none existed in the islands at the time. Santo Domingo's cabildo agreed to establish the convent of Santa Clara in 1545.[25]

The oidores of the audiencia wrote to the king in the late 1530s to inform him that the city had begun to build a stone house for a grammar school, for which they hoped to bring two *bachilleres* and a *repetidor*. In their opinion, "for the Indians and for the sons of your vassals, especially the orphans, this is a very important thing." They also noted that a Trinitarian named fray Antonio de Mendoza recently had arrived in Hispaniola with his fifteen-year-old legitimate son, apparently having intended to travel on to Peru. "Father and son preach and instruct the Indians and children ... with great results. From no other order has a more useful religious been seen." The city was helping with their expenses.[26] In 1541 Mendoza reportedly was teaching fifty students and hoped that the number soon would double, but whether his students included any Indians at that time is not clear.[27]

Despite these efforts, Christianization made only modest progress. The arrival of growing numbers of African slaves resulted in the substantial presence in the islands of new ethnic groups that for the most part were not Christian. In October 1538 the king wrote to the audiencia regarding the "many Indian and Black slaves" who had not been sufficiently indoctrinated in the holy faith. He urged the officials to specify a time when the city's slaves could gather in Santo Domingo's cathedral or one of its monasteries to receive instruction, and he charged ecclesiastical officials with enforcing the order. Whether they tried to implement this plan is not known.[28]

In the countryside, at least, officials worried about whether congregating Black slaves who labored on sugar estates to attend mass was worth the risk it might pose, "given that these gatherings could encourage uprisings and escapes."[29] Decades later, in 1568, oidor Licenciado Echegoyan wrote that Black slaves working on the ingenios were poorly treated and had not been baptized, so evidently little progress toward Christianization had taken place, even well after the middle of the century.[30] Although there are few indications that any systematic conversion efforts were directed toward Blacks, a complaint from oidores Zuazo and Infante in 1532 that "villainous" Blacks who had committed crimes were fleeing to monasteries, where "the friars hide and defend them," suggests that some enslaved Black people might have forged relations with the island's religious, notwithstanding the lack of a formal evangelization campaign.[31]

Neither the crown nor officials and clergy in the islands expected the regular orders to be solely responsible for evangelization efforts; the secular clergy participated as well. Bachiller Álvaro de Castro, who held a series of positions in the cathedrals of Concepción de la Vega and Santo Domingo, claimed that he personally baptized more than 4,500 "personas de indios" during the eleven months in which he had conducted his ecclesiastical visit in the 1520s, traveling 350 leagues over difficult terrain on foot and horseback.[32] In 1537 the king wrote to Puerto Rico's bishop, don Alonso Manso, saying that he had been told that the Indians on the island of Mona were "good Christians" but lacked a priest to instruct them; he told Manso to send a priest of good reputation.[33] When Bachiller Diego López went to Cuba to serve as dean in Santiago, he received permission to have several naborías for his service. He was expected to instruct them in Christianity.[34]

In the early years Spaniards also hoped that Christianized Indians would facilitate conversion. In 1511 don Diego Colón said that Miguel Díaz de Aux, whom he had appointed alguacil mayor of Puerto Rico, had asked permission to take some of his Indian slaves from Hispaniola "to minister to and catechize the other Indians of the said island." Díaz sought permission to take forty slaves to Puerto Rico, although he seems actually to have taken half that number.[35] Article IX of the Laws of Burgos stipulated that any encomendero who had fifty or more Indians should have a boy taught reading, writing, and the basics of Christianity so he could instruct the others. If there were one hundred Indians, then the encomendero should ensure that two boys would be so educated.

To what extent encomenderos complied with this mandate to educate boys is not known. Records for the hacienda de Toa and two other royal haciendas in Puerto Rico from later in that decade include lists of naborías and what they received in cacona, the goods distributed to workers, mainly in the form of clothing. A man named Martinillo "el cristiano" appears among the naborías of the cacique Francisco Aramana in 1514; in 1515 he was described as the "Christian who is in charge of the church on the said estate and instructs the Indians." In the list of October 2, 1515, Martinillo el cristiano appeared with six men from Hispaniola (Hayti) and one from Bimini, suggesting that he probably was not from Puerto Rico, although his place of origin was not mentioned.[36]

As more people were living on estates and in rural areas, their relative isolation from churches and clergy meant workers were unlikely to have much exposure to Christian instruction or to have been baptized. In March 1537 Cuba's lieutenant governor, Gonzalo de Guzmán, visited twenty estancias near Santiago, accompanied by the priest Sancho Seco, "in order to know if they are Indians brought up in the things of the faith." Most of the estancias had mixed workforces that included Cuban Indians who were part of the shrinking encomiendas, enslaved Indians who mostly originated outside of Cuba, and enslaved Blacks.[37]

The Blacks, perhaps because they were among the more recent arrivals in the island, were least likely to have been baptized, but regardless of whether they had been, most workers said that they did not receive any regular religious instruction. On the estancia that belonged to the widow of the deceased Andrés Ruano, one Black slave named Hernando said he was Christian, while another, Gonzalo, said he was not. Seco baptized Gonzalo. The Indian workers told Guzmán that they did not know the Pater Noster or the Ave María and that they received no religious instruction. Guzmán charged the estanciero Felipe Barbosa with responsibility for teaching them, perhaps a dubious choice, given that Barbosa lived with an Indian slave woman named Elvira with whom he had two children. Guzmán ordered that Elvira be sent to live in Santiago "to avoid the sin in which they are living," or he would prosecute him.

At the next estancia they visited, three out of the five Black men, two Black women, and four Black children living there had not been baptized. Guzmán told the owner of the estancia to take them to the church to be baptized and stipulated that all the workers, including two Cuban Indians, should be taught the Pater Noster and the Ave María. On the estancia of Juan del Castillo, the Black slaves said that they were Christian but had not been taught the prayers. Guzmán threatened Castillo with a fine of 3 pesos if the workers did not learn the prayers, and he stipulated that they must not work but instead must attend mass on Sundays and holidays. In contrast to this moderate fine, Guzmán ordered that Black slaves who missed Sunday mass should be brutally flogged, notwithstanding that they probably were at least as likely to miss mass because their masters required them to work as because they chose not to attend.

Via the notary who accompanied them, Guzmán notified Leonor de Medina, the wife of treasurer Lope Hurtado, that she must have "a Spaniard at the said estancia who will show them the things of our holy faith." Only at one estancia, that of Bernaldino de Quesada, did the workers say that someone taught them the prayers in the evenings. At another, when seven enslaved Blacks were asked whether they knew the "things of our holy faith," they declared that they "all had the desire to know them" but received no instruction; "some others"—presumably workers—who did know them had taught them a little. At the estancia of Antonio Velázquez, none of the Indian or Black workers knew the prayers.

The number of lay Spaniards in this period who could recite all the prayers and the catechism is unknown.[38] In a letter of October 1550, the dean of Concepción de la Vega described his efforts to promote greater familiarity with the prayers as follows:

> Most of the Spaniards in this bishopric don't know the church prayers. I told the priest of this church that on Sundays, after general confession and before the ceremony of absolution, he should announce that on one Sunday everyone will say the Padre Nuestro and Ave María with him, on another Sunday the Credo, and on another the Salve Regina, so that those who don't know them will learn, and also to tell them during mass when they should stand, be seated, or kneel. The priest didn't dare do it and said he would rather leave his office than to do it. I decided to act as priest for three Sundays in order to lead the way for the priest, and on the first they were so disturbed that I thought they would stone me, had not three good men been close at hand who said it was well done what I did and that there was great need for it.[39]

Given the dean's apparently strained relations with many vecinos and his fellow clergymen, the story merits some skepticism, although Spanish residents' familiarity with the basic prayers may well have been tenuous.

The approaches already discussed do not exhaust the varied means by which Spaniards sought to make progress toward Christianization of non-Spaniards.

Women, probably mainly upper-class married women, might be tasked with religious instruction. In 1513 governor Ovando sent two cacicas to be instructed by the wife of an unnamed vecino, and in the Repartimiento of 1514 officials placed an Indian woman named Luisa, whose Spanish husband had died, with veedor Gaspar de Astudillo, "so that his wife will have her with her in their house, and teach her to embroider and about the things of the faith." No additional service was to be required from her.[40] Although piety in upper-class women was highly prized, their religiosity did not necessarily exceed that of men; recall that Guzmán had to remind Lope Hurtado's wife to have someone at their estancia who would instruct the workers in Christianity.

Another means by which Spaniards sought to instill Christianity in the Indians was to take or send them to Spain. Starting with Columbus's first return voyage, Europeans took Indigenous islanders with them to Spain in the hope that they would learn enough Spanish to serve as interpreters. In 1512 the Dominican order announced plans to establish a school in Seville in which Indigenous boys would be educated to be missionaries; the archbishop of Seville would be responsible for maintaining the school. Members of the order were to bring children to study there after "accustoming them first to the foods of Castile."[41]

Religious justification for this appropriation of Native lives became more common over time and sometimes was used in cases where the mestizo children of Indigenous women and Spanish men were removed from their mothers. The wealthy entrepreneur Rodrigo Manzorro took his daughter doña Elvira, who almost certainly was a mestiza, to Castile in 1518 in order to "instruct her in the matters of our holy faith." He died there, and she married Francisco de Barrionuevo, returning with him to Hispaniola.[42] In 1529 the queen wrote to the lieutenant governor of Cuba, Gonzalo de Guzmán, that the eight Indians he had sent had arrived in Seville and that she had sent them to "certain monasteries in order that they be taught the things of the faith."[43] The previous year, Cuba's procuradores had protested the plan to remove the sons of caciques from the island, suggesting that the caciques would view it as "great harm."[44]

The uncoordinated and sporadic efforts to convert Indians and Blacks in the islands mostly failed, as officials and clergy were well aware. Cuba's procuradores complained in 1528 that the Indians had no interest in converting and spent their Sundays performing *areitos* (ceremonial dances) and playing games.[45] In discussing the brief and unsuccessful attempt to establish an "experimental" community of "free" Indians in Puerto Rico, Baltasar de Castro wrote to the king in 1520 that the reason for the experiment was "to see if they would be capable of living civilly and receiving Christian doctrine, and they did not benefit at all but rather forgot the catechism that had been shown to them."[46] However, while the Puerto Rican experiencia ostensibly was meant to promote a Christian lifestyle for its residents, there is no evidence that a priest ever was appointed to serve there as stipulated, possibly because of the shortage of clergy on the island in those early years.

In Cuba, Francisco Guerrero, the priest assigned to an experimental community established near San Salvador de Bayamo, exploited the community for his own financial benefit, lived openly with an Indian woman he had taken from her husband, and almost never said mass. Several boys between the ages of five and eight, whom he was supposed to instruct in Christianity, he instead put to work in his stable caring for the horses, over the protests of their parents.[47] Given that no effort was made, in either the Puerto Rican case or the Cuban, to ensure that the Indians designated for the experiencias were Christian or that they would receive instruction in Christianity, it is hardly surprising that Christianity did not take hold in these communities. The experiencias, then, offer yet another example of a failed (and, in truth, decidedly tepid) approach to fostering the spread of Christianity.[48]

Ultimately, of course, the high levels of mortality that reduced Indigenous populations to remnants of their former numbers more or less solved the problem of ineffective evangelization, at least of the Indians. In 1537 the king wrote to officials in Santo Domingo that there were several houses in the city belonging to the crown that had been built with the express purpose of generating rental income to be used to support "certain chaplains who reside in the pueblos of the Indians." He noted, however, that because so many deaths had occurred among the Indians, there was no longer a need for the rents, and he ordered the houses to be sold.[49]

Establishing the Church

Given the inconsistent commitment to evangelization in these years, it seems that the establishment of the church as an institution, with cathedrals, churches, monasteries, and schools staffed by members of the clergy, had far more to do with encouraging the formation of a full-fledged Iberian society in the islands than with converting Indians or Africans. As we have seen, representatives of the religious orders arrived steadily in Hispaniola in the early decades and subsequently began to establish themselves in the other islands. In July 1511 the crown instructed Juan Cerón, who was the alcalde mayor of Puerto Rico, and Miguel Díaz de Aux, the alguacil mayor, to establish a Franciscan monastery on the island and to start, as soon as possible, construction of a chapel for the sacrament dedicated to St. John the Baptist. At the time, the island was called San Juan, and indeed, St. John's Day fell not long before the crown issued the order.[50]

Not until 1529 did some Franciscans relocate from Hispaniola to Cuba with the intention of establishing a monastery, but they protested to the king about the treatment they received at the hands of the bishop. Apparently, the "good people" of the island had donated money to help them get a start, but the bishop, fray Miguel Ramírez, treated them badly and tried to force them to leave.[51] The king instructed officials to give the friars their help and support, but as late as 1532 lieutenant governor Manuel de Rojas wrote that there were only two Franciscan "frayles sacerdotes," who recently had come to the island with the oidor Licenciado Vadillo. They hoped to build a monastery in Santiago, for which the cabildo had donated a plot (*solar*), but Rojas questioned whether the city could support it, given the small number of vecinos, most of whom were poor. One witness in the deposition that Rojas prepared regarding the derelict state of churches and other problems on the island said that the two Franciscans had a "small old house of thatch" and had built a small church, also of thatch, in which they said mass. They were hoping more friars would join them. Witnesses agreed that the city could support only a small number of friars, perhaps four or five, but saw their presence as beneficial.[52]

In September 1533 the king reiterated the importance of building a monastery of stone, and two years later he directed that a special tax (sisa) be levied on all of the island's residents to raise 200,000 maravedís for the completion of the monastery.[53] In 1538 Ramírez's successor as bishop, don Diego Sarmiento, evidently used all means at his disposal to force the Franciscans out of the monastery, alleging that the order had failed to obtain the proper diocesan authorization for its establishment. The king had to instruct yet another bishop to leave them in peace.[54]

Given their long presence in Hispaniola, one would expect the Franciscans to be well established and supported there, but in 1544 the friars found it difficult to obtain the funds needed to rebuild their church in Santo Domingo.

Their first church was a small wooden building, poorly constructed because, as witnesses who recalled it from the time it was founded, after Ovando and the friars arrived in 1502, explained, "the *oficiales* who were there at the time were not as skilled at masonry as they are now."[55] Several years later, in August 1508, a hurricane destroyed the recently constructed stone walls of a new church, along with most of the city's buildings, and construction started again.

By the 1540s, the needs of the city's vecinos had outstripped the church's capacity. The church could not accommodate the numbers of people who might wish to attend mass, and no available tombs remained, although in the past some prominent vecinos had chosen the church for burial. The adelantado don Francisco de Garay, for example, had financed the construction of the main chapel, where he and his relatives were buried. Given the "great and excessive" costs of both materials and masons, the construction of a new church "of middling grandeur," which included replacing the rotting wooden roof with a vault, was expected to exceed 12,000 pesos. The friars themselves lacked any property or rents, ordinarily going door to door to beg and living on whatever charity the city's residents could provide.[56] They had raised 600 pesos toward the church's construction. Witnesses cited the general impoverishment of many of the city's vecinos, who "are in need because of the times and the little gold that is being collected," as the reason for the difficulty in raising the necessary funds.

Dominicans also maintained a continuing presence, although possibly a smaller one than the Franciscans. In April 1531 the queen instructed officials in Puerto Rico to provide 200 ducados for the construction of a Dominican monastery in San Germán.[57] Several years later padre Gil de Santacruz asked the crown to cover the costs of passage for seven Dominicans he was taking with him "for the instruction of the Natives of those parts."[58] In 1547 eight men who had entered the order in Hispaniola and then gone to Spain to study asked for permission to return to the island. They were to travel in the company of four other religious whom the provincial wished to send there.[59] Don Luis Colón established a Dominican monastery in La Vega, Jamaica, around 1540 called Nuestra Señora del Socorro. In 1557 the Dominican provincial in Santo Domingo ordered the monastery abandoned, but at Colón's request the crown interceded. It ordered that four or five men be sent to staff the monastery and that any ornaments that might have been removed be returned.[60]

The Mercedarian order was present in the Greater Antilles, although only in Hispaniola. Santo Domingo's cabildo wrote to the king in 1534 that the "order of our Lady of Mercies" had in the city "a very devout house.... There are always [those] in it who are well endowed in knowledge and conscience and very good life." They had begun construction of a "very sumptuous church" that could not be completed without royal assistance. Padre fray Francisco de Bobadilla, the provincial vicar of the order, who had lived for many years in Tierra Firme and Nicaragua, founded monasteries there and in Panama, and assisted Francisco Pizarro, would give the king a full accounting of the order's work.[61]

In 1540 fray Alonso de Escobar, the comendador of the Mercedarian Order in Santo Domingo, said that the order had maintained a monastery there for many years but needed more people. He asked the crown for a license authorizing six religious of his order to come to Hispaniola annually. Escobar said that the monastery had done well but that the need to send friars to Spain to study had drastically reduced their numbers on the island.[62] Some time after this the vicar Bobadilla wrote to the crown complaining that members of the order had left the monastery and were wandering around the island. The queen instructed Hispaniola's officials to apprehend them and return them to the monastery.[63] A few years later, however, Santo Domingo's cabildo reported that the monastery had been revitalized with the arrival of fray Juan de Cueva as *visitador general* of the order, who brought with him fray Amador de Aguiar. Although by 1549 the order had built its monastery of stone, the church remained unfinished.[64]

The crown had concerns about not only the viability of the orders but also their character. In 1542 the king called upon audiencia officials to provide all necessary "favor and assistance" to fray Jacobo de Tastera, the *comisario general* for the Franciscan Order in the Indies, who had complained about the behavior of members of the order in Hispaniola and Cuba. Tastera alleged that many religious no longer were observant and had failed to set the positive spiritual example they were expected to provide.[65] The Dominicans in Hispaniola received a warning from the king the following year regarding their acceptance of inappropriate donations and bequests. He reprimanded them for having distanced themselves from the "holy and good purpose in which for so many years they had persevered" in the service of both Spaniards and Indians. He instructed them either to rid themselves of whatever property and goods they had received or to use them for "pious" purposes.[66] In 1547 the king addressed the *padre general* of the Order of San Francisco, saying that he had received a report from officials in Santo Domingo complaining that the Franciscan monastery had few friars and that those who were there were not educated. He asked that "some learned religious" be sent.[67]

The secular branch of the church grew quickly both in size, with the arrival of increasing numbers of clergymen, and in complexity, as cathedrals needed to be staffed by canons and other dignitaries who formed the cathedral's cabildo, or chapter. The expansion of the secular church was particularly notable in Hispaniola, which initially had two bishoprics, in Concepción de la Vega and in Santo Domingo. Although those two soon came to be held by one churchman, the cathedrals of both cities in these years continued to function as such. Puerto Rico and Cuba faced greater difficulties than did Hispaniola in filling dignitaries and benefices, but even in Santo Domingo the cathedral chapter struggled to fill all the positions, and most of the time fell short.[68]

These shortfalls in staffing ultimately hinged on insufficient financial resources, a problem that worsened over time as the Spanish population contracted and tithes followed suit.[69] Qualified clergymen abandoned their positions because of the modest salaries offered, usually 100 pesos annually, to try their luck on the mainland. In a letter of October 1550 the dean of Concepción de la Vega recounted the departure of a number of canons, one of whom had left for Peru saying, "Here one dies of hunger." Another had returned to Spain, while a third allegedly persuaded a married woman to leave her husband and departed with her for Peru.[70]

The need for more clergy grew as demographic and settlement patterns changed and more people were living in areas underserved by the church. In 1518, for example, Puerto Rico's treasurer, Andrés de Haro, complained that the bishop, don Alonso Manso, was away in Castile and that there were only two priests on the entire island, one in each town.[71] When officials in Puerto Rico briefly tried to create the experiencia in which the Indians on the royal hacienda of Toa would be supervised by a priest and a mayordomo, there is no evidence that a priest was ever appointed, probably because none was available.[72] The procuradores of Cuba's towns complained in 1528 about the "considerable lack of spiritual things because of there being few priests and not one educated preacher, and those who are there mostly are inadequate both for Spaniards and for the conversion and instruction of the Indians."[73]

In a deposition about the state of the church in Cuba in 1532 a man named Juan Rodríguez Gallego, who had lived in Santiago for fourteen years, argued that, because of the distances that separated them, each of Cuba's towns should have two priests rather than just one. Even Santiago only had two priests. He alleged that the island struggled to retain priests because their salaries were so low.[74] In Asunción (Baracoa) a Trinitarian friar served as parish priest. In a letter of 1528 the procuradores of Cuba's towns suggested that Indians working at mines actually were well situated for conversion efforts "because they are in the company of many Spaniards, among whom there always are some priest or priests who communicate with and benefit the Indians a great deal."[75]

The king wrote to the bishop of Santo Domingo, Fuenmayor, regarding complaints that the clergy sent by the bishop to rural churches served more as mayordomos than as priests and "concern themselves more with properties than souls." The king noted, as well, that he had been informed that the clergy in the cathedral of Concepción de la Vega did not comport themselves with appropriate "devotion and honesty."[76]

Over time, as more clergy became available, rural estate owners not infrequently took religious matters into their own hands, building churches or chapels on their property and hiring priests. In 1532 the queen instructed the bishop of San Juan not to prevent vecinos of San Germán from hiring clergymen to say mass on their estates or in "pueblos de las minas." Manso wanted to limit the conduct of mass to San Germán, but the queen insisted that if he failed to provide priests to visit the rural communities, the vecinos themselves could arrange for mass to be said.[77]

The survey of Hispaniola's ingenios and rural estates conducted by Alonso de Ávila in July 1533 aimed to collect information on rural populations for the purpose of establishing churches or chapels and assigning clergy to them. Ávila suggested, for example, that if a priest resided at the ingenio of Sanate in the eastern province of Higüey, he could serve Sanate, which employed one hundred Blacks and twenty Spaniards, as well as another nearby ingenio with eighty Blacks and fifteen Spaniards, all the labradores who lived in the area, and "mucha copia de negros e indios de las estancias" (an abundance of Blacks and Indians on the farms). Diego Caballero employed a priest to serve his ingenio near Santo Domingo and the surrounding area. Ávila himself was owner of one of three ingenios on the floodplain of the Nizao River that together employed 250 Blacks, "some" Indians, and sixty Spaniards. He recommended that a priest be hired to reside at his ingenio, as it was in the center of the area and "has a church and everything necessary."[78]

Ingenio owners and other residents of the countryside argued that part of the tithes they paid should be used to support rural churches and their clergy.[79] According to Genaro Rodríguez Morel, sixteen churches were built on ingenios in Hispaniola in the first half of the sixteenth century, with seventeen priests receiving appointments. Of these, "eleven were to be remunerated by the vecinos, or rather using the tithes collected in the areas and places they served."[80] Inexplicably, Hernando Gorjón, who made the largest charitable donation of any individual in the period to establish a *colegio*, church, and hospital in Santo Domingo, failed in his effort to have the wooden church he had built at his ingenio recognized as a parish, which would have allowed him to retain the tithes to pay for the church and the priest who performed the sacraments.[81]

Although the need to expand the clerical presence in the countryside probably was most pressing, the growing population of Santo Domingo needed a second parish, which by 1545 came into existence as Santa Bárbara, "although with great difficulty," because neither the bishop nor the cathedral dean and cabildo were willing to provide funds.[82] In 1546 people in the city complained that the cathedral's clergy had started to build a bulky tower for the cathedral that loomed over the main plaza, to the detriment of both the city and the fortress, so expanding the cathedral's presence apparently claimed higher priority than providing an additional venue where Santo Domingo's residents could attend mass.[83]

Private wealth also underwrote the elaboration of churches, with donations usually taking the form of ornaments or the construction or embellishment of chapels. A canon of Santo Domingo's cathedral, Diego del Río, in 1543 donated *una custodia de plata dorada* worth 1,000 ducados to the church in honor of Corpus Christi.[84] The *protonotario* don Pedro Martín, who had served as abad in Sevilla (Jamaica), left 800 pesos to build a church of stone there. Unfortunately, even with an additional 800 pesos from the crown, the funds were insufficient to complete construction.[85]

In 1537 don Diego Colón's widow, doña María de Toledo, offered to have the *capilla mayor* of Santo Domingo's church rebuilt, arguing that the existing one was too small. She wanted to move the remains of her father-in-law, Christopher Columbus, from the *monasterio de las Cuevas* near Sevilla so that he could be buried in the chapel along with his brothers. Her son don Luis Colón, the third admiral, received permission from the crown to place the family arms and images in the chapel, reserving the highest place for the royal arms.[86]

While serving as dean in Concepción de la Vega, Bachiller Álvaro de Castro proposed building a chapel where mass could be said at dawn "so that the Indians and other working people can go to hear it before leaving for work." He promised to provide from his own belongings ornaments of silk and a silver chalice and hoped to serve as the first chaplain. Castro claimed to have had numerous churches built "by my diligence and work" during the visit of inspection of Hispaniola that he conducted while serving under bishop Pedro Suárez de Deza.[87]

A community's wealth from mining also could underwrite investment in its church. A notable example was that of the church and monastery at La Mejorada, one of the few mining towns in Hispaniola still thriving in the 1530s. Castro, who was treasurer of Santo Domingo's cathedral in 1533 when he testified in a deposition compiled by the town, boasted of the church's ample inventory of ornaments, citing the generosity of the vecinos. He explained that the church had been rebuilt several times, beginning with simple bohíos and finally, upon his orders as ecclesiastical visitor, was reconstructed of masonry with the help of the vecinos and "their people" (that is, servants and slaves). The town had started to construct a chapel of stone, which was destroyed in a storm, but since then the townspeople had made considerable progress toward building a stone, earth, and brick chapel for the monastery, and a church of the same materials. They also had constructed a similar building to serve as lodging for the friars, with a refectory on the ground floor and space on the second floor for cells in which ten or twelve young religious might study grammar and logic. Most of this was possible because of the generous alms the vecinos had donated.[88]

In the 1520s and 1530s the varying presence, construction, and staffing of churches was perhaps one of the most consistent indicators of the relative wealth or poverty of towns and smaller communities. Lack of funding, or perhaps the mismanagement of funds, affected construction of the cathedral in Santiago in Cuba, which got under way in the late 1520s. By 1532 2,000 pesos had gone into the project, which appeared to require at least an additional 2,000 pesos to be completed.[89] The bishop had left the island to return to Castile, leaving the cathedral roofless and "hopeless" (sin remedio). Lieutenant governor Manuel de Rojas resorted to borrowing 500 pesos from the city's funds (maintained in the arca de tres llaves) to complete the roof of wood and tile so that what had already been built would not be destroyed by the frequent storms that the island experienced.[90]

Lives of the Clergy

Like other immigrants to the islands, members of the clergy moved around, seeking optimal situations. Their careers were somewhat distinct from those of lay Spaniards in that they often initially arrived bearing a "presentation," or royal authorization to serve in a specified benefice. Although there is no way to know for certain, given the number of benefices that needed to be filled through the 1520s and 1530s, it is possible that the majority of secular clergy who went to the islands in those years did so with an appointment in hand, although that does not mean that they remained in the first position they held, or that they took up the specified position at all.

Before arriving in Hispaniola Bachiller Juan Díaz had served in the Canary Islands, where he was vicar, and in other ecclesiastical offices for some ten years before accepting a benefice as vicar and visitor in Salvaleón de Higüey, a position he subsequently left in hopes of gaining an appointment in Santo Domingo.[91] Diego de Medina served for five years as vicar in Cubagua before taking up a benefice in La Yaguana in the 1530s. While living in Cubagua, he had visited Isla Margarita and the coast of Tierra Firme "many times" to administer the sacraments, baptize the children, and instruct the Indians. He claimed to be a member of the Order of San Pedro and had been ordained in Seville. He was hoping to become a canon of Santo Domingo's cathedral.[92]

As the numbers of clergy available to hold positions increased, competition for these positions probably increased as well. The ordained priest Francisco de la Serna held only a chaplaincy in 1547 when he hoped to obtain the position of choirmaster in the church of Concepción de la Vega or a benefice in the church in La Yaguana.[93] The incumbents in both places had died, leaving vacancies. Francisco de Ledesma left the town of Portillo in Palencia to go to Cuba. In 1535 he asked to be appointed to take charge of the failing experiencia of San Salvador de Bayamo in Cuba after the incumbent, the priest Francisco Guerrero, was accused of major infractions in his management of the experiencia and another priest in San Salvador, Juan Valero, was himself accused of offering Guerrero a bribe of 120 castellanos to leave.[94] The king granted Ledesma a benefice in Havana, which in 1535 probably was not much of a prize.[95]

Residents contended that Caribbean-born *hijos patrimoniales* trained for the priesthood should receive preference in the granting of ecclesiastical appointments. Contador Álvaro Caballero argued that benefices should be reserved for native sons because the majority of people who came to Hispaniola did so with the intention of enriching themselves and returning to Spain; giving preference to the native-born would help to retain valuable contributors to local society. This aspiration became more realistic as it became possible for young men to pursue their studies in Hispaniola rather than having to go to Spain to do so.

In 1537 an ordained priest named Gonzalo de Moya, who called himself "hijo patrimonial de la iglesia catedral" (native son of the cathedral church) of Santo Domingo, prepared a probanza (deposition). He claimed to have served in the cathedral for more than fifteen years, first as "mozo devoto" (probably altar boy) and then as sacristan. He was hoping to obtain the position of maestrescuela and suggested that any vacancy should be filled by an hijo patrimonial, or a vecino of the city, rather than by someone from elsewhere. Moya's father, Luis de Moya, was the *maestre mayor* of construction for the cathedral. He apparently first had gone to Hispaniola on his own and then, several years later, around 1519, had returned to Spain for his wife. Gonzalo himself had not been born on the island, although he had been there from an early age. His family's long residence in Hispaniola and his and his father's close association with the cathedral would have made him seem close to a native son.

Another priest, Jerónimo de Quintanilla, claimed that his father was one of the islands' first settlers and that he had arrived with him in 1502. He had lived for twenty-seven years in Hispaniola, Puerto Rico, and Cubagua, where he worked as vicar and *preceptor de gramática*. In 1529 he said that he wanted to return to Hispaniola, "where it could be said he is a native," taking with him some relatives. He was seeking the *arciprestazgo,* or archpriesthood. One witness testified that one of his sons had studied grammar with Quintanilla and then became a friar.[96]

Juan de Bardecí was a true hijo patrimonial. Born in Hispaniola, he had a successful ecclesiastical career in the islands. By 1549, at the age of twenty-three, he already was canon in the cathedral of Santo Domingo and had been appointed abad of Jamaica by almirante don Luis Colón.[97] His father was the longtime prominent official and entrepreneur Lope de Bardecí, who had been close to don Diego Colón. Juan de Bardecí said that he had studied "grammar, logic, and philosophy" in schools on the island as well as in Santo Domingo's Dominican monastery.[98] Santo Domingo's cabildo supported Juan de Bardecí's appointment, noting that it would "give reason for other hijos patrimoniales to be encouraged to study" and that "it truly seems that he was born to be a priest."[99] They also supported the appointment to the cathedral of Juan Lebrón, who was the son of regidor Jerónimo Lebrón and grandson of Licenciado Cristóbal Lebrón, who was appointed oidor in 1521.[100] In 1550, Diego Caballero advocated on behalf of his son, who had qualifications in grammar and logic and was studying canon law and hoped to obtain a position in the cathedral.[101]

The best-documented clerical career of the period was that of Bachiller Álvaro de Castro, against whom a number of charges were lodged, resulting in a lengthy judicial inquiry and extensive testimony regarding his activities in Hispaniola, compiled in 1532.[102] At the time, he had been living in Hispaniola for about twenty years. Although it can be difficult to distinguish rumor and innuendo from fact, similar statements from several witnesses suggest that he had multiple relations with women, both married and unmarried, Spanish and Indian; that he had extensive economic involvements; and that his relationships with a number of other ecclesiastics, especially in Concepción de la Vega, were highly acrimonious. Castro's summary of his accomplishments, in addition to the ecclesiastical visit, baptisms, and construction of churches discussed earlier, included having built two stone houses in Concepción and then another two or three in Santo Domingo; establishing what he called the first "cátedra de theología en este mundo nuevo" (chair of theology in the New World), with fray Tomás de San Martín as the school's first chair, for which he had donated 120 pesos of rent annually; having brought his orphaned nieces and nephews to Hispaniola at his own expense, and the Bachiller Morales to teach his nephews grammar;[103] forming a partnership with the Genoese merchant Pedro Benito Basinana in Seville to import two hundred Black slaves to work in the mines of Cibao; and maintaining for several years a butcher shop with a slaughterhouse and corral to supply the miners and their workers. In a letter of September 1532 Castro claimed that he had been denounced, arrested, and imprisoned for a month and a half by the provisor Francisco de Mendoza because of his partnership with Basinana, which Castro defended as providing an important service to the crown through the revenue generated.[104]

Castro's detractors emphasized his unimpressive background. Canon Cristóbal Deza said that his father was a meat cutter and his mother a shopkeeper. He had known him for twenty-four years, both in Castile and in Hispaniola, and contended that Castro was not an educated man and had acquired the title of bachiller as a sort of joke. Pedro Palomo, a vecino of Concepción de la Vega, who also had known him in both Castile and Hispaniola, said Castro came from a family of labradores and had never earned a higher degree. Castro had worked in Palencia as the steward of a canon and subsequently served in the same capacity under future bishop Pedro Suárez de Deza, whom he accompanied to Hispaniola. According to Palomo, while Castro was still in Palencia, a young woman came to the bishop's house asking for "el bachiller." When they asked whom she meant, she said Castro. Everyone there enjoyed a good laugh at Castro's expense and from that time on began calling him bachiller, "more as mockery of him and not as an honor."[105]

Regardless of his background or education, which Castro never addressed in refuting the charges, he clearly was capable and possessed tremendous energy. He must have favorably impressed his patron, the bishop Pero Suárez de Deza, who made him canon and provisor in Concepción de la Vega. He also served there as dean and was a *comisario* of the Holy Office. Notwithstanding the charges brought against him, he continued to hold positions in the cathedral chapters of Concepción and Santo Domingo, including that of archdeacon in Santo Domingo, and in 1543 received the royal appointment of "protector of the Indians" charged with administering the changes mandated by the New Laws. He died shortly thereafter and never exercised the office.[106]

Castro's actions on behalf of the Holy Office were controversial. The maestrescuela of the cathedral, Antonio Marques, contended that the punishment of a woman named Ana de Ribera, who received one hundred lashes while being paraded through the streets on an ass, was excessively brutal and had far more to do with the personal vindictiveness of Castro and others than with her actions. Following her punishment, she was permanently exiled from the island. Although none of the witnesses described her ostensible offense, in Marques's opinion, many others had done the same as or worse than she, but no one else had incurred similar punishment. Pedro Palomo pointed to the lack of due process in her case and deemed the punishment to have been "without pity or any mercy. . . . It seemed to him an inhumanity and cruelty and he saw that it caused scandal and gossip in this city."[107] Witnesses also mentioned the arrests on behalf of the Inquisition of two vecinos of Santiago de los Caballeros whose property was sequestered and implied that the seizures were improper, although in those cases, again, they provided no details.

Castro's sometimes violent and vindictive actions were addressed in chapter 3, but they were not the only aspects of his behavior that attracted criticism.

He frequently abandoned clerical dress—and apparently clerical conduct as well—to participate in games during fiestas or to ride in the countryside. During the fiesta for Santiago in the town of that name, Pedro Palomo witnessed Castro, armed with a lance, "ride on horseback many times and skirmish with the other horsemen and shout like the others," behavior he judged to be utterly inappropriate for a canon and provisor. He reported that Castro rode and even raced with other horsemen during fiestas in Concepción de la Vega and that he participated in mock skirmishes between groups calling themselves Moors and Christians.[108] Witnesses agreed, however, that conditions in the countryside were such that it was understandable that Castro would wear ordinary attire when he left the city to visit his mines or estancias. Also controversial was his involvement in maintaining a retail store in Concepción and selling merchandise in the city, especially during the periodic smelting of gold, when officials, miners, and merchants converged and debts were settled. Probably the greatest portion of the testimony against him in the proceso, however, focused on his numerous and sometimes fraught relationships with women, which will be discussed in chapter 6.

Álvaro de Castro certainly was not the only ecclesiastic who stirred up controversy and bad feeling. As early as 1509, Diego Colón complained of the "great dissolution" of the clergy "because many of a dissolute lifestyle [*mala vida*] have come and some renounce their habits, doing things of laymen, playing canes [a form of jousting] and going about in the woods with the women they want."[109] The dean of Concepción de la Vega wrote to the king in 1550 complaining about the activities of a canon from Seville, Pedro Vaca, whom he called "the most dissolute man who has come here." He alleged that Vaca had organized "a mutiny with certain wild men, and they agreed that on a particular night they would attack the city and burn some houses, as they are thatch, and kill and rob and from there go directly to La Yaguana and take a ship to go . . . to Tierra Firme and then to join with Pizarro." The news that Gonzalo Pizarro was already dead ostensibly stymied the aspiring rebels, whom the dean said numbered more than thirty.[110]

The reliability of this report is questionable. In 1547, while bishop (soon to be archbishop) don Alonso de Fuenmayor was still in Spain, the king instructed him to return to Hispaniola, in particular to deal with problems caused by the dean of Concepción de la Vega (unnamed but presumably the same man), who "by his ambition and licentious greed" had driven everyone away.[111]

Pero Vaca (or Baca) himself had prepared an información in 1544 in which witnesses testified to his charitable efforts, noting that he customarily aided travelers and other poor people by offering them hospitality and money.[112] Perhaps these beneficiaries of Vaca's generosity, apparently mainly transients, were the "wild men" of the dean's allegation.

If not guilty of criminal behavior, two successive bishops of Cuba, fray Miguel Ramírez and Diego de Sarmiento, became embroiled in local politics to the detriment of their spiritual mission. Ramírez was appointed bishop of Cuba and abad of Jamaica in 1530. Although he died in 1534 and so served only briefly on the island, he forged a close alliance with lieutenant governor Gonzalo de Guzmán. The latter granted the bishop a repartimiento of Indians, which as an ecclesiastic he was ineligible to hold. When he was ordered to give up the repartimiento, Ramírez arranged to have it assigned to his niece's husband, a man named García López, who shared with the bishop the profits from the gold the Indians mined.[113] Ramírez boasted that he was beholden to no authority but the pope and that only at the pope's instruction could he be required to testify about any matter.[114]

The Carthusian fray Diego Sarmiento arrived in Cuba in 1536 as the island's new bishop. Sarmiento's hostility to the Franciscans in the monastery in Santiago has been mentioned, and other aspects of his behavior attracted the strong disapproval of the crown as well. The king expressed grave disappointment in Sarmiento's performance in a letter of January 1541, writing, "We are informed that since you arrived in that island you have done and consented that your officials should do things that are inappropriate and very prejudicial to our subjects and others, in disservice and prejudice to our jurisdiction."[115] Sarmiento had failed to take other clergymen with him to the island, with the result that the cathedral had nothing more than a provisor and a priest, the reason being, according to the king, that Sarmiento had claimed all the rents and tithes, leaving nothing to support the cathedral chapter, the physical structure (*fábrica*) of the cathedral, or the hospital. At his behest, Sarmiento's criados and Black slaves had become involved in confrontations with local officials. He also claimed inquisitorial powers, which he did not possess, and under that pretext had his men forcibly arrest the royal factor in Cuba, Baltasar de Castro, who was placed under house arrest for a time. The king instructed the alcalde mayor to look into whether Sarmiento had been acting as inquisitor, and he warned Sarmiento to limit his exercise of office to the functions of prelate.

Dr. Alonso Manso, bishop of San Juan, was the longest-serving bishop of the era. He had studied theology in Salamanca and was the first bishop to go to the Indies, arriving at the end of 1512 and serving as bishop until his death in 1539.[116] After a visit to Spain in 1519, he was appointed *inquisidor apostólico general de las Indias*. In Puerto Rico he maintained a circle of officials to support the work of the Holy Office, including a secretary, constable, and notary.[117] He founded the parish of Nuestra Señora de los Remedios in San Germán and initiated construction of San Juan's cathedral, purchasing Black slaves to mine gold to help defray the costs.[118] In the 1530s he also for some time served as the prior of the Dominican monastery and briefly as lieutenant governor.[119]

Although Manso's reputation was nowhere near as scandalous as that of the two Cuban bishops, he did not entirely avoid criticism. He made some effort to intercede on behalf of Sancho Velázquez, who went to Puerto Rico in 1514 to serve as *juez de residencia* and, with Juan Ponce de León, as *repartidor de indios*. Velázquez acted as justicia mayor, or governor, of the island until Licenciado de la Gama began the residencia of his term in office and brought numerous charges against him, some of which are discussed in chapter 4. Bishop Manso allowed Velázquez's house to be declared the Inquisition's jail, where Velázquez died in May 1520.[120]

A decade later the king noted that Manso was housing several prisoners of the Inquisition in the building where gold was smelted, the treasurer lived, and the arca de tres llaves containing the royal gold and pearls was stored. He ordered Manso to move the prisoners.[121] In 1534 there were complaints that Manso's "criados, slaves and other ecclesiastical persons of that island [Puerto Rico] commit crimes for which they should be punished," but the bishop would not allow judicial officials to move against them.[122]

Manso's successor in 1542 was don Rodrigo de Bastidas, a man who, if not actually born in the islands, had a long career in the Caribbean. His father, the adelantado Rodrigo de Bastidas, was the founder of Santa Marta. Bastidas (the younger) was ordained in Seville and then served as dean in Santo Domingo and as bishop of Coro in Venezuela before being consecrated as Puerto Rico's bishop.[123] Around 1546 the audiencia in Santo Domingo appointed him captain general to organize, in conjunction with the cabildo, the island's defense against the French.[124] He served nearly as long as Manso before stepping down in 1567; he died in 1570. He had a reputation for judiciousness and piety and spent much of his considerable personal wealth in the exercise of his office.

The first bishop to reach Hispaniola was don Pedro Suárez de Deza, who arrived at the end of 1513 or beginning of 1514 consecrated as bishop of Concepción de la Vega. Perhaps alone among the early bishops, he seems to have taken the situation of the Indians seriously. He opposed the enslavement of the island's Indians, although he advocated that captive Caribs be brought to Hispaniola to work in their stead. He was one of the first ecclesiastics to advocate the ordination of Indians as priests, and he hoped to conduct a census of Indians and to register their births, deaths, and baptisms, although there is no record of its having been undertaken. His tenure on the island was brief, as he left Hispaniola in 1518 and died before he was able to return.[125]

The two bishops who probably had the greatest impact on Hispaniola during the period were Sebastián Ramírez de Fuenleal and Alonso de Fuenmayor, both of whom headed the combined bishoprics of Concepción and Santo Domingo as well as serving as president of the audiencia. Ramírez de Fuenleal had a varied career, serving in Santo Domingo only from the end of 1528 to the beginning of 1531, when he departed the island to become president of the second audiencia of Mexico. He eventually returned to Spain, where he served on the Council of the Indies and later as bishop of Cuenca. Hispaniola almost certainly would have benefited had he stayed there longer. He was an active administrator, concerning himself with both the situation of the Indians and the island's faltering economy.

His successor, Licenciado Alonso de Fuenmayor, arrived in Hispanola in 1533 and was a very different sort of bishop and official. Well connected in Spain—he was related to the wife of the influential royal secretary Juan de Sámano—he surrounded himself with people whom Rodríguez Morel characterizes as "arrogant, although with much influence in Castile." Many found Fuenmayor himself to be arrogant; members of the cabildo alleged that he made his decisions in an "impassioned and emotional way."[126]

Fuenmayor left for Spain at the end of 1544, returning three years later as archbishop, the position in which he served until his death in 1554. In a letter of October 1549, canon Juan Tarifeño complained bitterly about Fuenmayor's bullying ways as archbishop. He suggested that although the island had not fared well during Fuenmayor's absence, the situation had deteriorated further following his return. He alleged that the archbishop's main interests were eating and drinking and that he was known to eat before saying mass. He characterized his mayordomo as "un infierno" and said the same of his dean in Concepción. More serious complaints were that Fuenmayor monopolized revenues from tithes and claimed for himself any donations made to the cathedral chapter. He bullied the cathedral's cabildo, at times threatening with shackles and imprisonment those who disagreed with him. Tarifeño concluded, not without some melodrama, that he wished to inform the king "that if he [the archbishop] learns that I have written this, I fear to die in chains."[127]

If the ecclesiastical establishments of Hispaniola, Puerto Rico, and Cuba suffered from insufficient financial support and sometimes-dubious leadership, oversight of the church in Jamaica was even more tenuous. Fray Miguel Ramírez, who hardly distinguished himself as bishop of Cuba, also was abad of Jamaica. Following his death, Licenciado Amador de Sámano, brother of the royal secretary, received the appointment in 1535, but he did not arrive in Jamaica until 1539 because of "uncertain" conditions at sea caused by the ongoing conflict with the French. There also was a delay in conveying the bulls authorizing his appointment, which Sámano's brother could not send because of the "little security that there was at sea because of the French corsairs." Sámano had been instructed to leave for Jamaica as soon as possible, notwithstanding the delay.[128]

When he finally arrived in the island, his reception was anything but welcoming. Pedro Cano, the island's lieutenant governor, together with other vecinos, went to his house to demand that he show the bulls, declaring that without them he would not be allowed to exercise jurisdiction. They accompanied this assertion with "many disrespectful words" and other actions "worthy of punishment." A priest named Juan Cano had been exercising the office of *juez eclesiástico* solely on the basis of an appointment made by the town council of Sevilla. In all likelihood he was related to the lieutenant governor, whom the king instructed to appear before the audiencia in Santo Domingo to face criminal charges after the Council of the Indies had reviewed the case. The king instructed Sámano to arrest Juan Cano and send him to the bishop of Cuba along with a deposition detailing what had happened. The fate of neither Cano is known.[129] Licenciado Sámano died in Aragón in or by 1549 and so might not have stayed long in Jamaica.[130]

Education

In addition to the educational efforts directed at Indigenous children already discussed, residents in the islands tried to ensure the availability not only of basic schooling but also of higher levels of education. Friars and priests probably provided most of the schooling for the children of the islands' residents, but they did not monopolize it; laypeople also were involved in education. Francisco Quemado, for example, testified that he had lived in the Indies for fifteen or sixteen years, mostly in Cuba, although he also had spent time in New Spain and Hispaniola. His only source of income in Cuba was his employment by Santiago's cathedral as sacristan and the work he did "in teaching some boys to read and write."[131] Cuba acquired a "maestro de gramática" in the 1540s in the person of Miguel Velázquez, who had been sent by his father to study in Seville and Alcalá and returned to serve as the first *maestro de capilla* as well. He played organ and was proficient in plainsong (*canto llano*).[132]

Even primary instruction required teaching materials. A married couple named Inés de la Peña and Francisco de Pedraza, a swordsmith (*espadero*), brought to Santo Domingo a large collection of books and pamphlets that must have belonged to Inés de la Peña's father, as they formed part of her dowry. Although most of the nearly 130 books fell within the category of religious and exemplary literature and devotional works, there were classical works as well, including a book by Petrarch, others about Queen Dido and Roman history, a biography of Charlemagne, the very popular *Amadís of Gaul*, and a song book. Notably there were nearly one hundred children's primers (*cartillas de mostrar a leer muchachos*) that likely were intended for sale. Inés died in 1521, and an auction was held in 1525 as part of a suit over claims to her dowry.[133]

The most concerted effort to establish a seminary for higher education got under way in the late 1530s when wealthy ingenio owner and longtime resident of the island Hernando Gorjón announced that he would donate his ingenio near Azua, Santiago de la Paz, with everything that belonged to it to establish a colegio and a hospital for the poor, in which they would receive care and food free of any charges.[134] The hospital would have a church and three chaplains to say mass and perform the sacraments for the sick.[135] Students in the colegio, which was to have two professorships, would "read all the sciences" and pay no fees.[136] He also stipulated that dowries of 150 pesos from the rents of the ingenio should be provided for two or three "needy young women" to be chosen by the regidores of Santo Domingo. The recipients would be known as "daughters of señor Santiago, because this will be the devotion of the said colegio and hospital."[137] In 1538 Santo Domingo's cabildo wrote to the king about the importance of establishing such a school, not only for the youth of Hispaniola but also for students from "all these territories," so that they could avoid both the expense and the possible risks of the journey back to Spain to pursue their studies there. The cabildo claimed that a growing number of young men had neither a place to study nor "lords, as in those kingdoms, whom to serve," and as a result, "they go astray."[138]

Gorjón purchased four lots in Santo Domingo from treasurer Miguel de Pasamonte and another two from merchant and ingenio owner Benito de Astorga; these were next to another eight solares that Gorjón already owned in the same block.[139] Gorjón had the highest ambitions for this project, asking the crown to concede to the colegio the same privileges that the University of Salamanca enjoyed.[140] In return for his bequest, Gorjón aspired to, and received, the royal concession of the habit of Santiago at the rank of *caballero de espuelas doradas* (knight of the golden spur), conferred by don Luis Colón in 1540.[141] Gorjón also received the patronage of the colegio and hospital and of the church at his ingenio dedicated to Santiago.[142] He died in 1547, at the age of sixty-five, and was buried in the Franciscan monastery. The colegio came into existence and subsequently became the core of the university that was officially established in 1558.[143]

Hernando Gorjón was an unusual figure in the early Spanish Caribbean. During the forty-five years or so that he lived in Hispaniola, he never married and apparently had no children; no presumptive heirs stepped forward to contest his donation to found the colegio. He never served in an important office, nor did he establish close ties with any political faction on the island, but he was one of the island's most successful and wealthiest vecinos. Although he aspired to the distinction and status that the royal concession of the habit of Santiago conferred, his commitment to elevating island society by establishing the colegio is undeniable.[144]

One of the few other substantial bequests to the church in Hispaniola in this period that, like Gorjón's, was not primarily intended to enhance the status of or provide a burial site for the donor's family, was Bachiller Álvaro de Castro's bequest in his will of his stone houses and four solares in Santo Domingo. Valued at 4,000 ducados, the house was intended for the planned convent of Santa Clara. The city council had informed the king in 1545 of the need for a convent, citing the "multitude of women and orphans." The council sent to Spain for four nuns of Santa Clara for the convent, which was to be affiliated with the Franciscan order. In 1547 "some elderly religious women of good conduct and living" traveled from Spain. By 1556 sixteen daughters of leading vecinos of Hispaniola had entered the convent and more than 10,000 pesos had been spent on the church, sleeping quarters, and related construction.[145] Fernández de Oviedo alleged that several regidores in Santo Domingo had redirected funds intended for the "guerra de los negros" to the convent, where they had placed their daughters and other female relatives.[146]

A vecina of Santo Domingo who traveled to Spain in 1556 left her house and six Black slaves to establish a Dominican convent. The crown questioned whether a city of five hundred vecinos that already had a cathedral, three monasteries, a convent, and two hospitals needed a second convent.[147] Some years later, in 1568, oidor Licenciado Echegoyan wrote that Santo Domingo had two convents with around 180 nuns in "great need."[148]

Local Religious Life

Far less is known about religious life in the islands than about the church and its clergy. Spaniards were well aware that the Indians continued to adhere to their own beliefs and traditions to whatever extent possible. The Laws of Burgos (1512) endorsed the continuation of the Indigenous areitos, or ceremonial performances of song and dance embodying myth and history, suggesting possible Spanish ambivalence about their significance, the challenges of eliminating them, or both.[149] Chronicler Gonzalo Fernández de Oviedo, known for his deep-seated dislike of the Indians, greatly admired their areitos and described the call-and-response patterns of verse and dance in which both men and women participated, sometimes together and sometimes separately. He also described an areito performed for Anacaona (whom he called a "great lady"), in which three hundred unmarried young women performed.[150]

For the majority of laypeople in the Iberian world of the time, probably the most important aspects of religious life were participation in fiestas and the maintenance of local cults.[151] When people crossed the Atlantic, they left behind the cofradías, shrines, and religious vows that, because they usually were specific to their communities and associated with particular holy places and people, could not easily be replicated or transferred. The volatility of the early years in which Spaniards settled in the islands, the rapid rise and fall of fortunes, and the tendency of men, especially, to move around most likely made the establishment of cofradías difficult, other than in the largest towns.

The creation of shrines associated with holy sites or objects depended, of course, on the perception or experience of some form of divine apparition or intervention. A cult came into existence in connection with a cross that was erected when Columbus founded the city of Concepción de la Vega. The story, recorded around 1528 or 1529, was that several thousand Indians had gathered to knock the cross down but failed to do so. At the top of the cross, "a woman from Castile, very beautiful," appeared to protect it. People carved off so many pieces of the cross—which in turn were fashioned into crosses and often taken to Castile—that "it is held as a miracle that it hasn't been finished off."[152] A shrine was built there.

Fernández de Oviedo claimed that the cross had cured many people of their illnesses. In his version of the story, on Columbus's second visit to Hispaniola, twenty or so men, mainly sailors, cut the tree and fashioned a cross around eighteen or twenty hands (*palmos*) high. He claimed that the cross was "held in much veneration," not only for the miracles associated with it but also because, notwithstanding storms or wind, it never had rotted or fallen down, nor had the Indians been able to harm or remove it. He said that they had tried to knock it over and drag it off, but when all their efforts failed, they looked upon it with respect.[153] In 1539 the king ordered that a chapel be built to protect the cross, with which "God has seen fit to work so many miracles," from the elements.[154]

For Spaniards in the Greater Antilles, attending church and participating in fiestas probably afforded welcome occasions to socialize and to participate in entertainments that were not necessarily religious in nature. In 1510 the king wrote that he had been informed that governor Ovando had issued an ordinance stipulating that the vecinos of Hispaniola should go to town on "holidays and Sundays and Pascuas," which he characterized as the main reason "for the great expenditures that they have made there." The king went on to explain that, because they had to go to town so frequently, the vecinos purchased mares in order to avoid walking and as a result went into debt. They also bought on credit the equipment needed to participate in jousts on holidays. The king suggested that these unnecessary expenses could be avoided by establishing a church "como hermita" (probably meaning here a small chapel) in the countryside.[155]

Given the probably meager social life that the countryside afforded—not to mention that most men surely wanted a mare or mule for transportation—it seems unlikely that this royal directive dissuaded people from going to town on holidays. Licenciado Cerrato, who went to Hispaniola in 1547 to conduct a residencia of the audiencia, tried to curtail Santo Domingo's customary celebration of Corpus Christi. When the island's representatives complained, the king wrote to Cerrato (probably echoing the words of the procuradores themselves) that "since the discovery of that city of Santo Domingo, it has been the custom to celebrate with great solemnity the days of Corpus Christi with various games and inventions that accompany the procession ... in the celebration of the said holiday, which is something ... by which God is served, and that the costs involved always have been divided among all the commonwealth." Cerrato wished to limit the observance of the holiday to just the procession but, pending appeal, the city continued to celebrate it as always. The king had little sympathy for Cerrato's austerity program.[156]

In addition to religious holidays, military triumphs also provided occasions for festivities. In 1533, the king wrote to officials in Cuba thanking them for arranging for processions and prayers in honor of "my victory over the Turk."[157]

The establishment and growth of the church in the Greater Antilles responded to and reflected many of the same factors that structured nearly every other aspect of life in the early Spanish Caribbean. Over time, declining revenues and fortunes meant less wealth to invest in cathedrals, churches, and monasteries and to pay the clergy salaries that were high enough to persuade them to remain. Clergy, especially bishops, became involved in, and were affected by, political conflicts and rivalries. Vast and rapid demographic changes—the drastic reduction in Indigenous populations, the arrival of growing numbers of Africans, the departure of Spaniards seeking opportunities elsewhere—changed the nature of the church's early mission in the islands. As mining declined and sugar and cattle grew in importance, economic change combined with demographic transformation to create a shift in settlement patterns, which fostered an increased need for a clerical presence in the countryside that was not consistently met.

If high levels of Indigenous mortality and Europeans' overwhelming focus on using the islands' people to pursue their economic enterprises to a great extent stymied a systematic effort to evangelize the Indians, it appears that almost no effort was made to convert Blacks. What emerged in this period, then, was a sort of bare-bones version of an Iberian Catholic church that mainly catered to the Spanish residents of the Greater Antilles, with understaffed cathedral chapters, insufficient clergy to fill all the benefices in the islands' towns and rural communities, few priests available to preach, and a seminary that only took shape toward the end of the period examined here.

5

Transitions

The speed of change in the first fifty or sixty years following the arrival of Europeans in the Caribbean has given rise to the general impression that economic decline and demographic catastrophe overwhelmingly defined the decades after 1520 or so, resulting in the virtual elimination of the islands' Indigenous peoples and the exodus of Spaniards, who flocked to the mainland in search of new opportunities. Although there is truth to this picture, the reality was more complicated. Some towns shrank noticeably or disappeared, but others actually grew, and efforts to recruit settlers for the Caribbean continued. As gold mining became less central to island economies, the agricultural sector, especially sugar production and cattle ranching, expanded and helped to sustain a transatlantic trade that did not rely solely on the extraction and export of gold and pearls. To some degree, then, island economies became more diverse and stable as they adjusted to the shrinking labor pool.

Despoblación

Populations on the islands of the northern Caribbean overall were decreasing by the 1520s as a result of high levels of mortality among Indigenous groups and departures of Europeans for other destinations. The timing of the *despoblación* (depopulation) that worried officials and the crown varied a good deal, given that Spaniards established themselves in Puerto Rico, Jamaica, and Cuba more than a decade and a half after they began to occupy Hispaniola. In general, however, the increasingly limited opportunities in gold mining and the high cost of investment in sugar production led many Spaniards to seek opportunities elsewhere, especially following the extension of Spanish dominion over central Mexico in the early 1520s and the Andean region in the 1530s.

Indeed, both the lure of opportunities opening up elsewhere and active recruitment in the islands for multiple expeditions to the mainland drew substantial numbers—of Africans and Indians as well as Spaniards. In 1532 the lieutenant governor of Cuba, Manuel de Rojas, wrote to the king complaining about "all the Spaniards and Indians who have been taken in the fleets [*armadas*], by which the island has been left depopulated," a situation he partly blamed on inequities in the distribution of repartimientos, which had left many people with little access to labor. He noted that some residents had left for New Spain, "taking with them their naborías and Indians who were commended to them, and the rest they sell . . . under the pretext of selling their haciendas."[1] The following year Rojas wrote about the excitement that news from Peru had produced. He noted that as he was writing, two ships were being loaded in the port of Santiago to sail to Nombre de Dios and that many people hoped to board the ships secretly.[2] During his tour of inspection of the island, when he reached the town of Trinidad in mid-March 1533, he found it "depopulated and lost."[3]

In 1534 San Juan's bishop, don Alonso Manso, together with the prior of the island's Dominican monastery and the lieutenant governor, expressed their concern that people on the island who were in debt wanted to leave for Peru. The following year, treasurer Juan de Castellanos noted the numbers of people leaving Puerto Rico for that destination. Officials complained that because of their debts, people were hiding in the montes or stealing boats and leaving the island, taking with them their Black slaves.[4]

Recruitment for the many expeditions that were organized to go to the mainland could be controversial. In 1529 members of Santo Domingo's cabildo complained that during the previous year, Pedro de Vadillo had received a license from the audiencia to take "vecinos, settlers, and other people in great quantity of over three hundred men" to go to Santa Marta, while factor Juan de Ampies received a license to recruit one hundred men. Licenciado Castañeda and another man received a license to take three hundred men to Nicaragua, "for which reason the island is very depopulated."[5]

Oidores Espinosa and Zuazo responded that some of these reports were exaggerated and that they had only provided licenses for people in transit, such as merchants who were on their way elsewhere. They noted that Pedro de Vadillo had been sent to relieve the expedition in Santa Marta and that Juan de Ampies had taken the one hundred men to settle Curaçao. Ampies had a royal license to load brazilwood and to take ten or twelve people to do that, along with "other delinquents exiled from this island, and disobedient people who it would be convenient to exile," so clearly at least some departures were not just sanctioned but welcomed. The oidores did admit that there had been irregularities; Ampies sent his son in his place but then accompanied him without authorization.[6]

In 1528 and 1529 audiencia officials issued many licenses to individuals, couples, and small groups, mainly to go to New Spain, Nicaragua, and Honduras. These included, for example, Cecilia Lucero, her daughter, and a nephew, who planned to join Lucero's husband, Diego de Jaramillo, in New Spain; Juan Moreno and Francisco Díaz, who said that they had come from Castile with the intention of continuing on to New Spain; Catalina Rodríguez, traveling with her two sons and a nephew to New Spain to join her husband; and Juan de Frías, who was traveling to New Spain with his "muchacho esclavo negro," Juanico, and an Indian slave named Marina.

Thus, even as concerns about depopulation were mounting in the late 1520s, the audiencia continued to allow or even encourage people to leave the islands for other destinations. Given that the alternative would have been to impose far more severe restrictions on people's choices about where to live, and that expeditions to other locales potentially could yield positive gains for the treasury or investors (including, of course, many officials), audiencia officials for the most part continued to allow people to move around much as they wished. The concern about the extensive recruitment activities of men like Pedro de Vadillo and Juan de Ampies hinged on their targeting of experienced and economically active men, such as estancieros and miners, rather than the kind of people officials might have hoped would move on to other destinations. In fact, people from all levels of society left the islands, and it is impossible to know how effective the system of issuing licenses to leave actually was.

For Spaniards, especially those who owned property and held repartimientos, the decision to uproot and relocate could be complicated. Juan Suárez de Peralta, the brother of Hernando Cortés's first wife, Catalina Suárez, remained in Cuba when Cortés left for Mexico in order to look after his brother-in-law Cortés's properties. He had gone to Hispaniola early and received a repartimiento there, but he later joined Diego Velázquez in the conquest of Cuba, where he also received a repartimiento.[7] In Cuba he was known as a "grandísima lengua" who had extensive dealings with the island's Indians.

Andrés de Tapia, who also lived in Hispaniola and Cuba before relocating to Mexico, testified that Juan Suárez had lived with his first wife in Cortés's house in Santiago and was in charge of Cortés's affairs ("haciendas y minas y casa"). After Cortés's departure, Suárez apparently paid off some of Cortés's debts and equipped a ship to go to his aid, taking men and horses. According to one witness, after the fall of Tenochtitlan, Cortés entreated his brother-in-law to go back to Cuba and to bring Catalina to join him in Mexico. Suárez returned from Cuba with two ships, which were wrecked along the coast, resulting in considerable loss of life and cargo, although he and his sister survived. Suárez remained in Mexico, where his active career included participating in viceroy don Antonio de Mendoza's campaign in Nueva Galicia during the Mixton War, to which he contributed four Blacks, six horses, and six Spanish criados, at the cost of 6,000 pesos. Juan Suárez de Peralta became a wealthy man in New Spain. His sister did not share his good fortune.[8]

Population numbers for the period are scarce, and estimates often were impressionistic. Santo Domingo's cabildo estimated the number of residents in December 1537 at a little over five hundred vecinos, "entre vecinos y moradores" (between citizens and residents).[9] One of the few systematic counts was undertaken in Puerto Rico by lieutenant governor Francisco Manuel de Lando in 1530 and 1531. Essentially, Lando's report is an inventory of Indian and Black slaves and servants on the island, not a true census. Since very likely almost all Spaniards held at least an Indian slave or servant or two, the inventory offers a reasonable approximation of the numbers of Spanish residents, together with their slaves and servants. Not included, of course, were Indians or Blacks on the island who evaded Spanish control. There were several hundred Spanish residents living in the two main towns of San Juan and San Germán and in the countryside; more than two thousand Black slaves, about a fifth of them women; around seven hundred Indian slaves; and a little more than three hundred naborías, possibly the island's surviving Native inhabitants, although there is no way to know whether they were indigenous to the island or people brought from elsewhere.[10]

Accountant Álvaro Caballero, who acted as Hispaniola's procurador to the royal court in 1540 and 1541, reported to the king that Santo Domingo and other towns of Hispaniola altogether had barely one thousand vecinos (in this context, meaning permanent Spanish residents), six hundred of them in Santo Domingo and another four hundred in ten other towns, numbers that seem plausible. Although Caballero noted that some towns near Santo Domingo, such as Buenaventura and Santa Fe de Izagua, were nearly depopulated, he pointed out that considerable numbers of people were living on farms and sugar estates, some of them with as many as a hundred Spaniards and several hundred "negros e indios."[11] Another report of around the same time said that most of Hispaniola's towns (apart from Santo Domingo) had no more than twenty-five or thirty vecinos.[12]

The movement of population in Hispaniola away from the older towns and into rural areas reflected the declining importance of gold mines and the expansion of the agricultural sector with the establishment of ingenios, cattle ranches, and small farms. It is very likely that shifting demographic patterns also reflected Indigenous and African preferences for rural life and small-scale agriculture. Cuba and Jamaica probably were home to at most one hundred to two hundred Spanish vecinos, at least some of whom were married to Spanish or perhaps mestiza women. A 1528 report from the audiencia stated that there were eighty Spaniards living in the two Jamaican towns of Oristan and Sevilla and that Santiago, the principal town in Cuba, had perhaps fifty vecinos.[13] The numbers of Indians had fallen precipitously everywhere, and African-descended and mixed-race people constituted a majority by the 1540s, at least in Hispaniola and Puerto Rico.[14]

Officials often mentioned depopulation in general terms, but the effects of population movement and reduction varied a good deal from town to town and from one island to another. Although raiding and trading expeditions constantly departed from Hispaniola, its larger population compared to the other islands (which probably included higher numbers of transients, given that Santo Domingo was the principal port in the period) might have mitigated the impact of these departures to some extent. In contrast, the organization of major expeditions in Cuba (those of Cortés and Pánfilo de Narváez to Mexico in 1519 and 1520 and of Narváez and Hernando de Soto to Florida in 1528 and 1539) would have had a relatively greater and therefore more negative impact on Cuba's smaller population.

Contraction and Growth of Towns

The report of 1528 from the audiencia to the crown detailed the population reduction in many of Hispaniola's towns, principal among them Concepción de la Vega, which its founders had expected would be a major urban center because of its location near productive goldfields. It was the site of the first bishopric (later joined to that of Santo Domingo) and of an ambitious building effort that included construction of a fort, church, and Franciscan monastery in stone, along with twenty-five or thirty other buildings.[15] By 1528, however, the numbers of vecinos had fallen from two hundred to perhaps a tenth of that number, with those remaining described as "old and unmarried and without children." Santiago's one hundred vecinos had decreased to just eight, who mainly lived on their rural properties "and not in the manner of a town," Salvaleón de Higüey's population had decreased from one hundred to fifteen vecinos, San Juan de la Maguana's from 150 to fifteen, and so on.[16] Although it is impossible to gauge how accurate this report is, the much-reduced numbers it offers accord with other observations made during the period.

Manuel de Rojas's report on his visit of Cuba's towns and mines in 1533 to 1534 pointed to some significant differences in their situations. He found Trinidad to have lost some three-quarters of its vecinos after Narváez recruited people there for his expedition to Florida. When Rojas visited, there were maybe eleven or twelve vecinos and a Mercedarian friar who performed mass in a "very small and poor" house. Trinidad also lacked alcaldes and regidores and, in Rojas's opinion, just about anything that constituted a town. In addition to those who had already left with Narváez, other vecinos were considering departing for Peru, while some had moved to the neighboring town of Sancti Spíritus. Trinidad's residents begged Rojas to require the former vecinos who had moved to Sancti Spíritus "with their households and cattle and Indians" at the orders of the previous lieutenant governor, Gonzalo de Guzmán, to return.[17]

In contrast, when Rojas arrived in Sancti Spíritus two weeks later he found twenty-five or twenty-six vecinos with four regidores, two alcaldes, a procurador, a constable, and a town hall. There also was a "good church," for which he had brought a priest from Santiago. Yet there, too, the vecinos held few Indians and talked about leaving for Peru. They had some slaves "of those who come to this island from other nearby lands." Only three vecinos still mined gold, while the others made a poor living from growing yucca and hunting. A plan to merge the two towns had been debated. Rojas thought it would be advantageous to do so, but he left the decision to the crown. The question went unresolved, and both towns exist today.[18]

Thus, the population reduction in some towns did not necessarily mean that all the "missing" vecinos had left the islands. An información of 1533, for example, reflected the growth and success of La Mejorada de Cotuy in Hispaniola.[19] Although it was founded in 1503, Cotuy only gained recognition as a *villa* (town) in 1518. It was a mining town that in 1533 boasted a substantial eighty or ninety vecinos, most of them married to Spanish women and collectively holding some five hundred enslaved Black and Indigenous people. The town seems to have grown at the expense of Buenaventura and Bonao, which were located twelve and seven leagues away, respectively, and which according to the información had been depopulated. There were only two or three vecinos living on their estancias in Bonao, and Buenaventura retained only an inn, whereas formerly there had been "many people of honor with many Indians and stone buildings." Because it had not been recognized as a town until 1518, La Mejorada's residents did not receive allotments of Indians in the Repartimiento of 1514 and depended instead on their slaves to provide labor for the gold mines. They argued that, because Buenaventura had lost so many people, eight or ten leagues of its *término* (municipal district) should be transferred to La Mejorada. Most of the witnesses were long-standing vecinos who had lived in the town for fifteen years or more and had raised their families there. Some formerly had lived in Bonao or Buenaventura.

The vecinos of the prosperous town took pride not only in their healthy children and families but also in their contributions to the island's welfare, pointing out that they had constructed roads to Santo Domingo, Concepción de la Vega, and elsewhere at their own expense and had built a church and a Franciscan monastery. Bachiller Álvaro de Castro, the treasurer of Santo Domingo's cathedral at the time of the información, testified that the town's church had the most complete inventory of *ornamentos* of any in the island and that the vecinos were the most generous in donating items to the church. La Mejorada seems to have been prosperous and stable, and the Spanish community probably was more socioeconomically homogeneous than was the case in towns where encomenderos resided.

The apparently successful efforts to repopulate the port of Montecristi on the island's northern coast also contradict the picture of general decline in Hispaniola. In 1545 the king made an agreement with Francisco de Mesa, a vecino of Canaria, to organize a settlement at Montecristi, authorizing him to take his wife and children, together with thirty married vecinos and their families, to Hispaniola. The capitulación promised him the title of governor and gave him authority to distribute lands in line with the customary practices of the audiencia, with the stipulation that those receiving them must stay for eight years. Mesa, however, could not grant sites for ingenios, a prerogative reserved by the crown, which delegated to the audiencia the right to designate land and water for ingenios.[20] A jurisdiction of thirty leagues (later reduced to fifteen) was designated for the pueblo, and Mesa had authority to name regidores, escribanos, and alguaciles. Mesa himself would serve as alguacil mayor for his lifetime, as well as governor with full judicial power in the town.

Mesa and the other settlers received permission to move their households without paying the *almojarifazgo* (duty on imports and exports), and each could take six Black slaves without paying the usual fees. If the town failed to come into existence, however, the settlers would have to pay the fees. Any additional vecinos who emigrated from Spain or the Canaries over the course of the following decade also would be exempt from paying the almojarifazgo on what they brought. In addition to land, each vecino would receive twenty cows from the royal herds, which they could not sell during the specified eight years. The king ordered the construction of a church, to be supported by the tithes collected in the town.[21] Francisco de Mesa anticipated recruiting the majority of the settlers in the Canary Islands, where many residents were natives of Portugal. The king agreed that Portuguese families could be included "without any impediment"; indeed, he thought their presence would be "very beneficial for the said town." If he fulfilled the terms of his contract, Mesa would receive sites for two ingenios.

The capitulación that the crown issued to Francisco de Mesa did not represent the first effort to settle Montecristi. About ten years earlier, around 1533, a Pedro de Bolaños had obtained authorization to undertake an even more ambitious colonization plan, arriving in Hispaniola with seventy labradores. The audiencia judges were impressed that "Bolaños has done much with little aid or resources."[22] Disillusion with Bolaños seems to have followed, however, at least in Spain. In June 1534 the officials of the House of Trade in Seville concluded that Bolaños had attempted to defraud the crown by presenting "mariners and cabin-boys and passengers going to Hispaniola" rather than bona fide settlers. Subsequently, however, when the group of seventy potential vecinos assembled, officials determined that there were married men among them, and they all affirmed that they were not seamen or travelers but rather intended to settle in Montecristi.[23]

Unfortunately, the records consulted provide no specifics regarding the long-term success of either colonization scheme, but in the 1550s and 1560s Montecristi was a functioning port and considered to be one of the more prosperous towns in Hispaniola, with a substantial Portuguese presence.[24] The evidence of La Mejorada and Montecristi, then, suggests that anxieties about depopulation did not take into account geographic shifts in patterns of settlement. While several of the earliest towns in Hispaniola clearly were no longer viable, at least some were growing, although possibly mainly at the expense of others.

Recruitment of settlers and colonization schemes were nothing new. As chapter 1 recounted, the crown initiated one such effort as early as the time of Ovando's fleet. In 1529 the crown announced an initiative to grant concessions to people who would establish new settlements in Hispaniola, essentially endorsing a plan proposed by oidores Zuazo and Espinosa the previous year.[25] The new settlements would have a minimum of fifty married vecinos, half free people and half enslaved Black people, to be recruited in Spain or Portugal "or from other places that have our license to go to settle" in the Indies. Each would have a church built of stone, with a priest, as well as a stone fort. Every new vecino would receive two cows, two oxen, fifty sheep, a mare, ten pigs, two calves, and six hens. Within five years of the settlement's establishment, the vecinos would be responsible for building at least twenty-five stone houses. New communities would be located at least ten leagues from Santo Domingo and would have a *término* (district) of two leagues; those located farther away from Santo Domingo would have three leagues. The founders of the new settlements would be recognized as hidalgos "de solar conocido" (with established noble lineage) and caballeros.

Although the cédula specifically referred to the establishment of new settlements in Hispaniola, Asencio de Villanueva, a prominent resident of Puerto Rico, in 1534 proposed creating a new community on the island between San Juan and San Germán, much along the lines of the audiencia's plan, with twenty-five married vecinos and twenty-five married Black slaves. Villanueva had arrived in Puerto Rico in 1510 and served there as alguacil mayor and then *receptor* for the Inquisition. He grazed cattle on his estates and had planted wheat, barley, vegetables, grapevines, and fig and other trees. The new town would be called Villanueva.[26]

Whether this town came into existence is not known (it does not seem to have done so), but other men also were interested in recruiting settlers. In 1535 Puerto Rico's treasurer, Juan de Castellanos, offered to recruit thirty men with their wives and households who would be obliged to stay on the island for five years. He also proposed sending an additional fifty single men. In May 1537 Castellanos received the congratulations of the king for taking fifty men to the island. Castellanos arranged to send another group of twenty-five men.[27] In 1546 Álvaro Caballero asked that the crown reverse its order that only married men be allowed to go to the Caribbean, citing the "great lack of people, especially farmers and workers for the countryside and city" (gente de servicio del campo y ciudad).[28]

A different kind of recruitment effort got under way in 1532 when the king decided to send Francisco de Barrionuevo to Hispaniola with a force of two hundred men to make a final push to end the lengthy campaign against Enrique. The recruiters targeted a number of towns in southern Spain, promising free passage, board, and salary along with any plunder they managed to take, including slaves; the men were told that should they succeed in capturing Enrique and his people, they could take the captives back to Spain to sell as slaves. This promise came to naught, both because officials on the island immediately judged Barrionuevo's 180 recruits, most of whom were farmers, inadequate to the task and because negotiations resulted in a treaty recognizing the autonomy of Enrique and his community, not their enslavement.[29]

The Rise of the Ingenio

In a letter of April 1544 to the king, Melchor de Castro, the escribano de minas, wrote that mining was in decline. In the previous year Hispaniola had produced only 20,000 pesos of gold. Castro blamed the low yield partly on the decreasing numbers of Black slaves, many of whom he said had been sent to work in the mines in Cabo de Honduras, and partly on the dangers posed by bands of escaped Blacks active in the mining areas. In contrast, however, he noted that in 1543 the island had exported 110,000 *arrobas* of sugar and sixty thousand to seventy thousand cowhides, together with sheepskins, canafistula, and "other things all of which are very valuable."[30]

Just as the notion of despoblación has failed to take into account internal shifts in settlement patterns and the growth of a decidedly mixed rural population, processes that were under way in the 1520s through the 1540s, so too did the economy prove more resilient than is usually assumed. Though the Greater Antilles had ceased to produce enough gold to generate great fortunes for the crown and some prominent vecinos, the diversification of the economy helped to stabilize it at more modest levels. The rise of sugar production ensured that a small group of entrepreneurs (including, of course, many officials) would continue to enjoy wealth, status, and influence.[31]

The establishment of sugar estates and the rapid expansion of cattle herds surely were the most important economic developments of the period, although they had almost opposite effects on settlement patterns in the islands. In the earliest years, access to gold mines in many cases dictated the location of towns; now, ingenios became important nuclei of new communities in the countryside. Cattle, in contrast, proliferated and tended to disperse into the unsettled, "wild" parts of the islands, although they often played a vital role on sugar estates as well.[32] The physical plant of a sugar estate encompassed the ingenio or refinery itself as well as housing for workers and buildings for storage or dedicated to auxiliary trades such as blacksmithing. Diego Caballero's ingenio on the Nigua River included a church "very well adorned with everything necessary" and a settlement of more than sixty houses of stone and thatch, in which a priest and more than twenty Spaniards and 150 Blacks and Indians lived. In 1538 he received permission to build a fort and tower there. Caballero clearly aspired to do more than produce sugar. He had planted wheat and vineyards that he claimed were growing well, and he was interested in experimenting with the production of dyes and cultivation of mulberries to make silk.[33]

Hernando Gorjón, who arrived in Hispaniola with Ovando in 1502, owned an ingenio in Azua, probably one of the first established on the island, with 150 "Spaniards and Blacks," a number he expected to increase.[34] In 1540 Gorjón's estate included an iron forge, a water-powered sawmill, a gristmill, a stand of canafístula trees as well as orange and other fruit trees, another three caballerías of irrigated land, a herd of three thousand cattle and a flock of three thousand sheep, a "labranza de comer" (food-producing farm) that fed the people of the ingenio, and sixteen carts with thirty-two oxen. He also had built a wooden church and employed a priest.[35]

The description of Juan de Villoria's ingenio near Higüey, which in 1533 had one hundred slaves and twenty "cristianos," makes it clear that ingenios not only became significant nuclei of population in the countryside but also acted as anchors for further agricultural development unrelated to sugar; alternatively, smaller farmers might have raised foodstuffs or sugarcane to help supply the ingenio. Genaro Rodríguez Morel writes of Villoria's estate, "At this date... on the outskirts of this ingenio, there were haciendas belonging to Spanish farmers, forty in all.... These small farmers did not rely on Black slaves or Indians. ... The proliferation of these agriculturalists in the sugar-producing areas gave rise to small-scale peasant agriculture that would end up consolidating in the mid-sixteenth century with the incorporation of the cultivation of ginger into colonial agriculture."[36] Located near an ingenio in the Higüey region that employed eighty slaves and fifteen Spaniards were twenty-five estancias that were farmed without any slaves. A similar pattern took shape in Puerto Rico, where, by 1550, rural settlements clustered around Alonso Pérez Martel's ingenio La Trinidad, in Toa, and others were located near two ingenios owned by Gonzalo de Santa Olalla: Santa Ana in the north and Valle Hermoso in the southwest.[37]

Sugar production in the Caribbean got under way earliest in Hispaniola, by around 1515, and expanded fairly rapidly, especially as the crown started to make funds available to lend to people who agreed to establish ingenios. The crown also provided other forms of financial assistance to ingenio owners, such as eliminating taxes on importing necessary tools and equipment. Notwithstanding these forms of royal support, in the 1540s there still were fewer than forty ingenios on the island.[38] Even with the assistance the crown provided, establishing a sugar mill was a major undertaking that was financially out of reach for the majority of vecinos.

Benito de Astorga, for example, rose from shopkeeper to merchant and finally to ingenio owner. His connections to some powerful people in Hispaniola, such as treasurer Miguel de Pasamonte, whom Astorga once served as criado, and his close friend Melchor de Castro, the escribano de minas, probably helped him to obtain a loan. By 1530 Astorga's sugar mill had become a substantial enterprise, with a labor force of sixty enslaved Black people and fifteen Spanish men, but its construction almost perfectly exemplified Murphy's law: anything that could go wrong, did. Building a dam for irrigation took two years, for instance, and the main irrigation canal was twice built incorrectly, taking altogether three and a half years from inception to successful completion. Much of the wood that was cut for the construction of the water-powered sugar mill subsequently proved to be rotten, damaged, or of the wrong size and had to be replaced. Worse yet, a fire destroyed not only all the wood to be used to build the refinery but also a number of carts, thirty huts in which slaves were housed, and two other lodgings, along with cut wood and a field of cane, sparing only a couple of small shacks and a kitchen. As a result, Astorga lost his crop of sugar, as the cut canes could not be ground. He claimed to have spent

10,000 to 12,000 castellanos in building the ingenio, much of it borrowed, and in 1533 petitioned the crown for an additional loan.[39]

Ingenios were much slower to appear in Puerto Rico. Tomás de Castellón established the first one near San Germán in 1523, with its own port on the Bay of Añasco. Within a few years he died, already deeply in debt.[40] In 1535 Juan de Castellanos, representing San Juan, asked the crown to provide loans of 2,000 pesos to a few vecinos to establish ingenios because of the decrease in gold production. Recipients of the loans would be required to grind half the cane produced by vecinos who would receive land near the ingenio as well as access to water for irrigation. In return the ingenio owners would retain half of the vecinos' canes.[41]

In 1542 Gonzalo de Santa Ollala, a vecino of San Juan, was building two ingenios, one that used water power and the other a *trapiche* that relied on horses, for which he hoped to receive a loan. In a deposition he explained that he had reassigned the slaves who had been mining gold to work on the construction of the mill and so had lost most of his income from mining. In addition some fifty of his slaves had died and needed to be replaced. He stated that he had purchased all the necessary equipment for the two ingenios and had hired a sugar master and other skilled workers, whom he feared he would have to fire if he failed to receive a loan. Santa Olalla claimed to be the first to build an ingenio near San Juan, although one witness mentioned that Rodrigo Fránquez had built a smaller one, probably a trapiche.[42]

In 1549 San Juan regidor Alonso Pérez Martel said that he was building "a powerful water-powered ingenio for grinding sugar ... that is useful and beneficial for the vecinos of this city." He already had imported and paid for copper cauldrons and other equipment from Castile, had planted more than fifteen thousand *montones de cañaverales* (mounds for sugarcane), and had begun to harvest and refine sugar. He had carts and numerous horses and some thirty-five Black slaves and had hired a *maestro mayor* named Pantaleón Bernaldo.[43] That same year the vecinos of San Germán asked the crown for loans to build four "ingenios de caballos," arguing that their presence would help to expand the population in that part of the island. The town's vecinos also lobbied for the construction of fortifications, arguing that with half a dozen ingenios, "each ingenio needs many tradesmen, and with these and the said fortress the town will populate." They mentioned that the only ingenio nearby was located two leagues from San Germán.[44]

Jamaica also lagged well behind Hispaniola, but there, too, a small number of ingenios came into existence. In 1532 don Antonio de Garay, the son of adelantado Francisco de Garay, said that his father had left two sugar ingenios in the island, one of which was in operation. The other was only partially built and could not be completed because he lacked the necessary workers. He asked for permission to take cauldrons and equipment for the ingenio, together with whatever he needed for his household and provisions for himself and his criados, up to a value of 1,500 pesos, without paying the almojarifazgo when he returned from Spain to Hispaniola.[45] In the mid-1530s the treasurer of Jamaica, Pedro de Mazuelo, started building an ingenio near the southern coast of the island, close to where he proposed moving the town of Sevilla. Mazuelo asked permission to bring up to fifty Black slaves, male and female, from Spain or Portugal, free of fees; he received permission to bring thirty-three.[46]

For reasons that are not clear, Cuba was the slowest of the islands to turn to sugar. In 1534 Gonzalo de Guzmán asked permission to bring fifty male and female Black slaves, free of any fees, so that he could build an ingenio. He suggested that the "island would receive much benefit because it would be reason that other sugar ingenios would be established." He received a license to bring fifty slaves from Portugal or Cabo Verde over the course of two years, with the stipulation that they not be Wolof.[47] He had four years to build the ingenio and would be liable to pay the full tax on any slaves he imported if he failed to finish during the specified time period.[48]

Whether Guzmán started to build the ingenio before his death in 1540 is not known. In his recent study of sugar production in early Cuba, Alejandro de la Fuente concludes that there is no solid evidence that the island was producing sugar before the late sixteenth century.[49] The explanation for Cuba's late entry into sugar cultivation may lie in the smaller numbers of Black slaves who reached the island in the period, compared to Hispaniola or Puerto Rico.[50]

In Hispaniola, at least, the crown clearly saw ingenios as playing a role in stabilizing rural populations and as being vital to the island's economy.[51] The king wrote to president of the audiencia, Licenciado Cerrato, in 1546 regarding the indebtedness of ingenios that had belonged to the factor Juan de Ampies, the Pasamontes (Miguel and his nephew Esteban), and Francisco de Tostado. Lacking willing buyers for any of the ingenios, the audiencia considered selling off their assets, mainly the slaves and equipment, as best they could, but the officials worried that the result would be to "depopulate one-third of this island."

They decided instead to work out a plan for the repayment of the debts, "so the ingenios will remain intact."[52]

Beyond the Sugar Economy

While ingenios might have fueled the export economy of Hispaniola and signified a new source of wealth for a small number of entrepreneurs in the islands, they accounted for only some of the population growth in the countryside. A report of 1533, compiled by Alonso de Ávila for the purpose of determining the need to create new parishes, documented the presence of substantial rural populations in at least some parts of Hispaniola, especially in the area closest to Santo Domingo. In the riberas de Cocoimagua y el Cacay, "very populated with farms and herds of cattle," Ávila found more than seven hundred people, including Spaniards, Blacks, and Indians. There were "haciendas de labradores" (farms) near the ingenio de Santiespíritus on the Cacay River, twelve leagues from Santo Domingo, while near Diego Caballero's ingenio on the ribera de Yuca there were "many properties of vecinos ... [with] two hundred people." In the ribera de Hayna, only three leagues from Santo Domingo, some four hundred people were living on farms, while at the confluence of the Nigua and Yamán rivers, where there were five ingenios, there "are many farms ... in all of which there are at least seven hundred Blacks and two hundred Indians and 150 Spaniards because it is the most populous river shore that there presently is in this island." The report documents other, similar clusters of rural population.[53] In 1537 Santo Domingo's cabildo wrote to the king that although some towns, such as Buenaventura, had depopulated, within the city's término, "which has many populated river banks and valleys.... there are ... in some of them more than one hundred Spaniards and six hundred Blacks and Indians, and *this without the sugar ingenios*" (emphasis mine).[54]

Small farms and ranches surrounded the islands' towns. Typically, people who sought vecino status would receive an urban lot (solar) and a grant of agricultural land (caballería). Luis Hernández, a vecino of Santo Domingo, testified in a deposition for doña Isabel de Maraver that they were neighbors "both in the estancia as well as in the house of residence" in the city.[55] When in March 1537 Gonzalo de Guzmán, lieutenant governor of Cuba, conducted his visita of the estancias near Santiago with the priest Sancho Seco, they went to more than twenty estates, one of which belonged to Guzmán.[56]

Rural establishments ranged from modest to fairly substantial. Urban residents might have spent much of their time on their estancias, although many employed estancieros to oversee their rural properties. Testimony of 1522 regarding the episode in which some vecinos of Sancti Spíritus briefly formed a commune in protest of the reassignment of repartimientos in Cuba includes a number of references to people being on their estancias rather than in town. After several of the ringleaders of the *comunidad* (commune) were arrested, authorities sequestered and inventoried their properties. Diego Mendes, who acted as procurador for the comunidad, owned an estancia with three bohíos, three thousand *montones de yuca,* five new and old axes for cutting firewood, thirty-three *bateas* (for washing gold), twenty-three bars of iron, seven pickaxes (mostly old), two draft horses and a mule, twenty-seven *cargas* of salt, ten hens, a rooster, and twenty chicks. He owned another estancia where he kept pigs. Hernán López's estancia was only slightly more substantial, with three bohíos and a separate kitchen, thirty fowl "large and small," five draft horses and another horse and saddle, two iron axes, two "duhos de asentar" (indigenous carved wooden stools) and other chairs, and eight thousand montones de yucca, among other items. He owned two estancias with pigs.

Some vecinos owned their estancias jointly. Alonso de Vargas and Luis Hernández, for example, together owned an estancia with twenty thousand montones, "todo viejo" (all old, or mature), and another estancia with around one thousand pigs. At the time, these rural establishments might have been mainly oriented toward supporting households or workers at gold mines, either by supplying them directly or by selling them foodstuffs on the local market.[57] With their thatched structures and principal crops of yucca, the estancias incorporated strong Indigenous influences. Hernán López's inventory included two Native-carved *duhos*. In all likelihood, mundane items such as cookware and eating implements that were not listed and bateas for washing gold also were Indigenous-made.

Potentially, at least, the islands could support a variety of crops. Some Spaniards, such as Diego Caballero, were eager to import familiar plants, especially ones they hoped would have commercial success. In 1534, when the treasurer Lope Hurtado left Spain for Cuba, he took with him a man named Juan González, along with his mother, whom he called labradores, to plant wheat and other crops.[58] A few years later a man named Juan de Oribe asked for land in order to raise spices such as pepper, cinnamon, cloves, and ginger.[59] Representing Hispaniola in 1541, the accountant Álvaro Caballero argued for the necessity of growing olive trees, mulberries, and other plants and asked the king to stipulate that all ships departing for the island carry one or two tubs with trees and plants, the costs of which would be paid by the island.[60]

In his "natural" history, Gonzalo Fernández de Oviedo was effusive in his praise of the variety and potential of the plants and trees of the Caribbean. He mentioned the "very beautiful groves" of canafistula, which he said was worth four ducados per quintal (hundredweight), excellent cotton, brazilwood in the Bahoruco mountains (which he claimed no one bothered to cut), and "great woods and groves of the tree of guayacan," which he wrote had considerable therapeutic properties.[61] In 1510 don Diego Colón had been informed of the existence of "dos montes de una fruta que llaman piñas" (two groves of a fruit they call pineapples), which he prohibited anyone from entering. The king, however, declared that the fruit "should be commons for all, and that everyone should be able to take them to put in their farms and estancias, and take advantage of them as something shared."[62] A number of fruit trees brought from Castile flourished, including citrus and figs as well as pomegranates, as did garden crops such as lettuce, radishes, cabbages, carrots, eggplant, and melons, and herbs, including parsley, cilantro, and mint.

Of the plants thought to have medicinal properties, the two that were of greatest commercial interest in this period were balsam and canafistula. Balsam was prized in the Mediterranean world for a variety of uses and healing qualities.[63] A man named Antonio de Villasante was mainly responsible for generating interest in Hispaniola's balsam. In 1528 he obtained a monopoly to exploit it, on the condition that he prepare and present a report on the tree and how to "obtain the liquor." He presented his report to the Council of the Indies a few months later, explaining that his wife, a cacica and Christian, and her family had taught him about the therapeutic qualities of various plants on the island. Although physicians in Spain debated whether the Hispaniola balsam was identical to the plant from Egypt with which they were familiar, and concluded that it was not, experiments nonetheless demonstrated its effectiveness.[64] Asencio de Villanueva, the receptor of the Inquisition, who in 1533 was at court representing the bishop of San Juan and pursuing his colonization plan, also asked for a license to "collect and cultivate" balsam.[65] Vecinos of Hispaniola and Puerto Rico objected to the monopoly assigned to Villasante on the basis that they needed balsam to treat the illnesses and injuries of their slaves and Indians and that having to travel to buy it from Villasante would result in unnecessary cost and harm.[66]

When the accountant Álvaro Caballero was at court in 1541 representing Santo Domingo and the other towns of Hispaniola, he described the successful cultivation of canafistula, which at one time sold for 30 pesos per quintal. He noted that it had proliferated to such an extent that the price dropped to 2 and then 1.5 pesos per quintal, at which point the bishop and president don Sebastián Ramírez made an agreement with the regidores of all the islands' towns to establish a central warehouse where the growers of canafistula might store their product under the management of a mayordomo or factor. This person would take charge of selling the product on behalf of the collective. They implemented this system in 1529 and 1530, sending all the canafistula to Seville, where they were able to sell it at the decent price of 16 pesos per quintal, much cheaper than the canafistula imported from Alexandria, which sold at 35 or 40 ducados per quintal. In those two years they sold all the canafistula shipped to Seville. Unfortunately, when Ramírez de Fuenleal left Hispaniola for New Spain the collective fell apart, producers reverted to selling on an individual basis, and the price dropped to just one peso per quintal. As a result, many growers abandoned its cultivation. Caballero proposed reviving the collective.[67]

In these years, then, although sugar dominated as a transatlantic export crop, other commodities remained important for both local consumption and export. A vecino of San Germán in Puerto Rico, Rodrigo de Sanlúcar, "who is among its first conquerors and settlers," asked for and received royal permission to farm and graze cattle on the uninhabited small island (*isleo*) of Desecheo, thirteen miles off the coast of the larger island. By the early 1530s he had planted yucca, sweet potatoes, and other crops there, and he hoped to bring cattle. In 1535, Sanlúcar referred to his "ingenios de caçabi" and claimed that he had built ships. The word *ingenio*, normally used for a sugar estate, suggests substantial commercial production of yucca. In recognition of his efforts the crown conceded Desecheo to Sanlúcar and his heirs.[68]

Livestock

Like much of the Americas, with the exception of the plains of North America and the Andean region, the Greater Antilles lacked large grazing animals before Europeans introduced them. Old World livestock found grassy fields and woods with no natural predators apart from humans. Fernández de Oviedo discussed the proliferation of cattle, horses, sheep, and pigs on Hispaniola, noting that large numbers of the cattle and swine had become feral. He also mentioned the importation of dogs and domestic cats from Spain, many of which also had become "wild" (*bravos*) in the woods.[69] Possibly some horses were becoming feral as well; in 1537 Santo Domingo's cabildo reported that Blacks who carried out uprisings and assaults in the Higüey region were doing so on horseback.[70]

The economic impact of cattle and horses on the islands was considerable, if mixed. The exchange of Indigenous slaves from Pánuco in New Spain for cattle and horses from Hispaniola is well documented.[71] In 1529 oidores Espinosa and Zuazo declared that they had given a license to Captain Diego Albítez to take to Nicaragua some forty mares and horses that he had bought on the island, along with a few slaves to care for the animals. They noted "the great benefit that results for this island and its vecinos and settlers in favoring those who buy livestock and cattle to take them away from the island."[72]

In 1533 lieutenant governor Manuel de Rojas wrote to the king regarding the export to New Spain of horses and mules bred in Cuba and mentioned exchanging "bestias y otras cosas" (beasts and other things) for slaves from Pánuco and Yucatan. He stressed the importance of opening roads to connect Sancti Spíritus and Trinidad to Puerto del Príncipe so that vecinos could move their livestock overland to be exported, "because the livelihood of those two towns is the raising of horses and mules" for New Spain.[73] Gonzalo de Guzmán, Cuba's former lieutenant governor, who in 1539 was serving as veedor de fundiciones (overseer of smelting), wrote that the main business of the vecinos of Santiago was the sale of cattle and other items to the ships headed for Tierra Firme, which provided them a good living.[74] Although Puerto Rico figures less frequently (in the records, at least) as a source of livestock, in 1534 Juan de Ibarra, a vecino of the island, stated that he planned to sell or take horses and cattle from his hacienda to sell in "some islands and provinces."[75] Martín de Aguilar, a vecino of San Juan, in 1536 had "one hundred breeding mares with their purebred horses [*caballos de casta*] as sires" grazing in two different sites. He complained that other people were grazing their "yeguas y caballos ruines" (worthless mares and horses) in his pastures, compromising the quality of his horses.[76]

The rapid proliferation of cattle fostered intense conflicts over where and how they should graze. Herds in Hispaniola reached huge proportions. Rodrigo de Bastidas, who succeeded don Alonso Manso as bishop of Puerto Rico and whose family owned substantial properties in Hispaniola, was said to have owned sixteen thousand head of cattle in 1535 and twenty-five thousand in 1547.[77] The big stock raisers, who claimed cattle herds of ten thousand, fifteen thousand, or twenty thousand or more head, or more than three thousand mares, probably had little idea of the actual numbers of animals they grazed, because "these cattle are not gathered or pastured or even branded as in Castile."[78] Herds in Puerto Rico did not reach anywhere near the same numbers. There, a typical herd more likely numbered a thousand or fewer, more in line with Castilian practice.[79] There is no information on the size of herds in Cuba, which possibly more closely resembled the size of herds in Puerto Rico than in Hispaniola. Nonetheless, the island experienced conflicts over how close to Santiago cattle could be grazed and complaints about cattle destroying "the haciendas of conucos and maize fields."[80]

Regardless of herd size, in all the islands conflicts arose over access to pastures and woods, the size of ranches, damages that roaming cattle inflicted on crops, and how close to towns cattle should be allowed to graze. In Castile, access to municipal commons, which normally included some pasture land, and to montes, which were wooded and usually hilly areas used for a variety of purposes, typically was a right enjoyed by all the vecinos of a particular place. As a result, even people who did not own any land could keep and graze some animals. Many municipalities also guaranteed vecinos the right to stubble graze their animals on privately owned or rented land following harvests.[81]

The situation in the Greater Antilles, however, was different. As in Andalucía, cattle were more common than sheep, meaning that the laws and customs that regulated sheep grazing, and especially the transhumant movement of sheep in Castile, did not transfer to the Caribbean.[82] Feral cattle (*ganado bravo*), however, were familiar from southern Spain and Portugal.[83] Medieval scholar C. J. Bishko underscores the significant differences "between municipal and seigneurial cattle ranching in medieval Iberia.... The distinction finds reflection not merely in disparity of size between town ranching outfits and those of the nobles, monasteries, and military orders at the top of the industry, but in differences of organization, land use, and pasturage and marketing rights. Seigneurial ranching operated far more freely than municipal, which partly explains why the cabildos of the Indies had so much difficulty imposing livestock controls upon the new colonial classes."[84]

The distinction that he makes suggests the socioeconomic divisions that emerged as wealthy and powerful men increasingly monopolized large tracts of grazing land that they often did not fully use. Historian Francisco Moscoso points out that the herds of cattle on the northern coastal plains of Puerto Rico "were in great disproportion to the enormous size of the ranches that occupied several leagues." An ordinance of 1519 had decreed that cattle ranches (*hatos*) had to be at least one league apart, and they had taken up most of the land near San Juan. As of 1542 the island's contador, Martín Erguiluz, owned four hatos, alcalde Francisco de Aguilar owned three, regidor García de Villadiego three, and treasurer Juan de Castellanos four. Each hato controlled four square leagues of land.[85] Led by longtime resident Hernando de Lepe, a group of smaller holders, whom Moscoso calls "campesinos estancieros," attempted to introduce reforms in the 1540s that would reduce the size of the hatos.[86]

There were complaints in Hispaniola as well. In 1541 the king said that he had been informed that "there are in it [the island] many people who occupy thirty leagues of land and will not allow within that space that anyone build a corral or bohío or bring their cattle and they sell their lands publicly." He reiterated that the "pastos montes términos y aguas" (pastures, woodlands, districts, and water) should be held in common in perpetuity and that all residents should be able to graze their cattle freely.[87]

In Santo Domingo, in 1546, vecinos complained that "rich people enjoy the district and pastures of the said city and . . . the poor cannot have or use the pastures and water, even though they are commons, and for this reason the land is depopulating." They asked that everyone have access and be able to graze their cattle together, as they said they had done in the past, and that the "haciendas and *estancias de pan*" (properties and farms producing bread) be guarded, as also had occurred in the past.

In 1547 there were more complaints about damage to crops from cattle. The result was that smaller farmers sometimes were unable to survive and ended up selling their land to the big cattle owners, "so that the rich and the cattle owners possess the properties of others and sell their bread as they wish," pushing up prices.[88] The dean of the cathedral of Concepción de la Vega complained that some people wished "to have the city as a corral for cattle and the church a pen for calves." He claimed that they kept their cattle so close to the city that they "come to us at night to bawl in the streets and knock over the houses, which are mostly of thatch." He said that the cattle had destroyed gardens and estancias.[89] In 1555 vecinos of Concepción de la Vega complained that their regidor, Juan Daza, was holding on to funds that had been earmarked to support the "house of the banner of Christ" (la casa de la Bandera de Cristo), which he was using to keep animals.[90]

There can be little doubt that, as in Puerto Rico, the conflict over commons reflected class tensions and resentments. Although historian Gabriel de Avilez Rocha makes an interesting case for the development of an unregulated and mostly separate cattle economy in unassigned "wild" parts of islands inhabited by maroons, the rise of the cattle economy in more settled areas tended to exacerbate socioeconomic differences, as was true for sugar and gold.[91] It is telling, for example, that Moscoso has found that, from the mid-1540s on, some of Puerto Rico's wealthiest men converted into sugar ingenios land along the north coast that had been devoted to cattle ranches.[92]

Nonetheless, some men who might be considered part of the middle group in island societies did well in the increasingly mixed rural economies. In Cuba in the 1520s and 1530s, for example, brothers Diego and Hernando Alonso raised cattle, made carts, provided meat, and maintained inns and roads along the twenty-five leagues that separated Bayamo and Santiago. Their venta de Higuan and three other inns provided food for travelers.[93]

Mining

Mining did not come to an abrupt halt, although it changed over the years, and certainly by midcentury it no longer dominated the economy of the Greater Antilles.[94] They continued to produce gold, and vecinos continued to search for new sources of gold and for other metals, especially copper. The success of La Mejorada hinged on its proximity to the mines of Cotuy, which in the 1530s were considered to have the richest veins of gold in Hispaniola. Fernández de Oviedo commented on the rivers in Hispaniola that carried gold, "among which rivers, the one called Cotuy is extremely rich."[95]

Antonio Rodríguez, an escribano who was one of the town's first settlers and had lived there for thirty-two years, testified in 1546 that the eighty or ninety vecinos collectively owned more than five hundred Black and Indian slaves who mined for gold.[96] Bachiller Álvaro de Castro apparently persuaded the bishop and president of the audiencia to authorize the creation of a company named Espíritu Santo, to which each of La Mejorada's vecinos would contribute a Black slave or two to work the mines, but the plan faltered when assistance in the form of equipment that they anticipated receiving from the audiencia did not materialize. The town's residents were unwilling to "give their Blacks for the said company, thinking it was a joke," and in any case, after bishop/president Ramírez's departure from the island, nothing more came of the proposal. Castro, at least, was certain that a "gran cantidad" (large amount) of gold still could be mined there.[97]

Fernández de Oviedo wrote at length about gold mining in Hispaniola, addressing "how gold is mined here by our Spaniards" and emphasizing that it required a great deal of labor. Gold was found and collected in rivers, along their banks, and in the mountains. In his opinion the largest amounts of gold were to be found in the montes. Fernández de Oviedo explained in detail the arduous labor required to clear the ground of trees, vegetation, and rocks, and then to dig out and wash a shallow area before digging more deeply. Workers used wooden bateas fabricated on the island to wash the earth, work that was done mainly by enslaved Indian and Black women, who sat on the shore with their legs in the water up to their knees. Women also prepared food and brought it to mine workers.[98] In Puerto Rico by the 1530s most of the gold extracted was in the mountains, where slaves and miners had to undertake treks of several leagues over difficult terrain, carrying supplies on their backs. Officials worried that "as a result of the excessive work, it could be that said slaves will rebel."[99]

The early years of mining in the islands, by far the most productive ones, did not receive much systematic attention from scholars until recently. Jalil Sued Badillo's thorough study of the early Puerto Rican mining economy addresses the organization of the industry as well as labor and production. Because of the close connections between Hispaniola and Puerto Rico, his book also includes material on Hispaniola.[100] Hispaniola's eastern province of Higüey, where Juan Ponce de León had been active, lacked gold, so the residents of the area became involved in gold mining in Puerto Rico; it was both easier and more profitable to transport their Indian workers the short distance to Puerto Rico than to move them to mining sites elsewhere in Hispaniola. In 1518 vecinos of Salvaleón asked permission to use their Black and Indian slaves to collect gold on the neighboring island.[101] Spaniards' unequal access to Indigenous labor in Hispaniola encouraged people to leave the island, and

Puerto Rico was near at hand. The first fundición (smelting) there took place in October 1510, with 168 participants; in May 1511 with 248; and in August 1512 with 310. In 1519, after the conclusion of the island-wide conflict, a total of 375 miners participated. The first fundición in San Germán took place in 1513, with 359 people.[102]

On the gold-producing islands (Hispaniola, Puerto Rico, and Cuba), periodic fundiciones were pivotal events attended by royal officials, miners, their workers, and merchants. Miners paid off their debts and contracted new ones. Sued Badillo describes merchants descending "like wolves" to recover money owed to them, sometimes insisting on crowding into the foundry itself so as to witness the actual smelting. Their merchandise included everything from wine and cheese to imported cloth, slaves, and musical instruments.[103] Cuba's treasurer, Lope Hurtado, in 1533 requested the grant of a lot near Santiago's foundry in order to build a shop (*tienda de mercader*).[104]

Royal governor Ovando established two fundiciones in Hispaniola, one at Concepción de la Vega and another at Buenaventura, subsequently adding a third in Santo Domingo. In the early years the island's gold production averaged 300,000 pesos annually.[105] By the 1540s fundiciones still took place every two months in Santo Domingo but only once a year in Concepción, where officials were obliged to stay thirty days. Since by this time there was little gold to smelt in Concepción, the king directed that only one oidor needed to go, accompanied by the deputies of the other two.[106] In Cuba, fundiciones probably took place in Santiago only once a year, scheduled during the dry season (October to March) so as to avoid the difficulties of overland travel and risky navigation along the coast that characterized the rainy season. Given the island's size and the challenges of travel, the representatives (procuradores) of the towns took advantage of the annual fundición to meet.[107]

In the earlier years, especially, the actual *casas de fundición* were unimpressive bohíos that predictably often went up in flames. After moving the fundición among several venues, in 1525 royal officials in San Juan finally purchased a house from Baltasar de Castro for 1,000 pesos. As described in Lando's 1530 census, the house, built of masonry ("cal y canto"), had a tile roof. A second story was added in 1537 to serve as lodging for royal officials. Casas de fundición could be fairly rudimentary, and since they were used for only part of each year, they tended to fall into disrepair. The main investment was the forge, which consisted of a brick chimney, oven, and roof.

Up to 6,000 pesos of gold could be smelted on an average day. During a period generally lasting from a week to a month, various officials registered miners, weighed gold, took the royal fifth, and returned the gold to its owners.[108] A royal cédula of 1512 authorized the elaboration of chains, bracelets, and "other things of gold for women" at the fundición.[109] According to Sued Badillo, Puerto Rico produced a verifiable 1,852,603 pesos de oro from 1509 to 1546 (information for four years is missing), while Hispaniola probably produced 1.5 million to 2 million pesos from 1505 to 1517, and 1,777,317 pesos from 1520 to 1540, with both islands continuing to produce gold throughout the remainder of the sixteenth century. Levi Marrero's estimate for Cuba's gold production from 1515 to 1547 is 624,115 pesos, but the data for Cuba are even more incomplete than data for Puerto Rico.[110]

In addition to other royal officials who oversaw the fundición were officers specifically associated with mining. Baltasar de Castro served as Escribano Mayor de Minas de la Española until he was sent, in 1514, as factor to Puerto Rico, where he served in various offices until his death in 1540. His brother Melchor de Castro served in the same position in Hispaniola for more than thirty years, ultimately renouncing the office in favor of his nephew, Pedro de Castro Maldonado, the son of his brother Baltasar.[111]

Each island had an official fundidor. The first man who served in that capacity in Puerto Rico was a German named Jerónimo de Bruselas, who was married to a Spaniard. His appointment included the position of *marcador de indios esclavos* (brander of Indian slaves).[112] In Hispaniola, too, the positions of fundidor and marcador de indios coincided. Hernán Pérez de Almazán held the position in the 1530s, renouncing it in favor of his nephew, don Luis Pérez Almazán, in 1537. He apparently did not take the office, as in 1540 Hernán Pérez passed it to his brother don Juan Pérez de Almazan. The royal concession of the title named him "fundidor y marcador mayor de todo el oro y plata que se fundiere y marcan en todas las casas de la fundición de la Isla Española" (chief smelter and marker of all the gold and silver smelted in the foundries in Hispaniola). His son don Pedro Pérez de Almazán assumed the office at his death in 1545. A man named don Pedro Niño held the office in Puerto Rico in the 1530s. Given their apparent social standing (don Juan Pérez was lord of the town of Maella in Aragón), it is not surprising that this position was one of the most lucrative of those associated with the gold economy.[113]

The existence of multiple officials registering and overseeing the smelting of gold is no surprise, given the potential for fraud in disclosing how much gold had been mined. In 1532 Blas de Villasante denounced Pedro Diez Maldonado, the miner he had hired to oversee operations at a newly discovered gold mine at the source of the Caguana River, near his ingenio in the district of San Germán in Puerto Rico. Although according to Villasante the mine had produced 4,000 pesos of gold under Maldonado's direction, he claimed that, assisted by his brother Juan Maldonado, Pedro Diez had hidden an additional 2,000 pesos of gold among the rocks and debris near where his workers were washing the gold.[114]

Fraud and evasion of payment of debts could come into play at the fundiciones as well. In Puerto Rico, at least, no one could be imprisoned or detained for debt as long as the smelting continued, as signified by the presence of the bellows. As the bellows were being shut down, the people who were desperate to evade their creditors would flee to the countryside. The queen stipulated that creditors could ask for bonds (*fianzas*); anyone who failed to provide one was subject to arrest.[115]

The intensive labor and other investments that mining required limited the possibilities for small independent miners. In 1532 a man named Juan Rodríguez Gallego, who had lived in Santiago for fourteen years, said that although he owned nine or ten Black and Indian slaves, "he wouldn't dare to collect gold having to pay the *quinto* [the royal tax], even if the mines were good, as they are, because supplies have gone up in price."[116] As Sued Badillo suggests, "The era of the independent miner ... was giving way to mining as an enterprise of owners of a good number of slaves with sufficient capital to invest." He points out that the crown itself was the main beneficiary of gold mining, taking its cut of 20 percent until 1522 and 10 percent thereafter and directly holding mines and encomiendas.[117]

A partnership formed in Puerto Rico in November 1522 by two prominent men, Sancho de Arango, a regidor of San Juan, and Asencio de Villanueva, the vecino of San Germán who some years later would propose the colonization plan discussed previously, suggests the advantages enjoyed by men of some means, although they were operating on a relatively small scale. The partners' agreement included ten Black male and female slaves. Their total investment came to 1,400 pesos, which included an Indian woman whom they jointly purchased as a slave. Villanueva committed one-third of his Indians and agreed to live at the hacienda where the mine was located. Arango did not have to live there "except at my pleasure, when I might go and be there." An Indian woman named Beatriz, who belonged to Villanueva, could live at the estate with her children gratis while the partnership endured, which they specified would be for as long as they both remained on the island.[118]

The quest for other metals that could be mined profitably became of greater interest as gold yields declined.[119] In 1539 the tirelessly ambitious Álvaro de Castro asked for a grant of land three leagues in length and one in width near the headwaters of the Ozama River (Hispaniola) to graze his cattle, "where he has discovered many arroyos of gold and silver and copper and blue and many other colors and he has built roads to enter and leave the mines."[120] When Asensio de Villanueva was making his plans for his proposed new colony in Puerto Rico in the mid-1530s, he asked for permission to take with him "some miners and persons who know how to discover mines and silver and copper and other metals."[121] Fernández de Oviedo wrote that the prominent Lope de Bardecí claimed to have found and smelted iron near the Niçao River in Hispaniola, but there is no other evidence of iron being found in the Greater Antilles in any quantity.[122]

The most important discovery of copper in the islands took place in Cuba in 1530, three leagues from Santiago. Silversmith Luis de Espinosa, a vecino of Santiago, in 1534 received a concession to establish a foundry to smelt copper near the site of the discovery and permission to transport all the necessary equipment to mine and smelt copper. Named fundidor of copper for his lifetime, he also received permission to take with him from Spain people who could build the foundry.[123] Espinosa was in Santiago in 1537 but apparently made little progress on the project. In 1540 a Flemish miner named Gaspar Lomans stopped in Cuba on the way to New Spain and, after seeing the "sierra del cobre" (mountain of copper), decided to stay on the island. He soon recruited his friend Johan Tetzel from Nuremberg to join him, and Tetzel finally launched a serious effort to mine Cuba's copper.

Although an estimated 90,000 pounds of smelted copper were produced from 1540 to 1546, Tetzel decided to return to Germany to consult experts on the best method of extracting the metal from the rock in which it was found. He went back to Santiago in 1547 with six miners he had recruited and significant concessions from the crown, including an exemption from paying the *quinto real* for ten years, after which he would pay only one-twentieth of the ore's value for the following ten years. He also received a monopoly on smelting and the right to cut all the trees needed for firewood. People in Santiago who were interested or possibly already involved in copper mining became incensed when they learned that Tetzel did not intend to share with them "the secret of how to smelt it" and that he—an outsider—essentially had obtained a monopoly from the crown. Under pressure from the governor, Dr. Gonzalo Pérez de Angulo, Tetzel agreed that he would teach "everything about the skill of collecting, smelting, and reducing the copper to any slave who was handed over to him within a year and a half, during which period they would work for him" and he would maintain them. The arrangement seems to have been successful, as Tetzel renewed the *asiento* (contract) in 1571.[124]

Another important mineral resource found in the islands was salt. Fernández de Oviedo mentions several sources of salt in Hispaniola: in the north, near Montecristi; in Puerto Hermoso, fifteen leagues from Santo Domingo, on the south coast, which supplied the city; and "a mountain of salt [that is] almost crystalline... near the great lake of Xaragua, fourteen or fifteen leagues from the town of San Juan de la Maguana."[125] Puerto Rico also boasted significant salt mines. Tomás de Castellón rented the monopoly of Puerto Rico's salt for three years for 500 pesos a year, while his brother Jácome de Castellón, a vecino of Hispaniola and associate of prominent Genoese merchants in Seville, rented the salt mines of Hispaniola and Araya on the coast of Venezuela. Thus, the Castellón brothers, who also were active in Cubagua's pearl fisheries, monopolized much of the salt produced in the Caribbean. After 1515, however, the *salinas* of Araya proved cheaper to work and became the main source of supply for the Greater Antilles, and the salt mines of the islands began to decline.[126]

The period of the 1530s and 1540s and the demographic and economic trends that affected the Greater Antilles during that time have not received a great deal of attention from Anglophone scholars. During those years Spaniards in the Indies were establishing themselves on the mainland and, at least superficially, the Caribbean diminished in importance as an arena for Spanish activity. Yet mercantile activity was booming, imports of African slaves were increasing, and sugar estates and cattle ranches were producing significant exports. Toward the end of this period, however, some important shifts were occurring. Havana was emerging as Cuba's leading city by around 1550, and in subsequent decades it, together with Cartagena de Indias, would overshadow Santo Domingo as the Caribbean's principal ports, even as Santo Domingo, for the most part, retained its institutional dominance.[127]

Little is known about whether, and in what form, aspects of the Indigenous economy survived. Spanish encomenderos transformed yucca, maize, and aje into commercial crops, although the Indians continued to produce those staples for their own subsistence as well. I have not found evidence that Spaniards were producing cotton commercially during this period. The Laws of Burgos stipulated that Indigenous workers must be provided with hammocks, although possibly Indigenous production was insufficient to support that mandate.[128]

The same partial transformation of Indigenous into postcontact commercial production might have occurred with Native fisheries. Las Casas wrote that the bay of Xagua in Cuba, which had a narrow entrance, had an expanse of ten leagues of open water containing three small islands. Within the bay, the Indians had constructed open cages that trapped tens of thousands of fish, which they could remove with nets when they wished.[129] Did the Indians maintain, or did the Spaniards appropriate, these fisheries? Presumably the Spaniards would have found them to be of interest, given the scale of commercial fishing off the Iberian coast and Atlantic islands near Africa.[130]

It is possible, however, that Spaniards were not exploiting the potential for fishing, as in 1541 the king responded positively to a request that the "working people in that island who are Black and Indian slaves" be allowed to eat meat on fast days and Saturdays "because of the great lack of fish."[131] In the early years, at least, "it was more economical to import cheap fish from Seville than to fish" in Puerto Rico, so salted and smoked fish supplemented rations of cassava bread.[132] Fernández de Oviedo, however, mentions fishing off Mona Island, specifically noting the "good red lobsters, which are better than the others."[133] The unanswered questions regarding fishing in the Caribbean suggest that there is much still to be learned about how Europeans both exploited and eschewed the region's natural resources and the extent to which Indigenous agricultural and marine traditions and technology endured.

6

Women and Family

The experiences of Spanish women in the early Spanish Caribbean aligned closely with those of Spanish men. Women faced the same physical hazards and challenges that men faced, including transatlantic travel, inclement weather, and the predations of corsairs, hostile Indians, and rebellious Africans. They strove to create stability for themselves and their families, established and lived in ethnically diverse households filled with relatives, servants, and slaves, and dealt with the vicissitudes of rapid economic change, reversals, and decline.[1] In a sense, the most basic way in which the experiences of Spanish women differed from those of their male counterparts is that they left behind a far more limited and often only indirect record of their lives and activities in the documents that survive. This scarcity of evidence about women's lives is due in large part to the nature of the records that remain for the period, which are mainly administrative and financial, but also to certain legal and sometimes customary impediments to women's ability to function independently of men's authority. This is especially true of married and underage women.

Notwithstanding those limitations, and given the volatility of the early Spanish Caribbean, in which men moved around a great deal in search of opportunities, women frequently found themselves heading households, directing economic activities, and even occasionally exercising public functions.[2] Women in the Caribbean generally moved around far less than did men, and if they did move, it most likely was to places where husbands or other relatives resided and awaited them. As was true in an earlier frontier situation, when territory opened up to Christian settlement and new towns were founded during the Reconquista of the Iberian Peninsula, women symbolized and embodied stability and continuity; town charters (*fueros*) sometimes offered men incentives to marry.

Women's roles, however, certainly were not limited to the symbolic. Historian Heath Dillard has documented the crucial part that women played in founding new towns in medieval Iberia and ensuring that they flourished. Women, she writes, "played indispensable roles as settlers, wives of colonizers, mothers of successive generations of defenders, and vital members of the new Hispanic communities."[3] The role of Spanish women in the Caribbean was no different, notwithstanding the presence of Indigenous and Black women. There, too, the crown viewed the presence of Spanish women as a means to promote stability and adopted policies to encourage marriage.[4] In 1513, the king wrote to Diego Colón that "we are astonished" that he had refused to allow women from Hispaniola to join husbands who had gone to Cuba.[5]

From a relatively early time Spanish women were living in significant numbers in the larger towns of the Caribbean. When officials compiled information for the Repartimiento of 1514 in Hispaniola, barely twenty years after Columbus's first voyages, there were Spanish women living in all of Hispaniola's towns except Salvatierra de la Sabana in the west. Not surprisingly, the largest number of women, forty, were recorded as living in Santo Domingo, followed by nineteen in Salvaleón de Higüey and eleven in Concepción de la Vega. Most of them were married women who were not listed by name; officials simply indicated whether the vecinos of each town were married to women who were living in Castile, from Castile but living in Hispaniola, or Indigenous. A total of twenty-three women appeared independently in the Repartimiento, however, usually receiving assignments of one or two naborías (Indigenous servants). In some cases these were widows or women whose husbands were absent, while in other instances their marital status is not known.[6]

These numbers for Spanish women in Hispaniola in 1514 are almost certainly low. The marital status of royal officials usually was not noted, for instance, although their wives often accompanied these men to the Indies, and they in turn most likely brought their sons and daughters as well as their female servants, none of whom would have been included in the Repartimiento of 1514. The actual number of Spanish females of all ages who were living in Santo Domingo, then, easily could have been two or three times or more the number that appeared in the Repartimiento.

Even so, the Repartimiento provides solid evidence that within twenty years of the beginnings of Spanish settlement of the island, the numbers of adult Spanish women residing there had become substantial. Spanish women who crossed the Atlantic to live in Hispaniola, and later in the other islands, could expect to find themselves in the company of women whose background was similar to their own. Their households, of course, would have included Indigenous, African, and mixed-descent slaves and servants, who constituted the majority of the female population of the towns.[7]

Notwithstanding reversals in fortune and the frequent departure of Spaniards for other destinations or to return to Spain, many Spaniards married and raised their families in the islands. Rodrigo de Tamayo went to Cuba with Velázquez, where the priest Andrés Denis married him to Inés de la Jardina in Santiago. They had several children, including their son Andrés de Tamayo, born in Cuba about 1525. He married Ana Velázquez, and their children also were born in Cuba.[8] Pedro Gallego, the founder of the town of Compostela de Azua, who received the title of mariscal in 1526, had been married to Inés González Vivas for twenty-five years by the time of his death in 1532; their son Luis Gallego was born around 1512. Pedro Gallego, whose wife survived him, was buried in a chapel in the Franciscan monastery in Santo Domingo he had built at his own expense.[9] Francisco Alegre went to Puerto Rico around 1533 with his father, Hernando Alegre, and married María Mansa, the niece of bishop don Alonso Manso, around 1541.[10] Some marriages in the islands created or perhaps bolstered alliances between prominent families, as occurred with the families of Gonzalo Fernández de Oviedo and don Rodrigo de Bastidas; they created two *mayorazgos* (entails) to be attached to the two family surnames (Oviedo and Bastidas) in perpetuity.[11]

Spanish Women in the Islands

Most women probably traveled to the islands with husbands or other family members, or as servants. In 1533 Diego Portillo took with him to Cuba a married sister with her husband and two unmarried daughters, along with sons and nephews, for a total of ten people.[12] In 1534 Hernando de Lepe, who had lived in Puerto Rico for twenty-two years, was in Spain and declared that he was returning to the island, taking with him a brother and sister who already were married and had homes in San Juan, along with another brother, Gonzalo de Lepe, with his wife and children. The entourage also included a Juan de García with his wife and children and an unmarried sister; Salvador Martín and his wife and two unmarried nieces; and Alonso Pabón with his wife and children. In 1538 Salvador Martín and his wife, Beatriz de Lepe, obtained a license to go to Puerto Rico with their two daughters and two sons.[13] Although single men continued to travel to the Caribbean, the number of women and girls was approximately equal to the number of men and boys in these family entourages.

Because of the overall scarcity of information about women's lives in the documents and histories of the period, the relatively small number of cases in which women's stories can be recovered in some detail offer valuable insights into their experiences and the complex milieus in which they lived. Three such women, all named Isabel, lived during the period that is the focus of this book. Although one of them might never actually have gone there, the Caribbean decisively shaped the lives of doña Isabel Núñez de Andrada, doña Isabel de Maraver, and Isabel de Mayorga. Their stories are discussed in some detail.

The first of the three to arrive in Hispaniola was doña Isabel Núñez de Andrada, who went to Hispaniola in circumstances that all but ensured her a prosperous future. She was the niece of Jerónimo de Agüero, don Diego Colón's former tutor, who remained Colón's lifelong close advisor and associate. When the king summoned Colón to court in 1514, Colón designated his wife and Agüero to act in his name.[14] Doña Isabel went to Hispaniola as one of doña María de Toledo's ladies. Described as *"pequeña"* ("little," but probably meaning young) in 1509, she was an orphan and most likely under the age of fourteen.[15] With neither of her parents living and her brothers also apparently quite young, Isabel's well-connected maternal uncle Jerónimo de Agüero probably acted as the effective head of the family and surely was responsible for arranging his young niece's place among the virreina's entourage.

Isabel married Lope de Bardecí in Hispaniola around 1515.[16] Bardecí had arrived a few years earlier and became a prominent figure in the island, closely associated with Diego Colón. Given the polarized politics of that period, Bardecí's alliance with Colón meant he was not universally trusted.[17] He served as lieutenant governor of Hispaniola in the 1520s and 1530s, though not continuously. He was the compadre of the influential Diego Caballero, longtime secretary of the audiencia, for whom he testified enthusiastically in 1538 regarding his ingenio, calling the secretary "muy gran poblador en esta isla" (very great settler of this island).[18] Bardecí was a wealthy and successful entrepreneur, at one time owning a store in Santo Domingo in partnership with Lucas Vázquez de Ayllón and participating actively in the traffic in pearls and Indigenous slaves in the southern Caribbean.[19]

Jerónimo de Agüero and his niece Isabel belonged to a family with close ties to the crown based in the town of Zebreros near Ávila in Castile. Isabel was the daughter of Jerónimo Núñez and Francisca de Agüero. Núñez was a trusted retainer of King Fernando who fought in various campaigns and suffered a mortal wound in Navarra while serving under the Duque de Alba. His father, Pedro García Núñez, had served as governor in Asturias. In restitution for a church he had destroyed in order to arrest "certain criminals," he was said to have built five churches in Ávila as well as a house, which Pedro Nuñez, brother of Jerónimo Nuñez, inherited.

Agüero brought his own entourage of relatives and criados to Hispaniola, thus establishing a strong connection between his hometown of Zebreros and Santo Domingo that lasted for some years.[20] The entourage included other family members and people from their hometown with whom they had longstanding ties. Doña Isabel's sisters Catalina Núñez and Francisca de Agüero accompanied her to Hispaniola, as did their cousins Jerónimo and Antonio de Agüero, the sons of Jerónimo de Agüero.[21] Jerónimo de Agüero (the younger) testified that when he went to Hispaniola in 1526, his father already had died. His cousin doña Isabel's husband, Lope de Bardecí, took him into their household.

A number of other townspeople from Zebreros also went to Hispaniola. Catalina Núñez's husband, Juan de Henao, accompanied her to Hispaniola. Francisca Núñez (no relation) was seventy-five years old in 1550 when she testified that she and her husband, Cristóbal Yáñez, a barber, also had gone with them, in 1509, and subsequently returned to Zebreros. Vicente de Bejar "el viejo" had served doña Isabel's parents as a youth, before going to Santo Domingo; he later returned to Zebreros, around 1530. And Diego Sacristán, also a vecino of Zebreros, knew the family and spent some time in Santo Domingo.

Lope de Bardecí and doña Isabel Núñez de Andrada both were alive in 1550 when their son Juan de Bardecí was named abad of Jamaica by don Luis Colón, the son and heir of Diego Colón, and Bardecí at least was still living in 1560 when he testified in the información of Pero Vásquez de Ayllón and stated that he was more than sixty years old.[22] Notwithstanding the many years she spent in Santo Domingo, and despite her husband's prominence, little more is known of Isabel's life.[23] Her son Juan probably was in his late twenties when he prepared two depositions, in 1549 and 1550. These informaciones omitted mention of any siblings. As a young girl and then a bride in Hispaniola, doña Isabel had lived surrounded by her siblings, cousins, and people she knew from her hometown, and as an elite Spanish woman she would have been a respected figure in Santo Domingo society. In 1532 the priest Cristóbal de Deza, canon of the cathedral of Concepción de la Vega, testified that Bachiller Álvaro de Castro, who at the time also was a canon of the cathedral, had placed Catalina, "*india lucaya*" (a Lucayan Indian), in Bardecí's household while Castro was in Castile. He had seen Catalina at mass with doña Isabel, so Isabel must have taken charge of Catalina's religious instruction. Unfortunately for Catalina, Castro removed her from Isabel's care after he returned to Hispaniola.[24]

The Situation of Widows

The experiences of doña Isabel de Maraver (or Malaver) were far different from those of doña Isabel Núñez. The life of doña Isabel de Maraver vividly illustrates the uncertainties of living in the islands, even for a well-born Spanish woman, and vulnerability of widows, as well the multiethnic context in which Spanish women lived in the Caribbean. She probably did not have much say in her family's decision to migrate to Hispaniola or in her marriage to a resident of the island, Gonzalo de Guzmán. Doña Isabel de Maraver arrived in Hispaniola in 1515, a few years after doña Isabel Núñez de Andrada, as part of a family entourage that included her parents, Juan Guillén and María de Maraver, five sisters, a brother, and several criados, possibly having already married Guzmán earlier that year.[25]

Her father must have had connections at court, which would explain a generous (but ultimately empty) royal promise of 120 Indians in encomienda to each of Guillén's daughters. Had such encomiendas still existed on the island, they would have constituted valuable dowries for the young women, but after the redistribution of available Indigenous workers was carried out in Hispaniola in 1514, none remained to be assigned. The result was disastrous for the sisters. Two never married, and the husband of a third abandoned her in 1519 when the dowry did not materialize. Another sister, doña María de Maraver, died, leaving two sons whose father left them behind when he relocated to New Spain.[26] Isabel's husband, Gonzalo de Guzmán, was bitterly disappointed that she failed to provide the anticipated dowry and made it clear that it had been the only reason he had agreed to the marriage.[27]

Guzmán went to Hispaniola as part of the large party that accompanied royal governor frey Nicolás de Ovando in 1502. His friend Luis Hernández testified on his behalf in 1527, when Guzmán prepared a petition asking to be relieved of a debt of 600 pesos that he claimed he could not repay because he was poor and had been sick for several years.[28] Luis Hernández was the couple's neighbor in both the city and the countryside. Among the witnesses who testified on Guzmán's behalf and had known him for many years were a number of leading men of early Hispaniola. Guzmán, however, apparently had been unable to use those connections to achieve a stable economic situation for himself. He might have been more closely allied to the Colón faction than to the royal party dominated by the treasurer Miguel de Pasamonte. Men close to Colón who testified for Guzmán and later for his widow included Lope de Bardecí (who, as mentioned, married doña Isabel Núñez de Andrada, the niece of Diego Colón's tutor) and Diego Colón's secretary, García de Aguilar.

Guzmán at one time held an encomienda, but it had become worthless as the Indians died or fled.[29] In the Repartimiento of 1514 he received only nine *naborías de casa* (servants).[30] In a deposition compiled by the city council of Santo Domingo in 1515, Guzmán testified to protest the assignments that had been made in the Repartimiento, in which treasurer Miguel de Pasamonte ultimately played the deciding role. Guzmán specifically complained that Benito de Astorga and another man, named Pedro de Llanos, had received Indians because they were the criados of Pasamonte, even though they were unqualified to be encomenderos. He said that Llanos should not have received anything because he was well known to be a "very bad person," and Astorga because he had been a shopkeeper, "and because both are married in Castile, and because they are inconsequential men [de poca manera] that haven't had any Indians."[31] Whatever the reason, Guzmán seems to have ended up on the wrong side in the island's often turbulent political struggles.

After Guzmán died, his widow, Isabel, petitioned to have their debts forgiven. Her husband had owed 666 pesos and 4 tomines de oro to the crown, and she owed an additional 108 pesos to private parties. The testimony for the *información de su pobreza* that she executed in 1531 revealed her household's poverty. Guzmán had left only a rural property on the Hayna River, which was described as being of very little value. Around three hundred head of cattle worth about 200 pesos grazed on the estancia. Some sheep had been sold for 30 pesos to pay to enclose the house lot in the city on which stood two old thatched houses where they lived.³²

The widowed Isabel's household included her father, said to be very old and ill (her mother had died ten years before); two unmarried sisters; two of Guillén's grandsons and another "niño huérfano de padre y madre" (child orphaned by both father and mother), probably the son of her sister María de Maraver; two mestiza girls born and raised in her house, "hijas de indias cristianas" (daughters of Christian Indians), whom she hoped to marry "as her own daughters"; two "very old" Black slaves named Diego and Bartolomé, and a third who was missing a hand;³³ and two young Black girls, the daughters of one of the Black slaves, who also had been born in her house and whom Isabel also considered to be like her daughters. She had no children from her marriage, or at least none who survived. Luis Hernández also mentioned that "una india naboría vieja" (an old Indian woman servant) also was living in doña Isabel's household.³⁴ Significantly, nearly everyone in the crowded household other than Isabel herself was too old, too young, or too ill to work. It is notable that, although her father was still alive, Isabel clearly functioned and was recognized as the head of household.

A number of witnesses to Isabel's deposition were people to whom she owed small sums that she had been unable to repay. Some of the debts were fairly recent, others long-standing. She owed the pharmacist Antonio de Gibasa, together with another pharmacist named Ordóñez, 35 pesos de oro for medication for her husband and other members of her household. Sympathizing with her situation, Gibasa, like others, such as the carpenter Anton García, who had built some doors for her house and was owed 10 pesos, did not press her for payment. Antonio Hernández, whom she owed 7 pesos for work on part of the wall surrounding her property, said that he had not tried to collect the debt "so as not to bother her," because it was clear that she did not have the money. She owed the estanciero "de la dicha estancia" (of the said farm) 50 pesos.

Some debts that her husband had incurred before his death included money owed for merchandise purchased from Juan de la Serna, a small loan of 32 pesos Guzmán had taken from Dominican friar Francisco Ramírez, and 21 pesos he owed to the mason Maestre Lorenzo for work done on his house, which his widow, Francisca Jiménez, tried to collect from Isabel. It is possible that Francisca also faced financial hard times and could not afford to excuse the debt.

Genoese merchant Esteban Justinian testified that Isabel still owed him 9 pesos from a larger debt her husband had incurred seven years previously, but he too had not tried to collect them, "being as she is an honorable person and knowing of her as is notorious she has no possibility of repaying the said pesos."

What became of this large and impoverished household is not known. Perhaps in her midthirties in 1531, Isabel, saddled with debts and nearly propertyless, was unlikely to have remarried. The young mestiza and Black girls she was rearing perhaps ended up as servants in other households as she hardly could have provided dowries for them. Her nephews, assuming they survived to young adulthood, might have followed in the footsteps of other Spanish residents of Hispaniola who abandoned the island to seek opportunities elsewhere in the expanding Spanish-controlled territories of the mainland. The household, with its diverse residents bound by complex relationships, in some ways constituted a microcosm of the Spanish Caribbean society of the times: ethnically mixed, ensconced in a nominally Spanish society that itself was socioeconomically and ethnically diverse, beset by hard times as a result of the demise of the Indigenous population that initially had formed the main productive base for the island's economy, and unlikely to experience any reversal of fortune.

The trajectory of Isabel de Maraver and her family was downward. They arrived in Hispaniola with a pledge of royal support, reasonably high social status, and expectations that relocating to the other side of the Atlantic would yield advantages for them all. Nothing worked out as expected. Isabel and her family did not benefit from the island's early boom period. Instead, they lived through its demographic and economic decline and rapid transformation to a much more modest and increasingly ethnically mixed society. Yet although Isabel de Maraver's economic situation was dire, and certainly she did not have the life she might have anticipated, she nonetheless forged ties of genuine affection and domesticity, rose to the challenge of marshaling her ramshackle household through hard times, and in doing so, at least earned the respect and sympathy of her neighbors and acquaintances.[35]

As seen in Isabel de Maraver's story, a widow's situation usually depended on her husband's economic success or failure during his lifetime,[36] although the island's most prominent widow, doña María de Toledo, was wealthy in her own right. In 1544 she returned to Santo Domingo from Spain, bringing with her an entourage that included two women, doña Jerónima de Chaves and

Lucía de Luyando, and four men. The men probably were married, as they received permission to take whatever they needed for themselves and their wives and households.[37] She also obtained royal permission to take with her three clerics, "her chaplains."[38] Thus, more than thirty years after she began her life in Hispaniola, doña María returned to the island, where her son don Luis, the third admiral, still lived. She outlived her husband by more than twenty years, mostly spent in Hispaniola, and died in 1549.

Other widows also seem to have managed well enough. In 1515 Beatriz Sánchez, the widow of Francisco de Herrera and a vecina of San Juan de la Maguana in Hispaniola, received authorization to retain the sixty people her husband had held in encomienda.[39] Doña Florencia de Ávila, the widow of factor Juan de Ampies, in 1546 arranged to repay her husband's 6,000 to 7,000 ducados in debt in installments of 1,000 ducados annually over a period of ten or twelve years.[40] As was discussed in chapter 1, the widow of Lucas Vázquez de Ayllón also was able to cover his debts and in the end regained her house in Santo Domingo. Doña Juana de Carvajal, the widow of Juan de Tiedra, apparently remained a wealthy woman, as in 1545 she sought permission to leave Hispaniola for Peru, taking with her "her Black and Indian slaves and servants."[41]

For many widows, though, even if they were able to retain property or the rights to a repartimiento—which often they only succeeded in doing through litigation—maintaining themselves and their children in the Caribbean was not easy or assured. In 1532 Isabel de Ávila, vecina of San Juan, declared that she and her husband, Diego Gilante, had lived for a long time in Puerto Rico and that she had been left a widow with two daughters, ages two and four, and a son who was seven. She hoped to return to her native city of Seville to place her daughters in a convent and to have her son pursue his studies. Permission was granted.[42]

Catalina Méndez, the widow of Melchior Mata, who referred to herself as "hija de español e india" (daughter of a Spaniard and an Indian woman), in 1545 wanted to take her children to Guadalcanal in Andalucía, where she hoped to marry her two daughters to the sons of "her" neighbors; perhaps she was referring to neighbors of her husband's family. She claimed that she was always sick in Hispaniola.[43] Juana Méndez, the widow of Esteban de Roça, asked permission to take her children and possessions to join her mother and brothers in Mexico City, as she said she no longer had a single relative left in Santo Domingo.[44] In 1540 Catalina de Collantes, the widow of Hernando de Henares, declared that she was ill and wanted to sell her property and return to Spain.[45]

Ana Marques, the widow of the longtime porter of the audiencia, Pedro de Vidaguren, petitioned in 1546 to be allowed to continue to live in the lodgings in the house of the audiencia, where they had resided while her husband served as portero.[46] Her husband had earned a meager living. His original salary was only 20,000 maravedís, and in 1543 he said that he had served for nearly twenty years "with much work and little salary." The crown conceded an additional 10,000 maravedís annually. Not long before his death, he renounced his office in favor of his son Pedro, but as Pedro was under eighteen when his father died, someone else would have to serve until he was of age.[47]

Beatriz de San Pedro decided in 1537 to return to Hispaniola after her husband Alonso de San Pedro died.[48] Not only widows but also some single women also preferred life in the Greater Antilles. Catalina Morena declared that she wanted to remain in San Juan to marry and live, after her father, Pedro Moreno, the former lieutenant governor of Puerto Rico, died.[49] In 1529 Francisca Hernández, a vecina of Seville, asked permission to go to live in San Juan, taking her daughter, whom she hoped to marry there, as well as two slaves, without paying the usual fees.[50] In one case a woman living in Santo Domingo did not go to live with her husband, Pedro López de Angulo, in Puerto Rico. He held an encomienda there and in 1531 asked permission to retain it, notwithstanding his trips to see his wife.[51]

Fractured Marriages

Many men moved to the islands without their spouses, a decision that could destroy marriages and ruin women's lives, even if those outcomes were unintentional. Although the length of her husband's absence was somewhat unusual, the situation of Francisco Flores, a vecina of Ciudad Rodrigo, was not atypical. In 1533 she said that she had married Marcos Martínez twenty-eight years before. Only three years after they married, he departed for the Indies, since which time he had not written to her or sent her any financial support. To make matters worse, she had heard that he had remarried in Jamaica. She asked the king to order him to sell his goods so that he could return to Spain to take up married life with her, or at least to send her some part of his possessions.[52] In 1538 Ana de Mendonedo petitioned the crown for a similar reason. She had married Pelayo Briceño around 1504 and he had departed for Cuba about fourteen years later. During those twenty years he had neither returned nor sent her anything.[53]

Women refused to accompany or join their husbands for a variety of reasons, including their own or their children's health, as discussed in chapter 2. In 1536 Rodrigo Romero, a vecino of Asunción (Baracoa) in Cuba, said he was unable to bring his wife to join him because he was ill. He sent her money so she could make the journey. Contador Pedro de Paz, who was in Spain at the time, offered to bring her, along with another relative, but she refused, saying she was old and sick and would likely die at sea.[54]

Men failed to bring or send for their wives for reasons of their own, even though the crown reiterated with some frequency that married men must not remain in the Indies without them.[55] In 1533 Inés López stated that her husband, Francisco de Espinosa, who was in Puerto Rico, ostensibly had arranged for her and their children to travel to the island with Asencio de Villanueva, who was in Spain at the time. Espinosa, however, whether deliberately or not, seems to have sabotaged the reunion by failing to furnish his wife the means to make the journey.[56]

In 1534 Cuba's lieutenant governor, Manuel de Rojas, not only summoned and questioned a number of men who were living on the island without their spouses but also had to account for why his own wife remained in Spain.[57] Cristóbal de Verdejo, who had been there for fourteen or fifteen years, explained that his wife, Ana Rodríguez, with whom he had a son and daughter, lived in the bishopric of Cartagena. He had sent her a small sum of money before departing from Seville, all that he could spare, and later 25 pesos with a merchant in 1525. He claimed to be too ill to return to live with her but finally had accumulated 400 pesos in cash or slaves and thought that within two years he would be able to send for her. Francisco Quemado offered a lengthy explanation of the various sums of money, totaling around 300 pesos, that he had sent to his wife from Cuba, New Spain, and Hispaniola over the course of the fifteen or sixteen years they had been separated. Now that he had returned to Cuba, he could not afford to send for her. When he had tried to make arrangements for her to join him in New Spain, where he had arranged a marriage for their daughter in Veracruz, she flatly refused to come.

With regard to his own situation, Manuel de Rojas testified that he had lived in Cuba for fourteen years and once had traveled back to court, at which time he had been able to visit his wife and children and see to their situation. Since then, he had written and sent money "many times," and one of his younger sons, Gómez de Rojas, had joined him. Around the time he was appointed lieutenant governor, he had planned to travel again to Spain to see his daughter married and to arrange for his wife and other children to travel back to Cuba with him. He had been unable to do so, however, because of the substantial amounts of his own money that he had spent on "the pacification of this island and on other things that have arisen relating to its welfare and good governance and the implementation of justice."

In his defense he described at some length the actions he had been forced to take against "certain rebellious Indian slaves," for which he had equipped, at his own expense, a patrol of four Spaniards, a Black, and ten or twelve Indians, who pursued the Indians unsuccessfully, as a result of which he had to recruit, provision, and compensate several other such patrols. Whether because of the financial strain of his duties as lieutenant governor, the economic difficulties that even well-situated Spaniards in the islands faced as the result of the decline of gold mining and loss of Indigenous labor, or (most likely) a combination of the two, by 1544 Rojas was in such financial straits that he decided to travel to Peru to visit his brother, Gabriel de Rojas. He hoped that Gabriel could offer him some assistance in arranging the marriages of his daughters who were still in Spain, both of whom at that time were over the age of thirty. Rojas himself was over sixty-five by then.[58]

The strains on marriages and odd accommodations that sometimes resulted from long-distance separations are vividly illustrated in the story of a man named Benito de Astorga, who was married to the third Isabel mentioned at the beginning of the chapter. Astorga went to Hispaniola in the early years and traveled back and forth between the island and Spain, at some point marrying Isabel de Mayorga in his hometown of Astorga, a city in the north central province of León, located on the old pilgrimage route to Santiago de Compostela. Not a great deal is known of Benito's background and early years in Hispaniola, including the exact date of his arrival. He claimed to be one of the first settlers of the island and that he went there while frey Nicolás de Ovando was governor. At one point he stated that he arrived in Hispaniola with Ovando, but more likely it was a few years later.[59]

He probably was in his teens when he emigrated; in testimony of 1515, he was referred to as "mozo," a boy. In the same testimony witnesses noted that Benito was the criado, or retainer, of the powerful and influential treasurer of the Indies, Miguel de Pasamonte. For years he maintained close relations with Pasamonte and his nephew, Esteban de Pasamonte, who became treasurer of

Hispaniola after his uncle's death. Astorga very likely went to Hispaniola as Miguel de Pasamonte's servant or employee around 1508.[60]

Once on the island, Astorga for a while operated a shop in Santo Domingo selling cloth, groceries, and other items. His close ties with Pasamonte accounted for his name appearing in the testimony amassed against Rodrigo de Alburquerque, the man commissioned by the Spanish crown to conduct the Repartimiento of 1514. Several people complained that Astorga should not have received any Indians, as he was a mere shopkeeper (*tendero*) and a man of little ability (one witness referred to him dismissively as "un Astorguilla," who had been assigned nine naborías only by virtue of his connection to Pasamonte.[61] By 1515 he had become more directly involved in the import business and was traveling back and forth between Castile and Hispaniola. In the course of those transatlantic journeys he surely visited his hometown, and there he married Isabel de Mayorga, who continued to live in Astorga, probably remaining in her family's home.[62]

As was true for many other Europeans on the island, Benito de Astorga's fortunes were closely tied to those of Hispaniola. His connection to Pasamonte probably helped him to gain a foothold there. During the prosperous years of Hispaniola's early gold rush, Benito apparently did well enough as a shopkeeper to become a successful participant in the transatlantic trade.[63] One of his acquaintances on the island testified that Benito de Astorga "came from Castile many times."[64] He also invested locally in some property, but then Hispaniola's economy began its downturn. When Benito returned to Hispaniola after a trip to Spain in 1521, he planned to divest himself of his properties and go back to Spain to take up married life in Astorga, using whatever capital he had accumulated to start a new phase of his life.

Treasurer Esteban de Pasamonte later testified that while Benito was in Castile, he wrote to let him know that he would find at court a commission for certain offices in Hispaniola. Given Benito's heretofore somewhat marginal status on the island, holding office could have meant a significant boost in prestige. He was not to be swayed, however, and he wrote back to Pasamonte that "he had no desire to live or remain in these parts other than that he wanted to come and sell what he had in this island and go to live with his wife in Castile."[65] His friend Luis Hernández (the same man who had testified for Isabel de Maraver) mentioned that when Benito went back to Hispaniola in 1521, the two of them discussed returning together to Castile to live.

Initially Benito's plan seemed likely to work. He sold a cattle ranch (hato) and a Black slave to another resident of the island, but he could not find a buyer for his other properties.[66] At that point, he seems to have decided that he would not return to Castile and, according to his own declaration, he "very affectionately begged his wife to see the benefit of coming to this island to make a life with him." He gave up his mercantile business and began to invest in the construction of a sugar estate and mill, for which he purchased Black slaves and necessary equipment.[67] He bought a house in Santo Domingo and, in expectation of his wife's arrival, furnished it with curtains, wall hangings, and a bed.

Isabel de Mayorga, however, failed to see the appeal of living in Santo Domingo. Most likely she and Benito had always planned for him to return home, so when she married she did not anticipate going to the Caribbean. Thus commenced Benito de Astorga's dogged and ultimately futile effort to convince her to join him, a campaign for which he solicited the aid of nearly a dozen friends and acquaintances, both men and women, who wrote letters, talked to people who knew Isabel and her family, offered to make travel arrangements or to accompany her to Hispaniola, or actually visited the town of Astorga to try to persuade Isabel to join her husband.

The details of Benito de Astorga's efforts to bring his wife to the island are known because his failure to do so eventually came to the attention of the audiencia. The court ordered Benito to produce her or pay a fine. While many married immigrants made only perfunctory efforts to bring their spouses, Benito's attempts to convince his wife to come actually had gotten under way before the case came before the audiencia, and they were quite persistent.

In his deposition of 1527–1528, Benito de Astorga stated that he had sent three different men—Melchor de Castro, the notary of mines; Diego de Alcántara; and Alonso de Aguilar, nephew of audiencia judge Licenciado Rodrigo de Figueroa—to Astorga to talk to Isabel and inform her in detail about his property and possessions "so she could come and live at her pleasure." In 1525 Isabel and her brothers wrote that she would go to Seville. Benito sent money to Luis Hernández de Alfaro, a resident of Seville active in the transatlantic trade, who agreed to make arrangements for Isabel's journey. Luis Hernández de Alfaro's son Juan de Alfaro, who in the 1520s was living in Hispaniola,[68] confirmed that his father had received money from Benito and that Isabel had written to his father in Seville telling him that she would go there to embark.

Treasurer Esteban de Pasamonte mentioned that he had seen a letter from Luis Hernández de Alfaro saying that Isabel de Mayorga had written indicating that she planned to make the journey with the wife of Licenciado Espinosa (an oidor of the audiencia), who was going to Hispaniola. Women avoided traveling alone as they were at risk of sexual and other kinds of violence.[69] Benito's friend and fellow merchant Rodrigo de Marchena also had seen letters from Luis Hernández de Alfaro in Seville, "in which he said that every day he was waiting there" for Isabel. Marchena testified that at the time that Luis Hernández was expecting Isabel to arrive, he had been about to leave for Seville to bring his wife and household back to the island. He had arranged with Benito de Astorga to bring Isabel to Santo Domingo along with his own wife.[70]

Of the three men who went to talk to Isabel in Astorga, Benito's friend Melchor de Castro played the most active part. Between 1521 and 1526, he made at least two trips to Castile, during which he traveled twice to Astorga to talk to Isabel and her family, carrying letters from her husband. In 1528 Castro claimed to have known Benito for eighteen years and Isabel for twelve, so possibly he had been in Spain and met her around the time that Benito and Isabel married. Castro testified in January 1528 that two and a half years previously he had traveled, at Benito's request, from Burgos to Astorga and that, in the presence of her mother and brothers, Isabel had promised to come to Seville in five months. Esteban de Pasamonte was in Castile at that time and later said he saw Melchor de Castro in Toledo on his way to Astorga; on his return to Toledo, Castro told Pasamonte that Isabel was going to meet him in Seville. She planned to be there at Christmastime of 1526, with two of her brothers.

She failed to meet Melchor de Castro in Seville, however, and after he returned to Santo Domingo he complained that Isabel and her brothers had made a fool of him. By this time, Benito was beginning to feel much the same. Agueda Hernández, the wife of his longtime friend Luis Hernández, said that she had heard Benito de Astorga speak to her husband "complaining of... how badly she [Isabel] had acted."[71]

Yet this was not the end. After failing to meet Melchor de Castro in Seville, Isabel wrote to her husband that if his cousin Hernando de Ponferrada, who was married and living in La Palma in the Canaries, would come for her, she would go to Hispaniola with him and one of her brothers. Both she and Astorga sent letters to Ponferrada, who left La Palma for Seville and from there went to Astorga for her. Isabel and her "mother and relatives" again deliberated as to whether she should go and finally decided that she would not. Ponferrada returned to Seville and then went back to La Palma with letters from Isabel and her family, which he sent on to Benito in Hispaniola.

Other friends on the island wrote to Isabel during this time, urging her to join her husband. Luis Hernández encouraged Isabel to come, saying that her husband was "very rich and that she would be treated well." He also assured her that Benito had never had a mistress or children. Abel Meléndez, a native of the town of Astorga, who had been living in Santo Domingo for about three years when he testified in 1527, said he had known Isabel de Mayorga for years and that before coming to the island had heard a great deal about Benito from his and Isabel's relatives as well as from Benito's friends and acquaintances who had visited Astorga. Meléndez claimed that he actually wrote many of the letters that Benito sent to Isabel and her family and to Luis Hernández de Alfaro and had prepared the account of what the latter would provide Isabel for her journey.

In 1526 audiencia judge Licenciado Sepúlveda left Santo Domingo for Spain, offering to go to Astorga to talk to Isabel de Mayorga and carrying more letters from Benito and others to her. Sepúlveda wrote to his fellow judge, Licenciado Zuazo, and to María de Beltriana, the wife of treasurer Esteban de Pasamonte, asking them to assure Benito that he would do as promised.[72] Subsequently, fray Tomás de Berlanga, the prior of the Dominican monastery of Santo Domingo, told María de Beltriana that he had spoken with Sepúlveda when he was in Castile and that the latter mentioned that he had fulfilled his pledge to Benito. Sepúlveda also wrote directly to María de Beltriana himself.

When Esteban de Pasamonte was in Spain in 1525, he too made inquiries on Benito's behalf. He tried to find a brother of Isabel de Mayorga who was said to be residing at the royal court, but he failed to do so. He talked to a retainer of the Marqués de Astorga, who said that he knew Isabel and would urge her to join her husband in Santo Domingo. Pasamonte also spoke with Benito's cousin Hernando de Ponferrada, who had journeyed in vain from La Palma to Castile, as well as to Melchor de Castro in Toledo and Luis Hernández de Alfaro in Seville. Pasamonte's wife, María de Beltriana, also wrote to Isabel, via Licenciado Sepúlveda, encouraging her to make the journey to the island. When she went to Hispaniola in 1523, she had expected Isabel to travel with her.

In May 1533, when the high court was about to fine him because of his continued separation from his wife, Benito de Astorga obtained a copy of the deposition of 1527–1528 regarding his efforts to bring her to Hispaniola to present to the audiencia. By then, it surely was clear to all that she was unlikely to join her husband on the island. The intervening years, however, had been busy ones for Benito as he poured his remaining capital and energy into developing a sugar mill and estate five leagues from the capital city of Santo Domingo.[73]

When he first arrived in Hispaniola, Benito de Astorga was a young man of undistinguished background, possibly with little education. Meléndez's statement that he actually wrote many of the letters that Benito sent back to Spain suggests that Astorga might not have been highly literate. Nonetheless, he made considerable economic gains and clearly had friends and defenders, some of whom numbered among the island's most influential figures. His compatriot Abel Meléndez noted that Melchor de Castro had offered to help Benito "because they were and are such good friends."[74] Castro was a longtime officeholder and important figure in local society; by 1543 he had served as chief notary for the mines for thirty years.[75] It is likely that Astorga and Castro emigrated to the island together in 1507 or 1508, and this was perhaps the source of their close bond, since they were not from the same town. Benito de Astorga was on friendly terms with high-ranking officials, including audiencia judges and the prior of the Dominican monastery in Santo Domingo, and on speaking terms with the wives of officials and others.

Astorga's efforts to convince his wife to join him, although quite determined for a while, on the whole reflected motives that probably were more pragmatic than uxorious. Having made up his mind to stay in Hispaniola when he was already married in Spain, the best—indeed only—course open to him was to persuade his wife to join him there. The considerable money and energy he put into his sugar estate suggest that, regardless of his wife's unwillingness to emigrate, he was more concerned with forging an economic base on the island than with pursuing married life. Experiencing one major setback after another in the construction of the sugar mill, he might have decided it was a losing proposition and returned to Astorga to try to make a life there. That he did not do.

One can only guess at the reasons for Isabel de Mayorga's reluctance. If she was unwilling to sacrifice the comfort (or at least security) of hometown and family to make a life with her husband in a distant outpost of the empire, neither did she demonstrate any antipathy for him. She remained in contact with Benito, writing frequently in response to his letters, and ostensibly seriously entertained the possibility of going to join him, on several occasions actually promising to do so. Her family may have played a significant role in persuading her not to leave home, but there is no way to know why this was so. Isabel had several opportunities to go to Hispaniola with other women who were traveling with or going to join their husbands; she considered, and rejected, a number of options for making the journey.

She and her family might have had some specific concerns about her future in the Caribbean. Perhaps Benito's economic prospects appeared uncertain. Together with the great distance involved and the prospect of Isabel's never returning home, even to visit, her family might have judged the implications of her departure to be unacceptable. Whatever the reasons, Isabel and her family weighed the alternatives and concluded that emigration was not in her (or their?) best interest. It is possible that, reassured by her husband's new prosperity and status as the owner of a sugar mill, she eventually decided to join him, but the evidence is ambiguous.[76]

Sexuality, Marriage, and Irregular Unions

The stories of the three Isabels suggest that Spanish women's choices and experiences could be varied and unpredictable; in all three cases, however, their marriages proved pivotal in setting the course of their lives. The experience of a woman named Beatriz de Salas, however, suggests the vulnerability of women who lacked a male protector. A good deal is known about what happened soon after Beatriz arrived in Hispaniola because the relationship between her, her daughter, and the flamboyant cleric Bachiller Álvaro de Castro came under particular scrutiny when charges were brought against Castro in the early 1530s.

Beatriz was a widow and *beata* (a laywoman living under religious vows) who arrived in Hispaniola in April 1531 with her daughter Inés de Salas and Inés's husband, Juan Merchante (or Merchan). Castro claimed that he had come to Beatriz's aid and persuaded the bishop to allow her to live in a bohío located on his property.[77] This arrangement did not last long, however, and Castro offered the three of them accommodations in another bohío near his house. He later claimed that he had provided them with everything they needed. He hired Beatriz's son-in-law to work as his estanciero, meaning Merchante (conveniently) left town to work on the estancia.

Castro testified that Beatriz and Inés were his criadas, or servants. Inés had cared for him during two or three illnesses, but Castro insisted that there was nothing improper about their relationship and that he treated her like a daughter. (Inés died shortly before Castro's deposition was taken, in August 1532.)[78] Beatriz de Salas testified in May 1531 that Castro had seduced her daughter in her husband's absence. Several times when she left home, she returned to find Inés with Castro in his house, and once she went to look for her between nine and ten o'clock at night and found them together. When she became upset and argued with them, Castro took her by the arm and escorted her back to her own house. Her daughter did not return until midnight. Soon after that, Castro brought Inés's husband back to town and they all argued, following which Castro ordered Beatriz to vacate the house. Castro sent Inés and her husband to the estancia, where Inés became ill. She returned to the city, where she ended up staying with Castro's niece Leonor de Castro, the wife of Martín de Landa, and refused to visit her mother. She died soon after.[79]

Castro's relations with women can only be considered predatory. Rumors of them abounded, although some appear to have been consensual, if inappropriate. The barber Pedro Palomo, for example, claimed that Castro was involved with a Spanish woman, both before and after she married, who became pregnant with his child while she was still single. She asked Palomo to bleed her, which he did, not suspecting that she was pregnant; only later did he realize that she had hoped to abort the child. He failed to mention whether she succeeded.[80]

Violence, however, marked Castro's relationship with a young Lucayan woman, Catalina or Catalinica. He had raised her from the time she was a child, making his actions particularly disturbing. Castro had been away from Hispaniola, and when he returned, according to Cristóbal de Deza, he discovered that she was pregnant. Believing that Catalina had had relations with another man, he beat her so severely in a jealous fury that she miscarried at seven months and died soon thereafter.[81]

Although the existence of unions marked by irregularities of some sort often generated comment, they were common enough, even within the Spanish group, to suggest that the circumstances of life in the islands might have fostered flexibility and variability in male–female relationships. Juan Ponce de León married a young woman named Leonor, the daughter of an innkeeper in Santo Domingo, soon after he went to Hispaniola in 1502. The fact that she used her husband's surname suggests that her own family did not rank high socially.[82]

Bachiller Juan Roldán, who arrived in Santo Domingo in 1512, maintained a long romantic involvement with his housekeeper, María de Ávila, described by one witness as "vieja" (old). When she died in 1520, he refused to leave the house for more than a week and arranged for her to be buried "very honorably" in the cathedral. She in turn made Roldán, whom she called "su amigo," her heir.[83]

In 1519 a witness testified that Puerto Rico's treasurer, Andrés de Haro, kept a woman named Isabel de la Feria, with whom he had a son, in her father's house, and that in addition he had "another Indian woman" with whom he had a son. Since these women apparently were Haro's servants, the witness, Sancho de Arango, was uncertain whether they should be considered his mistresses. The testimony was part of the residencia of Licenciado Sancho Velázquez, who himself allegedly had "two or three Indian mistresses" in his house. Garcí Troche, the island's alguacil mayor and future son-in-law of Juan Ponce de León, maintained a mistress named Mejía, with whom he had a son, until a month before he married. Likewise, procurador García Hernández was said to have a Spanish woman as his mistress, with whom he had a son, while the sacristan Francisco Quemado had a daughter with a Black woman named Cristina. Both men were fined for being "amancebados" (cohabiting), because both were married.[84]

Santo Domingo's cabildo complained about the marriages that the veedor of the audiencia and fellow regidor Gaspar de Astudillo had contracted (serially, it seems) "con tres buenas mujeres sacadas de lugares públicas" (with three good women taken from public places). Presumably, the "public places" to which they referred were taverns, or possibly brothels, and the cabildo members considered the women to be the opposite of "good." They asked the king to appoint officials of higher quality, alleging that "there are plenty of people who have eschewed marrying in this city, seeing that he [Astudillo] holds these offices and that the wives he has had, and has, who are of the quality already mentioned ... something that is a huge affront for all the good men of the city."[85]

When the lieutenant governor of Cuba, Manuel de Rojas, conducted his visit of the island's towns and mines in 1533, he found in Puerto de Príncipe "everyone living together unmarried [amancebados], some with their own naborías and others with their female slaves and others with the daughters of Spaniards and women of this country, in such peace and tranquility as if they were under God's blessing." The somewhat wistful tone of that observation might have reflected the many years that Rojas spent on the island without his own wife. He said that he persuaded some of the men to marry their domestic partners.[86]

From the earliest years Spanish men made Indigenous women their sexual partners, whether the women were willing or not. Just how coercive these relationships were is often impossible to determine from the documentary record, other than anecdotally. Some of these relationships led to long-term, stable cohabitation or marriage with children, but others were ephemeral and produced children whose fate was uncertain.

Testimony compiled during Rojas's visit underscores the varied domestic arrangements that characterized society in Cuba's small towns in the 1530s.[87] Juan de Espinosa had been a vecino of Sancti Spíritus for eighteen or nineteen years and was married to an Indigenous woman; they had three children. Alonso de Reyna was not married but had a little girl, very likely mestiza. Miguel de Ranay, who had lived altogether for fifteen years in either Trinidad or Sancti Spíritus, said he recently had married an Indigenous woman. Jorge Velázquez described his wife as "a woman of this country, daughter of a Spaniard." Their only child had died. Alonso de Cepeda had a daughter with his Indigenous wife, who herself had married and had a little boy. Juan Rodríguez de Córdoba's Indigenous wife had died, leaving a daughter who had married in the town. He also had two "bastard sons," presumably also mestizo. Sebastián de la Fuente also had a daughter with his Indigenous wife, and she too had married locally. Alonso de Oviedo, who was a regidor, also was married to "a woman who is Native of this country, daughter of a Spaniard," with whom he had a little girl; in addition, he had another illegitimate daughter. The wealthiest local vecino, Vasco Porcallo de Figueroa, never married but had several mestizo children, probably by more than one Indigenous woman. Within a generation or two of their founding, then, the populations of these small towns had become notably mixed.

Marriages between Spanish men and Indigenous women could foster novel relationships, as seen in the arrangements that Juan Millán tried to make on behalf of his Indigenous wife's relatives and other Indians. Millán, who owned an estancia near Santiago in Cuba, declared in 1536 that he wanted to leave the island with his wife and family. Before leaving, however, Millán sought to make arrangements for eight of his naborías, among whom there was one named Alonso, who was his wife's nephew. Alonso and his wife were practicing Christians who worked a piece of land and lived on their own. Millán petitioned the king, asking that Alonso and his wife be allowed to remain free, along with the other naborías "in his company." The king agreed and stipulated that Alonso and his wife would remain free as long as they provided to the crown the tribute or "moderate service" required, and that the other naborías could stay with them, possibly salvaging something of their original kin group or community.

There was a specific reason why Millán sought a formal royal order to protect his wife's relatives. A Spaniard named Bernardo de Quesada and other men were treating "certain Indians, relatives of my wife, being free," as if they were slaves. The king instructed the bishop of Cuba that they should be allowed to remain free if they paid the required tributes. Millán, then, was trying to ensure that if he left Cuba, his wife's people would receive some protection and guarantee of their freedom and could continue to live and work together. Millán also intervened on behalf of one of his Indians, named García, "who said that if he could marry, he would be a very good Christian." He asked for permission to marry whomever he wanted as long as she was not a slave. Millán said he would provide him a farm and a house in which to live.[88]

Notwithstanding the almost unavoidable assumption that most relationships between Spanish men and Indigenous women were coercive in some (or large) measure, Millán's efforts on behalf of his Indigenous wife's kin betoken a marriage based on feelings of affection and obligation, which must have existed in some instances. Perhaps another such case was that of Martín de Solís, a vecino of Santo Domingo, who in 1517 obtained a license to bring a "moza india" named Catalina Bastidas with him to Spain. She had been raised in his house and brought up among his own children. He wanted to take her to Spain because she was "a good woman and to better instruct her."[89]

The informality and frequently ephemeral nature of relationships between Spanish men and Indigenous women could result in siblings who shared only a father. García de Alquívar, vecino of Buenaventura in Hispaniola, received a license in 1515 to take his sons Rodrigo and Pedro, whom he had with two Indian women, Beatriz and María, to Spain. A man named Pedro Fernández Bermejo, originally from the Montes de Toledo, made his will in October 1527 in an inn on the highway to Seville. He said he had been married to "Guiomar, india, natural de [Native of] la isla Cuba," by then deceased, and left as his heirs two sons by different women in Cuba, whom he had fathered while still single. Pedro was his *hijo natural* by a Cuban Indian woman named Leonor, and the other son was Pedro Bermejo, whom he had with Juana de Antón Martín, who might have been Spanish or mestiza herself.[90]

Family and Children in a Multiethnic Society

Notwithstanding the growing numbers of mixed progeny from Spanish–Indigenous marriages and nonmarital unions, the term *mestizo* almost never appears in the documents of this period. Francisco de Barrionuevo, who lived for many years in Puerto Rico, Hispaniola, and later Tierra Firme, went to Santo Domingo tasked with trying to end the prolonged "rebellion" of Enrique. In a letter to the king in August 1533, he complained about the poor character of the mestizos on the island, calling them "badly inclined... naturally turbulent and mendacious and friends of any evil." He suggested that they were liable at any time to rebel, along with Indians and Blacks. He suggested that they—or at least children eight years old and younger—should be sent to Spain, where they would learn to live as good Christians, and then return to the island. It is unlikely that anyone in either Castile or Hispaniola took his proposal seriously. It should be noted that Barrionuevo married a wealthy mestiza heiress, doña Elvira Manzorro, when she traveled to Spain with her father.[91]

The situation and treatment of mestizo children varied considerably depending on the domestic arrangements of the parents—and often on the wealth and status of Spanish fathers. Catalina Sedeño was the daughter of Antonio Sedeño and an Indian woman named Madalena, whom Sedeño claimed they had conceived when both were single.[92] When Sedeño died, he left Catalina an enslaved Black woman named Isabel, who was to be part of her dowry, along with other items. A man named Martín Ventura had taken Isabel and refused to hand her over to Catalina.[93]

Francisco Marmolejo also must have been recognized by his father, Alvar Hernández Marmolejo, a vecino of Seville, who conceived him with "una india natural de Española" (an Indian woman native to Hispaniola). Francisco Marmolejo asked permission to sell his property in Hispaniola in order to remain in Seville where he was a vecino, because in the island he had been very ill.[94]

Hernando de Isla was a vecino of San Germán in Puerto Rico whose daughter by an Indian woman was only five years old when he died. In 1526 his cousin Juan de Isla, a *jurado* (member of the city council) of Seville, petitioned the crown, saying that Hernando had made his daughter his universal heir "by word and in front of witnesses," appointing Vasco de Tiedra and another unnamed vecino executors of his will. Tiedra apparently had persuaded an alcalde ordinario to name him her tutor and guardian, allowing him to benefit from her possessions rather than administering them for her, "nor is the said minor well treated." Juan de Isla asked that local officials be instructed to see that Vasco de Tiedra administer her inheritance properly and treat her well. He did not send for her, however.[95]

A number of mestizo children ended up in Spain, often removed from their Indigenous mothers and taken or sent there by Spanish fathers or other relatives or guardians.[96] They appear in the records because, until 1524, the crown did not permit mestizos to travel to Spain without special license.[97] In 1513 Juan García Caballero received a license to bring to Spain the two sons he had by "una india" in Hispaniola. Two sons of Violante Velázquez, a vecina of Cuéllar, died as they were returning to Spain from Cuba, leaving her as their universal heir. One of her sons had ordered that the "hijos naturales que tenía pequeños" (his young illegitimate children) be brought to Spain to live with their grandmother, along with all their property.[98] Juan Calvillo, who in 1535 had lived in Cuba for fourteen years, said that he had a six-year-old daughter with an Indian woman who was "single and free." He wished to take or send the daughter to Spain to live with his mother and siblings so that his mother "would instruct her in the things of our holy faith."[99] A vecino of Puerto Rico named Juan Pérez de Ramales said in 1541 that he had in his care the nine-year-old son of Martín de Orellana, who had died. He wanted permission to bring the boy to Spain, with his property, so that he could live with his relatives there. Mari Saez de Limpias, a vecina of Segovia, sought to bring her nephew, whom her brother Juan de Limpias, who had died in San Juan, had fathered with an Indian woman. As her brother's heir, she wanted to bring the six-year-old boy "to raise him and make him my heir because of having no children" and planned to send someone to the island to get him.[100] In none of these examples do the records indicate whether the mothers of these children were alive or how they were to be persuaded or forced to surrender them.

In some instances, however, efforts were made to keep children with their mothers. García de Matienzo, a vecino of Puerto Rico, said that he owned an Indian slave named Francisca who had a son who was free. The son apparently had traveled to Spain with his aunt, and Matienzo wanted to take Francisca with him to Spain as well. He received permission to bring her, if she agreed to go. Teresa de Aldana, a vecina of Alcántara in Extremadura, hoped to bring her granddaughter, the child of her son Lucas de Sayavedra with an Indian woman, together with the girl's mother, to Spain. She too received permission to arrange to have her granddaughter's mother accompany her, if the woman was willing.[101] When García de Valero received permission to bring his daughter with an Indigenous woman to Spain, the girl's mother, Luisa, petitioned to be allowed to go with her daughter "to raise her and look out for her on the voyage and live in those kingdoms in her company."[102]

The existence of children conceived outside of marriage by men who had wives or other heirs in Spain could create legal complications. In one instance a Spanish woman named Pasquala Pérez stated that her husband, Juan de Soria, had gone to Cuba and lived there for many years before dying around 1523. She claimed, in 1532, that he had left as heirs his brother Juan Escribano and a "bastard son of his who he had with an Indian woman" and that she was entitled to half of the inheritance. From the Cuban perspective, the situation appeared to be quite different, however. A Juan de Soria claimed to be the son of Juan de Soria, who had been a vecino of San Salvador de Bayamo, and stated that his father had made him and his brother Pedro de Soria, his sons with "doña María, both being single and free," his universal heirs. Juan de Soria's brother Pedro had died, meaning that by the terms of their father's will, he would inherit the property his father had left in San Salvador, "up to 2,000 ducados," which he had not yet received. Further complicating this murky picture, Juan de Soria also stated that his mother, doña María, wanted to travel to Spain, bringing with her "his brother, son of another husband." They received permission to go to Spain and to bring their property with them.[103]

This situation certainly raises questions. If Juan de Soria had indeed married Pasquala Pérez before leaving Spain, how could his son claim that his father was "single and free" when he conceived his sons in Cuba? Who was doña María? Was she Indigenous? If she had married after Soria's death, why did she want to leave Cuba to bring her son to Spain? The records do not answer these questions. In 1535 Juan de Soria received a license to return to Santo Domingo.[104]

It was not uncommon for Spaniards in the islands to have no legitimate children to inherit what they left. A priest named Diego Mejía and his brother Gonzalo Mejía, residents of the town of Ribera, which belonged to the Order of Santiago, in 1531 wanted to bring their eight-year-old nephew, Diego, to live with them in Ribera. Their brother García, the boy's father, had died, making Diego his universal heir.[105] Francisco de Ávila, who had lived in Hispaniola since 1508, served in various official positions, and amassed substantial properties, asked for royal permission in 1541 to create a mayorazgo for his hijo natural, Pedro de Ávila.[106] In neither case is it known whether the boys were mestizos, but in all likelihood they were.

The experiences of Spanish women in the Greater Antilles varied considerably, as suggested by the lives of the three women, coincidentally all named Isabel, highlighted here. Two of them—doña Isabel de Maraver and doña Isabel Núñez de Andrada—emigrated to Hispaniola at a young age, with their families or members of their families. Although the third, Isabel de Mayorga, perhaps never went to Hispaniola despite the persistent efforts of her husband (and his friends and acquaintances) to convince her to join him, their stories unfolded during the same years.

The two Isabels who lived out their lives in Santo Domingo almost certainly would have known each other, although the economic difficulties that Isabel de Maraver and her family faced, notwithstanding their relatively high social status in Castile, probably meant that the two women did not move in the same social circles. Doña Isabel Núñez's status as one of the virreina's ladies and the niece of Diego Colón's tutor and trusted advisor, Jerónimo de Agüero, together with her marriage to the well-placed and wealthy Lope de Bardecí, guaranteed her a place in the highest ranks of Santo Domingo society.[107]

Not all Spanish women who went to or were born in the islands during this period enjoyed such assurance of status and wealth, but many lived well enough. A small number exercised administrative duties and wielded power. The virreina doña María de Toledo, for instance, acted in the name of her young son Luis Colón during his minority, and doña Isabel de Bobadilla served as governor of Cuba in the absence of her husband, the adelantado Hernando de Soto. By virtue of the capitulación that her father, the oidor Marcelo Villalobos, obtained for the settlement of Isla Margarita in 1525, his eldest daughter, doña Aldonza de Villalobos, became *gobernadora* of the island following his death two years later. She was just seven years old, and her mother, doña Isabel Manrique, received authority to govern until doña Aldonza came of age or married.[108]

Below that level, however, many other Spanish women avoided the poverty into which Isabel de Maraver and her household sank, and they probably lived reasonably comfortable lives. Indeed, one observer complained, "In this city [Santo Domingo] there isn't a shoemaker or other tradesman who doesn't have his wife and children covered with silk, and all of them on mules.... In this city alone there are two hundred mules with velvet bridles and cloth coverings."[109]

At the other end of the socioeconomic spectrum were the many women who traveled to the Caribbean as servants or slaves. The contador of Cuba, Pedro de Paz, received permission in January 1536 to take with him to the island "two white slaves," and his daughter doña María a *mulata* slave, provided they were already Christian and at least twelve years old. He had brought with him from Cuba two Black slaves, María and Francisca, whom he was ordered to take or send back to the island.[110]

Unmarried or widowed women who emigrated might have been particularly subject not only to mistreatment but also to accusations of immorality or sin. The protection that the cleric Álvaro de Castro offered the beata Beatriz de Salas after she arrived in Hispaniola with her daughter and son-in-law proved treacherous, and his inappropriate attentions to her daughter destroyed what little family she had. Elvira Pinelo faced accusations of being a procurer and a witch during the residencia of Licenciado Sancho Velázquez in Puerto Rico, although Velázquez claimed she was a baker and pastry maker.[111] And, as mentioned in chapter 4, Ana de Ribera suffered at the hands of the Inquisition brutal punishment that many vecinos thought was unjustified.

If in these societies women who did not enjoy the protections of male relatives, employers, or other patrons were especially vulnerable to abuse, no one was more at risk of sexual exploitation and violence than the nonwhite women of the Greater Antilles, especially enslaved women. The extent to which they commonly suffered the sexual predations of men is reflected in an ordinance of 1544 stipulating that "anyone who keeps a slave or Indian woman for an entire day or night away from the house of her owner, if that person is of low status, he will receive one hundred lashes, and if it were a maestre or someone of higher status, he would pay 20 pesos of gold; and if by day or night she is taken forcibly to use her basely, he will be fined according to the law regarding the rape of women."[112]

The lives of Indigenous and Black women, for the most part, can be discerned only indirectly. As discussed here, some Indigenous women surrendered their children to their Spanish fathers, probably having little choice but to comply. Indian women who married Spanish men at least had the advantage of raising their children and perhaps remaining where (or close to where) they themselves had grown up; but they at times might have had little choice in their marriage partners. In Puerto Rico's hacienda de Toa community the cacica doña María, who succeeded her uncle Caguas at his death, married Diego Muriel, the former mayordomo and eventual owner of the hacienda; the agreement stipulated that the Indians would be "commended" to Muriel if they married. The bishop of Santo Domingo, Sebastián Ramírez de Fuenleal, arranged the marriage, saying that doña María had no other source of protection.[113]

A notable aspect of the situation of Indigenous women after Europeans arrived in the Caribbean was the sharp increase in the number of women chiefs, or cacicas. Whether women chiefs existed in the Greater Antilles before contact continues to be debated, and it is unlikely that either documentary or archaeological evidence will emerge to settle the issue. The growing numbers of cacicas in the postcontact years may have hinged on declining numbers of caciques, who had been the particular targets of early military campaigns in Hispaniola, or of Spanish preferences for dealing with women chiefs, or both. Nearly thirty cacicas appear in the Repartimiento of 1514 in Hispaniola, with the greatest concentration in the region of Higüey, which experienced extensive early conflict. However, apart from Anacaona, the famous wife of Caonabo, a leading cacique, and sister to Behecchio, whom she might have succeeded as ruler of the rich province of Xaraguá, there are few indications that cacicas exercised any real authority, which possibly, for Spaniards, was the point.[114]

The lives of Black women in the islands during this period are possibly even more opaque than those of Indigenous women. A complaint of 1542 regarding robberies routinely perpetrated by Black men, some gains of which went to pay their owners and some to purchase their own shoes and clothing, included the intriguing allegation that two or three hundred Black women in Santo Domingo, known as *ganadoras,* sold the stolen items in the city and all over the island.[115] It would be useful to know whether these women were enslaved, free, or a mixture of the two, as there is little information from the period about manumission or the presence of free people of African descent.[116]

Not only are the lives of non-European women largely inaccessible to us but also the nature of relationships across ethnicities can be difficult to discern.

The 1530 will of Pedro de Vadillo, a vecino of San Juan de la Maguana in Hispaniola and cousin to the oidor Licenciado Juan de Vadillo, reveals that many of the ties he formed on an individual basis in Hispaniola crossed ethnic lines. Vadillo had inherited 130 pesos of gold from an Indian woman named Teresa, wife of Juan de Paredes; he in turn ordered that masses be said for her soul and that of her father, the cacique Gómez, and that indulgences be purchased for her and her parents. He left 50 pesos to Juanico Negrillo, the "son of the Indian Teresa, whom I brought up," and stipulated that the freedom of an Indian slave named Juanica be purchased and that she receive 30 pesos as a dowry. The mestiza Elena and María, daughter of the cacique Luis, were to receive 100 pesos and 50 pesos, respectively, for their dowries. He left 100 pesos for the "bastard mestiza daughter" of his friend Juan Fernández, Isabel de las Varas, to marry or enter a convent, and 100 pesos to the daughter of his naboría Teresa and Diego de Jaen (probably also mestiza) if she would stay in San Juan de la Maguana, and 25 pesos if she left.[117]

Vadillo's bequests suggest ties of affection and mutual obligation that crossed ethnic and class lines but probably did not reflect any special empathy with the situation of the island's Indians. His understanding of the gulf that separated Europeans from the island's Indigenous, Black, or mixed-race majority most likely remained strongly colored by assumptions of European superiority. Many Spaniards, especially people from the southern part of the Iberian Peninsula, had worked and lived near or with slaves from Africa or the Canary Islands, Muslim captives, and converted Muslims and Jews. The racially diverse households and cross-ethnic fictive and actual kinship ties that emerged in the Caribbean, therefore, might have been less radically distinct from what Spaniards knew from home than is often assumed.

The demographic realities of the Greater Antilles, however, were quite different. At least initially, Indigenous peoples far outnumbered Europeans, and within a few decades African, African-descended, and mixed-race people would do the same. Spaniards always constituted a minority within Caribbean populations, and as a result they established a regime based on coercion. Their ascendancy left non-European women particularly vulnerable to sexual violence and predation and to the forfeiture of their children.

Ties of domesticity and affection that formed among people who were mutually dependent and living in close contact, as seen in the eclectic household of Isabel de Maraver, at times may have mitigated the extremes of exploitation and inequality, but they might not have been the norm. The first repartimientos assigned in Hispaniola formalized the practice by which some Spaniards inserted themselves into Indigenous households and kinship networks, thus gaining access to Indigenous labor and resources. There are indications, as seen in Juan Millán's relations with the naborías who actually were his Indigenous wife's relatives, that these earlier relationships continued to affect the nature of encomiendas, although probably only in a minority of cases.

After the death of his mestiza wife, doña Elvira Manzorro, Francisco de Barrionuevo petitioned to retain her encomienda, arguing that the eighteen or twenty naborías were her relatives. Doña Elvira also was named the main heir to the property of a Spaniard named Francisco de Teca, further underscoring the complex interethnic relationships that took shape in the earliest years in Hispaniola.[118] In 1538 the widow of oidor Marcelo de Villalobos, doña Isabel Manrique, stated that when her husband died, the four or five Indians who remained in their encomienda had been "raised and born in his house, and the two women were married, one to a Christian Spaniard and the other to an Indian, who now live in . . . freedom, and the other three or four, although they wanted to let them go, they did not want to leave because they had been brought up in their house and [their] having given them there everything they need and if they were to leave they would be lost and some people might brand them as slaves."[119] After several decades of rampant exploitation and devastating mortality, some survivors clung to what remained of familial ties, even across ethnic lines, in the vastly altered world of the Greater Antilles.

Conclusion

CARIBBEAN CONNECTIONS

Looking at the formation of society on the four large islands of the Greater Antilles—Hispaniola, Cuba, Puerto Rico, and Jamaica—from the time Europeans arrived in the early 1490s up to around the middle of the sixteenth century, highlights the connections that bound them, as well as their differences and similarities. The most obvious differences, of course, were in timing. During the decade and a half following Columbus's second voyage, Spaniards focused their efforts on Hispaniola while they continued to reconnoiter the Caribbean and surrounding littoral.

Even after Spaniards began to extend their control over the other large islands, starting in 1508, Hispaniola's early precedence endured. In the first half of the sixteenth century, Santo Domingo was the main seat of government for the region and eventually for an archbishopric, as well as its principal port. The island maintained the largest European population throughout the period, produced the greatest yields of gold, had the most sugar ingenios and largest herds of cattle, and imported the highest numbers of African slaves, and most likely of Indigenous slaves as well. Santo Domingo's cabildo boasted of its primacy, writing to the king in 1537, "Being this island Hispaniola the mother head of everything here and whence it has been discovered and populated and maintained, all of this ocean sea and where Your Majesty has placed his royal audiencia and chancellery, and being the port and gateway of this New World and the strength and defense of the Indies, and where the trade and commerce is for all of them and by whose ordinances and customs all the rest is ruled and governed."[1]

Socioeconomically and politically, the other islands developed along much the same lines as Hispaniola, but later and on a more modest scale.[2] Jamaica was exceptional in that it lacked gold mines and as a result attracted smaller numbers of potential settlers, although the crown must have thought that it had some value as a source of provisions, because it did not declare Jamaica "useless," nor did it make the island a target for slave raiding. Instead, the king turned it over to the third admiral, Luis Colón.

Although the connections between Hispaniola and Puerto Rico, especially in the earliest years, were particularly strong, each of the islands developed in ways that reflected differences in Indigenous cultures and population sizes, topography, resources, location, access to trade routes and other ports, royal ordinances, numbers of Europeans and Africans, and rates of Indigenous population decline and introduction of captive Indian slaves or servants from elsewhere. The result was the formation of a set of closely interrelated but distinctive island societies with their own elites, sets of officials, class struggles, personal and political rivalries, patterns of interaction with Indigenous and African-descended peoples, and ecclesiastical establishments.

The diversity of early Spanish Caribbean societies ensured that in nearly all settings, from Spanish-headed households to mines, ingenios, farms, and ranches, people of European, African, Indigenous and, increasingly, mixed origins lived and worked in close proximity in both towns and countryside. For many Spaniards, ties to home remained strong and active, and some people traveled back and forth across the Atlantic frequently. Italians, Germans, and Portuguese joined Spanish merchants and settlers in the Caribbean.

The connections among the islands, and between the islands and the neighboring mainland, fostered constant movement, which provided some coherence to the region as a whole. Indigenous slaves from Honduras, Mexico, Tierra Firme, and Yucatan who were captured and sold, or acquired in exchange for cattle and mares from the islands, arrived in large numbers. Although the great majority of slaves brought from across the Atlantic were of African origin, in the early years they often arrived from Castile or Portugal and were joined by much smaller but still perceptible numbers of "white slaves" of Muslim (probably Iberian) origin. From the time that Europeans arrived, bringing their ambitions and biases along with their livestock, material culture, church, and diseases, the new societies that took shape in the islands were diverse, complex, and dynamic.

Given its geographic location and institutional predominance in this era, Hispaniola acted as the hub of the Greater Antilles. Not only did the entradas that led to the occupation of the other islands originate there but also the movement of people—Spaniards and Indians alike—and goods among the islands tended to center on Hispaniola. When Miguel Díaz de Aux left Hispaniola for Puerto Rico in 1511, he sought and received permission to bring with him his Indigenous and Black slaves, along with "cassava bread and corn, pigs, cows, dogs."[3] Encomenderos and miners in the southeastern region of Higüey in Hispaniola took their workers and slaves to labor in the gold mines in Puerto Rico.

The people who lived in the Caribbean before Europeans arrived moved readily from island to island, forging and maintaining connections among them, and this movement did not cease following contact. In 1515 the king instructed the lieutenant governor of Cuba, Diego Velázquez, to return to Hispaniola the "Indians and naborías who went with Hatuey, who was the leader who went there." Velázquez demurred, responding that they were all "rooted in the land, which they consider to be their home [la tiene por su natural], and they are all married with principal women, and they [the women] with principal men of this land [Cuba], and they have children and grandchildren"; they should be allowed to stay where they were. The king at the same time instructed Velázquez to send "certain caciques and Indians who killed some Spanish Christians who came from Castilla de Oro" to Hispaniola to be punished.[4] The voluntary and involuntary relocation of Indians from one island to the other continued throughout the period. In April 1542 the crown noted that during the two previous years, the third admiral, don Luis Colón, had taken twenty-two free Indians from Jamaica and brought them to Santo Domingo as slaves to work as pearl divers. The king instructed that they be taken from the admiral and freed.[5]

Spaniards, especially officials, moved from one island to another or to the nearby mainland. Audiencia officials conducted residencias on other islands or in Panama or Tierra Firme, and men participated in entradas and returned with captive slaves to sell, or instead met their end at the hands of hostile Indians, as did Juan Ponce de León and Lucas Vázquez de Ayllón in Florida, or even of rival Spaniards, as did don Rodrigo de Bastidas. For the most part, however, apart from becoming involved in trade (which nearly everyone did, in one way or another), most Spaniards on an individual basis focused their economic efforts on a single island rather than attempting to maintain enterprises in more than one. Even on a particular island the majority probably confined their economic activities primarily to one locale, much as was true in Spain itself. Diego and Hernando Colón and Miguel de Pasamonte, all encomenderos on Hispaniola, also acquired encomiendas on early Puerto Rico, but that was not the norm.⁶

The careers of officials below the level of the audiencia judges also could take them from one island to another or to the mainland and back. In 1519 Licenciado Antonio de la Gama accepted appointment as *juez de residencia* for San Juan in place of his father, who declined the commission, saying he was too elderly and ill to undertake it. The following year de la Gama married Isabel, the daughter of Juan Ponce de León. After her early death, he married Isabel de Cáceres, the wealthy widow of Miguel Díaz de Aux and a vecina of San Germán. They went to Panama, where de la Gama conducted the residencia of the governor, Pedro de los Ríos, whom he succeeded as governor of Castilla de Oro. From there, his career took him to Peru, then back to Panama to serve on the newly created audiencia, and then again to Peru with Licenciado Pedro de la Gasca, the designated president of the audiencia in Lima. He died in Peru some time before 1555.⁷ Francisco de Barrionuevo pursued a multilocal career in Puerto Rico, Hispaniola, Tierra Firme, and Panama and returned to Spain at least twice. Chronicler Gonzalo Fernández de Oviedo served the crown for a number of years in Panama before settling in Santo Domingo as the warden of the city's fortress, where he died in 1557.

Not all travel within the region was officially sanctioned. People sometimes attempted to evade officials or creditors by fleeing one locale for another. The lieutenant governor and accountant of Nicaragua, Licenciado Castañeda, in 1537 fled to La Yaguana in Hispaniola to avoid Rodrigo de Contreras, the newly appointed governor of Nicaragua, who was to conduct the residencia of his term in office.⁸ Hernando de Soto's long-term partner, Hernán Ponce de León, avoided settling business affairs with Soto's representative in Panama, but ironically, when he tried to depart for Spain, a storm forced him to land in Cuba. There Soto's wife, doña Isabel de Bobadilla, awaited.⁹

Peru's wealth and the turbulent early years that followed the capitulation of the Inca emperor Atahuallpa resonated strongly in the islands. In 1537 Santo Domingo's audiencia responded to a plea from the bishop of Tierra Firme to provide aid because of the turmoil caused by "uprisings of the Natives" in Peru, dispatching the brother of audiencia president and bishop Fuenmayor, Diego de Fuenmayor, with 150 men and seventy horses and sending, in another three ships, an equal number of men and 120 horses to Panama, whence they would go to Peru.¹⁰

Ten years later, officials in the islands again responded to reports of trouble in Peru, in this case news of Gonzalo Pizarro's rebellion. In June 1547, Santo Domingo's cabildo reported having sent 180 men to aid President la Gasca, a force that included one hundred arquebusiers, twenty gunners, and sixty horsemen. Another two hundred men "of the sea and land" joined them, likely determined to reach Peru in hopes of benefiting from the suppression of the rebellion. They received 500 castellanos in aid. The cabildo sent an additional thirty-eight horses worth 1,440 pesos and seventy-four pack mules that cost 1,450 pesos, along with five Black slaves at the cost of 440 pesos to care for them. Individual participants took with them another 180 horses and mules. In addition, officials in Hispaniola provided forty arrobas of gunpowder, 180 arquebuses, and other arms. All in all, this was a major expedition that included a large ship and five caravels provisioned with biscuit, yucca, corn, wine, meat, oil, and vinegar. The report did not note whether the expeditionary force included Indians or Blacks (apart from those designated to care for the animals), although it is difficult to imagine that it did not.

The audiencia ordered royal officials in Puerto Rico to provide 5,000 pesos to underwrite the relief expedition and received from them 2,000 pesos in reales, but the remainder, which was supposed to be delivered in gold, had not arrived by the time the expedition was dispatched. Officials in Cabo de la Vela (on the Caribbean coast of what today is Colombia) sent four boxes containing 600 marcos of pearls, which arrived at Hispaniola's port of La Yaguana. The total estimated costs of the expedition topped 12,000 pesos, and officials in Hispaniola were forced to cover a shortfall in funds by borrowing from the bienes de difuntos.[11]

As the expedition was about to leave, President la Gasca's handpicked leader, captain Felipe Boscan, died suddenly and was replaced by Diego Caballero, brother of the accountant Álvaro Caballero, who had been the company's *alférez* (ensign). The fleet was set to depart on May 11, with admiral don Luis Colón as its general, but bad weather forced a delay. The ships left the next morning with an unexpected additional passenger, Colón's wife, the *duquesa*. In the end, the expedition went no farther than Panama, as la Gasca sent word that he needed no additional aid. On the way back to Hispaniola, Colón and the expeditionary party struggled with illness and French corsairs, which delayed their return for some weeks.[12]

The close and continuing ties between the Greater Antilles and Spain figure throughout this history. They linked people in the Caribbean with their

Iberian hometowns, relatives, and friends as well as with the court, conveying letters, petitions, and royal responses along with streams of royal ordinances and official reports, bringing staples and luxuries to the islands in exchange for gold, pearls, sugar, therapeutic drugs, and leather hides. The traffic of goods and people between Spain, the Canaries, and the Caribbean was such that residents in the islands had little difficulty finding relatives or acquaintances from home to testify on their behalf when necessary; indeed, they frequently went to the Caribbean in the company of people from home.

A relative of Juan Ponce de León, Juan González Ponce de León, who claimed to have acted as his kinsman's interpreter in early forays to Puerto Rico, including a possibly apocryphal expedition that supposedly went to the island in 1506, prepared a deposition in Mexico City in 1532.[13] He had gone to New Spain with Pánfilo de Narvaéz twelve years earlier. His witnesses included several lifelong companions. Francisco Rodríguez testified that he had known Juan González for more than fifty years, first as his next-door neighbor in Seville, then in Hispaniola, Puerto Rico, and Mexico, and had served his parents as criado because his own parents were poor. Lucas Gallego also had been the criado of Juan González's parents and had helped to raise him until he was twelve or thirteen years old. Gallego, who was around sixty-five years old when he testified, said that he had been in Tierra Firme with Juan de la Cosa and had returned to Santo Domingo when the expedition was preparing to go to San Juan. Although he was unwell, when Juan González begged him to go with him, he "couldn't tell him no"; subsequently, he also accompanied González to New Spain. Gonzalo Suárez also was a close neighbor and friend in Seville; he and González had grown up and gone to school together.[14]

When Bachiller Juan Díaz, hoping to secure a position in the cathedral, prepared a deposition in Santo Domingo in 1544, several men testified that they knew him from Spain. Pedro Prieto had known Díaz for forty years; they had grown up together in San Pedro de Vegas in the jurisdiction of Ponferrada and he had known Díaz's parents and grandparents. Arias Vuelta had known his brothers. Juan Montañés knew him from his own home in the kingdom of Asturias and knew his father's brother and other relatives. Two other witnesses knew Díaz from the time he had lived in the Canaries, before he left for the Caribbean.[15]

Cleric Rodrigo Tenorio prepared a deposition in 1545. Originally from La Palma in the Canaries, witness Juan Rodríguez Gallego had seen him conduct mass in Seville, while Bartolomé Sánchez Sandoval was acquainted with Tenorio's parents, brothers, and other relatives in La Palma, having lived there himself "many times." Juan Pérez Rendón was born in La Palma and grew up with Tenorio.[16] In 1545 witnesses for Gonzalo Hernández said that they knew his parents in Zalamea de la Serena. Hernando Botello was a vecino of the town and had known Gonzalo since he was born, and Alvar Arias testified that he witnessed the marriage of Gonzalo's parents in the town of Hornachos.[17]

The careers of these men are a reminder that mobility and relocation, often several times over the course of a lifetime, were crucial to the construction and operation of Spain's empire, strengthening connections among distinct locales and reinforcing the ties of common interest or friendship that facilitated communication and the maintenance of networks of acquaintance, kinship, and economic interest over time and distance. It also should be remembered that, especially after the early gold rush years, the numbers of Spaniards in the islands at any given time were small, so it is not surprising that they would be well aware of acquaintances and kinfolk who were close at hand.

It is impossible to estimate the numbers of people who spent time in the islands during the first half of the sixteenth century, even if they did not remain there to live. Merchants and ship captains made multiple trips to the Caribbean and might live there for months at a time, as also was true for crew members, who sometimes took advantage of their stays, in the early years at least, to join in the quest for gold.[18] Among the Europeans who spent some time in the Caribbean were many non-Spaniards. Foremost were Portuguese, who often arrived as merchants or ship captains bringing cargoes of slaves from Cabo Verde or elsewhere. In 1541, for example, a vecino of Seville, Gaspar de Torres, received authorization to send to the islands 1,200 Black slaves "in Portuguese ships with Portuguese people." Portuguese ships could return with cargoes of sugar, hides, and any other merchandise they wanted, as long as they went to Seville.[19]

Probably more numerous were the Portuguese who went to the islands to settle. As early as 1502, Fernando and Isabel granted permission to four Portuguese to go to Hispaniola to live, presumably as part of the large group that accompanied governor Nicolás de Ovando.[20] In 1518, when representatives of Hispaniola's towns prepared a list of requests to be made to the crown, among them was that "Portuguese and other nations come to settle these parts, becoming citizens [*naturales*] of the kingdoms and settling permanently in this island [Hispaniola], with the exception of Genoese and French."[21] When the crown announced, in 1529, a plan to encourage the recruitment of settlers and the organization of new settlements, it welcomed Portuguese colonists alongside Spanish vecinos. It was common knowledge that the Portuguese had played an important, even leading, role in settling the Canaries. In 1541 the king noted that "the major part of them [the Canary Islands] are populated by Portuguese because most of the masters and sailors are also Portuguese, who are considered to be native because they are vecinos and natives of those islands."[22] It is no surprise, then, that both the crown and Spaniards in the islands turned to Portugal when they sought more settlers.

In April 1531 Charles V responded to a complaint from residents of Cuba that the people who had left Spain for the island or other parts of the Indies "have not had the diligence that is needed.... The Portuguese, natives of the king [sic] of Portugal or his islands could come to these islands.... Swearing perpetual vassalage and permanence in that said island, they would be given caballerías of land where they could settle and work.... For the present, we give permission and authority to any married Portuguese ... so that within six years ... they can go to that island and settle in it, taking their wives and households." The king instructed island officials to treat the Portuguese settlers "as citizens, settlers [and] natives of our kingdoms."[23]

A letter of 1535 to the Council of the Indies, referring to the Portuguese in Hispaniola, noted that "there are some married men who are vecinos, and more than two hundred single men, specialists in sugar, in the ingenios, farmers, carpenters, masons, blacksmiths, and all the trades in all the communities and they are very useful."[24] Around that time the treasurer of Jamaica, Pedro de Mazuelo, asked the crown to send thirty married Portuguese vecinos, "farmers and working people," to settle in the new town he proposed establishing.[25] As discussed in chapter 5, by around the middle of the sixteenth century and beyond the town of Montecristi on Hispaniola's northern coast had attracted a substantial number of Portuguese settlers, who possibly arrived mainly from the Canaries rather than from Portugal itself.

Given that the French nearly always arrived in the islands with hostile intent, it is not surprising that they were not welcome. The objection to the presence of the Genoese is more difficult to explain. Most of the Italians who went to the Caribbean in these years did so as merchants and merchants' factors. Some settled there and "naturalized," just as did the Portuguese. While many fewer in number than the Portuguese, they were prominent figures. The Genoese played an important role not only in the slave trade to the Caribbean but also as financiers to the crown, for expeditions, and in the establishment of the sugar industry.[26] They also provided personal loans for prominent men who were active in the early Spanish Caribbean, including Juan Ponce de León, Hernando de Soto, Gonzalo Fernández de Oviedo, and of course Columbus.[27]

Not surprisingly, some Genoese arrived with Columbus, or soon thereafter. Rafael Cataño traveled to Hispaniola as Columbus's accountant in 1493 and remained there; he was joined by his brother Juan in 1503. Cataño even received eleven naborías in the Repartimiento of 1514. The Genoese invested in sugar ingenios in Hispaniola and Puerto Rico and sent sugar to Europe in exchange for imported goods.[28] Perhaps surprisingly, given the mercantile emphasis on liquidity, some invested in real estate as well. The influential Genoese merchant/financier Bernardo Grimaldi, who formed a partnership with two Sevillians in Santo Domingo, had a house built in Santo Domingo, hiring masons and carpenters in Seville to send to Hispaniola, along with bricks.[29] Jácome Castellón built several houses in Santo Domingo that he rented out, and he purchased other urban lots there.[30] Bernardo Grimaldi's nephew Jerónimo Grimaldi formed a partnership with Jácome Castellón in 1513 to trade in salt; in 1515 they rented the Venezuelan salinas of Araya.[31]

The first English ship to reach Hispaniola arrived in Santo Domingo's harbor in November 1527, having fled cold temperatures and imminent starvation in Newfoundland, where several members of the crew perished and the ship's pilot apparently died at the hands of local people. Reports and testimony about this episode reflect, above all, surprise and uncertainty; hitherto, Englishmen barely had been present in the Caribbean. Although the ship arrived heavily armed, there is little indication that their intentions were hostile. The men were hungry and desperately in need of supplies of all kinds.

The ship's arrival occasioned much deliberation on the part of audiencia officials and other prominent vecinos, who, upon realizing that the English brought potentially desirable merchandise, seemed on the verge of working out the terms of trade, until the warden of the fort ordered a shot to be fired—in warning, or greeting, or both. The English captain feared they were in danger and hastily departed, subsequently launching a smaller boat with thirty armed men, who went ashore to commandeer water, food, and other supplies, ransacking some estates on the coast north of Santo Domingo and literally stealing the clothes off the backs of some residents.[32]

Two pilots, Antón Martín and Pedro de Montiel, and others who testified about the episode seem to have been more skeptical than the officials about English motives for sailing to Santo Domingo. Given the difficulty of locating Santo Domingo's harbor—which even Spanish pilots missed on occasion—it seemed hardly credible to them that the English ship could have ended up there serendipitously. The two pilots recounted the conversation they had with the ship's owner when they and the alguacil mayor boarded the ship, where the owner entertained them graciously. They were on the ship when the warden, Francisco de Tapia, who had been unable to obtain a clear response when he sent messengers to the audiencia officials asking them what he should do, ordered the cannon to be fired. The pilots attempted in vain to reassure the ship's owner that the shot was routine and an attack was not imminent.

The question of how these men conversed says much about the cosmopolitan nature of the maritime world of which the Spanish Caribbean quickly became a part; no one mentioned any problems in communication. Crews sailing out of Europe most likely were polyglot. The ship's captain and a couple of sailors had disembarked and were allowed to move freely around the city for a couple of days. Local residents, no doubt curious about the strangers, treated them courteously. Diego Martel testified that he had invited the two sailors to lodge with him. They explained that their ship had brought cloth to trade and that they were hoping to find someone—"a man skilled in the sea"—who could guide them back to England. The episode had no repercussions, although the king reprimanded audiencia officials for not having seized the ship.

The men who sailed on it were not the first Englishmen to reach the islands, which might explain the general lack of alarm in Santo Domingo at the ship's appearance. Starting with the reign of Henry VII, there was a good deal of trade between Spain and England, in which such Caribbean products as dyewoods, hides, and sugar figured. Several mercantile families from Bristol established themselves in Spain in the early sixteenth century, and a trader named Thomas Malliard was sending merchandise to Santo Domingo by 1509. By the 1520s some English merchants were maintaining factors in Santo Domingo, who might have been a source of information for people back in Europe. It is possible that the pilot or master of the English ship that arrived "accidentally" in 1527 knew something (or perhaps a good deal) about the Caribbean as a result of the voyages of Sebastián Cabot.[33]

Islands are distinctive spaces, simultaneously open to outside influences and to both friendly and hostile arrivals but also sharply delimited and at a remove from other places, as the words *isolated* and *insular,* both derived from the Latin for *island,* suggest. Some Spaniards in the Caribbean struggled with their distance from the metropolis, both physical and sociocultural, and continued to look to Spain for honors and concessions, even as they forged their lives and careers in a very different setting. Prominent vecinos and officials such as the brothers Melchor and Baltasar de Castro petitioned the crown for coats of arms, which would commemorate the roles they played in combating hostile Indians (Baltasar in Puerto Rico) or Blacks (Melchor in Hispaniola).[34] Hernando de Gorjón obtained the habit of the Order of Santiago in recognition of his contributions toward the establishment of a colegio and hospital in Santo Domingo. Hernando de Lepe, longtime resident of Puerto Rico, also petitioned for a coat of arms.[35] Other men aspired not only to secure honors but also to return home to enjoy them, as in the case of the mariscal Diego Caballero.

The impossibility of replicating a Spanish society in the radically distinct circumstances of the islands did not stop Spaniards from trying to maintain a European lifestyle. Certainly there were men like Antonio de Villasante, who married an Indigenous woman, learned to speak her language, and obtained valuable information about the properties of balsam from his wife and Indigenous in-laws in Hispaniola. The great majority of Europeans who worked and lived in the islands, however, apparently made little effort to learn an Indigenous language; this was even true of someone like Manuel de Rojas, who had extensive dealings with the Indians during his lengthy sojourn in Cuba. The majority of bilingual people in the islands during this period most likely were Indigenous, not Spanish. Lucas Vázquez de Ayllón, for example, mentioned two Indigenous men who lived for some time in the house of governor Ovando, Diego Colón and Alonso de Cáceres, "who were always raised with Spaniards and [were] great interpreters of the language."[36]

The non-Spanish people with whom they lived challenged and baffled Spaniards. In the Interrogatorio Jeronimiano, for example, Juan de Ampies testified that Blacks terrorized the Indians, raping women and girls and forcing them to flee to the montes. Treasurer Miguel de Pasamonte, on the other hand, expressed his concern about having Blacks on the islands, "the Indians being such good friends of theirs."[37] It seems clear that relations between Blacks and Indians varied a good deal and were largely situational, ranging from friendly interaction and cooperation to abuse and exploitation.

The records of the period provide constant reminders of the enormous gulf of incomprehension that separated Spaniards from the people they exploited and relied upon to sustain their households and enterprises. Although probably no more than a tiny minority of Indians in the islands received a formal education from the clergy, the king worried that Spaniards were taking works of popular and profane literature such as *Amadís de Gaula*, "and others of this type of deceitful stories," to the Caribbean. From this, he suggested, "would follow many difficulties because the Indians who learn to read, if they were given these, they would abandon wholesome books" that instructed them in spiritual matters. Instead, this genre of literature would induce them to adopt bad customs and vices and even cause them to suspect that Spaniards themselves had little regard for scripture and devotional writing. Although the risk surely was minor, to be on the safe side the king instructed that no Spaniards should keep such profane books at home, nor should Indians be allowed to read them. Of the many ways in which Spaniards inflicted harm on the Indians, exposing them to *Amadís de Gaula* surely ranked low on the list.[38]

How Indians or Blacks viewed Spaniards is nearly impossible to glean from the historical records. Archaeological work, however, has produced some intriguing evidence about which items that arrived with Europeans might have been of particular interest to the islands' Indigenous residents. A number of caves in the present-day Dominican Republic, for example, contain depictions of European people, animals, and objects, including ships, horses, and human figures with spades or lances.[39]

Testimonial evidence from Indigenous witnesses appears only rarely in documents of the period. Indians, however, were summoned to testify in connection with the establishment of the experiencias in Cuba and Puerto Rico in the 1520s. Although limited, the testimony in the Puerto Rican case provides some insight into how Indians responded to and viewed the regimen that Spaniards imposed on them.

The Indigenous witnesses claimed that during the years that the people laboring at the hacienda de Toa were part of an encomienda assigned to Blas de Villasante, he systematically overworked them. Two men, Perico Ogooy and Diego Bayma, stated that they had fled to the woods because of overwork and bad treatment. When they heard that Diego Muriel, who formerly had served as mayordomo and had gone to Spain to ask the crown to transfer control of the hacienda and its workers from Villasante back to him, had come back, "they returned to work because he treats them well." They said that, while they were in the monte, when they heard the cannon shots announcing the arrival of ships, they would go to the estancia to see whether Muriel had returned. The Indigenous witnesses claimed that people died from overwork and that Villasante forced them to work even when they were ill, saying, "It's nothing."[40]

The Spanish witnesses, neighbors who lived close to the hacienda de Toa and were familiar with it and its people, confirmed what Diego and Perico had said regarding the poor treatment they had received at Villasante's hands. Juan Cancer testified that when Muriel was in charge, he did not force the Indians to work more than they wished but would reward those who worked extra. He noted also that the location of the Indians' bohíos was "very sickly and unhealthy," which accorded with the Indians' claim that they would be better off if they were relocated to the hill where a corral for the hogs had been built. Cancer's brother Baltasar also thought that the bohíos should be moved to the higher site, where it was "mas airoso y vistoso" (airier and brighter). An estanciero named Jerónimo Gallardo who worked nearby claimed that he had helped to bury some of the Indians who died at Toa and that they were among the best and youngest workers. Toa's Black swineherd, Diego Pérez, also believed that Villasante's bad treatment was responsible for many deaths.[41]

The Indians' testimony, confirmed in every detail by their Spanish neighbors, reflects their awareness of differences among the Spaniards with whom they had to deal and what they understood to be the norms regarding their treatment. They knew that the food and clothing they received was of the worst quality and probably inadequate in quantity and that they were not supposed to be forced to work into the night or when they were ill. In addition the testimony of local Spaniards, mostly estancieros, suggests that they were acquainted with many of the Indians on an individual basis and were well aware of conditions and changes at the hacienda de Toa.

The kind of mundane interaction among Spaniards and Indians that the testimony suggests might have fostered, at least in some situations, less aggressively exploitative relations, and perhaps a degree of mutual accommodation. The fact that the young Indian men who fled the hacienda to escape Villasante's harsh regimen returned upon learning of Muriel's return, together with Muriel's tempering of labor demands, suggests that at least some Indians and Spaniards thought an accommodation could be made. While the devastating mortality that destroyed the people laboring at Toa by the early 1530s eliminated any possibility that a different type of relationship could take hold and endure, perhaps it might have done so had the Indians survived in sufficient numbers to maintain their communities.

Neither Indigenous people nor their way of life disappeared entirely from the Greater Antilles, although by the middle of the sixteenth century their survival and the strength of their presence varied considerably. Yet the undermining and destruction of their communities and of Indigenous leadership, with all that implied for the fracturing of sociopolitical organization and the disruption of daily life, meant that the Indians lost a basic and crucial instrument that might have allowed them to deal collectively—and perhaps more effectively— with their Spanish overlords.

The outcome of Enrique's famous revolt is worth considering in this regard. Spanish officials ultimately negotiated and signed a treaty with Enrique, the only such agreement made with an Indigenous group in the first half of the sixteenth century and well beyond. This was done largely for practical reasons, given the great expense the Spaniards had incurred in organizing and equipping patrols to find and destroy the rebellion over the course of many years. It is also likely that Enrique's success in negotiating a treaty hinged in some measure on the size and cohesion of the community of several hundred people he led, which observers described as being tightly under his control.

Subsequently, Spanish authorities would conclude similar agreements with groups of Black maroons who formed autonomous communities in the Caribbean and elsewhere in Spanish America, but not with Indigenous groups. This difference in treatment may suggest that, once the Native communities of the large islands no longer functioned effectively as collective entities, they lost any leverage in dealing with Spaniards. The result in the Greater Antilles was not so much the erasure of Indigenous lives and ways as their increasing integration into a racially mixed and largely rural population that existed at some remove from the Hispanic societies of the towns.

If the Indians saw their sovereignty and freedom of movement and choice quickly erode after Europeans began to establish themselves in the islands, the Caribbean, in contrast, at least initially offered considerable latitude for ambitious Spaniards who enjoyed advantages—good connections, skills, favorable timing—that helped them to get a start. Within Spanish society, perhaps no one exemplifies more fully both the possibilities of the islands and their distance (and difference) from the Iberian society of Europe than Bachiller

Álvaro de Castro. He appears throughout this book in many guises—as a high-ranking and hard-working ecclesiastic, as a successful entrepreneur with multiple economic interests, and as a generous patron of the church. Yet he also readily resorted to violence to punish and intimidate other Spaniards, quarreled with his fellow clerics, seduced vulnerable women, and so severely injured his young Indigenous ward, Catalina, whom he had impregnated, that both she and her unborn baby died. The distinctive juncture of law, the church, criminality, and economic opportunism that characterized Castro's career permeated Spanish society in the Greater Antilles. Their convergence and interaction allowed men like Castro, whose credentials were dubious at best, or Benito de Astorga, who got his start in Hispaniola as a lowly shopkeeper, to respond to the opportunities offered by settling in the islands and to flourish.

Although, as in Spain itself, Europeans in the Caribbean were split between a wealthy and well-connected minority and much larger numbers of people who often struggled to find their way in these new societies, the socioeconomic divisions and patterns that emerged within Spanish society in the early Greater Antilles in some ways were quite distinct from those of Iberia. These differences were reflected in everything from the improbable leadership of Columbus, a non-Spaniard with a maritime and commercial background, to the outsize influence of officials like treasurer Miguel de Pasamonte or audiencia secretary Diego Caballero, whose political power hinged not on their social status but on their connections and economic success, their heavy reliance on the labor of Indians and Africans in their households and in nearly all their economic enterprises, and the marriage alliances forged between Spanish men and Indigenous or mestiza women. Spaniards in the Caribbean also adopted and adapted to new foods, drugs, housing styles, and modes of transport.

With few exceptions (such as the virreina doña María de Toledo), Spain's high-ranking nobles did not participate in settling or governing the islands, nor did they play a role there in the early sixteenth century. With the establishment of the encomienda, the Spanish crown instead found the means to reward those whom it wished to favor by providing access to Indigenous labor. This concession allowed the recipients to develop the economic enterprises that would ensure the success and profitability of the crown's new possessions, without delegating too much authority to a group that might challenge or dilute the crown's power. The crown further stymied the rise of potential rival power bases in the Caribbean by placing its own officials on municipal councils, by interceding at moments of contention through the appointment of special judges or other officials to conduct special inquiries (pesquisas) or routine investigations (residencias), and by concentrating decision-making authority in the hands of the Council of the Indies. Although the Spanish enterprise in the Caribbean often is pictured as a failed experiment, in fact the crown succeeded in devising ways to benefit considerably from its human and other resources while avoiding making substantial financial investments or conceding any significant devolution of authority.

The sense of inevitable failure that has attached itself to our understanding of the history of the Greater Antilles in the first half of the sixteenth century stems to some degree from concerns at the time about depopulation, external attacks, the threat from "rebel" Indians and Blacks, and the decline in gold mining constantly reiterated in official correspondence and reports of the period. Certainly these factors affected the nature of life and society in the Caribbean; mainland destinations, Peru especially, appeared to offer much greater possibilities for economic success and stability for Spaniards than did the islands. Indeed, the "failure" motif dates to the very outset of Columbus's undertaking, when he lost first the *Santa María* and then the men left behind in Hispaniola, following which his first town, La Isabela, built at great cost to his sick and starving men, was abandoned.

Yet the disarray and suffering of the earliest years gave way to a period of considerable success (at least from the point of view of the crown) in the first couple of decades of the sixteenth century. During this period, Spaniards founded towns, organized the extraction and export of substantial quantities of gold, established sugar estates and cattle ranches, expanded their territory to include all the large islands of the Greater Antilles, and engaged in a lively regional and transatlantic commerce that linked the islands to the mainland, the Atlantic islands, and Spain itself. The wealth, manpower, and resources of the Greater Antilles underwrote Spanish occupation of the mainland. In the Caribbean Spaniards developed a template for their relations with Indians and Blacks as the institutions of encomienda and chattel slavery were gradually codified and the legal underpinnings of a new sociocial hierarchy took shape, all of which they transferred to the societies of the mainland.

Moreover, the Greater Antilles remained important in their own right and represented much more than just a transitional phase in the larger colonial project. The mineral wealth that initially made them economically viable and important to the crown was no longer significant after the first half of the sixteenth century. By the end of the century, their economies were much more modest, their populations far more mixed, and their security ever more threatened by the increasing territorial ambitions of other European powers than had been true before 1550. Nonetheless, the stability of society achieved there in those early decades allowed Spain to maintain a dominant presence in the region for centuries.

GLOSSARY

abad	highest-ranking ecclesiastic in the absence of a bishop
adelantado	leader granted civil and judicial powers by the crown
aje	a kind of sweet potato
alarife	master builder
alcaide	warden of a fort or jail
alcalde mayor	district magistrate
alcalde ordinario	magistrate of the first instance
alférez	ensign
alguacil	constable
alguacil mayor	chief constable
almojarifazgo	duty on imported and exported goods
almotacen	inspector of weights and measures
alzado	literally "risen up," in revolt
amancebado(a)	cohabiting without being married
arca de tres llaves	chest requiring three keys
arcediano	archdeacon
arciprestazgo	archpriesthood
areito	Indigenous ceremonial dance and song
armada	squadron, fleet
arroba	weight of approximately 25 pounds
asiento	site; contract
audiencia	high court
bachiller	holder of a bachelor's degree
batea	wooden tray for washing gold

beata	laywoman living under religious vows
behique	shaman
bienes de difuntos	property or funds belonging to deceased persons who died intestate
bohío	Indigenous house
boticario	pharmacist
bravo	wild
caballería	unit of agricultural land, slightly more than one hundred acres
caballero	noble; horseman
cabildo	council (of a town or cathedral chapter)
cacica	Indigenous female ruler or chief
cacicazgo	chiefdom
cacique	Indigenous male ruler or chief
cacona	goods, mostly clothing and shoes, provided as compensation to Indigenous laborers
campesino	peasant
capilla	chapel
capitulación	license, charter
carcel	jail
carga	three or four *fanegas*
casa fuerte	strong house, fort
casa poblada	large household
castellano	Castilian language; Spanish unit of currency worth 480 maravedis
cédula	decree, ordinance
chancillería	chancellory
chantre	choirmaster
cimarrón	Black or Indian living outside of Spanish authority
cofradía	confraternity, lay brotherhood
colegio	college, seminary
comendador	commander of a military order
comisario	deputy
compadre	godfather of one's child

GLOSSARY

comunero	member of a commune
comunidad	commune
confianza	trust
contador	accountant
conuco	agricultural field
corregidor	royal representative to a municipality
criado	servant, retainer
cristiano	Christian; during this period, someone who was culturally Hispanic
cuadrilla	gang, militia patrol
cuentas	accounts
despensero	steward
despoblación	depopulation
doliente	sickly
ducado	Spanish unit of currency worth 375 maravedis
duho	Indigenous carved stool
encomendero	holder of an encomienda
encomienda	grant entitling holder to the labor of a specified Indigenous group
entrada	expedition, incursion
esclavo	slave
escribano	scribe, notary
estancia	rural estate
estanciero	foreman or owner of a rural estate
experiencia	experiment, experience
factor	agent, factor
fanega	approximately 1.5 bushels
fiel ejecutor	public inspector
fiscal	prosecutor
flota	Indies fleet
fortaleza	fort, fortress
fraile	friar
fuero	town charter
fundición	foundry; smelting

fundidor	smelter
ganado	cattle
ganadora	woman vendor, possibly of stolen goods
gobernador/a	governor
gramática	grammar; study of Latin
hacienda	property; treasury
hato	cattle herd or ranch
hermandad	brotherhood, league
hermita	shrine, hermitage
hijo natural	child of parents who are not married
hijo patrimonial	native son
información	deposition
ingenio	sugar mill
juez	judge
justicia	justice
labrador	farmer
labranza	farmland
ladino	Spanish-speaking
lengua	interpreter
licenciado	holder of an advanced university degree
maestrescuela	cathedral dignitary who taught divinity
manso	docile, tame
maravedí	smallest unit of account in Spanish currency
marcador	assayer, brander
marco	weight of gold, silver, or pearls
mariscal	marshal
mayorazgo	entail
mayordomo	steward, manager
mesta	stock raisers' association
mestizo/mestiza	someone of European and Indigenous parentage or descent
monte	woodland
montón	mound used to cultivate yucca and other crops

GLOSSARY

morisco	Muslim convert to Christianity or a descendant
mozo	boy, servant, "the younger"
mulato/mulata	person partly of African descent
naboría	Indigenous dependent or servant
natural	native, citizen
naturaleza	place of origin
oficial	tradesman, artisan; official
oidor	audiencia judge
padrino	godfather
paja	straw, thatch
personero	representative of a town's vecinos
peso de oro	unit of currency worth about 450 maravedis
pesquisa	inquiry
piña	pineapple
preceptor de gramática	grammar instructor
probanza	literally "proof," deposition
proceso	criminal case
procurador	deputy, delegate
propios	properties belonging to a municipality
provisor	vicar-general
quintal	hundredweight
quinto	royal tax, originally of one-fifth
real	monetary unit worth 34 maravedis
receptor	receiver of sequestered property for Inquisition
regidor	town councilman
repartimiento	allotment of Indigenous labor (synonymous with encomienda)
repetidor	repeater (person who had students repeat lessons)
rescate	trade or exchange, often coercive or unequal
residencia	judicial review of an official's term in office
Reyes Católicos	Catholic monarchs, Fernando and Isabel
ribera	riverbank, shore
sacerdote	priest

sagrario	sanctuary
salina	salt mine, saltworks
sisa	excise tax
solar	urban lot
tapia	earthen wall
tejar	tile works
tendero	shopkeeper
teniente	lieutenant, deputy
término	district of a municipality
tesorero	treasurer
tienda	store (also a small building used for varied purposes)
trapiche	sugar mill using animal power
vara	staff, rod
vecino	citizen, head of household, neighbor
veedor	overseer, inspector
venta	inn
viejo	old
virreina	vicereine
visitador	visitor, inspector

NOTES

Introduction

1. The testimony is in AGI Patronato 177 N. 1 R. 12; for a longer discussion of the Cuban *experiencia,* see Altman, "Failed Experiments."

2. See especially the studies in Hofman and Keehnen, *Material Encounters.*

3. See Altman, "Revolt of Enriquillo" for a detailed discussion of the revolt and the scholarship on Enrique. He was notorious at the time, and officials in Santo Domingo continued to refer to his rebellion well after his death. He has barely figured in the Anglophone historiography until recently. Guitar discusses him in "Cultural Genesis."

4. These terms were very similar to those of future agreements with groups of runaway African and African-descended slaves.

5. There certainly are exceptions, as the reader will see in the scholarship cited throughout the book. Yet the very limited Anglophone literature on these topics for the period suggests that they have not been a high priority among English-speaking scholars until recently.

1. Creating a Spanish Caribbean

1. The arrival of Europeans did not end Indigenous migrations to and around the Caribbean and circum-Caribbean, but no doubt affected them; see Yaremko, *Indigenous Passages.* Archaeological work in the islands has been extensive; see, for example, Rouse, *Taínos;* Keegan, *Taíno Indian Myth;* and a number of publications by Kathleen Deagan, including "Reconsidering Taíno Social Dynamics."

2. See, for example, Wilson, "Indigenous People"; and Keegan, Hofman, and Rodríguez Ramos, *Oxford Handbook.*

3. On the Indigenous slave trade, see Stone, "War and Rescate." Parts of northern South America and eastern Central America were particular targets of slave raiding in the earliest years. Rebecca Goetz is conducting research on the Indigenous slave trade, as discussed in her 2020 podcast entitled "Native Enslavement in the Caribbean" (part of the National Humanities Center's Discovery and Inspiration series).

4. Spanish jurist Juan de Palacios Rubios wrote the Requirement, versions of which already existed, based on the 1493 papal *Inter caetera* bulls of donation. See the discussion of law in chapter 3 of the present volume. For several perspectives on the origins, meaning, and historical significance of the Requerimiento, see Devereux, *Republics of Letters*, special issue, which is devoted to the topic.

5. William F. Keegan writes, "Taíno is not a specific way of life or a particular belief system; it is a social formation that incorporated distinct groups, allowing them to maintain their distinctiveness, while incorporating social groups in a regional political economy." Keegan, "'Classic' Taíno," 81.

6. The timing and nature of Spanish incursions and campaigns of conquest in the other islands also generated differences in the nature of relations to the Indigenous inhabitants they encountered; see Valcárcel Rojas, "Indigenous Material Culture," who writes, "The expansion to these islands . . . was undertaken with a perspective that reduces the time for negotiation and contact with the indigenous inhabitants, moving quickly to take control of the population, and to the imposition of forced labor. . . . In this environment, the European objects, the circumstances of their transfer, and the attitudes of the indigenous themselves at the moment of receiving them and using them, were all different. This results in diminished indigenous access to the goods used by Europeans for gifts and *rescate*—part of the so-called gift kit—and the expansion of the use of other kinds of artifacts" (103).

7. On Columbus, see Phillips and Phillips, *Worlds of Christopher Columbus*; and Varela, *La caída*. Columbus's father-in-law, Bartolomeu Perestrelo, was the first *donatario* of Porto Santo near Madeira. On the importance of Columbus's Portuguese and African experience, see Hair, "Columbus." There is, of course, a large body of scholarship on Columbus and a number of collections of documents relating to Columbus and his voyages; see, for example, Gil and Varela, *Cartas de particulares*. For English translations of some key documents, see Symcox and Sullivan, *Christopher Columbus*.

8. Ita Rubio, "Mercaderes ingleses."

9. For a recent study of German activities in Venezuela, see Tyce, "Hispano-German Caribbean."

10. Extensive archaeological work has been conducted at this site; see Florida Museum, "Material Remains," https://www.floridamuseum.ufl.edu/histarch/research/haiti/en-bas-saline/material-remains. The site today is about twelve miles west of Cap Haïtien and only about a mile and a half from the site where the Spanish founded Puerto Real in 1503.

11. Fernández de Oviedo, *Historia general*, Libro IV, cap. XXIII, 47–48.

12. See chapter 2 for a discussion of disease and health in the islands.

13. After La Isabela, the first fort to be built was Santo Tomás, followed by several others that stretched from La Isabela to the mouth of the Ozama River, where subsequently Santo Domingo would be built. See Varela, *La caída*, 29–30, who notes that all the forts were situated near rivers and had the resources to potentially support a garrison of men. These would have been simple palisaded structures.

14. See Varela's discussion of the witnesses and their testimony in her lengthy introduction to *La caída* and in the pesquisa transcribed by Isabel Aguirre in the second half of that book.

15. Deagan and Cruxent, *Columbus's Outpost*, 50–52, 54–70.

16. Varela, *La caída*, 28, 146–148. Briolanga Muñiz subsequently married a Florentine merchant named Francisco de Bardy, who was close to the Columbus family; see Arranz Marquez, *Don Diego Colón*, 1:74.

17. According to Rodrigo Manzorro, who testified in the pesquisa, Columbus allowed foodstuffs in the storehouse to rot rather than distributing them to the men. Manzorro claimed that fifty men starved in La Isabela; see Varela, *La caída*, 131–132, 255. He testified that he witnessed rotten food being thrown into the sea.

18. Varela, *La caída*, 44.

19. Varela, *La caída*, 53, 55.

20. Varela, *La caída*, 77.

21. See Mira Caballos, *Nicolás de Ovando*, 63, who argues convincingly for the figure of 1,200 instead of the generally accepted number of 2,500 passengers, based on his calculation of the tonnage of the ships and the other items they transported. On the makeup of the passengers, see Gil, "La gente de Ovando." Although Ovando usually is referred to as *comendador mayor* of the military order of Alcántara, he only received the title after he went to Hispaniola; see Fernández de Oviedo, *Historia general*, Libro III, cap. VI, 74.

22. Varela, *La caída*, 168, 171–172.

23. Columbus and his party landed at St. Ann's Bay and ended up near an indigenous village named Maima, close to where Spaniards later established Nueva Sevilla; see Henry and Woodward, "Contact and Colonial Impact," 85.

24. Sauer, *Early Spanish Main*, 136, 141.

25. Sauer, *Early Spanish Main*, 149.

26. Las Casas, *Historia de las Indias*, 3:275–301. Las Casas, always sympathetic to Columbus, was at a loss to explain Ovando's inaction. He writes that Méndez purchased the ship and supplies to relieve Columbus and his party in Santo Domingo and sent it to Jamaica before he departed for Spain in May 1504 (284). See also Fernández de Oviedo, *Historia general*, Libro III, cap. IX, 79–80. Neither Las Casas nor Fernández de Oviedo provides a date for Escobar's trip to Jamaica.

27. This document is transcribed in Varela, *La caída*.

28. Fernández de Oviedo, *Historia general*, Libro IV, cap. XXIII, 54–56. Archaeologist Samuel M. Wilson published a careful reconstruction of events that took place in Hispaniola during the 1490s, with particular attention to the interactions between Europeans and the island's caciques and native inhabitants, informed by archaeological evidence and ethnographic approaches. See Wilson, *Hispaniola*.

29. Some pacification of Hispaniola already had taken place before Ovando arrived; on the violence of the mid-1490s, see Wilson, *Hispaniola*, especially chapter 3. On Ovando's campaigns, see Floyd, *Columbus Dynasty*, 56–63; on the pacification of Higüey and Xaraguá, see Sauer, *Early Spanish Main*, 149. Sauer writes of Ovando that "the principal effort and success of his first two years was to gain control of the entire island, which he did by breaking its native political structure. The major chiefs were liquidated along with many of the lesser ones."

30. The most thorough study of the encomienda system in the Greater Antilles is Mira Caballos, *El Indio Antillano*. The book, based on extensive archival research, examines the establishment of encomiendas in each of the large islands as well as other topics related to the orga-

nization and exploitation of labor (including that of Africans) in the islands during the first fifty years of colonization.

31. For the reaction in one town in Cuba to the reassignment of repartimientos by Diego Velázquez, see Altman, "Vasco Porcallo," 74–77.

32. Archaeologist Roberto Valcárcel Rojas points out that in Puerto Rico and Cuba, the immediate move to impose a labor regimen on the Indigenous residents was not preceded by period of gift exchange or *rescate*; rather, "the link with the indigenous peoples originated from a position of domination.... In contrast with many parts of North and South America, in the Antilles the *rescate* did not develop into the consolidation of systems of interaction and the creation of new and large indigenous exchange networks, but rather, it collapsed or readjusted with the imposition of forced labor" (Valcárcel Rojas, "Indigenous Material Culture," 117).

33. For a full transcription of the Repartimiento of 1514, see Rodríguez Demorizi, *Los Dominicos*. Arranz Márquez, *Repartimientos y encomiendas* includes transcriptions of a number of other documents related to the Repartimiento. The number of Indians listed in the Repartimiento should not be assumed to reflect the entire Indigenous population of Hispaniola, as some people had fled into remote areas and children probably were underreported.

34. On the Hieronymites, see Mira Caballos, *El Indio Antillano*, 131–146; on the free communities or *experiencias*, see 155–157, 180–183, and 209–212. See also Altman, "Failed Experiments." For further discussion of the encomienda, the laws that amended it, and its impact on the Indians, see chapters 2 and 3 in the present volume.

35. Disease and demographic trends are discussed in chapters 2 and 5. Scholarly efforts to estimate population numbers at contact in the Caribbean and the rate of decrease under Spanish rule mainly have focused on Hispaniola. See Mira Caballos, *El Indio Antillano*, 33–35, who accepts relatively low estimates of around 100,000 for contact populations. Over the years, estimates have ranged as high as 8 million, but most scholars currently accept a figure of 100,000 to 400,000 for Hispaniola at contact. For a recent argument for lower figures at contact, based on genetic evidence, see the op-ed piece by David Reich and Orlando Patterson, "DNA Rewrites the Telling of the Caribbean's Past," *New York Times*, December 26, 2020. The turmoil and destructiveness of the Indigenous revolt that took place in Puerto Rico between 1511 and 1517 might have driven substantial numbers of people off the island, compounding the mortality from violence and disease and possibly accounting for the extremely small documented Indigenous population that remained on the island two decades after Spanish occupation began. Some scholars have argued for a higher level of Indigenous survival in Cuba than in Hispaniola or Puerto Rico. There are almost no population figures for Jamaica. For a discussion of postcontact population trends among all groups, see Mira Caballos, *El Indio Antillano*, chapter 1.

36. Rodríguez Demorizi, *El pleito Ovando-Tapia*, 22, 25, 252, 270. The suit, the records of which are in the Archivo General de Simancas, originated as part of the residencia that was taken of Ovando's term as governor; the rest of the residencia has been lost. According to Ovando's biographer Ursula Lamb, "It appears that what Tapia wanted was an indictment of Ovando's government and recognition of himself as a champion of royal prerogative.... Tapia's suit is ... a reflection on Ovando's entire conduct in office" (Lamb, "Christobal de Tapia," 428–429). Rodríguez Demorizi's discussion follows Lamb's article closely, even word for word in large part (although translated into Spanish), including her interesting analysis of how the testimony of Tapia's and Ovando's witnesses reflected differences in class and wealth.

37. Mira Caballos, *Nicolás de Ovando*, 87, 101.

38. Mira Caballos, *Nicolás de Ovando*, 102. The surnames of some of his favorites reflect their extremeño origins: Alonso de Hervás, Rodrigo de Trujillo, and Manuel de Ovando.

39. Mira Caballos, *Nicolás de Ovando*, 128–130, writes that he owned more than 300,000 *montones* of yucca and *ajes* distributed all over Hispaniola.

40. Arranz, *Don Diego Colón*, 85, 98–99. On the king's unhappiness with Ovando, see 100–101.

41. According to Otte, "La flota de Diego Colón," 476, Francisco de Garay, together with Miguel Díaz, owned half of one of the ships. Analyzing the list of cargos for twenty ships that were loaded in 1509 by Diego Colón and Diego Nicuesa, Otte affirms the "collective character of the transatlantic commerce: besides the merchants of Seville, the shipmasters, sailors, and passengers participated by taking to sell in the Indies wine, flour, fruit, domestic and foreign textiles, jewelry, construction materials, animals, and many other items" (479). All translations from Spanish are the author's.

42. Hernando Colón's collection of books made news in 2019, when the annotated catalog of his library, long thought to be lost, was found in Copenhagen. What remains of Colón's collection, perhaps one-quarter of his books, is housed in the Biblioteca Colombina in Seville's cathedral.

43. Las Casas, *Historia de las Indias*, 3:439–440.

44. Las Casas, *Historia de las Indias*, 3:433.

45. Arranz Marquez, *Don Diego Colón*, 108–109; Fernández de Oviedo, *Historia general*, Libro IV, cap. I, 98. See also Las Casas, *Historia de las Indias*, 3:434.

46. AGI Patronato 63 R. 24. Arranz, *Don Diego Colón* describes Pasamonte as "diligent and efficient, experienced in negotiations, a man of authority and knowledge, besides some less honorable qualities." He exercised "almost absolute power in the Royal Treasury" and corresponded with royal secretary Lope de Conchillos in secret code (111–112). Fernández de Oviedo, *Historia general*, Libro III, cap. XII, describes him as "honest and lacking in vices," adding that in the opinion of some "he never knew a woman carnally" (92), even though he died at an advanced age.

47. Eagle, "The Audiencia of Santo Domingo," 4. Complaints about the judges' misconduct led regent Jiménez de Cisneros to send Alonso de Zuazo to Hispaniola as *juez de residencia*, and the audiencia was suspended in 1518 (5).

48. Floyd, *Columbus Dynasty*, 144.

49. Floyd, *Columbus Dynasty*, 214–216. See Fernández de Oviedo, *Historia general*, Libro IV, cap. VII, 114–115. In 1537 doña María de Toledo received authorization from the crown to move the remains of both her husband and her father-in-law to Hispaniola to be placed in the Capilla Mayor of Santo Domingo's cathedral; see Rodríguez Morel, *Documentos*, 170. Their current location is still debated.

50. Marc Eagle writes that "it was only in June of 1528 that Charles sent new ordinances codifying the structure and duties of the Audiencia of Santo Domingo. . . . If the president of the audiencia was a letrado, he would act as a fourth oidor and have a vote in the cases heard in appeal" (*Audiencia*, 6).

51. Fernández de Oviedo, *Historia general*, Libro IV, cap. VII, 116. The *alguacilazgo mayor* would remain in his family line as part of their *mayorazgo;* see AGI Santo Domingo 868 L. 1 f. 186v.

52. Because Diego Colón was governor, the highest authorities in the individual islands were designated lieutenant governors.

53. Fernández de Oviedo, *Historia general*, Libro II, cap. XIII, 51–53. He refers to Catalina as "cacica," although whether she was recognized as ruler or was a high-ranking woman but not necessarily a chief is not known.

54. See the interesting description of the establishment of Darién, the first mainland settlement in what the Spanish would call Panama (although it was actually in the Chocó region of modern Colombia), in Sarcina, "Santa María de la Antigua del Darién," 175–196. Sarcina describes the initial occupation of the existing indigenous town of Darién by Spaniards, followed by the establishment of a Spanish town separate from but adjoining the indigenous one; see especially 177–181. Whether similar foundations took place in the Greater Antilles is not known. Five towns were founded in Panama between 1510 and 1522, starting with Darién; see Díaz Ceballos, "Negociación, consenso y comunidad política."

55. On the contraction of Hispaniola's towns, see the 1528 report of the audiencia oidores in Marte, *Santo Domingo*, 277–278; and discussion in Altman, "Towns," 32.

56. Sued Badillo, *El dorado borincano*, 55–56. In 1520 the town still had 150 vecinos. Sued Badillo writes that "it was also the seat of island and municipal government and the ecclesiastical capital of all the eastern Caribbean, including part of Tierra Firme."

57. For a good discussion of how the sites of Cuba's towns were chosen, see Davis, "Strategy," 294–314, especially 302–309. According to Hernández Mora et al., "Pueblo Viejo de Nuevitas," 157, the town of Puerto del Príncipe (today's Camagüey) moved to the site of Caonao in 1516 and then moved again in 1528, to its present location, because of an Indigenous uprising.

58. The names of islands slowly stabilized through a similar process. Cuba prevailed over Isla Fernandina and Jamaica over Santiago, but Hayti and Borinquen, both of which appear in early sixteenth-century documents, lost out to Isla Española and San Juan, which itself slowly shifted to Puerto Rico (with the main city becoming San Juan).

59. Fernández de Oviedo, *Historia general*, Libro VI, cap. I, 164.

60. Tió, *Nuevas Fuentes*, 282–283, 287–288. The testimony regarding the house and Juan Ponce de León is from a deposition of 1558 by his grandson Juan Troche Ponce de León, son of Garcí Troche. Francisco Juancho testified that Juan Ponce's "casa fuerte" was the only thing that protected many "Christians" during the Indigenous rebellion; see 295–296.

61. Rodríguez Demorizi, *El pleito*, 55, 100. Garay was the first to build a stone house in Santo Domingo.

62. Mira Caballos, "Urbanismo," 464–465.

63. Mira Caballos, "Urbanismo," 466–467 (quote is from AGI Contratación 5787 N. 1 L. 1 f. 36). Presumably, encomienda workers drafted for work on construction projects performed these duties in addition to their other labor obligations.

64. As quoted from the *Memorial por el Almirante* of 1509–1510, in Rodríguez Demorizi, *El pleito*, 62.

65. See Altman, "Key to the Indies," 21–22. Fernández de Oviedo became alcaide in 1533 and served in the post until his death in 1555. An audiencia official in the 1540s complained to the king that "this isn't a fortress . . . but rather a house that the Comendador Mayor had built in the style of those that they build in the pastures of Extremadura," a reference to Ovando's place of origin. AGI Santo Domingo 49 R. 1 N. 9a, transcribed in Rodríguez Morel, *Cartas de la Real Audiencia*, 51–52.

66. Rodríguez Demorizi, *El pleito*, 66–67.

67. Arranz, *Don Diego Colón*, 251. According to Mira Caballos, "Urbanismo," 459–460, most of the cathedral still lacked a roof in 1533, but construction, under the direction of Luis de Moya, who served as *maestro mayor* for more than twenty years, was nearly complete by 1540.

68. AGI Patronato 176 R. 1.

69. AGI Santo Domingo 2280 L. 2 f. 108v.

70. AGI Santo Domingo 2280 L. 2 ff. 115v–116r.

71. AGI Santo Domingo 2280 L. 2 ff. 24r–24v.

72. Rodriguez Morel, *Documentos*, 88.

73. See Damiani Cósimi, *Estratificación social*, 38–39, testimony of Juan Ponce de León's son-in-law Garcí Troche.

74. AGI Santo Domingo 2280 L. 2 f. 110r.

75. Quoted in Levi Marrero, *Cuba*, 2:372–373.

76. See Mira Caballos, "Urbanismo."

77. Quoted in Rodríguez Demorizi, *El pleito*, 75. Mira Caballos, "Urbanismo" notes that at the time that Geraldini wrote, Santo Domingo "was no more than a collection of houses of ephemeral materials around a single paved street, which was that of Las Damas, that numbered barely a dozen stone houses" (444).

78. Fernández de Oviedo, *Historia general*, Libro III, cap. IV, 97.

79. Fernández de Oviedo, *Historia general*, Libro III, cap. X, 84.

80. Rodríguez Demorizi, *El pleito*, 76–78.

81. Otte, "Una carta inédita," 443. Fernández de Oviedo accused three prominent officeholders—audiencia secretary Diego Caballero, accountant Álvaro Caballero, and inspector Gaspar de Astudillo, all three regidores—of having used more than 1,500 cartloads of lime in the construction of their houses, "of the largest and best in the city," for which they paid considerably less than full value, thus defrauding the city.

82. For a more detailed discussion of early port towns, see Altman, "Key to the Indies."

83. For a discussion of the numbers of emigrants to the islands in the first couple of decades of European occupation, see D'Esposito and Jacobs, "Auge y ocaso."

84. Las Casas, *Historia de las Indias*, vol. III, cap. XI, 120–121.

85. Marte, *Santo Domingo*, 25, 27. Diego Marquez was veedor and Rodrigo Alcazar marcador.

86. Gil, "Emigrantes," 265–266, 278.

87. For a good explanation of the process by which people obtained permission to emigrate, see Jacobs, "Legal and Illegal Emigration," 61–63. For a detailed discussion of the conditions and mechanisms of travel to the Indies, focusing on a later period than the one examined in the present book, see Rodríguez Lorenzo, "El contrato de pasaje."

88. Fernández de Oviedo, *Historia general*, Libro III, cap. II, 64. Las Casas, called them "gente vil" and criminals who abused and exploited the Indians (*Historia de las Indias*, vol. 3, Libro segundo, cap. 1, 26–27).

89. *Colección de documentos inéditos relativos al descubrimiento, conquista y colonización de las posesiones españolas en América y Oceanía sacados, en su mayor parte, del Real Archivo de Indias* (CDIAO), 39:13–14.

90. Marte, *Santo Domingo*, 40.

91. Gil, "La gente de Ovando," identifies nearly three hundred passengers who accompanied Ovando. More than 10 percent were *trabajadores* (workers) (256). Gil, "Emigrantes," 279, identifies more than twenty women, mostly *sevillanas*, among the more than 250 emigrants who went to Hispaniola in 1506, including the wives of several men already on the island.

92. AGI Indiferente General 418 L. 1 f. 78r. For a full discussion of women's experiences in the islands, see chapter 6 of the present volume.

93. Marte, *Santo Domingo*, 39. There were complaints, for example, that in the Repartimiento of 1514 unmarried men and married men living in Hispaniola without their wives had received encomiendas.

94. AGI Indiferente General 418 L. 1 ff. 33r–35v; Marte, *Santo Domingo*, 150.

95. *Colección de documentos inéditos relativos al descubrimiento, conquista y organización de las antiguas posesiones españolas y de ultramar*, 1:16; and Alegría, *Documentos Históricos*, 1:248.

96. CDIAO, 1:416–420.

97. Rodríguez Morel, *Documentos*, 145.

98. The complexities of these decisions and arrangements, both collective and individual, are addressed for a somewhat later period in Altman, *Emigrants and Society*, chapter 5.

99. AGI Patronato 63 R. 13, información of Juan Suárez de Peralta's son Luis Suárez de Peralta, in Mexico City, January 1560. Witnesses included men who had known Juan Suárez in Cuba, such as Jerónimo de Salinas, Andrés de Tapia, and Gutierre de Badajoz, as well as Gonzalo Gómez and Diego de Villapadierna, both of whom had been with him in both Hispaniola and in Santiago de Cuba and had seen Suárez depart.

100. AGI Patronato 18 N. 1 R. 2.

101. AGI Santo Domingo 9 N. 45.

102. He took with him a brother named Gonzalo de Lepe, with his wife and children; Juan Garcia and his wife, children, and an unmarried sister; Salvador Martín and his wife, Beatriz de Lepe, with four children and two unmarried nieces; and Alonso Pabón and his wife and children. See AGI Santo Domingo 2280 L. 2 ff. 71r–77v; and AGI Contratación 5536 L. 5 f. 139r.

103. AGI Santo Domingo 9 N. 40.

104. Otte, *Las perlas*, 111–114. He writes that Puerto Plata, in particular, was the base for the slaving expeditions to the "islas inútiles" and that the dominant role that the oidores, particularly Lucas Vázquez de Ayllón, played in these expeditions meant that other vecinos and entrepreneurs were all but excluded. Giménez Fernández, "Las Cortes" refers to Ayllón as "el converso anticolombista" (4–5).

105. Notary Diego de Herrera testified that Ayllón recruited people in his hometown of Toledo and that Hernán Vázquez, a regidor in Toledo and presumably a relative, invested in the expedition. AGI Patronato 63 R. 24.

106. Hoffman, *Florida's Frontiers*, 24–28. Ayllón's son Pero Vázquez de Ayllón prepared an información in Santo Domingo in 1560 in which he stated that his father took five ships; Hoffman says there were six. The información is in AGI Patronato 63 R. 24.

107. AGI Patronato 63 R. 24. According to Hoffman, *New Andalucia*, 82, the house in Santo Domingo was sold to oidor Licenciado Alonso de Zuazo for 1,700 pesos, to be paid over a period of ten years. When he failed to make the semiannual payments, Ana Becerra sued and regained the house. Hoffman discusses Lucas Vázquez de Ayllón's life, career, and expedition in detail in *New Andalucia*; see especially 41–47 and chapters 2 and 3.

108. Regarding archaeological work at En Bas Saline in Hispaniola, Valcárcel Rojas, *Archaeology*, writes that "the limited presence of European objects suggests a rejection of Spanish materiality and values.... Research at En Bas Saline leaves no doubt that the indigenous experience was not limited to the first moments of contact; but rather, it was diverse and did not always result in the assimilation of Spanish components" (15). Over time, this changed. Valcárcel Rojas, while noting that "the European material universe at El Chorro de Maíta [Cuba] was sparse," concludes that "nonetheless, it is clear that there is a strong insertion of this place in the process of indigenous–European interaction" (161).

109. See Valcárcel Rojas, *Archaeology*, 274–275. Based on his analysis of extensive archaeological evidence, he suggests the existence of "a limited Spanish influence that left space for indigenous agency, and seems to coincide with the historical comments regarding the tendency of Indians to recover their life schemes once they returned to their towns after the demora, as well as their desire to avoid dealing with the Spanish in these places" (325). A number of the studies in Hofman and Keehnen, *Material Encounters*, address these issues. Bernan and Gnivecki, for example, note indigenous "selectivity" in the incorporation of objects and that "indigenous and European items were often transformed physically and given new meanings and uses as they crossed cultural borders" (33) There is also the possibility that "the possession and circulation of European objects were controlled by indigenous elites"; see Fleehner, "Treating 'Trifles,'" 72.

110. Regarding burial practices, Valcárcel Rojas, *Archaeology* writes that "the indigenous population ... maintained mostly traditional mortuary practices and managed Christian ones in a not-so-formal way or connected them to the indigenous practices in syncretic ways in an ambivalent and strategic position that constructed a non-indigenous, but not really Christian, cemetery" (334).

111. See Altman, "Revolt of Enriquillo."

112. Fleehner, "Treating 'Trifles,'" 61.

113. See Rocha, "Maroons in the *Montes*" on the connections between Black maroons and the proliferation of cattle in Hispaniola and elsewhere.

2. Death and Danger in the Islands

1. Fernández de Oviedo, *Historia general*, Libro IV, cap. XXIII, 47–48. Anthropologist José Barreiro has published *Taíno*, a fictionalized autobiography of Diego Colón.

2. Fernández de Oviedo, *Historia general*, Libro V, cap. X, 156.

3. There is a sizeable literature on this topic; see, for example, Henige, *Numbers from Nowhere*; and a more recent study, Livi-Bacci, "Return to Hispaniola." Cook, *Born to Die*, 21–24, summarizes estimates for Hispaniola.

4. See Cook, *Born to Die*, 17, on illnesses found in the Americas prior to European contact; and Fernández de Oviedo, *Historia general*, Libro II, cap. XIV, 56. Cook, *Born to Die*, table 1.2 (58), lists the occurrences of epidemic diseases in the Caribbean from 1493 to 1525.

5. According to Gómez, "Hospitals," "Europeans' life expectancy in some Caribbean locales may have been severely limited, with as many as 45 percent of them not surviving their first year in the Americas" (213). See Cook, *Born to Die*, 63, on reports sent from Santo Domingo to the king on the illness of new arrivals to the island in 1520.

6. Guerra, "Earliest American Epidemic."

7. Guerra, "Earliest American Epidemic," 316. Although other historians have argued that the illness was malaria or yellow fever, Guerra makes a convincing case that it was swine influenza. He points out that passengers only became ill after they landed at the site of what would become La Isabela and came into contact with the eight hogs that had traveled on one of the ships; see 319, 322.

8. Fernández de Oviedo, *Historia general*, Libro III, cap. II, 64. The perception in Spain of the Caribbean as a place of high mortality might have endured for some time. In 1534 Francisco Quemado, a resident of Santiago in Cuba, explained that although he had made several attempts to have his wife join him and over the years had sent her money a number of times, she refused to come, "offering as an excuse that in these parts her father and a brother and other relatives had died and it would be the same for her if she arrived here." AGI Santo Domingo 10 N. 8.

9. Gil, "Emigrantes," 269.

10. Mira Caballos, "Sanidad."

11. Marte, *Santo Domingo*, 149; see also 21 for annual salaries earmarked for a physician (50,000 maravedís), surgeon (30,000 maravedís), and pharmacist (20,000 maravedís).

12. Mira Caballos, "Sanidad," 513.

13. In Alegría, *Documentos históricos*, 1:99 (from AGI Indiferente General 418 L. 2).

14. AGI Santo Domingo 868 L. 2 f. 42v.

15. See Mira Caballos, "Sanidad," 511–512, who writes that in 1506 Licenciado Hernando Becerra received an annual salary of 60,000 maravedís plus an encomienda of 150 Indians, granted by governor Nicolás de Ovando; surgeon Gonzalo de Vellosa received 50,000 maravedís in 1511, and Licenciado Barrera received the same in 1517, although he left his post and received a reduced salary of 30,000 maravedís when he later returned.

16. AGI Santo Domingo 1121 L. 1 f. 24v.

17. Mira Caballos, "Sanidad," 515.

18. AGI Santo Domingo 10 N. 13; and Santo Domingo 2280 L. 2 f. 102r.

19. Gil, "Emigrantes," 277–278.

20. AGI Santo Domingo 868 L. 2 f. 166r.

21. Pablo Gómez's recent study of hospitals in the sixteenth-century Caribbean focuses on the evolution of policies over time. He writes that "the crown clearly understood the need to develop a network of hospitals to accommodate the new circumstances of the Caribbean, especially in strategic places" (Gómez, "Hospitals," 218). By the latter decades of the sixteenth century, hospitals in the main ports, such as Santo Domingo and Cartagena, had expanded and become much more substantial and better organized entities, with administrators, surgeons, nurses, and visiting physicians as well as Black slaves, who not only performed the menial work of cleaning, doing laundry, and cooking but also themselves acted as "bona fide health providers" (220–221).

22. Mira Caballos, "Sanidad," 520. By the 1540s, however, Fernández de Oviedo, *Historia general*, Libro III, cap. XI, described the hospital as "very good . . . well built and endowed with a good income, where the poor are treated and helped" (87).

23. AGI Santo Domingo 1121 L. 1 f. 167r.

24. AGI Santo Domingo 1121 L. 2 ff. 127r-v.

25. AGI Patronato 18 N. 1 R. 2; AGI Santo Domingo 868 L. 1 ff. 255r–257r, 260r–265r, 270 r–271v.

26. AGI Santo Domingo 868 L. 1 f. 152v.

27. Mira Caballos, "Sanidad," 513, quotes Fernández de Oviedo, who observed that doctors and surgeons often arrived in Santo Domingo either lacking any documentation of their degrees and examinations or perhaps never having had such.

28. AGI Santo Domingo 10 N. 16. In 1537, the year of the deposition, Moya had held the post of "maestre mayor en las obras de la iglesia cathedral" for more than twenty years. He had lived in Santo Domingo for five years before returning to Spain for his wife. He then went back to the island with her. In 1525 Luis de Moya, *cantero*, paid 168 maravedis for a "libro sacramental" purchased at auction from the property owned by Inés de la Peña, who died in 1521; see AGI Santo Domingo 77 R. 2 N. 34.

29. AGI Santo Domingo 2280 L. 2 ff. 133r-v. The ingenio was built by Tomás de Castellón, whose brother, Jácome de Castellón, built an ingenio in Hispaniola. They were members of a Genoese family that had established itself in Toledo; see Pike, *Enterprise and Adventure*, 138.

30. On balsam see AGI Santo Domingo 77 N. 82 (Antonio de Villasante). Also see AGI Santo Domingo 868 L. 2 ff. 23v–24r for a 1541 report regarding the export of canafistula as a collective effort in 1529 and 1530, which *contador* Alvaro Caballero, as representative of Santo Domingo at court, recommended be revived. In his *Historia general* Fernández de Oviedo wrote extensively on the medicinal properties of a number of plants native to the Caribbean; see especially Libros V and XII of the Primera Parte. Spaniards eventually learned about their healing properties, either through experimentation or from the Indians. Mira Caballos, "La medicina indígena," 187–188, suggests that the Indians, especially the *behiques* (shamans), deliberately tried to keep this knowledge from them, but Spaniards soon were taking advantage of the new pharmaceutical possibilities. Mira Caballos writes, for example, that by 1530 large quantities of "palo de guayacán" were being used in the *hospital de las bubas* in Seville (193). See also Barrera, "Local Herbs."

31. Fernández de Oviedo, *Historia general*, Libro X, cap. 1, 362.

32. Gómez, *Experiential Caribbean* writes that in the seventeenth century, "black Caribbean healers' methods resonated with their contemporaries practicing in Europe, sub-Saharan Africa, and the Americas. Common treatments applied to people in seventeenth-century Caribbean locales included massages, cupping, power objects, cutting, potions, herbs, medications, and prayers" (80–81). The situation in the sixteenth century probably was much the same.

33. Mira Caballos, "Sanidad," 515, from AGI Indiferente General 421 L. 13.

34. AGI Santo Domingo 1121 L. 2 f. 191v.

35. AGI Santo Domingo 1121 L 1 f. 173v.

36. AGI Patronato 178 N. 1 R. 18.

37. AGI Santo Domingo 10 N. 30. See chapter 4 of the present volume for the dean of Concepción's diatribe against Vaca.

38. See Altman, "Spanish Women," 68–69.

39. AGI Santo Domingo 2280 L. 2 f. 35r.

40. AGI Santo Domingo 2280 L 2 f. 145v. On the lengthy stay in Spain of Cuba's treasurer Pedro de Paz, because of illness, see Lalor, "Two Doñas," 100.

41. AGI Santo Domingo 1121 L. 2 f. 88v. Whether he actually departed is uncertain. Lope Hurtado testified that had been jailed unjustly at the order of don Diego López in February 1537.

42. AGI Santo Domingo 10 N. 8, ff. 1r–1v. On the crown's efforts to ensure that married men who went to the islands did not permanently abandon their wives, see Altman, "Spanish Women," 59–60. See also chapter 6 of the present volume.

43. AGI Santo Domingo 10 N. 8 ff. 2v–3r.

44. AGI Santo Domingo 10 N. 8 f. 3r.

45. Fernández de Oviedo, *Historia general,* Libro XVI, cap. III, 469; Libro III, cap. X, 82.

46. See testimony in AGI Santo Domingo 9 N. 51.

47. Fernández de Oviedo, *Historia general,* Libro XVIII, cap. I, 581.

48. AGI Santo Domingo 1121 L. 2 ff. 28v–32v. Mazuelo was not a disinterested party in this petition, as he wanted to establish a sugar ingenio near the proposed site for the new town. On moving the site of Veracruz because of environmental factors, especially on concerns about disease, see Clark, "Environment," 198–199.

49. AGI Santo Domingo 10 N. 35.The word *conversación* had several meanings in the period. In this instance, I am guessing that, as an educated man, Díaz meant the absence of what might be called polite society in this isolated locale.

50. Quoted in Marrero, *Cuba,* 2:372–373.

51. AGI Patronato 176 R. 1, letter of 1518.

52. AGI Santo Domingo 2280 L. 1 ff. 5r–7r. On the experiencia, see Altman, "Failed Experiments."

53. On the revolt, see Farnsworth, "Revolt of Agüeybana II." It is possible that many of the island's people fled during the years of conflict.

54. In 1514 Juan Comerio was listed as *capitán* at Toa. See AGI Contaduría 1072 for the lists of people and what they received in *cacona* (goods provided in lieu of monetary compensation) from 1514 to 1519. Most anthropologists agree that succession in the chiefdoms of the Greater Antilles and the Bahamas was by preference matrilineal—that is, from a man to the son of his sister or possibly to his brother, although there were exceptions. Whether there were female rulers—whom Spaniards called *cacicas,* a feminization of *cacique*—prior to contact is debated. See Moscoso, *Caguas,* 101–102, 143–144; and Altman, "Cacicas."

55. The inventories are in AGI Patronato 175 R. 18.

56. AGI Patronato 175 R. 18.

57. Lieutenant governor Manuel de Lando mentioned the epidemics in his report of 1530–1531; they were taking place while he was compiling what amounted to a census of the island that, although somewhat incomplete, listed the Indians and Blacks working for Spaniards. See Damiani Cósimi, *Estratifación social* for transcription and analysis. The report is in AGI Santo Domingo 155 R. 1 N. 1. Muriel referred to the illnesses of the early 1530s as *viruelas* (smallpox) and *sarampión* (measles); AGI Santo Domingo 10 N. 4. Around this time, the same illnesses also killed many Indians in Cuba; see AGI Santo Domingo 1121 L. 1.

58. AGI Santo Domingo 10 N. 4.

59. Muriel stated that at the time Spaniards occupied the area, Caguas's people numbered around three thousand.

60. AGI Santo Domingo 77 R. 4 N. 52.

61. AGI 2280 L. 2 f. 10r. The ingenio had been founded by Tomás de Castellón, to whom the Indians had been assigned in encomienda. After his death, the ingenio and the encomienda passed to Blas de Villasante, who was married to Castellón's daughter, doña Theodora. After Theodora's death, Villasante married Catalina Suárez del Pozo; at his death, his daughter Juana de Villasante became heir to the ingenio.

62. AGI Santo Domingo 1121 L. 1 ff. 177v, 178r.

63. For a transcription of the Interrogatorio, see Rodríguez Demorizi, *Los Dominicos*, 273–354.

64. Rodríguez Demorizi, *Los Dominicos*, 280.

65. Rodríguez Demorizi, *Los Dominicos*, 309.

66. See, for example, Altman, "Vasco Porcallo," 78–79, on Porcallo's drastic punishment of Indians who ate earth, which Spaniards thought was a means of committing suicide.

67. Rodríguez Demorizi, *Los Dominicos*, 277–278.

68. Rodríguez Demorizi, *Los Dominicos*, 299.

69. AGI Santo Domingo 2280 L. 1 f. 20v.

70. AGI Santo Domingo 2280 L. 2 f. 178r.

71. AGI Santo Domingo 10 N. 27. Gonzalo de Santa Olalla did not explain the cause of the slaves' deaths and was mainly concerned with the impact on his ingenio. He not only wanted to replace the fifty or so slaves who had died but also hoped to acquire an additional twenty or thirty.

72. See Gómez, "Hospitals," 216.

73. Información of Diego Caballero, in AGI Santo Domingo 77 N. 118.

74. AGI Justicia 13 N. 1 R. 3.

75. AGI Justicia 11 N. 1 (1532). I am grateful to David Wheat for providing me with his notes and transcriptions of this document.

76. See Cook, *Born to Die*, 43, 52, 93. Cook suggests that although Spaniards in the early sixteenth century had some awareness of the efficacy of quarantine measures, as seen in efforts to prevent ships carrying passengers or slaves who were ill from either departing ports or making landings, they made few systematic efforts to impose quarantines in the period.

77. Fernández de Oviedo, *Historia general*, Libro IV, cap. II, 105, wrote that the epidemics that killed the Indians "seemed a great judgment of heaven" (un juicio grande del cielo).

78. AGI Santo Domingo 1121 L. 2 f. 117r.

79. AGI Santo Domingo 868 L. 2 ff. 40r, 50r.

80. AGI Santo Domingo 868 L. 2 ff. 136v–137r. On the funding and building of fortifications throughout the Caribbean, see Hoffman's authoritative *Spanish Crown*, 51–59. Hoffman's book remains the standard work on military defense during the period.

81. In 1531 the king instructed the Casa de la Contratación in Seville to send two brigantines to Puerto Rico "in pieces, along with sails, oars, and masts," together with the necessary arms to help the residents defend themselves from Caribs; see AGI Santo Domingo 2280 L. 1 ff. 94v, 99r (on the arms to be supplied). By June 1531 the brigantines had arrived but lacked some of what was needed to outfit them fully (f. 133r).

82. The deposition is in AGI Santo Domingo 11 N. 18.

83. AGI Santo Domingo 11 N. 18.

84. See Marte, *Santo Domingo*, 412–414, for two reports of clashes with "negros alzados" in San Juan de la Maguana and the Bahoruco, from Licenciado Cerrato in 1546; and AGI Santo Domingo 49 R. 16, N. 97 and N. 98, transcribed in Rodríguez Morel, *Cartas de la Real Audiencia*, 447–452. In February 1546 Cerrato reported that a group of Blacks led by a man named Diego de Guzmán had burned the *casa de purgar* of an ingenio and killed "una cristiana," and that the "cristianos" there had killed two of the Blacks' captains. In a letter of June 1546 Cerrato described other clashes in San Juan, Azua, and the Bahoruco and mentioned a captain from La Yaguana, although not by name.

85. See Marte, *Santo Domingo*, 430.
86. AGI Santo Domingo 11 N. 18 f. 16r. Presumably doña Catalina was ransomed.
87. AGI Santo Domingo 11 N. 18 ff. 12v, 16r.
88. AGI Santo Domingo 868 L. 2 f. 137v.
89. See Altman, "Key to the Indies."
90. AGI Santo Domingo 2280 L. 1 f. 90v.
91. AGI Santo Domingo 868 L. 1 f. 115v.
92. According to Hoffman, *Spanish Crown*, although historians often refer to two wars with the French during this period in the Caribbean (from 1534 to 1538 and from 1542 to 1544), it actually was one long conflict interrupted by "the ill-kept Truce of Nice from June 1538 to July 1542" (24).
93. On the attempted attack on Santiago, see Altman, "Key to the Indies," 19–20; on the attack on Havana, see Wright, *Early History*, 218–220.
94. AGI Santo Domingo 11 N. 15.
95. Hoffman, *Spanish Crown*, 40.
96. The muster is in AGI Santo Domingo 9 N. 28.
97. AGI Santo Domingo 9 N. 28.
98. AGI Patronato 175 R. 28.
99. Marte, *Santo Domingo*, 113.
100. Farnsworth, "Revolt of Agüeybana II."
101. AGI Patronato 176 R. 6.
102. The two terms Spaniards commonly used to refer to Indians and Blacks not under their control, *alzados* and *cimarrones*, have rather different implications. Whereas *cimarrón* connotes someone who was living beyond the constraints of the colonial regime, *alzado* literally meant someone who had "risen up," or rebelled against that regime, implying that at least nominally alzados had been under Spanish control. For an interesting discussion of the origins and use of the term *cimarrón*, see Rocha, "Maroons," 6–7.
103. Fernández de Oviedo, *Historia general*, Libro IV, cap. IV, 108–109. Castro's deposition of 1535 appears in AGI Justicia 1003 N. 5 R. 2. For his services, he requested hidalgo status and a coat of arms that would include a golden castle, from the doors and windows of which flames would be visible, and an ornamental border of silver "with six heads of Blacks, the necks bloody." Oviedo probably got much of his information about the revolt and its suppression from Castro, as many of the details in his account are the same. A revolt of Black slaves actually took place in Puerto Rico even earlier than this better-known one in Hispaniola; see Farnsworth, "Revolt of Agüeybana II," 37–38.

104. Altman, "Revolt of Enriquillo"; Utrera, *Polémica de Enriquillo*.

105. Marte, *Santo Domingo*, 347. In 1532 the audiencia estimated the costs at 40,000 pesos; see 360.

106. Rodríguez Morel, *Cartas del cabildo*, 70.

107. AGI Santo Domingo 9 N. 51 (1533). Castro stated that Romero several times had led patrols: "Ha corrido mucha parte desta isla y a tomado muchas quadrillas de indios cimarrones y negros con ellos que a sido la mayor cosa y causa de mas pacificacion que todas las guerras que se ha hecho de ocho o nueve años a esta parte" (He has traversed much of this island and has apprehended many gangs of Indian cimarrones and Blacks with them, which has been the most important thing and reason for more pacification than all the wars that have been waged here in the past eight or nine years).

108. Rodríguez Morel, *Cartas de la Real Audiencia*, 66, 81.

109. Erin Stone suggests that the slave revolt that began on Diego Colón's estate was connected to Enrique's revolt, although she does not provide any evidence of a direct relationship. Given the considerable official attention paid to Enrique's revolt and the resulting extensive documentation, if officials had known of a connection between the revolts, they surely would have commented on it. See Stone, "America's First Slave Revolt," where she writes that "within the mountains, the African slave rebels joined with a group of indigenous fugitives, or *indios negros*, led by cacique Enriquillo, who had rebelled himself in 1519. For the next fifteen years, these two diverse groups melded together, fighting the same enemy, perhaps even intermarrying, and creating their own distinct culture" (195) She also writes somewhat confusingly that the audiencia referred to the "larger maroon community as *indios negros*" in 1530, implying that the term referred to Blacks rather than "indigenous fugitives" (213, note 4). She also states that "both archaeological and documentary evidence suggests that the African and Indian revolts eventually became one" (196), but she fails to cite any documentary evidence for this conclusion. She discusses archaeological evidence that suggests that both Blacks and Indians lived in caves in the Bahoruco mountains in the early 1500s (206), but that does not constitute proof that rebel groups had united under Enrique's leadership.

110. Rocha, "Maroons," 4.

111. AGI Santo Domingo 868 L. 2 f. 245v. Rocha, "Maroons" states that "black men like Diego de Guzmán, Diego de Ocampo, and Sebastián Lemba established themselves across the Bahoruco valley. Colonial administrators were quick to point out that these settlements occupied the same areas as had Enriquillo decades prior" (9). *Ladino* meant that someone spoke Spanish or Portuguese and suggested a broader acculturation beyond linguistic ability.

112. See the deposition of lieutenant governor Manuel de Rojas in Santiago de Cuba in January 1533, in AGI Santo Domingo 9 N. 48.

113. In 1532 Guama was based near Asunción (Baracoa). He was reputed to have more than sixty men and reportedly was attracting Indians from all over the island. AGI Patronato 177 N. 1 R. 11.

114. The quote is "Rojas les dio cacona a los indios y negros abundosamente por manera que todos quedaron contentos y con voluntad de volver a ranchear" (Rojas compensated Indians and Blacks generously so they were happy and willing to patrol again). *Ranchear* is difficult to translate, as its meaning shifted depending on context.

115. In 1533 the king authorized Rojas to make war on and enslave "los indios que anduvieren alzados"; AGI Santo Domingo 1121 L. 1 f. 161v. Prior to that, apparently, the crown had forbidden the taking of slaves in these campaigns. In 1532 a seventy-year-old vecino of Santiago complained that "the island never will be secure unless His Majesty allows rebel Indians to be given as slaves"; AGI Patronato 177 N. 1 R. 11. Other witnesses agreed with him.

116. The transcription of this letter is in Marrero, *Cuba*, 1:235.

117. Marrero, *Cuba*, 1:236.

118. AGI Santo Domingo 10 N. 8. Possibly the kidnapped woman was Indigenous.

119. AGI Santo Domingo 1121 L. 2 f. 131v.

120. On doña Isabel Bobadilla as acting governor, see Lalor, "Two Doñas."

121. AGI Santo Domingo 118 R. 1 N. 71. See Altman, "Vasco Porcallo," 71.

122. AGI Santo Domingo 1121 L. 1 ff. 178v–179r.

123. AGI Santo Domingo 77 N. 50.

124. AGI Santo Domingo 1121 L. 2 ff. 80v–81r. Cuba had received far fewer slave imports by this time than had Hispaniola or Puerto Rico, so Guzmán probably was exaggerating the numbers.

125. AGI Santo Domingo 868 L. 2 f. 108r.

126. AGI Santo Domingo 77 N. 89.

127. AGI Santo Domingo 868 L. 2 f. 250r.

128. AGI Santo Domingo 868 L. 2 ff. 245v–246r. For Cerrato's 1544 letter, see AGI Santo Domingo 77 N. 90. My thanks to David Wheat for a copy of this document.

129. AGI Santo Domingo 2280 L. 2 f. 25r.

130. AGI Santo Domingo 2280 L. 2 f. 162v.

131. Moscoso, *Juicio al gobernador*, 79.

132. AGI Santo Domingo 2280 L. 2 f. 31v.

133. Fernández de Oviedo, *Historia general*, Libro VI, cap. III, 167–168. Given that he revised earlier versions of his history, it is surprising that he did not revisit this issue.

134. AGI Santo Domingo 77 R. 2 N. 37; and AGI Santo Domingo 2280 L. 1 f. 81r.

135. Murga, *Historia documental*, 1:299.

136. AGI Santo Domingo 2280 L. 1 f. 91r.

137. AGI Patronato 177 N. 1 R. 11.

138. AGI Santo Domingo 77 R. 3 N. 59. See Rodríguez Morel, "Sugar Economy," who writes, "By the 1520s a dam seventy meters long, one of the largest of its time, was constructed to provide waterpower on an *ingenio* near Santo Domingo on the Isabela River. The wealthy Castilian merchant Benito de Astorga, who spent 12,000 castellanos and some seven years in its construction, due in part to the technical mistakes made in the building of the dam, began this mill in 1525" (96).

139. Rodríguez Morel, *Cartas de cabildos eclesiásticos*, 77.

140. Mulcahy and Schwartz, "Nature's Battalions," 438, 441. Mulcahy and Schwartz cite naturalist Edward O. Wilson, who argues that tropical fire ants, probably the culprit, do not eat plants but rather host other insects that do. "Wilson speculates that the infestation developed after new homopterans arrived on the island, likely alongside plantains, which were imported from the Canary Islands in 1516" (442).

3. Government, Politics, and the Law

1. See Fernández Armesto, *Before Columbus;* and Aznar Vallejo, *La integración.*
2. According to Floyd, *Columbus Dynasty,* during the governorship of Nicolás de Ovando "the king became . . . the largest miner and encomendero on Española, as he would be on the other islands until the reforms under Charles V" (68). Rodríguez Morel "Cartas privadas," writes that "from an early time the island [Hispaniola] was enveloped in internal struggles between the clans of distinct factions" (215). In a letter of 1518, Miguel de Pasamonte, Alonso Dávila, and Licenciado Villalobos complained about Hispaniola's *bandos* (factions), one the bando of the king and the other of the admiral. *Colección de documentos inéditos relativos al descubrimiento, conquista y colonización de las posesiones españolas en América y Oceanía sacados, en su mayor parte, del Real Archivo de Indias* (CDIAO), 1:2. See also Fernández de Oviedo, *Historia general,* Libro IV, cap. I, 98; and Giménez Fernández, "Las cortes," 2, who states that he refers to these factions as "clans" and not parties, as they lacked any ideology. He contends that they pursued their own advantage and not the common good, very much to the detriment of the Indigenous population.
3. Giménez Fernández, "Las cortes," 5–6.
4. On the regulation, taxation, and organization of gold mining, see Sued Badillo, *El dorado borincano.* On royal policy on marriage, see Altman, "Spanish Women" and "Marriage, Family, and Ethnicity." On sex ratios for slave imports, see, for example, Scelle, *Histoire politique,* 768–769. On how cédulas sent to Santo Domingo's cabildo were handled, see Julián, "La documentación histórica."
5. On the work of the Hieronymites, see Floyd, *Columbus Dynasty,* 167–180. Giménez Fernández, "Las cortes" points out that after the death of Cardinal Cisneros, the Hieronymites in Hispaniola increasingly limited their focus to "the problem of the Indians . . . and remained on the margins of the political struggle" (9).
6. The contrast to the Canaries, where seigneurial rule was established on some islands, is notable. For interesting insights into the role of the nobility in the Canaries, see Lalor, "Women, Power," chapter 3, which focuses on doña Beatriz de Bodilla, governor and lady of Gomera.
7. See Marte, *Santo Domingo,* 103, 191; and Altman, "Spanish Women," 61. In 1512 the king encouraged the migration of "white slaves" (presumably *moriscas*) to the islands as potential wives for settlers. On the increasing numbers of cacicas, see Altman, "Cacicas."
8. See the testimony of Juan Mosquera and of Gonzalo de Campo in the Interrogatorio Jeronimiano, transcribed in Rodríguez Demorizi, *Los Dominicos,* 279–280, 282.
9. See Altman, "Revolt of Enriquillo"; and Utrera, *La polémica.*
10. There were some Blacks among Enrique's followers; see Stone, "America's First Slave Revolt." Black slaves in Puerto Rico had rebelled in in 1514; see Farnsworth, "Revolt of Agüeybaná II," 37.
11. See Altman, "Revolt of Enriquillo," 610–612.
12. Eagle, "Audiencia," writes that "while the Audiencia of Granada provided the crown with a model institution that provided justice by proxy for a recently conquered and relatively remote territory, the American audiencias should be considered adaptations of the tribunal rather than faithful copies of it" (9).
13. AGI Santo Domingo 868 L. 2 ff. 238v, 308v.

14. A residencia was the judicial review of an official's term in office. It originated in the Middle Ages but came into more general use under Fernando and Isabel, in conjunction with their extension of the system of appointing corregidores to serve in Castile's major towns and cities.

15. When Licenciado Grajeda was appointed oidor in 1543, his salary was specified as 300,000 maravedís. In addition, the king instructed the Casa de la Contratación to lend him 50,000 maravedís. AGI Santo Domingo 868 L. 2 ff. 173v–174r.

16. Marrero, *Cuba*, 1:237.

17. AGI Patronato 178 R. 10.

18. On the transition from this earlier form of municipal government that allowed vecinos to participate in choosing their local officials, see Altman, *Transatlantic Ties*, chapter 3.

19. AGI Santo Domingo 2280 L. 2 f. 106v.

20. AGI Santo Domingo 868 L. 1 f. 174v. In 1547 Gonzalo Fernández de Oviedo and capitán Alonso de Peña, acting on behalf of the town councils of Hispaniola, stated that the regidores received only 2,000 maravedís in salary. When an oidor of the audiencia conducted visits, a regidor was required to accompany him, incurring many expenses. They asked that when a regidor participated in these visits he be paid an adequate salary. AGI Santo Domingo 868 L. 2 ff.334v.

21. Rodríguez Morel, *Cartas del cabildo*, 127–128.

22. Rodríguez Morel, *Cartas del cabildo*, 129.

23. Rodríguez Morel, *Cartas del cabildo*, 23. Disagreements over who had the right to assign municipal lots surfaced in 1530 in a dispute over a house the oidor Dr. Infante had built near the fortress; see AGI Santo Domingo 9 N. 37.

24. AGI Santo Domingo 9 N. 37.

25. Rodríguez Morel, *Cartas del cabildo*, 76.

26. Rodríguez Morel, *Cartas del cabildo*, 66–67.

27. Rodríguez Morel, *Cartas del cabildo*, 109.

28. AGI Santo Domingo 868 L. 1 f. 188v.

29. As Rodríguez Morel writes in the introduction to his edited collection, *Cartas del cabildo*, "El modelo de ayuntamiento creado en las colonias estuvo mediatizado y deformado por el autoritarismo del poder real" (The model of the municipal council created in the colonies was influenced and distorted by the authoritarianism of royal power) (15).

30. Don Cristóbal de Sotomayor was named alcalde mayor of Puerto Rico, but after he died in the Indigenous uprising no one else was appointed alcalde mayor. In 1537 Hernando de Soto was instructed to appoint a lawyer as alcalde mayor for Cuba, at an annual salary of 200 pesos, presumably because Soto planned to lead an expedition to Florida. See AGI Santo Domingo 1121 L. 2 ff. 103v–104r. I have seen references in royal correspondence to corregidores but have not found any record of someone receiving such an appointment in the islands during this period; possibly the king simply assumed they existed in the Caribbean. Corregidores would appear in New Spain in a rather different guise, as district administrators over Indigenous communities not assigned to encomenderos. See Chamberlin, "Corregidor in Castile," 222–257. Chamberlin only discusses corregidores and residencias in Castile, and his main focus is on the reign of Philip II; there are no references to the Indies.

31. See Nader, *Liberty in Absolutist Spain*. She argues that even though many (but not all) municipalities had a lord—whether the king, a noble, or a high-ranking ecclesiastic—the municipalities themselves were self-governing.

32. Marrero, *Cuba*, 1:237.

33. AGI Patronato 177 N. 1 R. 17. The disappearance of municipal government in Trinidad probably resulted from the decision of a number of its vecinos to move to nearby Sancti Spíritus, which they had been encouraged to do by lieutenant governor Gonzalo de Guzmán.

34. For a longer discussion of this episode, see Altman, "Vasco Porcallo," 74–76.

35. CDIAO, 1:418.

36. AGI Santo Domingo 1121 L. 1 f. 122v.

37. CDIAO, 1:586.

38. AGI 868 L. 2 ff. 27r–27v.

39. Rodríguez Morel, *Cartas de los cabildos eclesiásticos*, 121.

40. Otte, *Las perlas*, 264–265.

41. See letter to the "rei principe" in Marte, *Santo Domingo*, 432. Fernández de Oviedo referred to Juan Caballero, Diego Caballero's son, who had become escribano of the audiencia and was asking for a regimiento "with which his father tyrannized this city because they never could deal with anything against the president and oidores that he did not direct them [to do]" (434). Fernández de Oviedo became regidor in 1549. See Julián, "La documentación histórica," 15–18, on conflicts between Fernández de Oviedo and Diego Caballero over matters concerning Santo Domingo's cabildo, including whether all present during cabildo meetings should sign off on the proceedings. Caballero wanted to limit the signatories to one alcalde and one regidor. Fernández de Oviedo also accused him of manipulating the yearly elections of officials to place his friends and relatives in those positions and of taking the cabildo's books to his house. Julián bases his discussion on Otte, "Una carta inédita."

42. Rodríguez Morel, *Cartas del cabildo*, 71.

43. Rodríguez Morel, *Cartas del cabildo*, 193–194.

44. AGI 868 L. 2 ff. 149r–149v.

45. AGI Santo Domingo 2280 L. 2 f. 118v.

46. AGI Santo Domingo 1121 L. 1 ff. 166r, 179v. In a 1528 letter to the king, the procuradores of Cuba's towns asked that the alcaldes "be elected every year by the votes of all the vecinos of each town, as it is done in many towns and villages of the kingdoms of Castile." AGI Patronato 178 R. 10.

47. AGI Santo Domingo 1121 L. 2 f. 80v.

48. AGI Santo Domingo 868 L. 2 f. 10r, 12r, 13r, 21r, 23r. In Castile, the mesta was an organization for people who raised sheep, not cattle. See chapter 5 for discussion of cattle raising in the islands.

49. AGI Santo Domingo 77 N. 6. See also Altman, "Vasco Porcallo," 79.

50. AGI Santo Domingo 1121 L. 1 ff. 39r–40r.

51. AGI Patronato 178 R. 10.

52. AGI Santo Domingo 2280 L. 1 ff. 181v–183v.

53. Rodríguez Morel, *Cartas del cabildo*, 111–113. According to a letter of 1537, construction had gotten under way but ran into difficulties in the attempt to build a pylon (*pilar*) in the river, which had halted work; see 136–137.

54. Lalor, "Two Doñas," 100.

55. AGI Santo Domingo 868 L. 2 f. 347r.

56. AGI Santo Domingo 2280 L. 1 f. 35v.

57. The información is in AGI Santo Domingo 9 N. 3.

58. AGI Santo Domingo 10 N. 39.

59. See Moscoso, *Lucha agraria*.

60. Lando's información of 1534 is in AGI Santo Domingo 10 N. 3.

61. Salvatierra's deposition is in AGI Santo Domingo 10 N. 53. Juan Ponce was the son of Garcí Troche and doña Juana, the eldest daughter of Juan Ponce de León. Troche had served as alguacil mayor, contador, and regidor in San Juan and also had been in charge of building the fort, where he then served as alcaide. His son Juan became alcaide in 1546. Juan Ponce de León's only son became a friar, so his family line continued through his daughters, who married two brothers, Garcí and Gaspar Troche, both of whom were prominent in Puerto Rico.

62. Wright, *Early History*, 101–102, 115. In 1538 Guzmán was the veedor de fundición in Cuba. Manuel de Rojas went to Jamaica in 1536 to audit accounts, but it is unclear how long he stayed; see Morales Padrón, *Spanish Jamaica*, 86.

63. Wright, *Early History*, 115.

64. AGI Santo Domingo 1121 f. 37v.

65. AGI Santo Domingo 1121 L. 1 ff. 35r, 37v.

66. AGI Santo Domingo 1121 L. 1 f. 27r, 44v–45r. The king responded that this complaint, as well as the complaints about the *visitadores* Guzmán had sent to Puerto Príncipe and Baracoa, should be referred to the juez de residencia, who did not arrive for almost another two years.

67. Marrero, *Cuba*, 1:234. The entire letter is transcribed, 234–239.

68. Marrero, *Cuba*, 1:235.

69. See AGI Patronato 177 N. 1 R. 13 for Rojas's report of 1532 of the repartimiento done by Diego Velázquez in 1522.

70. Marrero, *Cuba*, 1:235.

71. AGI Santo Domingo 1121 L. 1 ff. 68v–69r.

72. Rojas wrote about this in a separate letter to the king; see AGI Santo Domingo 99 R. 4 N. 16.

73. Marrero, *Cuba*, 1:235.

74. AGI Santo Domingo 1121 L. 2 ff. 162r–163f. According to Wright, *Early History*, Hurtado wrote "many pages of tiresome communications to his superiors" over the years but "seems . . . to have been that very rare creature . . . an honest man" (118).

75. AGI Santo Domingo 1121 L. 2 f. 165r. In 1528 a merchant and vecino of Santo Domingo, Pedro Gutiérrez, had obtained royal permission for him and a bodyguard to carry arms because of Gutiérrez's fears that people in Hispaniola intended to harm or kill him; see Rodríguez Genaro, *Documentos*, 58.

76. AGI Santo Domingo 1121 L. 1 f. 169v. There is nothing in the document about the reason for Pedro de Guzmán's murder or what he was doing in Cuba. Guzmán had assigned him a substantial encomienda of ninety people, which was reassigned to his nephew Juan Pérez on Pedro's death; see Mira Caballos, *El Indio Antillano*, 172, Cuadro XVIII. This was the same nephew who was living in Guzmán's house.

77. *Proceso*. This is a transcription of AGI Justicia 30. I have not found any indication of whether a sentence was handed down. His reputation does not seem to have suffered, and he continued to hold ecclesiastical offices in Concepción and Santo Domingo.

78. *Proceso*, 154–157. Pedro Palomo, a barber, accompanied Castro to the inn and said that Castro attacked the elderly innkeeper so quickly, cutting him around the head and neck, that he was unable to stop him. He did treat the victim's wounds, however; see 216.

79. *Proceso*, 174–175, 224.

80. *Proceso*, 151.

81. AGI Santo Domingo 10 N. 23; Santo Domingo 2280 L. 2 ff. 159v, 161v–163r, 176v–177v. Alonso de Molina and Pedro de Espinosa were partners in a gold mine. On this case, see also Gaspar Troche's información, which he presented to the audiencia in Santo Domingo in 1540; AGI Santo Domingo 10 N. 23.

82. Rubio, *Las casas*, 34–37, 40. He bases his account on AGI Justicia 5 N. 3. The three main perpetrators were accompanied by other unnamed criados.

83. CDIAO, 1:571–572. This extreme interrogation technique resembled modern waterboarding.

84. AGI Santo Domingo 2280 L. 2 f. 196v.

85. AGI Santo Domingo 868 L. 2 f. 62r.

86. Salazar received the concession of "una escribanía del número" in Santo Domingo in 1538. AGI Santo Domingo 868 L. 1 f. 124 r.

87. Trejo (or Trexo) was the son-in-law of another notary, Martín de Solís, who renounced his position in his favor; see AGI Santo Domingo 868 L. 1 f. 285r. Gutiérrez was Trejo's criado, and the real antagonism seems to have been between Salazar and Trejo. In 1550 Nicolás López was escribano de cámara of the audiencia; see Rodríguez Morel, *Cartas del cabildo*, 207.

88. Salazar's confession is in AGI Santo Domingo 10 N. 24. The inquiry was conducted in September 1541. See also Rodríguez Morel, *Documentos*, 201.

89. Rubio, *Las casas morada*, 10–13. Rubio's main interest in this brief publication, as suggested by its title, is to establish the location of the residences of Diego Caballero and other vecinos.

90. This also is part of AGI Santo Domingo 10 N. 24. For Salazar's probanza of March 1538 in Seville, which detailed the renunciation by Juan Ruiz of the escribanía pública in Santo Domingo in his favor, see AGI Indiferente General 1963 L. 8 f. 89v–90v; and Indiferente General 1092 N. 244. One witness stated that Salazar was the criado of audiencia secretary Diego Caballero, so he was well connected in Santo Domingo society. Another witness estimated Salazar's age to be twenty-eight or thirty. All the witnesses had spent time in Santo Domingo.

91. The mariscal Diego Caballero was the compadre, and probably a kinsman, of the secretary Diego Caballero in Santo Domingo, for whom Salazar had worked.

92. For a longer discussion of this incident, see Altman, "Vasco Porcallo." Manuel de Cáceres testified about the pursuit of Juan del Oliva.

93. Rubio, *Las casas morada*, 25–32.

94. Murga, *Historia documental*, volume 2, is a partial transcription of the residencia. Licenciado de la Gama was appointed to conduct the residencia after his father, Dr. Sebastián de la Gama, declined the appointment because of age and poor health.

95. Murga, *Historia documental*, 2:47, 69, 74–75, 157 ("por ser tanto su amigo y parcial, y porque le curaba todo lo que se ofrecía en casa del dicho Licenciado sin dineros" [75]).

96. Murga, *Historia documental*, 2:264–265. There is no other testimony about this allegation.

97. Murga, *Historia documental*, 2:284, 308–310, 316–317, 326. Vasco Troche was alguacil in San Germán. Whether he was related to the more prominent Troche brothers (Garcí and Gaspar) is not known.

98. The *arca de tres llaves* was a locked chest used to store valuable materials. It required three keys held by different officials.

99. Las Casas, *Historia de las Indias*, 3:374–375.

100. See Mira Caballos, "Las cuentas del tesorero," 79–222. He includes a transcription of the lengthy 1531 información. See also Mira Caballos, *Nicolás de Ovando*, 109–110.

101. Mira Caballos, *El Indio Antillano*, 269–270, 272.

102. After Esteban de Pasamonte died in 1535, a cousin, Juan de Pasamonte, briefly served as treasurer. Alonso de la Torre also was appointed alcaide of Concepción de la Vega. He was back in Spain in 1543 and died the following year. His son Juan de la Torre died in an entrada in Uraba in 1537.

103. On this family, see Fernández Chaves and Pérez García, "América como mecanismo." Diego Caballero got his start in Hispaniola as the criado of Bernardo Grimaldi, the wealthy Genoese merchant based in Seville; see Garrido Raya and Moreno Escalante, "La red mercantil," 10, 19.

104. AGI Santo Domingo 77 N. 72. I am grateful to David Wheat for a copy of this document as well as for the article "América como mecanismo," cited in the previous note.

105. Astudillo also mentioned that, just a few months earlier, a Genoese named Valian de Forne had brought thirty-six unregistered Black slaves that the royal officials "allowed to pass." He alleged that Torre "shows [himself] such an enemy that it has left me speechless" and had formed an alliance with the alcaide Gonzalo Fernández de Oviedo, one of his principal antagonists. Forne (or Fornari) was a member of the Genoese company that had purchased a concession to deliver four thousand slaves to the Indies. The license to export the slaves was given in 1518 to Laurent de Gouvenot, who then sold it to the Genoese company for 25,000 ducados; see Fernández Chaves and Pérez García, "La penetración," 206–207.

106. Rodríguez Morel, *Cartas del cabildo*, 150–151. In 1539, Astudillo was being sued by Lope de Bardecí, who was lieutenant governor of Hispaniola at the time; see AGI Santo Domingo 868 L. 1 f. 175v. Astudillo died by 1543. In 1532 he declared that he was more than thirty years old; see *Proceso*, 275. Given that he arrived in Hispaniola in 1508 and received an assignment of Indians in the Repartimiento of 1514, it is difficult to believe that he was born as late as 1500.

107. AGI Santo Domingo 2280 L. 2 ff. 25v–26r. Once Castellanos was back in Puerto Rico, he asked permission to go to New Spain "to recover certain property that an Ángelo de Villafaña is said to have taken worth 8,000 ducados." Despite the discrepancy in surname, this surely was the same man; see f. 69r.

108. A typical case was that of Antonia Palomeque, a vecina of Salamanca, whose father, Juan Yáñez Palomeque, died in Puerto Rico. In 1536 he accused Antonio Sedeño, "so color de ser su testamentario" (under the guise of being his executor), and others of having appropriated the property her father left for her; AGI Santo Domingo 2280 L. 2 f. 96v.

109. AGI Santo Domingo 2280 L. 2 ff. 61v–62r. The prior and friars of the Dominican monastery in Puerto Rico informed the crown in 1535 that there were "muchos bienes de difuntos" that were going unclaimed and asked that some of the accumulated funds be used to support the island's two churches.

110. Rodríguez Morel, *Cartas del cabildo ecclesiástico*, 121.

111. See Masters, "A Thousand Invisible Architects." Julián, "La documentación," writes, "Los súbditos de la corona española disfrutaban del derecho de poderse dirigir por escrito directamente al rey. Esta libertad era ejercida ... por obra de disposiciones legislativas que conferían, en fecha tan temprana como 1509, a colonos de la Española el uso de esa facultad" (The subjects of the Spanish crown enjoyed the right to write directly to the king. This freedom was exercised ... by virtue of legislative acts that, as early as 1509, conferred on the colonists of Hispaniola the use of this instrument) (11).

112. See Julián, "La documentación," 10, on cédulas sent to Santo Domingo in the early sixteenth century.

113. For a discussion of the events that led to the adoption of the Laws of Burgos, see chapter 4 of the present volume.

114. Mira Caballos, *El Indio Antillano*, 350–353.

115. AGI Santo Domingo 868 L. 2 f. 194r; see also 203v.

116. AGI Santo Domingo 868 L. 2 f. 223v. In Cuba, vecinos or officials were able to obtain a delay of the enforcement of the New Laws until 1553.

117. Marte, *Santo Domingo*, 409.

118. AGI Santo Domingo 868 L. 2 ff. 250v–251r.

119. AGI Santo Domingo 868 L. 2 f. 339r.

120. AGI Santo Domingo 868 L. 2 ff. 191v–192r.

121. Levi, *Cuba*, 2:353.

122. On the legal process involved in freeing slaves after the promulgation of the New Laws, see van Deusen, *Global Indios*.

123. AGI Santo Domingo 868 L. 2 ff. 240r–241r.

124. AGI Santo Domingo 868 L. 2 ff. 342r–342v.

125. Rodríguez Morel, *Cartas del cabildo*, 176. On the sale of Tairona captives on the island of Terceira in the Azores during the 1530s, see Rocha, "Azorean Connection," 262–265.

126. AGI Santo Domingo 868 ff. 241r–241v, 355v.

127. Franco, *Los negros*, 30–32. See the transcription in Saez, *La iglesia*, 237–249.

128. Ordinances of 1545 emphasized the need to catechize Black slaves. Saez, *La iglesia*, 276–277.

129. Alegría, *Documentos históricos*, 1:346–347.

130. Quoted in Marrero, *Cuba*, 1:217.

131. Altman, "Marriage, Family, and Ethnicity," 238–239

132. Saez, *La iglesia*, 232–233 (from AGI Indiferente 421 L. 12). For a discussion of an African man's successful suit to regain his freedom in the context of the Atlantic slave trade and the rise of plantation agriculture, see Turits, "Slavery and the Pursuit of Freedom."

133. AGI Santo Domingo 1121 L. 1 f. 158v.

134. AGI Santo Domingo 77 N. 98. For further discussion of the workers on these estancias, see Altman, "Marriage, Family, and Ethnicity," 244–247.

135. AGI Santo Domingo 868 L. 2 f. 225r.

136. Although construction of a fortaleza at La Yaguana was discussed for many years, in the 1540s officials concluded that it would not be practical. See the discussion of Pero Martín de Agramonte and his defense of the town in chapter 2.

137. See Fernández Chaves and Pérez García, "América como mecanismo," and many references to the members of this family in Otte, *Las perlas*. On Diego Caballero de la Rosa's duties as secretary, see Altman, "Key to the Indies," 10; and his deposition in AGI Santo Domingo 10 N. 5.

4. Church and Clergy

1. The regular orders are the subject of MacDonald, "Regular Clergy."
2. Also meaning "abbot," during this period the *abad* was the highest-ranking secular ecclesiastic in the absence of a bishop.
3. See MacDonald, "The Hieronymites."
4. Marte, *Santo Domingo*, 90.
5. For a discussion of this issue, see chapter 5 of Varela's long introductory essay in *La caída*, especially 99, 104, 107, 111–112. She calculates that by the time Francisco de Bobadilla conducted his pesquisa, or inquiry, in 1500, at least 1,500 Indians had been sent to Spain to be sold, the majority on behalf of Columbus himself. Some of them would be sent back to Hispaniola when the monarchs, probably mainly Queen Isabel, determined that Hispaniola's Indians were vassals of the crown and should not be enslaved.
6. Tibesar, "Franciscan Province," 378. He notes that these men "today would be called Belgians."
7. Tibesar, "Franciscan Province," 378; MacDonald, "Cemí and the Cross," 3.
8. Tibesar, "Franciscan Province," 380.
9. See MacDonald, "Cemí and the Cross," 3, 7–9. On Indigenous resistance to Christianity, see also Mira Caballos, "Los intentos evangelizadores," 431–433; he uses the words "disinterest" and "indifference" to describe the Indigenous response to conversion efforts.
10. Marte, *Santo Domingo*, 92.
11. AGI Patronato 178 R. 1.
12. Marte, *Santo Domingo*, 92–93.
13. Tibesar, "Franciscan Province," 380–381, 386. *Gramática* in this period meant instruction in Latin.
14. Las Casas, *Historia de las Indias*, 3:136–137.
15. MacDonald, "Cemí and the Cross," 11.
16. Las Casas, *Historia de las Indias*, 3:468–471.
17. See Las Casas, *Historia de las Indias*, 3:611–613. For a good discussion of Montesino's sermon, its impact on those who were in attendance, and the official response on the island and in Spain, see the introduction to Rodríguez Morel, *Cartas de cabildos eclesiásticos*, 22–26.
18. In March 1512 the king wrote to Diego Colón that he "had been astonished at what he [Montesino] had said, given that for it there was no basis in theology, canons or laws, according to all the lawyers." Indeed, his royal council recommended that not only Montesino but also all the Dominicans in Hispaniola be sent home forthwith to face punishment by their superiors. See Marte, *Santo Domingo*, 108–109.
19. Las Casas, *Historia de las Indias*, 3:634, 643, 737–739.
20. For a detailed discussion of the challenges that Indigenous languages posed for the regular clergy in New Spain (with particular focus on Oaxaca), see Farriss, *Tongues of Fire*.

21. Mira Caballos, "La educación," 53.

22. Rodríguez Morel, *Documentos*, 82–83. Fray Remigio knew Enrique and participated in the negotiations that ended his rebellion.

23. Mira Caballos, "La educación," 54.

24. AGI Patronato 275 R. 3; the queen noted the high mortality among the Indians on the island.

25. Mira Caballos, "La educación," 53. On the establishment of the *monasterio de monjas de* Santa Clara, see AGI Santo Domingo 868 L. 2 f. 356r (1547). Bachiller Álvaro de Castro had donated "unas casas y solares" worth more than 4,000 ducados for the convent, which was to be under the Franciscan Order. AGI Santo Domingo 868 L. 2 f. 295r.

26. *Colección de documentos inéditos relativos al descubrimiento, conquista y colonización de las posesiones españolas en América y Oceanía sacados, en su mayor parte, del Real Archivo de Indias* (CDIAO), 1:546–547. See also Rodríguez Morel, *Cartas del cabildo*, 148–149.

27. AGI Santo Domingo 868 L. 2 ff. 16r–16v. Mira Caballos, "La educación," 58, writes that all the students were "hijos de españoles," which might well have been the case, but the document actually does not state who the students were.

28. AGI Santo Domingo 868 L. 1 f. 153r.

29. Rodríguez Morel, *Cartas de los cabildos eclesiásticos*, 45; quotation from Alonso Dávila, regidor and representative of the city council.

30. CDIAO, 1:24.

31. Marte, *Santo Domingo*, 358. "Negros bellacos que han hecho delitos han tomado por costumbre huir a los Monasterios I los Frailes les esconden I defienden, de que viene mucho atrevimiento" (Villanous Blacks who have committed crimes have adopted the custom of fleeing to the monasteries, and the friars hide and defend them, for which comes much daring).

32. *Proceso*, 53. He claimed that no other cleric or bishop before or since had baptized so many souls.

33. AGI Santo Domingo 2280 L. 2 f. 137v. In 1568 oidor Licenciado Echegoyan wrote to the king that the Indians on Mona still had not been evangelized; see CDIAO, 1:23.

34. AGI Santo Domingo 1121 L. 2 f. 13r. López was a clérigo presbítero from the diocese of Cuenca; see AGI Santo Domingo 1121 L. 1 f. 190r.

35. AGI Santo Domingo 77 R. 2 N. 36.

36. AGI Contaduría 1072.

37. The visit is described in AGI Santo Domingo 77 N. 98. For a longer discussion of the composition of the workforce of the estancias, see Altman, "Marriage, Family, and Ethnicity," 245–247.

38. On successful post-Tridentine campaigns to promote religious education in the diocese of Cuenca in Castile, see Nalle, *God in La Mancha*.

39. Rodríguez Morel, *Cartas de cabildos eclesiásticos*, 124–125.

40. Marte, *Santo Domingo*, 307; Rodríguez Demorizi, *Los Dominicos*, 148. See also Altman, "Spanish Women," 71. Astudillo's wife, doña María de Fuentes, might have been known as particularly pious. She donated 3,500 pesos and some houses to the cathedral in Santo Domingo; see Rodríguez Morel, *Cartas de los cabildos eclesiásticos*, 67 (cuadro 2).

41. Marte, *Santo Domingo*, 110–111. There is no evidence that such a school came into existence.

42. Altman, "Spanish Women," 68–69. On taking mestizo children to Spain, see Mangan, "Moving Mestizos."
43. AGI Santo Domingo 1121 L. 1 f. 200r.
44. AGI Patronato 178 R. 10.
45. Mira Caballos, "Los intentos evangelizadores," 439.
46. CDIAO, 1:430.
47. AGI Santo Domingo 1121 L. 1 f. 178v.
48. See Altman, "Failed Experiments." Only when he attempted to reestablish the experiencia at Bayamo in the mid-1530s did Manuel de Rojas try to institute a method for ascertaining whether potential participants were or could become practicing Christians.
49. AGI Santo Domingo 868 L. 1, ff. 41v–42r.
50. Alegría, Documentos históricos, 1:275–276.
51. AGI Santo Domingo 1121 L. 1 ff. 22v–23 r.
52. AGI Patronato 177 N. 1 R. 11. Vadillo wrote that both the provisor, don Sancho de Céspedes, and the bishop had treated the friars badly. Vadillo also was highly critical of the way that Ramírez had handled the repartimiento of Indians in Jamaica and other matters there; see Rodríguez Morel, Cartas de la Real Audiencia, 96–97.
53. AGI Santo Domingo 1121 L. 1 f. 166v; Santo Domingo 1121 L. 2 f. 70r.
54. AGI Santo Domingo 1121 L. 2 ff. 144r–144v.
55. The deposition regarding constructing the new church is in AGI Santo Domingo 10 N. 32.
56. The Franciscans were a mendicant order, meaning that, in principle at least, they owned no possessions beyond their robes and sandals.
57. AGI Santo Domingo 2280 L. 1 f. 141v.
58. AGI Santo Domingo 868 L. 1 f. 26v.
59. AGI Santo Domingo 868 L. 2 ff. 370 v–371r.
60. Rodríguez Morel, Documentos, 265.
61. Rodríguez Morel, Cartas del cabildo, 108–109.
62. AGI Santo Domingo 868 L. 1 f. 238r.
63. See Rodríguez Morel, Documentos, 150.
64. Rodríguez Morel, Cartas del cabildo, 186.
65. AGI Santo Domingo 868 L. 2. ff. 145v–145r.
66. AGI Santo Domingo 868 L. 2.
67. AGI Santo Domingo 868 L. 2 f. 356r.
68. According to Rodríguez Morel, Cartas de los cabildos eclesiásticas, 16, the year 1540 marked one of the rare moments when the cathedral chapter was fully staffed under bishop Alonso de Fuenmayor. Rodrigo de Bastidas was dean, Álvaro de Castro archdeacon, don Diego Rodrigo Martel chantre, and don Alonso de Salas maestrescuela. The canons were Diego del Río, Alonso Monsalve, Licenciado Bartolomé Díaz, García de la Roca, Licenciado Tomás Franco de la Fuente, and the racioneros were Rodrigo de Quezada, Pedro Díaz de Fuenmayor (nephew of the bishop), Alonso de Madrid, and Francisco de Loaysa. For an explanation of the various positions, see Rodríguez Morel, 17, note 61.
69. Rodríguez Morel, Cartas de los cabildos eclesiásticos, 57, writes that toward the end of the first half of the sixteenth century, there probably were no more than six hundred Spanish vecinos in Hispaniola, about four hundred of them in Santo Domingo.

70. Rodríguez Morel, *Cartas de los cabildos eclesiásticos*, 122, 124.
71. AGI Patronato 176 R. 1.
72. See Altman, "Failed Experiments."
73. AGI Patronato 178 R. 10.
74. AGI Patronato 177 N. 1 R. 11.
75. AGI Patronato 178 R. 10. They added that there often was a visiting judge at the mines to see to the treatment of the Indians and "there they are better maintained and supplied with *caconas* than in any other estate."
76. AGI Santo Domingo 868 L. 1 ff. 197r–198r.
77. AGI Santo Domingo 2280 L. 1 f. 138r.
78. Saez, *La iglesia*, 267–270, includes a partial transcription of his report. Sanate belonged to Juan de Villoria.
79. AGI Santo Domingo 868 L. 2 f. 61v.
80. Rodríguez Morel, *Cartas de los cabildos eclesiásticos*, 48–50.
81. AGI Santo Domingo 868 L. 1 ff. 250v–251r.
82. AGI Santo Domingo 868 f. 248r. Santo Domingo's cabildo wrote to the king in September 1537 that the city "is growing in population, and for that reason it's necessary that it have two parishes"; see Rodríguez Morel, *Cartas del cabildo*, 139.
83. AGI Santo Domingo 868 L. 2 f. 316 v. The audiencia protested the construction of the tower to the king and apparently succeeded in having it stopped; see AGI Santo Domngo 49 R. 19, N. 124 ff. 1v–2r.
84. Diego del Río asked to be excused from paying taxes on the silver ornaments that he had brought with him from Seville, as they were a charitable donation and he was a clergyman. AGI Santo Domingo 868 L. 2 ff. 166v–167r.
85. AGI Santo Domingo 1121 L. 1 ff. 133r and 140r.
86. AGI Santo Domingo 868 L. 1 f. 91r, 203v, 205r. Colón was required to provide certain ornaments for the church and also had to promise to provide a "decent iron grate" for the chapel within fifteen years. The monasterio of Santa María de las Cuevas also was known as the monasterio de la Cartuja. Both Spain and the Dominican Republic still claim the remains of Columbus.
87. *Proceso*, 26–27, 53.
88. AGI Santo Domingo 9 N. 51.
89. AGI Patronato 177 N. 1 R. 11.
90. AGI Santo Domingo 1121 L. 1f. 163r.
91. His información was compiled in 1544; see AGI Santo Domingo 10 N. 35.
92. For his información of 1538, see AGI Santo Domingo 19 N. 19; and Santo Domingo 868 L. 2 f. 106r.
93. AGI Santo Domingo 10 N. 42.
94. See Ledesma's información in AGI Santo Domingo 10 N. 11. Gonzalo de Guzmán stated that he had known Ledesma's parents and grandparents well and that after he arrived in Cuba, Ledesma had lived with him and recited mass in his house.
95. AGI Santo Domingo 1121 L. 2 f. 51v. Only in the 1540s did Havana start to gain in importance, gradually displacing Santiago as Cuba's capital, in the 1550s.
96. AGI Santo Domingo 9 N. 34. In 1530 the queen recommended the appointment of Luis

de Aguilar as one of the canons of Santo Domingo's cathedral, noting that he was born and raised in Hispaniola and was the son of a vecino; see Rodríguez Morel, *Documentos*, 146.

97. Bardecí's información is in AGI Santo Domingo 10 N. 47. In 1546 he stated that he was twenty years old; see AGI Santo Domingo 74 R. 2. Don Luis Colón by this time had jurisdiction— "mero y mixto imperio e título de marques della"—over Jamaica; see Fernández de Oviedo, *Historia general*, Libro IV, cap. VII, 116.

98. On Juan de Bardecí's family, see another información he compiled, in 1550, in AGI Santo Domingo 10 N. 52.

99. Rodríguez Morel, *Cartas de los cabildos eclesiásticos*, 112. The letter from September 1549 was signed by García de Aguilar, Gaspar de Astudillo, Diego Caballero, Francisco Dávila, Juan Mosquera, Alvaro Carrillo, Luis de Santa Clara, Juan de Junco, and Gonzalo Fernández de Oviedo. See also AGI Santo Domingo 74 R. 2 for the cabildo's 1546 letter to the king.

100. Rodríguez Morel, *Cartas de los cabildos eclesiásticos*, 33–34. He points out that Santo Domingo's leading families were well represented on both the municipal cabildo and the cathedral chapters of Santo Domingo and Concepción de la Vega, mentioning the Caballero, Serrano, Tostado, Lebrón, and Bardecí families, among others. This situation "allowed the creation of a community of religious for the most part formed by creole hijos patrimoniales," although he points out that this phenomenon only came to full fruition in the seventeenth century (35).

101. AGI Santo Domingo 74 R. 2.

102. See *Proceso*. The discussion of Castro here is based on this document, unless otherwise noted.

103. *Proceso*, 235–238.

104. See Rodríguez Morel, *Cartas de cabildos eclesiásticos*, 86–91.

105. *Proceso*, 78, 119–120, 154.

106. AGI Santo Domingo 868 L. 2 ff. 194r, 237r, 240r. In his September 1532 letter to the king, written during the time that charges against him were being investigated, Castro sought permission to leave Hispaniola to return to "mi naturaleza" in Spain. He stayed on the island, however, reinforcing the inference that he was acquitted of any serious charges. See Rodríguez Morel, *Cartas de los cabildos eclesiásticas*, 90.

107. *Proceso*, 90–94, 119.

108. *Proceso*, 213.

109. Arranz, *Don Diego Colón*, 252–253.

110. Rodríguez Morel, *Cartas de los cabildos eclesiásticas*, 123–124. He referred to them as "ciertos hombres monteses."

111. AGI Santo Domingo 868 L. 2 ff. 371v–372r.

112. AGI Santo Domingo 10 N. 30. Vaca had been canon for twelve years when he compiled the información. It is unlikely that there were two canons named Pero Vaca in Concepción during the same years.

113. AGI Santo Domingo 1121 L. 1 ff. 29r–29v, 150r–151r. Licenciado Juan de Vadillo, who went to Cuba to conduct the residencia of Guzmán's term in office, wrote that the bishop waited until his niece arrived with her husband in the port of Santiago to give up his Indians, and he noted that there were others on the island who were far more deserving, given that his niece's husband was not a vecino or a settler but rather was living in the bishop's house; see Rodríguez Morel, *Cartas de la Real Audiencia*, 93.

114. AGI Santo Domingo 1121 L. 1 f. 162v.
115. AGI Santo Domingo 1121 L. 2 ff. 193r–195r.
116. Murga, *Historia documental*, 1:xxiv.
117. AGI Santo Domingo 2280 L. 1 f. 48v. Laypeople could fill these positions. A man named Buenaventura de Soto, who died in 1527, had served as alguacil, and in 1530 Juan López de Bienvenida was secretary. In the 1530s (perhaps earlier as well), Asencio de Villanueva was *receptor* (the person responsible for receiving sequestered goods); see AGI Santo Domingo 9 N. 32. In 1533 he was at court representing Bishop Manso, where he asked for six singers to form a choir for the cathedral; see AGI Santo Domingo 1121 L. 1 f. 175v.
118. AGI Santo Domingo 2280 L. 1 ff. 65v–66r.
119. AGI Santo Domingo 2280 L. 2 f. 22r.
120. Murga, *Historia documental*, 1:lviii, lxii.
121. AGI Santo Domingo 2280 L. 1 f. 96r (November 1531).
122. AGI Santo Domingo 2280 L. 2 f. 26v.
123. Bermúdez Bermúdez, *Don Rodrigo de Bastidas*, 110–112, 121–122.
124. Moscoco, *Juicio al gobernador*, 149.
125. Rodríguez Morel, *Cartas de los cabildos eclesiásticos*, 10, 13–14. The first bishop appointed for Santo Domingo was the Franciscan fray García de Padilla, but he died in Getafe before going to the island. According to Las Casas, *Historia*, 3:587, Deza was the nephew of Diego de Deza, a Dominican friar and archbishop of Seville.
126. Rodríguez Morel, *Cartas de los cabildos eclesiásticos*, 37–38. He points to the strong ties between the audiencia and the royal court: Licenciado Cervantes was related to the archbishop of Seville, Licenciado Vadillo was related to the wife of Dr. Beltrán, and Licenciado Guevara was related to a member of the Council of the Indies.
127. Rodríguez Morel, *Cartas de los cabildos eclesiásticos*, 114, 117–118. In a letter Tarifeño wrote the following year, he reiterated his claim that the cathedral chapter did not want to participate in votes for fear of the archbishop's retaliation; see 121.
128. AGI Santo Domingo 1121 L. 2 ff. 36v, 39r, 140v.
129. AGI Santo Domingo 1121 L. 2 ff. 151v–153r.
130. AGI Santo Domingo 10 N. 47.
131. AGI Santo Domingo 10 N. 8.
132. Marrero, *Cuba*, 1:201.
133. See AGI Santo Domingo 77 R. 2 N. 30. Esteban Mira Caballos has written about this collection in "Algunas consideraciones," although perhaps the term *library* that he uses is a misnomer. Inés's father, Antón Ruiz, was a locksmith and probably also had a bookselling business. Mira Caballos has transcribed the inventory (499–500) and describes the sale at auction of some of the books in 1525.
134. He included in the donation "an estancia I have in another part of the town of Azua with three caballerías of irrigated land and 3,000 feet of canafistula and large quantities of oranges and fruit trees and all the food-producing farmland with which the people of the said ingenio are sustained and maintained and an iron forge . . . with one hundred Black men and women . . . and sixteen carts and thirty-five oxen . . . and also three thousand cows and three thousand sheep." AGI Santo Domingo 868 L. 1 f. 264v.

135. AGI Santo Domingo 868 L. 1 ff. 255r–255v.
136. AGI Patronato 173 N. 1 R. 8.
137. AGI Patronato 173 N. 1 R. 8; see also Otte, "Una carta inédita," 445.
138. Rodríguez Morel, *Cartas del cabildo,* 146–147.
139. See Rodríguez Morel, "Cartas privadas," 218. In 1537 Gorjón had asked the city's cabildo for six solares for an orchard and an enclosure for chickens "as is suitable for this kind of building." AGI Santo Domingo 868 L. 1 ff. 270r–270v. The cabildo granted the solares, which were near lots owned by treasurer Miguel de Pasamonte. See also AGI Patronato 278 N. 2 R. 7.
140. Rodríguez Morel, "Cartas privadas," 16. The king made the request to the pope, who apparently did not act on it.
141. Rodríguez Morel, "Cartas privadas," 17.
142. AGI Santo Domingo 868 L. 1 f.256v.
143. On the disposition of Gorjón's ingenio and settlement of his debts, see AGI Santo Domingo 868 L. 2. See AGI Patronato 275 R. 68 for the royal authorization to establish the university in Santo Domingo "of all the sciences where the children of Spaniards and the natives of those parts would be taught the things of our holy Catholic faith and in the rest of the sciences and we concede the privileges and exemptions and freedoms and exemptions" of the university of Salamanca. See also Rodríguez Morel, *Documentos,* 267.
144. See Rodríguez Morel's perceptive discussion of Gorjón's life and career in "Cartas privadas."
145. AGI Santo Domingo 868 L. 2 f. 352. See also Rodríguez Morel, *Cartas del cabildo,* 169–170.
146. See Otte, "Una carta inédita," 444.
147. See AGI Santo Domingo 868 L. 2 ff. 295r, 356v; and AGI Santo Domingo 899 L. 1 ffs. 17v–18. See also Rodríguez Morel, *Documentos,* 244–245.
148. CDIAO, 1:35.
149. MacDonald, "Cemí and the Cross," writes, "Long after the arrival of the Europeans, the areito continued to be a significant act of memory, negotiation, and resistance for Caribbean Indians" (5). On the protection of the areitos in the Laws of Burgos (1512), see 17–18: "By protecting areitos, the Laws of Burgos were inadvertently protecting a potential medium for cultural transmission for Caribbean Indians."
150. Fernández de Oviedo, *Historia general,* Libro V, cap. I, 127. Anacaona, sister of one cacique (Behechio) and wife of another (Caonabo), was executed by governor Nicolás de Ovando. On aspects of her life and how she has been portrayed in early chronicles, see Moscoso, *Caguas,* chapter 7.
151. See Christian, *Local Religion.*
152. CDIAO, 1:464. This report was from the city of Concepción de la Vega.
153. Fernández de Oviedo, *Historia general,* Libro III, cap. V, 69. It is worth noting that he did not say that they venerated the cross, although they might have acknowledged its power.
154. AGI Santo Domingo 868 L. 1 f. 200r.
155. Alegría, *Documentos,* 1:159.
156. AGI Santo Domingo 868 L. 2 f. 326v.
157. AGI Santo Domingo 1121 L. 1 f. 163r.

5. Transitions

1. AGI Santo Domingo 99 R. 4 N. 17. The sale of a repartimiento or encomienda was illegal, but Spaniards evaded the prohibition by selling property and persuading or bribing officials to reassign rights to the repartimiento. See, for example, Lalor, "Two Doñas," 96, on the sale of an encomienda in Panama belonging to doña Isabel de Bobadilla.
2. AGI Santo Domingo 77 N. 50. Nombre de Dios was located on Panama's Atlantic coast.
3. For Rojas's visita, see AGI Patronato 177 N. 1 R. 18.
4. Both in AGI Santo Domingo 2280 L. 2; see also Murga, *Historia documental*, 1:44–45.
5. AGI Santo Domingo 77 R. 3 N. 52.
6. AGI Santo Domingo 77 R. 3 N. 52. Lope de Bardecí, the lieutenant governor of Santo Domingo, had prepared a deposition detailing the recruiting activities of Vadillo and Ampies in December 1527. One witness mentioned that he had heard that Vadillo had spoken to people in Concepción and Puerto Real as well as in San Juan de la Maguana, which had only about fifteen or twenty vecinos.
7. Juan Peralta was the son of Diego Suárez Pacheco, who went to Hispaniola with his wife, doña María de Marcaida, and family in the entourage of the virreina doña María de Toledo. Townsend, *Malintzin's Choices*, 136.
8. These details are in an información compiled by Suárez's son Luis Suárez de Peralta in 1560–1561, when Luis was twenty-three years old and petitioning for a regimiento in Mexico City. Juan Suárez probably died around 1554; AGI Patronato 63 R. 13. He apparently was married for a second time in Mexico, to doña Madalena de Esparsa. Catalina Suárez's fate in Mexico has been the subject of much speculation. She died not long after rejoining Cortés, but it is impossible to know for certain whether her husband was responsible for her death, as has been alleged from that time up to the present.
9. Rodríguez Morel, *Cartas del cabildo*, 143.
10. The report appears in AGI Justicia 106 N. 3 and has been transcribed and analyzed in Damiani Cósimi, *Estratificación social*. The report points to some interesting demographic differences between San Juan and San Germán; in San Germán, Indigenous slaves outnumbered Black slaves, and possibly a larger proportion of men were married to Indigenous women than in San Juan, although there is no way to know for certain.
11. AGI Santo Domingo 868 L. 2, ff. 21r and 10r. The figure of one hundred Spaniards on an estate is almost certainly exaggerated, although he might have been referring to several estates rather than one. Although the term *mestizo* seldom appears in official documents in this period, most likely some or even most of the "Spaniards" were mestizos. In 1538 Diego Caballero's ingenio and other properties in Hispaniola included a settlement with fifteen or twenty Spaniards and around 150 Indians and Blacks; see AGI Santo Domingo 77 N. 118. See discussion of his ingenio and Vasco Porcallo's estate in Cuba in Altman, "Marriage, Family, and Ethnicity," 235–236.
12. AGI Santo Domingo 868 f. 101v.
13. Marte, *Santo Domingo*, 279.
14. In the 1530 census of Puerto Rico, place of origin is noted for the wives of most married men in San Juan, although not in San Germán. Wives were described as being from Castile, liv-

ing in Castile, *de la tierra* (that is, Indigenous), or *española*. The last term is ambiguous and never defined. It could mean from Castile, but it also might have referred to women who were seen as culturally Hispanic but were born in the Indies, very possibly including mestiza women. The term *mestizo* does not appear in reference to either men or women. On the presence of Spanish women in the early Spanish Caribbean, see Altman, "Spanish Women"; Lalor, "Two Doñas"; Otte, *Las perlas*, 350–354; and chapter 6 in the present volume.

15. Marte, *Santo Domingo*, 277. On the extensive excavations at the original site of Concepción, destroyed by an earthquake, see Florida Museum, "Concepción de la Vega," floridamuseum.ufl.edu/histarch/research/dominican-republic/concepcion-de-la-vega. According to the website, "Concepción de la Vega had the richest, most diverse and most abundant material culture of any early sixteenth-century Spanish site excavated so far. This was undoubtedly related to the wealth brought to the city by gold. Such luxury items as clothing items and adornment, Venetian glassware, ornate furniture hardware, horse equipage and books are considerably more frequent here than at other sites." See also Kulstad, "Concepción de la Vega."

16. Marte, *Santo Domingo*, 278.

17. AGI Santo Domingo 77 N. 50.

18. For Rojas's report, see AGI Patronato 177 N. 1 R. 18. For a fuller discussion of the issues involved, see Altman, "Towns," 32–35.

19. AGI Santo Domingo 9 N. 51.

20. AGI Santo Domingo 868 L. 2 f. 261v.

21. AGI Santo Domingo 868 L. 2 ff. 263r–263v; also ff. 269r, 270v–275r.

22. Marte, *Santo Domingo*, 366.

23. AGI Indiferente General 1092 N. 45 imagen 3. Fernández de Oviedo, *Historia general*, Libro V, cap. X, mentions the arrival of "up to seventy farmers [labradores], and the majority of them with their wives and children, to settle in Montecristi and Puerto Real" (156). He noted that many subsequently left for Peru and alluded vaguely to poor leadership on the part of Bolaños.

24. Hoffman, *Spanish Crown*, 119–121. See AGI Patronato 172 R. 20 for a proposal to join Montecristi and Puerto Real. PARES lists the date of the document as 1521, but clearly that is an error; 1560s or 1570s would be more likely. Notwithstanding that uncertainty, the letter is further evidence that the towns were doing well; the justification for merging the towns was based on defensive needs, not population loss.

25. See *Colección de documentos inéditos relativos al descubrimiento, conquista y colonización de las posesiones españolas en América y Oceanía sacados, en su mayor parte, del Real Archivo de Indias*, 1:474–477. For the oidores' proposal, see Marte, *Santo Domingo*, 284–286, 290; and Altman, "Towns," 38–40.

26. AGI Santo Domingo 2280 L. 2 ff. 4r–7v. See also Villanueva's probanza of 1532 in AGI Santo Domingo 9 N. 35.

27. Castellanos first went to Hispaniola in 1505 as an adolescent and then participated in the conquest of Puerto Rico. He was still living in 1558, at which time he was sixty-five years old. See AGI Santo Domingo 2280 L. 2 ff. 52v, 65r, 90r; and Altman, "Towns," 40.

28. AGI Santo Domingo 74 R. 2. In 1551 the treasurer of Hispaniola, Alonso de la Peña, informed the crown that a number of potential settlers who planned to emigrate to the island had

to wait in Seville for so long before departing that they were forced to return to "their homes and origin" because of the cost; see Rodríguez Morel, *Documentos,* 230.

29. Mira Caballos, *El Indio Antillano,* 326–327, says that recruitment for Barrionuevo's expedition took place in southern Spain, targeting towns not far from Seville: Carmona, Osuna, Marchena, Lebrija, Utrera, Sanlúcar de Barrameda, Jerez de la Frontera, and Puerto de Santa María. See also Altman, "Revolt of Enriquillo."

30. AGI Santo Domingo 77 N. 89. Rodríguez Morel suggests that the annual export of hides to Sevilla reached 150,000; see "Cartas privadas," 213.

31. Genaro Rodríguez Morel is responsible for the most extensive recent research on sugar production in early Hispaniola. See Rodríguez Morel, *Orígenes de la economía;* and "Sugar Economy of Española."

32. See Rocha, "Maroons in the Montes." On the presence of cattle in connection with ingenios, see Rodríguez Morel, "Cartas privadas," 212–213.

33. AGI Santo Domingo 77 N. 118; and Santo Domingo 868 L. 1 ff. 115 v, 117r.

34. Gorjón was from the province of Huelva and probably was born around 1482; see Rodríguez Morel, "Cartas privadas," 203. Rodríguez Morel credits Gorjón with introducing some important changes in the construction and operation of water-powered mills for ingenios, which were quickly adopted by other leading ingenio owners, including Alonzo de Zuazo and Francisco de Tapia (217).

35. AGI Patronato 18 N. 1 R. 2, Santo Domingo 868 L. 1 ff. 250v, 255 r–v, 263v–264r.

36. Rodríguez Morel, *Orígenes de la economía,* 188.

37. Moscoco, *Juicio al gobernador,* 113.

38. Rodríguez Morel, "Sugar Economy," 89–92. Recipients of loans had to make certain guarantees about repayment and completion of construction within a specified period; a number of people had to request extensions. On the role of the Genoese in establishing sugar ingenios, see Pike, *Enterprise and Adventure,* 129–133, 137–138.

39. On the construction of the sugar estate, see AGI Santo Domingo 77 R. 3 N. 66 (executed in 1533); and AGI Justicia 13 N. 1 R. 3 (1533–1535). See chapter 6 for Benito de Astorga's efforts to bring his wife to Hispaniola.

40. Pike, *Enterprise and Adventure,* 143. Eventually, the heirs to the ingenio returned to Spain and rented it out, but in 1554 French corsairs arrived at the port, killed most of the slaves, and destroyed the estate.

41. AGI Santo Domingo 2280 L. 2 ff. 55v–5r.

42. AGI Santo Domingo 10 N. 27. In this period many sugar masters were being brought from the Canaries.

43. AGI Santo Domingo 10 N. 46. Pérez Martel had married doña Leonor Troche Ponce de León, a granddaughter of Juan Ponce de León, and built a stone house in San Juan for 2,000 pesos de oro.

44. AGI Santo Domingo 10 N. 48 ff. 3v, 6r.

45. AGI Santo Domingo 1121 L. 1 ff. 123v and 134r.

46. AGI Santo Domingo 1121 L. 2 ff. 27r, 29r, 32v.

47. Wolofs were associated, possibly inaccurately, with the slave revolt that began on don Diego Colón's estate in Hispaniola in 1522; see Landers, "Central African Presence," 234.

48. AGI Santo Domingo 1121 L. 2 f. 11v.
49. De la Fuente, "Sugar and Slavery," 116–117.
50. De la Fuente, "Sugar and Slavery," 117. On patterns of the early slave trade to the Caribbean, see Eagle, "Early Slave Trade." 141–142.
51. On the crown's worries in 1529 about the economic importance of the ingenios in Hispaniola, see Rodríguez Morel, *Documentos*, 97 (from AGI Patronato 275 R. 8 N. 8).
52. AGI Santo Domingo 868 L. 2 f. 296r.
53. From the partial transcription of Ávila's report in AGI Justicia 12 in Saez, *La iglesia*, 268–271.
54. Rodríguez Morel, *Cartas del cabildo*, 128.
55. AGI Santo Domingo 9 N. 42 (1531). For more on doña Isabel de Maraver, see chapter 6.
56. AGI Santo Domingo 77 N. 98. That visit is discussed in chapter 4. For a discussion of the workers on these estancias, see Altman, "Marriage, Family, and Ethnicity," 245–247.
57. AGI Patronato 295 N. 107. *Viejo* in this context probably means "mature" or "established." There is very little information on local markets and supply systems for the period.
58. AGI Santo Domingo 1121 L. 2 f. 9v.
59. AGI Santo Domingo 868 L. 1 f. 156v.
60. AGI Santo Domingo 868 L. 2 ff. 28v–29r.
61. Fernández de Oviedo, *Historia general*, Libro III, cap. XI, 85–86.
62. Alegría, *Documentos históricos*, 1:160. The existence of these extensive fields of pineapples in one location suggests that they were being cultivated.
63. Barerra, "Local Herbs," 165, notes that balsam was used as a purgative, for vision problems, to induce menstruation and childbirth, to heal wounds, and as an antidote for poison.
64. Barrera, "Local Herbs," 166–167, 170–174.
65. AGI Santo Domingo 1121 L. 1 f. 175v, AGI Santo Domingo 2280 L. 1 f. 189v.
66. Rodríguez Morel, *Documentos*, 86.
67. AGI Santo Domingo 868 L. 2 ff. 23v–24v. According to Pike, *Enterprise and Adventure*, 68, Franco Leardo and Pedro Benito de Basiñana, two Genoese merchants based in Seville who were involved in the import of sugar and hides, obtained a monopoly for the balsam and canafistula trade of Santo Domingo in 1528.
68. AGI Santo Domingo 2280 L. 1 f. 183r. AGI 2280 L. 2 f. Sanlúcar had served as alcalde in San Germán and owned a cattle ranch on the Guaviabo River.
69. Fernández de Oviedo, *Historia general*, Libro III, cap. XI, 85–86.
70. Cassá and Rodríguez Morel, "Consideraciones alternativas," 20.
71. See Chipman, "Traffic in Indian Slaves."
72. AGI Santo Domingo 77 R. 3 N. 52.
73. AGI Santo Domingo 77 N. 50.
74. AGI Santo Domingo 118 R. 1 N. 71. My thanks to Shannon Lalor for a copy of this document.
75. AGI Santo Domingo 2280 L. 2 f. 30r.
76. AGI Santo Domingo 2280 L. 2 f. 97r.
77. Moscoso, *Lucha agraria*, 98.
78. AGI Santo Domingo 868 L. 2 f. 101r.

79. Moscoso, *Lucha agraria*, 76.

80. AGI Santo Domingo 1121 L. 2 f. 78 r. The audiencia had issued an ordinance that cattle could not graze closer than six leagues to Santiago. Several prominent men had asked Manuel de Rojas to issue new ordinances, which the fiscal of the audiencia considered to be "very prejudicial to the republic of the said city."

81. On commons and other forms of land tenure in Castile, see Vassberg, *Land and Society*.

82. Andrew Sluyter's description of cattle raising in Andalucía is reminiscent of the increasingly uncontrolled movement of cattle into Hispaniola's montes: "As the floodwater of the Río Guadalquivir receded each spring, herders drove their stock into Las Marismas. . . . Largely untended during the long dry season, the animals became semiferal . . . As the rains returned each October, herders required horses to round up the semiferal stock before the Guadalquivir flooded and drive them up to the fresh regrowth of the hill pastures." Sluyter, "Ecological Origins," 162.

83. In his classic study, Charles Julian Bishko writes, "These range cattle of the *meseta* and Andalusian Plain gave rise to a characteristic Iberian and, later, Ibero-American phenomenon, the *ganado bravo* or unbranded wild cattle existing in some numbers on the fringes of the ranching industry as a result of loose herding methods and the frontier conditions of the cattle country. The co-existence of herded, branded cows and wild, ownerless ones was a regular feature of peninsular *ganadería vacuna* long before there appeared across the ocean the very much larger wild herds of Española, New Spain, Brazil, the River Plate, and other regions; just as the medieval hunts of *ganado bravo* by mounted hunters . . . anticipated the greater *monterías* and *vaquerías* of Cuba, Española and the pampas." Bishko, "Peninsular Background," 498–499.

84. Bishko, "Peninsular Background," 502. He points out that Castile's cattle raisers never established an organization similar to the sheep raisers' Real Consejo de la Mesta, although some municipalities had their own local mestas (503–504).

85. Mosoco, *Lucha agraria*, 57, 76–77, 139.

86. This conflict is the focus of Moscoso's *Lucha agraria*. See Murga, *Historia documental*, 1:201, 214–217, 219, 340–342, 352–360. The cabildo of the cathedral also weighed in on the controversy, which at some points seemed likely to end in violence. Lepe had traveled to court to report on the situation. In 1542 he was alcalde. Alonso de Molina stated that out of sixty vecinos in San Juan, fifty-two had an *asiento de ganado* (344).

87. AGI Santo Domingo 868 L. 2 ff. 84v–85r. In 1540 Francisco de Ávila, longtime resident of Hispaniola and regidor of Santiago, asked for five sites ("cinco asientos para ganados"), each "one league of land," to graze cattle in the valley of Ycagua, which had depopulated twenty-five years earlier; AGI Santo Domingo 868 L. 1 f. 231r.

88. AGI Santo Domingo 868 ff. 311v, 312v, 343r–v.

89. Rodríguez Morel, *Cartas de los cabildos eclesiásticas*, 107.

90. See Rodríguez Morel, *Documentos*, 242.

91. See Rocha, "Maroons in the *Montes*." In a letter he wrote in 1547 the dean of Concepción mentioned that vecinos from Concepción were abandoning the city to go the countryside, "fleeing to where the rebel Blacks hunt them [cattle] every day" (Rodríguez Morel, *Cartas de cabildos eclesiásticas*, 107).

92. Moscoso, *Lucha agraria*, 221.

93. AGI Santo Domingo 9 N. 45. Hernando had died by 1532. Because of the importance of the work they performed in maintaining inns and roads, the brothers had received fifty people in encomienda, who were under the authority of the cacique of Higuan.

94. Sauer, *Early Spanish Main*, writes that gold mining in the islands ended early, in Hispaniola during the time of don Diego Colón (the 1510s), and soon thereafter in Puerto Rico and Cuba as well. Although he suggests that the loss of native labor affected the mining economy, he argues that "the loss of cheap labor ... hastened the collapse but did not cause it" (197). Sauer seems to have concluded that the islands simply did not have extensive sources of the ore.

95. Fernández de Oviedo, *Historia general*, Libro VI, cap. VIII, 176.

96. Antonio Rodríguez's informacion of 1546 is in AGI Santo Domingo 10 N. 40; the información for the town is in AGI Santo Domingo 9 N. 51.

97. AGI Santo Domingo 9 N. 51 ff. 22r–22v.

98. Fernández de Oviedo, *Historia general*, Libro VI, cap. VIII. Alison Bigelow, *Mining Language*, points out that Fernández de Oviedo ignored or failed to grasp the rituals and meaning the Taíno associated with collecting gold, writing, "Taínos and Spaniards understood gold metals, and how to evaluate their meaning and worth, in radically different ways. . . . For Taínos, gold mining and refining occurred within a larger matrix of gendered social norms and cosmological principles of balance" (34). Bigelow points out that although he described the important work done by women, Fernández de Oviedo did not include any women in an illustration that showed workers panning for gold (75).

99. AGI Santo Domingo 2280 L. 1 ff. 181r–181v.

100. Sued Badilo, *El dorado borincano*.

101. Sued Badillo, *El dorado borincano*, 49.

102. Sued Badillo, *El dorado borincano*, 47.

103. Sued Badillo, *El dorado borincano*, 55, 285.

104. AGI Santo Domingo 1121 L. 1 f. 188v.

105. Sued Badillo, *El dorado borincano*, 80, 85.

106. AGI Santo Domingo 868 L. 2 f. 30r.

107. Marrero, *Cuba*, 2:14.

108. Sued Badillo, *El dorado borincano*, 338–341, 347.

109. Marte, *Santo Domingo*, 113.

110. Sued Badillo, *El dorado borincano*, 356, 358–359; Marrero, *Cuba*, 2:20.

111. Sued Badillo, *El dorado borincano*, 111–112.

112. Sued Badlllo, *El dorado borincano*, 127.

113. AGI Santo Domingo 868 L. 1 ff. 79v, 241f–v, 259v; and AGI Santo Domingo 868 L. 2 f. 277r. Don Juan Pérez de Almazán did go to Hispaniola to assume the office. According to Sued Badillo, *El dorado borincano*, 363, the fundidor received 1 percent of all the gold smelted.

114. AGI Santo Domingo 2280 L. 1 ff. 133v–134v. As often is the case in these kinds of allegations, there might have been more to the accusation than is possible to learn from the documents. Juan Maldonado was regidor of San Germán in 1533.

115. AGI Santo Domingo 2280 L.1 ff. 173r–173v.

116. AGI Patronato 177 N. 1 R. 11.

117. Sued Badillo, *El dorado borincano*, 334. The crown "was followed by the viceroy Diego

Colon and his family, which also received one-tenth of all the smelted gold belonging to the crown, besides direct benefits as producers." After 1519, "royal officials, big encomenderos, and those with the greatest access to slaves were the largest producers, and many of them were involved in other enterprises as well. Among them, they might have been able to monopolize sixty or seventy percent of all the gold smelted" (363).

118. See Sued Badillo, *El dorado borincano,* 281–283, for the transcription of the document establishing the partnership. In 1527 the price for a Black male slave was between 80 and 190 pesos, and for a woman it was 60 pesos; see 308. Although apparently Villanueva, at least, had access to Indian labor, there is no indication of how many Indian workers were available to be put to work in the mine.

119. Copper was discovered near Puerto Real soon after the town was established in 1503. In 1505 King Ferdinand sent tools, supplies, a German mining expert, and seventeen African slaves to exploit the mine, but it had only limited success. See Florida Museum, "History: Puerto Real, Haiti," https://www.floridamuseum.ufl.edu/histarch/research/haiti/puerto-real/history. According to Mira Caballos, "Las cuentas," 89, Ovando had several maestros brought from Spain but sent them back in May 1506.

120. AGI Santo Domingo 868 L. 1 f 291v.

121. AGI Santo Domingo 2280 L. 2 f. 71v.

122. Fernández de Oviedo, *Historia general,* Libro VI, cap. VIII, 177.

123. AGI Santo Domingo 1121 L. 2 ff. 15r, 16v–17v.

124. Marrero, *Cuba,* 2:24–32. Tetzel lived until 1576.

125. Fernandez de Oviedo, *Historia general,* Libro VI, cap. V, 173.

126. Sued Badillo, *El dorado borincano,* 194–196.

127. See Martínez-Fernández, *Key to the New World*. Although he was not the first to write about two distinct Cubas, he describes this phenomenon as emerging by the mid-sixteenth century.

128. Article XIX stipulated that within a year of being awarded an encomienda, the encomendero must provide each Indian a hammock. Indians were not to be permitted to exchange their hammocks for other items. The records of the hacienda de Toa for the late 1510s mention the distribution of hammocks but do not specify their source; see AGI Contaduría 1072. Mira Caballos, *El Indio Antillano,* 256–257, suggests that the precontact use of hammocks had been limited to the upper echelons of Indigenous society and, as a result, compliance with the general order to provide them was problematic.

129. Las Casas, *Historia,* 3:784.

130. See Rocha, "Pinzones," addressing the role that commercial fishing interests played in Columbus's first voyage. Columbus referred to fishing repeatedly in the diary of his first voyage. Rocha points out that fishing "continued to form part of the quotidian experience of maritime labor" and suggests that the way in which mariners' "understanding of longstanding Iberian social and political conventions for harvesting marine wildlife in Iberia and Atlantic Africa intersected with Taíno knowledge and expertise in Caribbean fishing, navigation, and maritime environments merits further scrutiny" (440).

131. AGI Santo Domingo 868 L. 2 f. 15v. Several years later, when Fernández de Oviedo and Alonso de Peña were representing Hispaniola, they again asked that slaves be allowed to eat meat

during Lent because of "the great lack of fish." Otherwise, the slaves would go hungry or become ill and die, or they would leave to search for food, as it was well known that "said island doesn't produce bread or wine." AGI Santo Domingo 868 L. 2 f. 320r and 327r. When an English ship unexpectedly arrived in Santo Domingo in 1527, the crew raided along the shore north of the city before departing and, among other things, commandeered from a fisherman 150 arrobas of fish (nearly four thousand pounds); AGI Santo Domingo 9 N. 21. Spaniards on Hispaniola may not have been exploiting this resource by the 1540s.

132. Sued Badillo, *El dorado borincano*, 326.

133. Fernández de Oviedo, *Historia general*, Libro XVI, cap. I, 465.

6. Women and Family

1. See Altman, "Spanish Women"; Enrique Otte, *Las perlas*, 350–354; and Lalor, "Two Doñas."

2. See Lalor, "Women, Power." There also were women who inherited encomiendas, although usually the grants passed quickly to their subsequent husbands. See Mira Caballos, *El Indio Antillano*, 223–225, which mentions, "It is in Cuba where we encounter the largest number of women who were beneficiaries of [a] repartimiento, perhaps because in this island the natives survived for more years and succession to the encomienda over several generations was more frequent" (224).

3. Dillard, *Daughters of the Reconquest*, 12.

4. For a discussion of how royal policies on marriage for Spaniards, Indians, and Africans in the islands differed, see Altman, "Marriage, Family, and Ethnicity."

5. *Colección de documentos inéditos relativos al descubrimiento, conquista y organización de las antiguas posesiones españolas y de ultramar*, 1:36.

6. See Altman, "Spanish Women," 62.

7. See Deagan, "Colonial Transformation."

8. AGI Santo Domingo 11 N. 28; Santo Domingo 1121 L. 2 ff. 154r–154v.

9. AGI Santo Domingo 77 R. 3 N. 59.

10. AGI Santo Domingo 10 N. 44. Francisco Alegre appeared in the muster of San Juan in 1541, declaring a horse, lance, and dagger; AGI Patronato 175 R. 28.

11. Bishop Rodrigo de Bastidas and his widowed mother, Isabel Rodríguez de Romera Tamaris, established an entail to which the son of Rodrigo's sister, doña Isabel de Bastidas, and her husband, Hernando de Hoyos, would succeed, taking the name Rodrigo de Bastidas. He married Juana de Oviedo, the daughter of Gonzalo de Fernández de Oviedo, and the two families agreed to join the families and retain the two entails, one attached to the *apellido* Bastidas and the other to Oviedo. See Bermúdez Bermúdez, *Don Rodrigo de Bastidas*, 122–129.

12. AGI Santo Domingo 1121 L. 1 ff. 152v–153r.

13. AGI Santo Domingo 2280 L. 2 ff. 16v–17v; AGI Contratación 5536 L. 5 f. 139r.

14. See Floyd, *Columbus Dynasty*, 137, 148.

15. See testimony of Francisco de Segovia in AGI Santo Domingo 10 N. 52.

16. AGI Santo Domingo 10 N. 47.

17. In 1518, for example, the cabildo of Santo Domingo refused to recognize Bardecí as procurador to the royal court and, with the support of Miguel de Pasamonte, elected Lucas Vázquez de Ayllón, but the Hieronymites rejected this choice and possibly neither man went to court. Marte, *Santo Domingo,* 255–256, 313–314. See chapter 3 of the present volume for a discussion of the political "clans" in early Hispaniola.

18. AGI Santo Domingo 77 N. 118.

19. Otte, *Las perlas,* 111, 118, 133, 196.

20. Witness Francisca Nuñez (not a relative) testified in 1550 that doña Isabel had gone to the Indies, "siendo pequeña de edad" (being young of age). See AGI Santo Domingo 10 N. 52.

21. Testimony of Francisco de Villalba, vecino of Avila and resident of Zebreros, AGI Santo Domingo 10 N. 52. This is one of two informaciones compiled by or on behalf of Juan de Bardecí, the son of doña Isabel Núñez de Andrada and Lope de Bardecí, around the same time. The first was executed in Santo Domingo in 1549, when Juan de Bardecí was a canon of the cathedral in Santo Domingo; AGI Santo Domingo 10 N. 47. The second was done at the behest of his uncle by marriage, Juan de Henao, in Zebreros in 1550; AGI Santo Domingo 10 N. 52. According to one witness, Isabel's brothers Francisco and Pedro Bravo also departed for the Indies, "siendo mozuelos" (being very young men), although it is not known whether they went to or remained in Hispaniola.

22. See AGI Santo Domingo 9 N. 21; Santo Domingo 77 R. 3 N. 52; and Santo Domingo 868 L. 1. For the información of Pero Vázquez de Ayllón, see AGI Patronato 63 R. 24.

23. In his lengthy letter of 1554, Fernández de Oviedo mentioned that Bardecí's wife (whom he did not mention by name) was related to both the wife of contador Álvaro Caballero and the wife of Juan de Junco. Otte, "Una carta inédita," 457.

24. See *Proceso,* 159. The term *lucaya* referred to the people of the Bahamas.

25. The license for the family's departure is in AGI Contratación 5536 L. 1 f. 398, dated October 1514. It is possible that not all the family members listed actually emigrated, or possibly not all of them survived the journey. In 1527 Guzmán claimed to have married Isabel in Castile; see AGI Santo Domingo 9 N. 17. This Guzmán is often confused with the Gonzalo de Guzmán who lived and made his career in Cuba during approximately the same years, but they most certainly are two different men. Guzmán said that he had married Isabel in Castile in 1515, but the number of witnesses in Santo Domingo who testified that they had witnessed the couple's marriage suggests that more likely the wedding took place in Santo Domingo. Those witnesses included Luis Hernández and Lope de Bardecí, along with Hernando de Carvajal and García de Aguilar, who were *padrinos de la boda.* Perhaps Guzmán had traveled to Spain and been betrothed to Isabel there.

26. By 1531 the husband of doña María, Gonzalo de Ocampo, apparently had died as well. AGI Santo Domingo 9 N. 42.

27. See Altman, "Marriage, Family, and Ethnicity," 230–232.

28. The debt was for a loan to establish a sugar mill and estate; see AGI Santo Domingo 9 N. 17. His having received such a loan means that he must have been considered one of the more substantial residents on the island at the time.

29. One witness suggested that the Indians had left to join the people in the Bahoruco, doubtless a reference to the "rebel" Enrique's community.

30. Rodríguez Demorizi, *Los Dominicos*, 153. Rodríguez Demorizi thinks that this is the same Guzmán who was so prominent in Cuba, but they were different men.

31. See transcription of the probanza in Arranz Márquez, *Repartimientos y encomiendas*, 467.

32. Isabel Maraver's información is in AGI Santo Domingo 9 N. 42; Gonzalo de Guzmán's información of 1527 is in AGI Santo Domingo 9 N. 17.

33. Witness Cristóbal de Santa Clara, who also testified for Benito de Astorga, provided the details about the slaves, two of whom he had previously owned. Bartolomé had been responsible for cutting off the hand of the third slave, who Santa Clara thought was named Pedro.

34. Nothing is known about Isabel de Maraver's brother, who was listed in the license they obtained from the Casa de la Contratación as traveling with the family. Possibly he stayed behind, or he traveled with the family but did not remain in Hispaniola.

35. On the forging of such ties, see Premo, "Familiar."

36. See Lalor, "Two Doñas" on doña Isabel de Bobadilla's situation after her husband Hernando de Soto's death.

37. AGI Santo Domingo 868 L. 2 f. 215r.

38. Rodríguez Morel, *Documentos*, 217.

39. AGI Indiferente General 419 L. 5 f. 448v.

40. AGI Santo Domingo 868 L. 2 ff. 293v–r.

41. AGI Santo Domingo 868 L. 2 ff. 232r–232v.

42. AGI Santo Domingo 2280 L. 1 ff. 107r, 110r, 156r.

43. AGI Santo Domingo 868 L. 2 ff. 264v, 301r. 333v. Somewhat confusingly, the statement from the man representing Catalina, Sebastián Rodríguez, referred to her having arranged her daughters' marriage in Seville, but the king's response to her petition mentioned that before he died she and her husband had hoped to go to live in Guadalcanal "where he was from . . . where he had many relatives."

44. AGI Santo Domingo 868 L. 2 f. 333v.

45. AGI Santo Domingo 868 L. 1 f. 246v.

46. AGI Santo Domingo 77 N. 133.

47. AGI Santo Domingo 868 L. 2 ff. 168r, 261r–v.

48. AGI Santo Domingo 868 L. 1 f. 102r.

49. AGI Santo Domingo 868 L. 1 f. 126r.

50. AGI Santo Domingo 2280 L. 1 f. 25v.

51. AGI Santo Domingo 2280 L. 1 f. 99v. It would be interesting to know whether he maintained some business dealings in Santo Domingo that his wife oversaw. Unfortunately, he offered no explanation for why she had stayed in Hispaniola. In 1527 Pedro López de Angulo was accused of murdering Nicolás Fajardo, a regidor of San Juan, but apparently never was brought to justice. See AGI Indiferente General 423 L. 12 ff. 49v–50r.

52. AGI Santo Domingo 1121 L. 1 ff. 143r–143v.

53. AGI Santo Domingo 1121 L. 2 f. 119r.

54. AGI Santo Domingo 1121 L. 2 ff. 60r–60v.

55. Vecinos in Puerto Rico argued that in order to afford to bring their wives, they would have to sell their haciendas; in December 1529, the crown gave them an additional two years. See AGI Santo Domingo 2280 L. 1 ff. 8v–9r.

56. AGI Santo Domingo 2280 L. 1 ff. 153r–153v.

57. This discussion is based on the testimony in AGI Santo Domingo 10 N. 8.

58. AGI Patronato 94 N. 2 R. 1.

59. In the 1527 deposition Benito de Astorga's friend Luis Hernández said that he had known Astorga for twenty-five years, which could mean that they both accompanied Ovando to Hispaniola in 1502; see AGI Santo Domingo 9 N. 20 (formerly Santo Domingo 9 R. 2 N. 18). Given a certain equivocation in his testimony as to whether or not he actually had arrived with Ovando, it seems more likely that Astorga went to the island some time after 1502. Astorga testified in the información compiled by Cristóbal de Santa Clara in the 1530s that he had witnessed Santa Clara serve as treasurer in 1507. For a transcription of this información, which appears in AGI Justicia 990 N. 1, see Mira Caballos, *Las Antillas Mayores*, 139 (appendix 4).

60. Boyd-Bowman, *Índice geobiográfico*, 163, lists Miguel de Pasamonte as holding office on the island in 1508. Pasamonte was Aragonese and close to Ferdinand. On his considerable influence in Hispaniola, especially between 1512 and 1517, see Mira Caballos, *El Indio Antillano*, 123. In the información of Cristóbal de Santa Clara Astorga testified that he was about fifty years old. Although the date of the testimony is unclear, if he made that statement in 1538 (rather than in 1531), he could have been born around 1488 to 1490 and hence in his late teens when he left Spain for Hispaniola. Mira Caballos, *Las Antillas Mayores*, 66–67.

61. In the deposition compiled in 1515 by Santo Domingo's city council, complaining about the assignments made in the Repartimiento, Gonzalo de Guzmán specifically complained that Benito de Astorga and another man, Pedro de Llanos, had received Indians because they were the criados of Pasamonte, even though they were unqualified to be encomenderos. The deposition is transcribed in Arranz Márquez, *Repartimientos y encomiendas*, 467.

62. As with his date of birth, there also are questions about the date of Benito de Astorga's marriage. In 1527, he stated that he had been married for twelve years, which would make 1515 the date of his marriage (AGI Santo Domingo 9 N. 20). In 1533 he clearly stated that he had gone to Spain and married in 1520 (AGI Santo Domingo 77 R. 3 N. 66). Witnesses who testified in the suit against Alburquerque in 1515, however, stated that Astorga was already married and that his wife was in Castile, so 1514 or 1515 seems the more likely date.

63. In his testimony in the información for Cristóbal de Santa Clara, Astorga stated that he was always present for the periodic fundiciones, or smelting of gold, which attracted merchants of all sorts. Mira Caballos, *Las Antillas Mayores*, 66. Astorga's close relationship with Melchor de Castro, longtime escribano de minas, also might have accounted, in part, for Benito's presence at the fundiciones.

64. AGI Santo Domingo 9 N. 20.

65. AGI Santo Domingo 9 N. 20. Unless otherwise noted, all the testimony regarding Benito de Astorga's efforts to convince his wife to emigrate comes from this deposition.

66. *Hato* could mean either a herd of cattle or the property where they grazed; in this case, it is not known whether he was selling land or just the animals.

67. On his sugar estate, see AGI Santo Domingo 77 R. 3 N. 66 (1533); and AGI Justicia 13 N. 1 R. 3 (1533–1535).

68. In 1527 Juan de Alfaro sent more than 17 marcos of silver to his father in Seville; see Otte, *Las perlas*, 421. Luis Hernández de Alfaro also received pearls from other sources in the 1520s

(see 410, 412). Mira Caballos, *Las Antillas Mayores,* appendix 3, 49–50, lists Luis Hernández de Alfaro as a shipmaster or proprietor who paid the almojarifazgo in 1506 and 1507.

69. See Altman, "Spanish Women," 72.

70. According to Otte, *Las perlas,* 196, Rodrigo Marchena maintained with his brothers Hernando Olivares and Francisco Martínez, who lived in Seville, a partnership called the Compañía del Puerto de Santa María. Marchena carried 4 marcos of pearls with him when he traveled to Spain in 1521 (see 411), and he continued to send pearls to his brothers and others in the 1520s (see 413, 420–421).

71. AGI Santo Domingo 9 N. 20.

72. Esteban de Pasamonte, who would be the heir to his powerful uncle Miguel de Pasamonte, went to Hispaniola in 1515 as a bachelor, so he either married in Hispaniola or returned to Spain at some point to marry.

73. Rodríguez Morel, "Sugar Economy," 96. Astorga's ingenio is also discussed in chapter 5 of the present volume.

74. AGI Santo Domingo 9 N. 20.

75. Marte, *Santo Domingo,* 401. In July 1543, Castro explained that the position entailed his ensuring that miners were properly licensed and that the royal fifth was paid when they brought their gold to be smelted.

76. Rodríguez Morel, "Sugar Economy," 94–95 (table 4.2), lists sugar mills built on Hispaniola before 1590. Benito de Astorga is listed as the owner of an ingenio on the Río Ibuaca. A "Señora de Astorga" also appears as an ingenio owner (there is no additional information). Could this be Isabel de Mayorga?

77. *Proceso,* 21. Regarding Beatriz de Salas, Castro testified that "la abrigó y socorró con cierta limosna e caridad secreta y suplicó a el señor obispo le diese por amor de dios un bohío questaba hecho en sus solares" (he protected and helped her with some alms and secret charity and asked the bishop for the love of god that he would give her a bohío located on one of his lots).

78. *Proceso,* 22.

79. *Proceso,* 226–229.

80. *Proceso,* 217.

81. *Proceso,* 136, 158, 183–184. Deza heard the story second hand; his informants believed that Castro had beaten Catalina because he suspected her of having had intimate relations with Pedro de Ulloa, Deza's nephew. Since Catalina was from the Bahamas, she might have been a slave, but she was not called such. Indigenous captives brought to Hispaniola from other islands who were not branded as slaves were called (somewhat confusingly) naborías, which in the early years was the term used for Native islanders who were part of the repartimientos assigned to Spaniards. Unlike slaves, naborías in principle had the right to choose for whom they would work and could not be sold, but given that they were required always to serve a master, their circumstances were not unlike that of slaves.

82. Fuson, *Juan Ponce de León,* 67, 144–145. Leonor died in 1519. Murga, *Historia,* 1:xxviii, suggests that Juan Ponce's wife might have been Indigenous and notes that her name was not mentioned in probanzas done by his grandsons Juan and Gaspar Troche Ponce de León. There is no way to know.

83. Rubio, *Datos para la historia,* 28–29. The discussion is based on the proceso in AGI Justi-

cia 43. Juan Roldán was the only son of pilot Alonso Pérez Roldán. In 1518 he was referred to as the *paniaguado* (retainer) of Miguel de Pasamonte. Marte, *Santo Domingo*, 255.

84. Murga, *Historia documental*, 2:38, 89, 123, 271, 274. Garcí Troche denied that the woman was his mistress while admitting that perhaps he had a son with her, "which could be because she's a woman and he's a man," an explanation that could hardly be refuted (234).

85. Rodríguez Morel, *Cartas del cabildo*, 151. The statement from the cabildo is difficult to interpret; Rodríguez Morel, *Cartas de los cabildos eclesiásticos*, 67 (Cuadro 2). Astudillo's wife was doña María de Fuentes. He died by 1543, after which there was another Gaspar de Astudillo serving as regidor on the cabildo. Exactly what the cabildo meant in referring to three scandalous marriages is unclear.

86. AGI Santo Domingo 77 N. 50.

87. AGI Patronato 177 N. 1 R. 18.

88. AGI Santo Domingo 1121 L. 2 ff. 90r–91v.

89. Quoted in Gil, "Los primeros mestizos," 19.

90. Gil, "Los primeros mestizos," 25–26. *Hijo natural* was the term used for a child who was born out of wedlock when both parents were unmarried.

91. AGI Santo Domingo 77 N. 69. Doña Elvira had held an encomienda of eighteen or twenty Indians whom Barrionuevo claimed were her relatives; he requested permission to retain them. Rodríguez Morel, *Documentos*, 71.

92. For a recent examination of one phase of Sedeño's career, see Perri, "Ambiguous Authority."

93. AGI Santo Domingo 2280 L. 2 f. 195r.

94. AGI Santo Domingo 868 L. 1 f. 258r.

95. AGI Indiferente General 421 L. 1 f. 141v.

96. See Mangan, "Moving mestizos"; and Gil, "Los primeros mestizos."

97. Mira Caballos, "La educación," 64. The royal cédula authorized a general license for Indian women who had children with Spaniards to travel with them to the peninsula; adults would have to continue to apply for licenses to go.

98. AGI Santo Domingo 1121 L. 1 f. 105v. Most likely the brothers, Bernaldino and Francisco Velázquez, were related to the first lieutenant governor of Cuba, Diego Velázquez; possibly they were his nephews.

99. AGI Santo Domingo 1121 L. 2 f. 62v.

100. These cases from July 1541 appear together in AGI Santo Domingo 2280 L. 2 f. 192v–193r.

101. AGI 2280 L. 2 f. 88v. She received permission in May 1557.

102. Rodríguez Morel, *Documentos*, 258. Permission was granted in 1556.

103. AGI Santo Domingo 1121 L. 1 ff. 106r, 110v–111v.

104. AGI Contratación 5536 L. 3 f. 249. He is listed as the son of Juan de Soria and doña María, "vecinos desta ciudad," meaning Seville. There certainly exists the possibility that there was more than one Juan de Soria in Cuba in those years, but the proximity of the cédulas regarding Pasquala Pérez and Juan de Soria in the legajo (AGI Santo Domingo 1121 L. 1) suggests that it is the same person.

105. AGI Santo Domingo 1121 L. 1 f. 56v. Very likely Diego's uncles in Spain were mistaken about his age, as a Diego Mejía, "vecino de la isla Fernandina," apparently petitioned to be al-

lowed to go to Spain "to pray to our lord" for his father's soul and to bring with him all his possessions; see ff. 90r–90v.

106. AGI Santo Domingo 868 L. 2 f. 53v.

107. Lope de Bardecí testified in doña Isabel Maraver's probanza of 1531 that he had known her and her husband for twenty years and had attended their wedding, so surely his wife knew them as well. AGI Santo Domingo 9 N. 44.

108. Otte, *Las perlas,* 269–271.

109. Marte, *Santo Domingo,* 397.

110. AGI Santo Domingo 1121 L. 2 ff. 63v, 99r. Paz suffered from a lengthy illness and never did return to Cuba, although in 1540 his wife, doña Guiomar de Guzmán, went there with an entourage of fourteen people, perhaps including these slaves. See Lalor, "Two Doñas," 101–102.

111. Murga, *Historia documental,* 2:279, 303, 329. At the time of the residencia, she was married to Andrés de los Ríos. In March 1533 a woman named Elvira Pinelo, widow of Francisco de Herrera, declared that she wished to go to live in Puerto Rico, taking with her a white slave; AGI Santo Domingo 2280 L. 1 f. 164v. The name is unusual enough that it might have been the same woman.

112. Franco, *Los negros,* 36.

113. AGI Santo Domingo 2280 L. 1 ff. 6v, 7r; Santo Domingo 10 N. 4. According to Muriel's deposition, the bishop interceded in the negotiation between Muriel and crown because the cacica doña María "andaba sin abrigo ninguno," that is, she lacked any protection.

114. See Altman, "Cacicas." Although Anacaona clearly enjoyed high status and influence, it is not clear that she ever was a chief. On Anacaona, see Wilson, *Hispaniola,* 120, 129–134; and Moscoso, *Caguas,* who devotes a chapter to her.

115. Marte, *Santo Domingo,* 397. The letter is recorded as being from arcediano *Alonso* de Castro, but surely it is Álvaro.

116. A petition of 1518 from Hispaniola to the king recommended that anyone who wished to free a Black slave should send him or her to Castile "to avoid difficulties." Giménez Fernández, "Las cortes," 32.

117. Parry and Keith, *New Iberian World,* 2:351–352.

118. Rodríguez Morel, *Documentos,* 69, 71–73.

119. Rodríguez Morel, *Documentos,* 175.

Conclusion: Caribbean Connections

1. Rodríguez Morel, *Cartas del cabildo,* 140–141.

2. According to Rojas, Samson, and Hoogland, "Indo-Hispanic Dynamics," "Events in Hispaniola had a pioneering character not replicated elsewhere, but which served to create strategies that accelerated domination in remaining spaces. This had the effect of foreshortening subsequent phases of interaction elsewhere" (20).

3. AGI Santo Domingo 77 R. 2.

4. AGI Patronato 178 R. 2.

5. AGI Santo Domingo 868 L. 2 f. 146v.

6. Sued Badillo, *El dorado borincano,* 279.

7. Murga, *Historia documental*, 2:cii, cvi, cx–cxii. Following the death of Puerto Rico's extremely wealthy treasurer Andrés de Haro, in 1519, Antonio de la Gama was accused by Haro's heirs of appropriating at least some of his possessions, including fifty-eight slaves ostensibly worth 200 pesos de oro each. He also was alleged to have turned Haro's two hundred Indians over to his brother Sebastián de la Gama. See AGI Justicia 7 N. 1; David Wheat generously shared his notes on and partial transcription of this text. The deposition suggested that the de la Gama brothers had only recently arrived in Puerto Rico when Haro died and were quite poor before gaining access to Haro's property.

8. AGI Santo Domingo 868 L. 1 ff. 54v–55r.

9. Lalor, "Two Doñas," 95.

10. AGI Santo Domingo 868 L. 1 ff. 54r–54v.

11. The description of the expedition is in AGI Santo Domingo 74 R. 2. Licenciado Pedro de la Gasca had been appointed president of Peru's audiencia and was sent by the crown to suppress Gonzalo Pizarro's rebellion, which he succeeded in doing in some measure by attracting a number of Pizarro's former supporters to his side.

12. See the información of canon Juan Bardecí, AGI Santo Domingo 10 N. 47.

13. The deposition is in AGI Mexico 203 and has been transcribed in Tió, *Nuevas Fuentes*.

14. Tió, *Nuevas fuentes*, 67, 79, 83–84, 98–99, 105.

15. AGI Santo Domingo 10 N. 35.

16. AGI Santo Domingo 10 N. 37.

17. AGI Santo Domingo 10 N. 36.

18. See Sued Badillo, *El dorado borincano*, 48. In an información presented in Seville in 1549 on behalf of the town of San Germán in Puerto Rico, Marcos Falcón testified that over the course of twenty-five years he had been in San Germán many times, while shipmaster Gonzalo Rodríguez, a vecino of Triana, had been in San Germán going back to 1509. Others testified along the same lines; see AGI Santo Domingo 10 N. 48.

19. AGI Santo Domingo 868 L. 2 f. 109v.

20. Marte, *Santo Domingo*, 39. On early Portuguese immigration, see D'Esposito, "Portuguese Settlers."

21. Giménez Fernández, "Las cortes," 31.

22. AGI Santo Domingo 868 L. 2.

23. AGI Santo Domingo 1121 L. 1 ff. 82v–83r.

24. Marte, *Santo Domingo*, 369.

25. AGI Santo Domingo 1121 L. 2 f. 27v.

26. According to Pike, *Enterprise and Adventure*, "No separation can be made between the commercial activities of the Genoese in Seville and their financial relations with the Spanish monarchs" (48).

27. Pike, *Enterprise and Adventure*, 102.

28. Pike, *Enterprise and Adventure*, 67, 71.

29. Garrido Raya and Moreno Escalante, "La red mercantil," 10–11. His nephew Jerónimo Grimaldi went to Santo Domingo in 1508 as Bernardo's factor (13). On Grimaldi, see also Otte, "La flota."

30. Pike, *Enterprise and Adventure*, 133.

31. Garrido Raya and Moreno Escalante, "La red mercantil," 17.

32. See AGI Santo Domingo 9 N. 21 for the testimony regarding this episode, discussed at greater length in Altman, "Key to the Indies," 23–24. See also Wright, *Spanish Documents*, 29–59; and de la O Torres, "Miedos," 277–278, who writes that the English ship sailed near the Isla de Mona, where a Spaniard named Gómez Navarro, thinking it was a Spanish vessel, went to meet it and was informed by the crew that they were Englishmen from London sailing for the English king.

33. Ita Rubio, "Mercaderes ingleses," 12–15.

34. On Baltasar de Castro, see AGI Santo Domingo 2280 ff. 73r–73v; and on Melchor, see AGI Justicia 1003 N. 5 R. 2.

35. AGI Santo Domingo 2280 L. 2 f. 200r.

36. Rodríguez Demorizi, *Los Dominicos*, 318.

37. Rodríguez Demorizi, *Los Dominicos*, 304, 308.

38. AGI Santo Domingo 868 L. 2.

39. Fleehner, "Treating 'Trifles,'" 66.

40. All the testimony, together with lists of Indians still alive and working at the hacienda de Toa in the late 1520s, is in AGI Patronato 175 R. 18. For a longer discussion of the experiencia, see Altman, "Failed Experiments."

41. AGI Patronato 175 R. 18.

BIBLIOGRAPHY

Archival Sources

Archivo General de Indias (Seville)
Contaduría
Contratación
Indiferente General
Justicia
Patronato
Santo Domingo

Database

"Spaniards Living in the Greater Antilles, 1493–1550." Biographical file compiled by Ida Altman. University of Florida Digital Collections, Digital Library of the Caribbean. https://ufdc.ufl.edu/l/AA00079036/00001.

Published Primary Sources

Alegría, Ricardo E., ed. *Documentos históricos de Puerto Rico*. Vol. 1, *1493–1516*. San Juan: Centro de Estudios Avanzados de Puerto Rico y el Caribe, 2009.

Arranz Marquez, Luis. *Repartimientos y encomiendas en la Isla Española (El Repartimiento de Albuquerque de 1514)*. Santo Domingo: Fundación García Arévalo, 1991.

Colección de documentos inéditos relativos al descubrimiento, conquista y organización de las antiguas posesiones españolas y de ultramar. Segunda serie. Isla de Cuba. Madrid: Real Academia de Historia, 1885.

Colección de documentos inéditos relativos al descubrimiento, conquista y colonización de las posesiones españolas en América y Oceanía sacados, en su mayor parte, del Real Archivo de Indias. Madrid: Imprenta de Manuel G Hernandez, 1883.

Damiani Cósimi, Julio. *Estratificación social, esclavos y naborías en el Puerto Rico minero del siglo XVI: La información de Francisco Manuel de Lando*. San Juan: Universidad de Puerto Rico, 1994.

Gil, Juan, and Consuelo Varela, eds. *Cartas de particulares a Colón y relaciones coetáneas*. Madrid: Alianza Universidad, 1984.

Marte, Roberto, ed. *Santo Domingo en los manuscritos de Juan Bautista Muñoz*. Santo Domingo: Ediciones Fundación García Arévalo, Inc., 1981.

Mira Caballos, Esteban. "Las cuentas del tesorero Cristóbal de Santa Clara (1505–1507)." In *La Española, epicentro del Caribe en el siglo XVI*. Santo Domingo: Academia Dominicana de la Historia, 2010.

Murga, Vicente. *Historia documental de Puerto Rico*. Vol. 1, *El concejo o cabildo de la ciudad de San Juan de Puerto Rico (1527–1550)*. Rio Piedras: Editorial Plus Ultra, 1948. Vol. 2, Seville, 1956.

———. *Historia documental de Puerto Rico*. Vol. 2, *El juicio de residencia, moderador democrático*. Santander: Aldus, 1956.

Proceso contra Alvaro de Castro, 1532. Patronato de la Ciudad Colonial de Santo Domingo. Santo Domingo: Editora Taller C. por A., 1995. Colección Herrera, Tomo 2.

Rodríguez Demorizi, Emilio. *Los Dominicos y las encomiendas de Indios de la Isla Española*. Santo Domingo: Editora del Caribe, 1971.

Rodríguez Morel, Genaro. *Cartas de la Real Audiencia de Santo Domingo (1530–1546)*. Santo Domingo: Archivo General de la Nación and Academia Dominicana de la Historia, 2007.

———. *Cartas de los cabildos eclésiasticos de Santo Domingo y Concepción de la Vega en el siglo XVI*. Santo Domingo: Patronato de la Ciudad Colonial de Santo Domingo and Centro de Altos Estudios Humanísticos y del Idioma Español, 2000.

———. *Cartas del cabildo de la Ciudad de Santo Domingo en el siglo XVI*. Santo Domingo: Patronato de la Ciudad Colonial de Santo Domingo and Centro de Altos Estudios Humanísticos y del Idioma Español, 1999.

———. "Cartas privadas de Hernando Gorjón," *Anuario de Estudios Americanos* 52, no. 2 (1995).

———. *Documentos para el estudio de la historia colonial de Santo Domingo (1511–1560)*. Tomo I. Santo Domingo: Archivo General de la Nación, 2018.

Saez, José Luis, SJ. *La iglesia y el negro esclavo en Santo Domingo. Una historia de tres siglos*. Santo Domingo: Patronato de la Ciudad Colonial de Santo Domingo, Colección Quinto Centenario, 1994.

Symcox, Geoffrey, and Blair Sullivan, eds. *Christopher Columbus and the Enterprise of the Indies: A Brief History with Documents*. New York: Bedford/St. Martin's, 2005.

Tió, Aurelio. *Nuevas fuentes para la historia de Puerto Rico.* San Germán: Ediciones de la Universidad Interamericana de Puerto Rico and Barcelona: Ediciones Rumbos, 1961.

Varela, Consuelo. *La caída de Cristóbal Colón. El juicio de Bobadilla.* Madrid: Marcial Pons History, 2006.

Secondary Works

Altman, Ida. "Cacicas in the Early Spanish Caribbean." In *Cacicas,* ed. Margarita Ochoa and Sara Guengerich. Norman: University of Oklahoma Press, 2021.

———. *Emigrants and Society: Extremadura and Spanish America in the Sixteenth Century.* Los Angeles: University of California Press, 1989.

———. "Failed Experiments: Negotiating Freedom in Puerto Rico and Cuba." *Colonial Latin American Review* 29, no. 1 (2020): 4–23.

———. "Key to the Indies: Port Towns in the Spanish Caribbean, 1493–1550." *The Americas* 74, no. 1 (2017).

———. "Marriage, Family, and Ethnicity in the Early Spanish Caribbean." *William & Mary Quarterly* 70, no. 2 (April 2013).

———. "The Revolt of Enriquillo and the Historiography of Early Spanish America." *The Americas* 63, no. 4 (2007): 587–614.

———. "The Spanish Caribbean, 1492–1550." *Oxford Research Encyclopedia of Latin American History,* July 30, 2018. https://doi.org/10.1093/acrefore/9780199366439.013.630.

———. "Spanish Society in Mexico City after the Conquest." *Hispanic American Historical Review* 71, no. 3 (1991): 413–445.

———. "Spanish Women in the Early Caribbean." In *Women of the Iberian Atlantic,* ed. Jane E. Mangan and Sarah Owens. Baton Rouge: Louisiana State University Press, 2012.

———. "Towns and the Forging of the Spanish Caribbean." In *The Early Modern Hispanic World,* ed. Kimberly Lynn and Erin Kathleen Rowe. Cambridge: Cambridge University Press, 2017.

———. *Transatlantic Ties in the Spanish Empire: Brihuega, Spain and Puebla, Mexico, 1560–1620.* Stanford: Stanford University Press, 2000.

———. "Vasco Porcallo de Figueroa: Ambition, Fear, and Politics in Early Cuba." In *The Spanish Caribbean & the Atlantic World in the Long Sixteenth Century,* ed. Ida Altman and David Wheat. Lincoln: University of Nebraska Press, 2019.

Altman, Ida, and David Wheat, eds. *The Spanish Caribbean & the Atlantic World in the Long Sixteenth Century.* Lincoln: University of Nebraska Press, 2019.

Arranz Marquez, Luis. *Don Diego Colón, Almirante, Virrey y Gobernador de las Indias*. Vol. 1. Madrid: Consejo Superior de Investigaciones Científicas, 1982.

Aznar Vallejo, Eduardo. *La integración de las islas Canarias en la Corona de Castilla, 1478–1526: Aspectos administrativos, sociales y económicos*. Madrid: University de Sevilla, Universidad de La Laguna, 1983.

Barreiro, José. *Taíno: A Novel*. Golden, CO: Fulcrum, 2012.

Barrera, Antonio. "Local Herbs, Global Medicines: Commerce, Knowledge, and Commodities in Spanish America." In *Merchants & Marvels: Commerce, Science, and Art in Early Modern Europe*, ed. Pamela H. Smith and Paula Findlen. New York: Routledge, 2002.

Bermúdez Bermúdez, Arturo. *Don Rodrigo de Bastidas. Adelantado de Santa Marta*. Bogotá: Fondeo Mixto de Promoción de la Cultura y las Artes del Magdalena, 2000.

Bernan, Mary Jane, and Perry L Gnivecki. "Colonial Encounters in Lucayan Contexts." In *Material Encounters and Indigenous Transformations in the Colonial Americas*, ed. Corinne L. Hofman and Floris W. M. Keehnen. Leiden: Brill, 2019.

Bigelow, Allison Margaret. *Mining Language. Racial Thinking, Indigenous Knowledge, and Colonial Metallurgy in the Early Modern Iberian World*. Chapel Hill: University of North Carolina Press, 2020.

Bishko, Charles Julian. "The Peninsular Background of Latin American Cattle Ranching." *Hispanic American Historical Review* 32, no. 4 (November 1952).

Boyd-Bowman, Peter. *Indice geobiogáfico de más de 56 mil pobladores de la América hispánica*. Vol. 1, *1493–1519*. México: Fondo de Cultura Económica, 1985.

Cassá, Roberto, and Genaro Rodríguez Morel. "Consideraciones alternativas acerca de las rebeliones de esclavos en Santo Domingo." *Anuario de Estudios Americanos* 50, no. 1 (1993): 101–131.

Chamberlin, Robert S. "The Corregidor in Castile in the Sixteenth Century and the Residencia as Applied to the Corregidor." *Hispanic American Historical Review* 23, no. 2 (1943): 222–257.

Chipman, Donald E. "The Traffic in Indian Slaves in the Province of Pánuco, New Spain, 1523–1533." *The Americas* 23, no. 1 (October 1966): 142–155.

Christian, William. *Local Religion in Sixteenth-Century Spain*. Princeton, NJ: Princeton University Press, 1989.

Clark, J. M. H. "Environment and the Politics of Relocation in the Caribbean Port of Veracruz, 1519–1599." In *The Spanish Caribbean & the Atlantic World in the Long Sixteenth Century*, ed. Ida Altman and David Wheat. Lincoln: University of Nebraska Press, 2019.

Cook, Noble David. *Born to Die: Disease and New World Conquest, 1492–1650*. Cambridge: Cambridge University Press, 1998.

Davis, Dave D. "The Strategy of Early Spanish Ecosystem Management on Cuba." *Journal of Anthropological Research* 39, no. 4 (1974): 294–314.

de la Fuente, Alejandro. "Sugar and Slavery in Early Colonial Cuba." In *Tropical Babylons: Sugar and the Making of the Atlantic World, 1450–1680*, ed. Stuart B. Schwartz. Chapel Hill: University of North Carolina Press, 2004.

de la O Torres, Rodrigo Alejandro. "Miedos y fenómeno de la piratería en el Golfo-Caribe durante el siglo XVI: Un ensayo de aproximación." *HistoReLo: Revista de historia regional y local* 11, no. 22 (2019): 267–300.

Deagan, Kathleen. "Colonial Transformation: Euro-American Cultural Genesis in the Early Spanish-Speaking Colonies." *Journal of Anthropological Research* 52, no. 2 (1996): 135–160.

———. "Reconsidering Taíno Social Dynamics after Spanish Conquest: Gender and Class in Culture-Contact Studies." *American Antiquity* 69, no. 4 (2004): 597–626.

Deagan, Kathleen, and José María Cruxent. *Columbus's Outpost among the Taínos*. New Haven, CT: Yale University Press, 2002.

D'Esposito, Franceso. "Portuguese Settlers in Santo Domingo in the Sixteenth Century (1492–1580). *Journal of European Economic History* 27, no. 2 (1998): 315–333.

D'Esposito, Franceso, and Auke P. Jacobs. "Auge y ocaso de la primera sociedad minera de América: Santo Domingo 1503–1520." *Mundos Nuevos/Nuevos Mundos*, 2015. https://doi.org/10.4000/nuevomundo.67723.

Devereux, Andrew W., ed. "Empire and Exceptionalism: The *Requerimiento* and Claims of Sovereignty in the Early Modern Mediterranean and Atlantic." *Republics of Letters* 5, no. 3, special issue (2018).

Díaz Ceballos, Jorge. "Negociación, consenso y comunidad política en la fundación de ciudades en Castilla del Oro en el temprano siglo XVI." *Investigaciones Históricas, época moderna y contemporánea* 38 (2018): 131–160.

Dillard, Heath. *Daughters of the Reconquest. Women in Castilian Town Society, 1100–1300*. Cambridge: Cambridge University Press, 1984.

Eagle, Marc. "The Audiencia of Santo Domingo in the Seventeenth Century." PhD diss., Tulane University, 2005.

———. "The Early Slave Trade to Spanish America: Caribbean Pathways, 1530 to 1580." In *The Spanish Caribbean & the Atlantic World in the Long Sixteenth Century*, ed. Ida Altman and David Wheat. Lincoln: University of Nebraska Press, 2019.

Farnsworth, Cacey. "The Revolt of Agüeybana II: Puerto Rico's Interisland Connections." In *The Spanish Caribbean & the Atlantic World in the Long Sixteenth Century*, ed. Ida Altman and David Wheat. Lincoln: University of Nebraska Press, 2019.

Farriss, Nancy. *Tongues of Fire: Language and Evangelization in Colonial Mexico*. New York: Oxford University Press, 2018.

Fernández-Armesto, Felipe. *Before Columbus: Exploration and Colonisation from the Mediterranean to the Atlantic, 1229–1492*. London: Macmillan Education Ltd., 1987.

———. *The Canary Islands after the Conquest*. New York: Oxford University Press, 1982.

Fernández Chaves, Manuel F., and Rafael M. Pérez García. "América como mecanismo de transformación y movilidad social en Sevilla moderna: Los Caballero de Cabrera." In *Pequena Nobreza de Aquém e de Além-Mar: Poderes, Patrimónios e Redes*, ed. Miguel Jasmins Rodrigues and Maia Manuel Torrão. Lisbon, 2011.

———. "La penetración económica portuguesa en la Sevilla del siglo XVI." *Espacio, Tiempo Y Forma, Serie IV, Historia Moderna* 25 (2012).

Fernández de Oviedo, Gonzalo. *Historia general y natural de las Indias, islas y Tierra-Firme del Mar Océano: Primera parte*, ed. José Amador de los Ríos. Madrid: La Real Academia de Historia, 1851.

Fleehner, Floris W. M. "Treating 'Trifles': The Indigenous Adoption of European Goods in Early Colonial Hispaniola (1492–1550)." In *Material Encounters and Indigenous Transformations in the Colonial Americas*, ed. Corinne L. Hofman and Floris W. M. Keehnen. Leiden: Brill, 2019.

Floyd, Troy S. *The Columbus Dynasty in the Caribbean, 1492–1526*. Albuquerque: University of New Mexico Press, 1973.

Franco, Franklyn J. *Los negros, los mulatos y la nación dominicana*. Santo Domingo: Editora Nacional, 1977.

Fuson, Robert H. *Juan Ponce de León and the Spanish Discovery of Puerto Rico and Florida*. Blacksburg, VA: McDonald & Woodward, 2000.

Garrido Raya, Enrique, and Valentín Moreno Escalante. "La red mercantil de los Grimaldi y su proyección desde Sevilla a la Española (1489–1517)." *Temas Americanistas* 19 (2012).

Gil, Juan. "Emigrantes a la isla Española en 1506." *Anuario de Estudios Americanos* 63, no. 2 (2006): 265–304.

———. "La gente de Ovando en los protocolos hispalenses." *Anuario de Estudios Americanos* 63, no. 1 (2006): 255–287.

———. "Los primeros mestizos indios en España: Una voz ausente." In *Entre Dos Mundos: Fronteras Culturales y Agentes Mediadores*, ed. Berta Ares Queija and Serge Gruzinski. Sevilla: Escuela de Estudios Hispano-Americanos, 1997.

Giménez Fernández, Manuel. "Las Cortes de Española en 1518." *Anales de la Universidad Hispalense* 15 (1954).

Gómez, Pablo F. *The Experiential Caribbean: Creating Knowledge and Healing in the Early Modern Atlantic*. Chapel Hill: University of North Carolina Press, 2017.

———. "Hospitals and Public Health in the Sixteenth-Century Spanish Caribbean." In *The Spanish Caribbean & the Atlantic World in the Long Sixteenth Century*, ed. Ida Altman and David Wheat. Lincoln: University of Nebraska Press, 2019.

Guerra, Francisco. "The Earliest American Epidemic: The Influenza of 1492." *Social Science History* 12, no. 3 (1988): 305–325.

Guitar, Lynne A. "Cultural Genesis: Indians, Africans, and Spaniards in Rural Hispaniola, First Half of the Sixteenth Century." PhD Diss., Vanderbilt University, 1998.

Hair, P. E. H. "Columbus from Guinea to America." *History in Africa* 17 (1990): 113–129.
Henige, David P. *Numbers from Nowhere: The American Indian Contact Population Debate*. Norman: University of Oklahoma Press, 1998.
Henry, Shea, and Robyn Woodward. "Contact and Colonial Impact in Jamaica: Comparative Material Culture and Diet at Sevilla la Nueva and the Taíno Village of Maima." In *Material Encounters and Indigenous Transformations in the Colonial Americas*, ed. Corinne L. Hofman and Floris W. M. Keehnen. Leiden: Brill, 2019.
Hernández Mora, Iosvany, Antonio Barroso Betancourt, Manuel García Palomino, and Osvaldo Jiménez Vázquez. "Pueblo Viejo de Nuevitas: nuevos referentes de investigación." *Memorias: Revista digital de historia y arqueología desde el Caribe colombiano* 20 (2013).
Hoffman, Paul E. *Florida's Frontiers*. Bloomington: Indiana University Press, 2002.
———. *A New Andalucia and a Way to the Orient: The American Southeast during the Sixteenth Century*. Baton Rouge: Louisiana State University Press, 1990.
———. *The Spanish Crown and the Defense of the Caribbean, 1535–1585: Precedent, Patrimonialism, and Royal Parsimony*. Baton Rouge: Louisiana State University Press, 1980.
Hofman, Corinne L., and Floris W. M. Keehnen, eds. *Material Encounters and Indigenous Transformations in the Colonial Americas*. Leiden: Brill, 2019.
Ita Rubio, María de Lourdes de. "Mercaderes ingleses en el Caribe durante el siglo XVI." *Sotavento* 5 (2000): 9–17.
Jacobs, Auke Pieter. "Legal and Illegal Emigration from Seville, 1550–1560." In *"To Make America": European Emigration in the Early Modern Period*, ed. Ida Altman and James Horn. Los Angeles: University of California Press, 1991.
Julián, Amadeo. "La documentación histórica de la época colonial de Santo Domingo y las causas de su desaparición: Esfuerzos por su recuperación." *Clío* 86, no. 193 (2017): 9–66.
Keegan, William F. "The 'Classic' Taíno." In *The Oxford Handbook of Caribbean Archaeology*, ed. William F. Keegan, Corinne L. Hofman, and Reniel Rodríguez Ramos. Oxford: Oxford University Press, 2013.
———. *Taíno Indian Myth and Practice: The Arrival of the Stranger King*. Gainesville: University Press of Florida, 2007.
Keegan, William F., Corinne L. Hofman, and Reniel Rodríguez Ramos, eds. *The Oxford Handbook of Caribbean Archaeology*. Oxford: Oxford University Press, 2013.
Kulstad, Pauline M. "Concepción de la Vega, 1495–1564: A Preliminary Look at Lifeways in the Americas' First Boom Town." Master's thesis, University of Florida, 2008.
Lalor, Shannon. "Two Doñas: Aristocratic Women and Power in Colonial Cuba." In *The Spanish Caribbean & the Atlantic World in the Long Sixteenth Century*, ed. Ida Altman and David Wheat. Lincoln: University of Nebraska Press, 2019.

———. "Women, Power, and the Expansion of Empire: The Bobadilla Women of Early Modern Spain, 1440–1550." PhD diss., University of Florida, 2019.

Lamb, Ursula. "Christobal de Tapia v. Nicolas de Ovando: A *Residencia* Fragment of 1509." *Hispanic American Historical Review* 33, no. 3 (August 1953).

Landers, Jane. "The Central African Presence in Spanish Maroon Communities." In *Central Africans and Cultural Transformations in the American Diaspora*, ed. Linda M. Heywood. Cambridge: Cambridge University Press, 2002.

Las Casas, Bartolomé de. *Historia de las Indias*. Vol. 3. Madrid: Imprenta de Miguel Ginesta, 1875; Project Gutenberg E-book.

Livi-Bacci, Maximo. "Return to Hispaniola: Assessing a Demographic Catastrophe." *Hispanic American Historical Review* 83, no. 1 (2003): 3–51.

MacDonald, Lauren E. "The Cemí and the Cross: Hispaniola Indians and the Regular Clergy, 1494–1517." In *The Spanish Caribbean & the Atlantic World in the Long Sixteenth Century*, ed. Ida Altman and David Wheat. Lincoln: University of Nebraska Press, 2019.

———. "The Hieronymites in Hispaniola, 1493–1519." Master's thesis, University of Florida, 2010.

———. "The Regular Clergy and Reformation in the Early Spanish Caribbean, 1493–1580." PhD diss., Johns Hopkins University, 2018.

Mangan, Jane E. "Moving Mestizos in Sixteenth-Century Peru: Spanish Fathers, Indigenous Mothers, and the Children In Between." *William and Mary Quarterly* 70, no. 2 (April 2013).

Marrero, Levi. *Cuba: Economía y sociedad*. Vol. 1. Puerto Rico: Editorial San Juan, 1972.

———. *Cuba: Economía y sociedad*. Vol. 2. Madrid: Editorial Playor, 1973.

Martínez-Fernández, Luis. *Key to the New World: A History of Early Colonial Cuba*. Gainesville: University Press of Florida, 2018.

Masters, Adrian. "A Thousand Invisible Architects: Vassals, the Petition and Response System, and the Creation of Spanish Imperial Caste Legislation." *Hispanic American Historical Review* 98, no. 3 (2018): 377–406.

Mira Caballos, Esteban. "Algunas consideraciones en torno a la primera biblioteca de Santo Domingo." In *La Española, epicentro del Caribe en el siglo XVI*. Santo Domingo: Academia Dominicana de la Historia, 2010.

———. *El Indio Antillano: repartimiento, encomienda y esclavitud (1492–1542)*. Seville: Muñoz Moya Editor, 1997.

———. "La educación de indios y mestizos antillanos en la primera mitad del siglo XVI." *Revista Complutense de Historia de América* 25 (1999).

———. "La medicina indígena en la Española y su comercialización." *Asclepio* 49, no. 2 (1997).

———. *Las Antillas Mayores, 1492–1550: ensayos y documentos*. Madrid: Iberoamericana, 2000.

———. "Los intentos evangelizadores del indio antillano (1492–1542)." In *La Española, epicentro del Caribe en el siglo XVI*. Santo Domingo: Academia Dominicana de la Historia, 2010.

———. *Nicolás de Ovando y los orígenes del sistema colonial español, 1502–1509*. Santo Domingo: Patronato de la Ciudad Colonial de Santo Domingo, 2000.

———. "Sanidad e instituciones hospitalarias en Las Antillas (1492–1550)." In *La Española, epicentro del Caribe en el siglo XVI*, 509–524. Santo Domingo: Academia Dominicana de la Historia, 2010.

———. "Urbanismo y arquitectura en los primeros asentamientos antillanos (1492–1550)." In *La Española, epicentro del Caribe en el siglo XVI*. Santo Domingo: Real Academia de la Historia, 2010.

Morales Padrón, Francisco. *Spanish Jamaica*, trans. Patrick E. Bryan with Michael J. Gronow and Felix Oviedo Moral. Kingston: Ian Randle, 2003.

Moscoso, Francisco. *Caguas en la conquista española del siglo XVI*. Río Piedras: Publicaciones Gaviota, 2016.

———. *Juicio al gobernador: Episodios coloniales de Puerto Rico, 1550*. Hato Rey: Publicaciones Puertorriqueñas, 1998.

———. *Lucha agraria en Puerto Rico, 1541–1545*. San Juan: Ediciones Puerto, 1997.

Mulcahy, Matthew, and Stuart B. Schwartz. "Nature's Battalions: Insects as Agricultural Pests in the Early Modern Caribbean." *William and Mary Quarterly* 75, no. 3 (2018): 433–464.

Nader, Helen. *Liberty in Absolutist Spain: The Habsburg Sale of Towns, 1516–1700*. Baltimore: Johns Hopkins University Press, 1993.

Nalle, Sara T. *God in La Mancha: Religious Reform and the People of Cuenca, 1500–1650*. Baltimore: Johns Hopkins University Press, 1992.

Otte, Enrique. "La flota de Diego Colón: Españoles y genoveses en el comercio trasatlántico de 1509." *Revista de Indias* 24 (1964): 475–503.

———. *Las perlas del Caribe: Nueva Cádiz de Cubagua*. Caracas: Fundación John Boulton, 1977.

———. "Una carta inédita de Gonzalo Fernández de Oviedo." *Revista de Indias* 15, no. 75 (1956), 437–458.

Parry, John H., and Robert G. Keith, eds. *New Iberian World*. 5 vols. New York: Hector & Rose, 1984.

Perri, Michael. "Ambiguous Authority: Juan de Frías and the Audiencia of Santo Domingo Confront the Conquistador Antonio Sedeño." *The Americas* 74, no. 4 (2017): 427–455.

Phillips, William D., Jr., and Carla Rahn Phillips. *The Worlds of Christopher Columbus*. New York: Cambridge University Press, 1992.

Pike, Ruth. *Enterprise and Adventure: The Genoese in Seville and the Opening of the New World*. Ithaca, NY: Cornell University Press, 1966.

Premo, Bianca. "Familiar: Thinking beyond Lineage and across Race in Spanish Atlantic Family History." *William and Mary Quarterly* 70 no. 2 (April 2013): 295–316.

Rocha, Gabriel de Avilez. "The Azorean Connection: The Trajectories of Slavery, Piracy, and Trade in the Early Atlantic." In *The Spanish Caribbean & the Atlantic World in the Long Sixteenth Century*, ed. Ida Altman and David Wheat. Lincoln: University of Nebraska Press, 2019.

———. "Maroons in the *Montes*: Toward a Political Ecology of Marronage in the Sixteenth-Century Caribbean." In *Early Modern Black Diaspora Studies: A Critical Anthology*, ed. Cassander Smith, Miles P. Grier, and Nicholas Jones. London: Palgrave Macmillan, 2018.

———. "The Pinzones and the Coup of the Acedares: Fishing and Colonization in the Fifteenth-Century Atlantic and Spanish Caribbean." *Colonial Latin American Review* 28, no. 4 (2019): 427–449.

Rodríguez Demorizi, Emilio. *El pleito Ovando-Tapia: Comienzo de la vida urbana en América*. Santo Domingo: Editora del Caribe, 1978.

Rodríguez Lorenzo, Sergio M. "El contrato de pasaje en la carrera de Indias (1561–1622)." *Historia Mexicana* 66, no. 3 (2017): 1479–1157.

Rodríguez Morel, Genaro. *Orígenes de la economía de plantación de La Española*. Santo Domingo: Editora Nacional, 2012.

———. "The Sugar Economy of Española in the Sixteenth Century." In *Tropical Babylons: Sugar and the Making of the Atlantic World, 1450–1680*, ed. Stuart B. Schwartz. Chapel Hill: University of North Carolina Press, 2004.

Rouse, Irving. *The Taínos: Rise and Decline of the People Who Greeted Columbus*. New Haven, CT: Yale University Press, 1992.

Rubio, Vicente. *Datos para la historia de los orígenes de la ciudad de Santo Domingo (Proceso Corvera-Roldán y Pasamonte-Roldán)*. Santo Domingo: Fundación García-Arévalo, 1978.

———. *Las casas morada del secretario Diego Caballero*. Santo Domingo: Fundación García-Arévalo, Inc., 1979.

Sarcina, Alberto. "Santa María de la Antigua del Darién: The Aftermath of Colonial Settlement." In *Material Encounters and Indigenous Transformations in the Colonial Americas*, ed. Corinne L. Hofman and Floris W. M. Keehnen, 175–196. Leiden: Brill, 2019.

Sauer, Carl O. *The Early Spanish Main*. Berkeley: University of California Press, 1966.

Scelle, Georges. *Histoire politique de la traite négriere aux Indies de Castille, contrats et traits d'assiento*. 2 vols. Paris: L. Larose and L. Tenin, 1906.

Sluyter, Andrew. "The Ecological Origins and Consequences of Cattle Ranching in Sixteenth-Century New Spain." *The Geographical Review* 86, no. 2 (April 1996): 161–177.

Stone, Erin. "America's First Slave Revolt: Indians and African Slaves in Española, 1500–1534." *Ethnohistory* 60, no. 2 (2013).

———. "War and Rescate: The Sixteenth-Century Circum-Caribbean Indigenous Slave Trade." In *The Spanish Caribbean & the Atlantic World in the Long Sixteenth Century*, ed. Ida Altman and David Wheat. Lincoln: University of Nebraska Press, 2019.

Sued Badillo, Jalil. *El Dorado Borincano: La economía de la conquista, 1510–1550*. San Juan: Ediciones Puerto, 2001.

Tibesar, Antonine S. "The Franciscan Province of the Holy Cross of Española, 1505–1559." *The Americas* 13, no. 4 (1957).

Townsend, Camilla. *Malintzin's Choices*. Albuquerque: University of New Mexico Press, 2006.

Turits, Richard Lee. "Slavery and the Pursuit of Freedom in 16th-Century Santo Domingo." *Oxford Research Encyclopedia of Latin American History*, September 30, 2019. https://doi.org/10.1093/acrefore/9780199366439.013.344.

Tyce, Spencer. "The Hispano-German Caribbean: South German Merchants and the Realities of European Consolidation, 1500–1540." In *The Spanish Caribbean & the Atlantic World in the Long Sixteenth Century*, ed. Ida Altman and David Wheat. Lincoln: University of Nebraska Press, 2019.

Utrera, Cipriano de. *Polémica de Enriquillo*. Santo Domingo: Editora del Caribe, 1973.

Valcárcel Rojas, Roberto. *Archaeology of Early Colonial Interaction at El Chorro de Maíta, Cuba*. Gainesville: University Press of Florida, 2016.

———. "Indigenous Material Culture in Indigenous Sites in Northeastern Cuba." In *Material Encounters and Indigenous Transformations in the Colonial Americas*, ed. Corinne L. Hofman and Floris W. M. Keehnen. Leiden: Brill, 2019.

Valcárcel Rojas, Roberto, Alice V. M. Samson, and Menno L. P. Hoogland. "Indo-Hispanic Dynamics: From Contact to Colonial Interaction in the Greater Antilles." *International Journal of Historical Archaeology* 17 (2013).

van Deusen, Nancy E. *Global Indios: The Indigenous Struggle for Justice in Sixteenth-Century Spain*. Durham, NC: Duke University Press, 2015.

Vassberg, David E. *Land and Society in Golden Age Castile*. New York: Cambridge University Press, 1984.

Wheat, David. *Atlantic Africa and the Spanish Caribbean, 1570–1640*. Chapel Hill: University of North Carolina Press, 2016.

Wilson, Samuel M. *Hispaniola: Caribbean Chiefdoms in the Age of Columbus*. Tuscaloosa: University of Alabama Press, 1990.

———, ed. *The Indigenous People of the Caribbean*. Gainesville: University Press of Florida, 1997.

Wright, Irene Aloha. *The Early History of Cuba, 1492–1586*. New York: Macmillan, 1916. Reprint, London: Forgotten Books, 2012.

———. *Spanish Documents Concerning English Voyages in the Caribbean, 1527–1568*. London, 1929.

Yaremko, Jason M. *Indigenous Passages to Cuba, 1515–1900*. Gainesville: University Press of Florida, 2016.

INDEX

Acebedo, doña Leonor de, 86
Africans, viii, 1, 4, 6, 10, 33–34, 35, 36, 46, 50–51, 66, 130; captive, 11; gender ratios of, 67, 96; illegal imports of, 90; trade in, 236n105. *See also* Blacks
Agramonte, Pero Martín de, 53–55, 58
agriculture, 2, 98, 142; commercial, 160; Indigenous, 16, 66, 160; small farms, 146–47, 152, 193. See also *estancias*; *ingenios*
Agüero, doña Catalina de, 81
Agüero, Francisco de, 49
Agüero, Jerónimo de, 18, 164–65
Aguiar, fray Amador, 112
Aguilar, Alonso de, 175
Aguilar, García de, 63, 167, 253n25
aje, 9, 64, 96, 160
alarife, 40. *See also* masons; stonecutters
Alba, Duque de, 18, 165
Alburquerque, Rodrigo de, 174
Alcántara, Diego de, 175
Alcántara, Order of, 13
Alegre, Francisco, 163
Alfaro, Juan de, 175, 255n68
almojarifazgo, 139, 145, 256n68
Alvarado, Diego de, 29
Álvarez Osorio, don Diego, 84–85
alzados, defined, 228n102
Ampies, Juan de, 133–34, 145, 170, 202
Anacaona, 69, 128, 189, 244n150
Andalucía, 10, 151, 170; cattle raising in, 249nn82–83

Andean region, 132, 149. *See also* Peru
Angulo, Dr. Gonzalo Pérez de, 159
Angulo, Pedro López de, 171, 254n51
Antequera, Spain, 28
appellate judges, xii, 19, 67, 90
Arango, Sancho de, 157–58, 181
archaeological evidence, 8, 12, 22, 33, 203, 217n28, 223nn108–9, 229n109, 246n15
areitos, 108, 128
arms, 54, 55–56, 65, 79, 82
Arriaga, Luis de, 28
Astorga, Benito de, 64, 127, 167, 206, 254n33; construction of *ingenio* of, 143–44; marriage of, 173–79, 255n62
Astorga, Spain, 174, 176, 177
Astudillo, Gaspar de, 90, 108, 181, 236n106, 257n85
Asunción. *See* Baracoa
Atlantic world, 4, 5, 6
audiencia
—of Lima, 195, 259n11
—of New Spain (second), 99, 124
—of Santo Domingo, xii, 31, 53, 71, 72, 73, 77, 78, 85, 86, 88, 95, 112, 123, 140, 171, 175, 181, 196, 200–201; establishment of, 19–20; judges of, 71, 76, 98, 104, 133–34, 177, 178, 194, 195; secretary of, 75; ties to royal court, 243n126
Ávila, Alonso de, 83, 114, 146
Ávila, doña Florencia de, 170
Ávila, Francisco de, 249n87

273

Ávila, Spain, 30, 165
Azores, 10, 95
Azua, Compostela de (Hispaniola), 22, 30, 58, 126, 142, 163

Bahamas, xi, 8, 11, 31, 46, 256n81
Bahoruco, mountains of (Hispaniola), 33, 58, 102, 148, 228n84
balsam, 29, 40, 148–49, 248n63; trade in, 248n67. *See also* Villasante, Antonio de
Baracoa (Asunción) (Cuba), 22, 77, 114, 172
Barba, Juan, 81, 82, 96
barbers, 38, 40, 165, 180. *See also* surgeons
Bardecí, Juan, 118, 253n21
Bardecí, Lope de, 30, 32, 118, 164–66, 167, 187, 236n106, 253n21, 253n25
Barrionuevo, Francisco de, 42, 108, 141, 184, 191, 195; recruitment for expedition to Hispaniola, 247n29
Basinina, Pedro Benito, 119
Basiniana, Esteban, 51
Bastidas, don Rodrigo de, 123, 151; as dean of the cathedral of Santo Domingo, 240n68; entail of, 163, 252n11
Bastidas, Rodrigo de (conqueror of Santa Marta), 32, 85, 90, 123, 194
Bayamo, 22, 109, 117, 186
beatas, 179
Becerra, Ana, 31–32, 222n107
Becerra, Francisco, 31
Behecchio, 69
behiques, 225n30
Beltriana, María de, 177
Berlanga, fray Tomás de, 177
Betanzos, Juan de, 93
bienes de difuntos, 91, 236n109
bishops, 37, 39, 99, 121–25, 130; of San Juan, 105, 114; of Santiago (Cuba), 110, 116, 183; of Santo Domingo, 47, 115; of Tierra Firme, 195. *See also* Bastidas, don Rodrigo de; Fuenmayor, don Alonso; Geraldini, Alessandro; Manso, don Alonso; Ramírez, fray Miguel; Ramírez de Fuenleal, Licenciado Sebastián; Sarmiento, fray Diego; Suárez de Deza, Pedro

Blacks, 2, 3, 4; children, 168, 169; communities of, 34; enslaved, 1, 3, 41, 46, 83–84, 85, 86, 89, 138, 168, 188, 194, 198, 254n33; on expeditions, 133, 196; illegal imports of, 90, 97; illness and death of, 50–51, 144; in *ingenios*, 50–51, 143, 144, 145; and labor in construction, 23, 26, 52; laws affecting, 95–97; maroon communities, 58, 141, 223n113; treaties with, 69, 205; marriages of, 96; in mines, 119, 123, 153, 157; mistreatment of, 62, 95–97, 105; numbers of, 125, 141; possible manumission of, 95–96; prices for, 251n118, 259n7; relationships with friars, 105; relations with Indians, 202; in revolt, 53, 55, 58, 62, 63, 69, 150; sales of, 50–51, 56; as settlers, 140; transatlantic trade in, 236n105; traveling with new migrants, 139; "trusted," 53, 58, 65; women, 83, 96, 184, 188–89. *See also* Africans; Christianization; labor
blacksmiths, 40, 142, 199
Bobadilla, doña Isabel de, 61, 187, 195
Bobadilla, Francisco de, xi, 12, 13, 27, 101
Bobadilla, fray Francisco de, 112
bohíos, 48, 83, 89, 102, 116, 147, 152, 155, 179, 204
Bolaños, Pedro de, 139
Bonao (Hispaniola), 30, 44, 138
books, 126, 203, 219n42
Bravo, Álvaro, 30
brazilwood, 134, 148
Bruselas, Gaspar de, 38–39
Bruselas, Jerónimo de, 89, 156
Buenaventura (Hispaniola), 22, 30, 38, 44, 77, 136, 138, 183; depopulation of, 146; Franciscan monastery of, 102; *fundición* in, 155

Caballero, Alonso, 90, 97
Caballero, Álvaro, 38, 76, 90, 97, 117, 135–36, 141, 148–49
Caballero, Diego (brother of Álvaro), 196
Caballero, Diego, "de la Cazalla" (*el mariscal*),

87, 90, 97, 202; relationship with Diego Caballero "de la Rosa," 235n91
Caballero, Diego, "de la Rosa" (secretary of the *audiencia*), 51, 55, 56, 75, 97–98, 119, 147, 164, 206; conflict with Gonzalo Fernández de Oviedo, 233n41; as *criado* of Bernardo Grimaldi, 236n103; *ingenio* of, 114, 142, 146, 245n11
Caballero, Hernando, 97
Caballero, Juan, 233n41
cabildos, 72–73, 76, 97, 152, 206; composition of, 242n100; of La Yaguana, 53; of Puerto del Príncipe, 77; of San Juan, 64, 80, 123; of Santiago, 77, 110; of Santo Domingo, 20, 58, 75, 78, 95, 112, 126–27, 133, 135, 146, 167, 181, 192, 196, 233n41
Cabo Verde, 6, 10, 51, 145
Cáceres, Alonso de, 79
Cáceres, Alonso de (Indigenous interpreter), 202
Cáceres, Isabel de, 195
cacicas, 23, 48, 68, 108, 189, 220n53, 226n54
cacicazgos, 9, 68
caciques, 3, 11,15, 23, 35, 62, 69, 190, 194, 250n93; education of sons of, 101–2, 108
cacona, 60, 106, 226n54
Caguas, 47
Calvillo, Juan, 185
Camagüey, 22
canafistula, 40, 142, 148–49, 248n67
Canary Islands, 5, 6, 10, 26, 27, 29, 45, 69, 117, 177, 190, 197, 198; conquest of, 66; seigneurial rule in, 231n6; settlers from, 138, 139
Cancer, Juan, 204
Cano, Juan, 125
Cano, Pedro, 125
canoes, 10
canons, 42, 75, 83, 103, 113, 117, 121
Caonabo, 189
Caparra (Puerto Rico), 22, 23, 44
Caribs, 8, 10, 35, 52, 63, 124
Carlos V. *See* Charles V (king)
carpenters, 24, 40, 95, 199

Cartagena de Indias, 159, 224n21
Carvajal, doña Juana de, 170
Casa de la Contratación (Seville), xi, 28, 29, 139
cassava. *See* yucca
Castañeda, Licenciado, 85, 133, 195
Castellanos, Juan 3, 42, 63, 78, 79, 90–91, 133, 140–41, 144, 152, 246n27
Castellón, doña Theodora, 50, 63
Castellón, Jácome, 159, 200
Castellón, Tomás de, 144, 159
Castile, 5, 14, 35, 37, 38, 43, 68, 78, 83, 108, 113, 119, 120, 129, 134, 144, 151, 167, 174, 175, 177, 193; women from, 162, 245–246n14
Castilla de Oro, 194, 195
Castillo, Juan del, 106
Castro, Bachiller Álvaro de, 59, 83–84, 88, 93–94, 105, 116, 138, 205–6; bequest of, 127; charges against, 242n106; ecclesiastical career of, 119–20; involvement in gold mining, 153–54, 158; relations with women, 166, 179–80
Castro, Baltasar de, 42, 109, 122, 155, 156, 202
Castro, Melchor de, 58, 62, 141, 143, 156, 175–78, 202
Castro Maldonado, Pedro, 156
Cataño, Rafael, 200
cathedrals, 99; of Concepción de la Vega, 42, 83, 105, 113, 114, 117, 119, 120, 124, 138, 152; of San Juan, 25; of Santiago de Cuba, 43, 116, 126
—of Santo Domingo, 24, 40, 83, 86, 87–88, 93, 94, 104, 105, 113, 115, 117, 118, 197, 221n67; *cabildo* of, 103, 124–25, 240n68, 242n100; donation to, 239n40
cattle, 18, 77, 78, 88, 91, 98, 130, 140, 141–42, 158, 159, 168, 175, 192, 193, 207, 223n113; export of cowhides, 141, 197, 201, 248n67; Iberian cattle raising, 249nn82–83; main discussion of, 149–53; ordinances regarding, 249n80. *See also* ranching
Ceballos, Francisco de, 32
Central America, 7, 46, 215n3

Cepeda, Licenciado, 53
Cerón, Juan, 110
Cerrato, Licenciado Juan López, 62, 93–94, 96, 130, 145
Cervantes, Licenciado, 75, 79
Chanca, Diego Álvarez, 37
chapels, 39, 110, 111, 115, 116, 129, 163
charity, 42
Charles V (king), 5, 11, 19, 20, 73, 92, 96, 102, 199
chiefdoms. See *cacicazgos*
Christianization: of Blacks, 104–5, 106–7, 131, 237n128; of Indians, 8, 42, 46, 92, 94, 95, 100–109, 113–14, 130
church, Roman Catholic, 8, 37; establishment of, 99–100, 109–16; relations with Indians and Blacks, 70. See also bishops; Christianization; churches; clergy; regular orders; schools
churches: establishment of parishes in rural areas, 114–15, 116; in Havana, 39; in La Mejorada, 116; in new settlements, 140; in Santiago, 110; in Santo Domingo, 63, 76. See also cathedrals; chapels
cimarrones, defined, 228n102. See also under Blacks (in revolt; maroon communities); Indians
clergy, 2, 13, 40, 66, 83, 87, 91, 203; chaplains, 170; salaries of, 113, 130; secular, 99, 105, 107, 109, 113–14, 117–25, 197; shortages of, 113–14, 131. See also bishops; Christianization; regular orders; schools
cofradías, 25, 41–42, 128
colegio, in Santo Domingo, 39–40, 126–27, 202
Colón, Bartolomé, 12, 13, 18; as *adelantado*, 21
Colón, Diego (brother of Columbus), 12, 13, 18
Colón, Diego (Indigenous interpreter), 35, 202
Colón, don Diego (second admiral), xi, 23, 24, 25, 28, 100, 101, 115, 118, 121, 162, 164, 165, 187; arrival of, 25, 27; death and burial of, xii, 19, 71, 219n49; as *encomendero*, 194; fleet of, 219n41; as governor, 18–19, 20–21, 37, 102, 105; revolt on estate of, 58, 69
Colón, don Luis (third admiral), 19, 20, 111, 115, 118, 127, 165, 170, 187, 193, 194, 196
Colón, Hernando (half brother of don Diego Colón), 18, 19, 194, 219n42
colonization schemes, 67, 138–41. See also Arriaga, Luis de
Columbus, xi, 1, 5, 7, 8, 10, 18, 37, 200, 206, 207, 251n130; burial of, 115, 219n49; and conversion of the Indians, 100; era of, 13–15, 20, 66; first voyage of, 11, 35, 108; fourth voyage of, 14; in Jamaica, 14; privileges of, 67; second voyage of, 11–12, 15, 27, 29, 36, 50, 129
Comerio, Juan, 47–48, 226n54
commons, 148, 151–53
commune, 74, 87, 147
Concepción de la Vega, 17, 18, 19, 22, 23, 30, 32, 38, 74, 84, 107, 162; cross in, 129; earthquake in, 64; Franciscan monastery in, 102, 137; *fundición* in, 155; population loss in, 136–37. See also cathedrals: of Concepción de la Vega
construction, 23–26, 40; in Concepción de la Vega, 137; of fortifications, 52; of *ingenios*, 143; of roads, 138. See also labor
Contreras, Rodrigo de, 195
convents, 104, 190; Dominican, 128; of Santa Clara, 127–28
conversion. See Christianization
copper: in Cuba, 153, 158–59; in Puerto Real, 251n119
Córdoba, fray Pedro de, 102
Coro (Venezuela), bishop of, 123
Corpus Christi, 115, 130
corruption, 71, 75, 79–82. See also crime; fraud
corsairs, 35, 52, 55, 56, 196
Cortés, Hernando, xii, 134, 135, 136
Cosa, Juan de la, 197
Council of the Indies, xii, 23, 24, 71, 102, 104, 125, 148, 199, 207
court, royal, 38, 68, 78, 174, 177; ties with *audiencia* in Santo Domingo, 243n126
cotton, 9, 148, 160

Cotuy. *See* La Mejorada
criados, 27, 28, 82, 83, 84, 85, 86, 87, 88, 122, 123, 255n61
crime, 82–89
crown, Spanish, 2, 5, 6, 8, 10, 24, 28, 29, 47, 53, 66, 68, 70, 72, 73, 74, 78, 91, 99, 127, 129, 130, 141, 194, 206–8; as *encomendero,* 231n2; providing loans for *ingenios,* 143–44; share of gold production, 157. *See also* Charles V (king); Fernando (king); Isabel (queen); Philip II (prince)
cuadrillas. See patrols
Cubagua, 93, 94, 117, 118, 159
Cuéllar, Cristóbal de, 89
Cuéllar, Diego de, 30, 79
Cueva, fray Juan de, 112
Curaçao, 133

Darién (Panama), xii, 20, 22, 220n54
de la Gama, Dr. Sebastián, 235n94
de la Gama, Licenciado Antonio, 79, 88, 124, 195, 259n7
defense, 52–57, 123. *See also* arms; fortifications
demography. *See* Indigenous people: demography and mortality of; population
Desecheo, island of, 149
Deule, fray Juan de la, 100–101
Deza, Cristóbal de, 83, 166, 180
Díaz, Bachiller Juan, 45, 117, 197
Díaz de Aux, Miguel, 21, 105, 110, 194, 195
disease, 35, 36, 40, 43–47, 51–52, 226n57. *See also* epidemics; Indigenous people: demography and mortality of; influenza; population; smallpox
Dominican Republic, 3
Dominicans, 16, 92, 99, 112, 168; arrival in Hispaniola, 102–3; church in Santo Domingo, 64; monastery in La Vega, Jamaica, 111; monastery in San Germán, 111, 133; monastery in Santo Domingo, 177, 178; proposed school in Seville, 108
dowries, 87, 126, 166

earthquakes, 64
Echegoyan, Licenciado, 104–5, 128
education. *See colegio,* in Santo Domingo; regular orders; schools; University of Santo Domingo
En Bas Saline (Haiti), 11
encomenderos, 68, 69, 70, 92, 105, 138, 160, 194–95
encomiendas, 1, 92–93, 207, 208; in Cuba, 49, 106, 133, 250n93, 252n2; establishment of, under Ovando, 15–16, 68; in Hispaniola, 49–50, 166, 167, 170, 191, 192, 257n91; in Puerto Rico, 47, 49, 97, 195. *See also* labor; Repartimiento of 1514; *repartimientos*
English, 6, 11, 200–201, 260n32
Enriquillo (Enrique): community of, 33; education with Franciscans, 102; revolt of, vii, xii, 3, 58–60, 69, 141, 184, 205; treaty with, xii, 58, 69, 103, 205
entradas. See expeditions
epidemics, 47, 48, 51, 226n57. *See also* disease; influenza; smallpox
Escobar, Alonso de, 112
Espinal, fray Alonso de, 101, 102
Espinosa, Licenciado, 25, 133, 140, 150
Espinosa, Luis de, 158
Espinosa, Pedro, 84
Esquivel, Juan de 20, 101
estancias, 51, 88, 89, 96–97, 106, 121, 146–47, 152, 153, 168, 204
estancieros, 41, 48, 96, 106, 134, 147, 152, 204
Europeans, 1, 3, 7–9, 12, 34, 35–36, 38, 45, 130, 132, 190, 199, 205, 223n5
evangelization. *See* Christianization
expeditions, 8, 33, 133, 134, 193, 196, 222n104
Extremadura, 17, 186, 220n65

farms. *See* agriculture; *estancias*
Fernández de Oviedo, Gonzalo, 15, 23, 36, 75, 90, 94–95, 128, 195, 200; in Darién, 22; entail of, 163, 252n11; as historian, 73; as *regidor* in Santo Domingo, 233n41
Fernando (king), 5, 13, 15, 17, 18, 19, 37–38, 67, 165, 199; concerns about conversion of Indians, 100, 101

fiestas, 128–30
Figueroa, Licenciado Rodrigo de, 28–29, 75, 78, 90, 175
fishing, 160, 251n130
fleets, 133
Florida, 7, 21, 32, 137, 194
forges, 155. See also *fundiciones*
Formicedo, Dr. Diego de, 38–39
fortifications, 36, 52, 220n60; *fortaleza* of Santo Domingo, 17, 18, 23, 200; forts in Hispaniola, 12, 216n13; in *ingenios*, 55, 142; in new settlements, 140
Franciscans, 49, 99, 100–102, 103, 127; churches of, 101, 110–11; monasteries of, 3, 63, 64, 102, 110, 122, 127, 163
fraud, 89–91, 157, 221n81
French, 52, 199; raids by, 54–56, 64, 123; war with, 228n92. See also corsairs
Frías, Licenciado, 85
Fuenmayor, Diego de, 195
Fuenmayor, don Alonso, 75, 78, 88, 99, 114, 121, 124–25, 195; appointed archbishop, 99
Fuentes, doña María de, 239n40
fundiciones, 17, 89, 121, 155–57, 255n63; of copper, 158; *fundidores*, 156, 158; overseers of, 17, 90

Gallego, Pedro, *mariscal*, 30, 63, 163
Garay, Francisco de, 18, 20, 23, 26, 30, 111, 219n41
García Caballero, Juan, 73, 185
Gasca, Licenciado Pedro de la, 195, 196, 259n11
Genoese, 6, 10, 199–200, 225n29; exporting slaves to the Caribbean, 236n105; merchants, 14, 51, 119, 159, 169, 236n103, 248n67
Geraldini, Alessandro, 25, 75
Germans, 6, 156; in copper mining, 158–59, 251n119; merchants, 11, 193
gold, 8, 9, 14, 92; figures on production of, 156; mining, 16, 21, 22, 25, 81, 98, 123, 132, 136, 142, 144, 147, 153–54, 173, 192, 197, 207, 250n94, 250n98; smelters, 89; smelting, 67. See also *fundiciones*

Gorjón, Hernando, 30, 39–40, 202, 247n34; bequest of, 115, 126–27, 142
government: absenteeism of officials, 78; municipal, 72–74; royal officials, 71–72, 74. See also *audiencia*; *cabildos*
Granada, Spain, 20, 71, 100
Grimaldi, Bernardo, 200, 236n103
Grimaldi, Jerónimo, 200
Guacanagarí, 11, 35
Guadalcanal, Spain, 170, 254n43
Guama, 60
Guerrero, Francisco, 109, 117
Guillén, Juan, 166
Gulf of Paria, 94
Gutiérrez, Pero, 86
Guzmán, Diego de, 228n84, 229n111
Guzmán, doña Guiomar de, 258n110
Guzmán, Gonzalo de (lieutenant governor of Cuba), 38, 60–62, 76, 80–82, 96, 106, 108, 122, 137, 145, 146; death of, 45; as *veedor de fundiciones*, 150
Guzmán, Gonzalo de (*vecino* of Hispaniola), 30, 166–68

Haiti, 11
hammocks, 251n128
Haro, Andrés de, 24, 46, 88, 113, 181, 259n7
Hatuey, 194
Havana, 39, 74, 117, 159; fortifications in, 52; French attack on, 55–56
Hernández, García, 181
Hernández, Luis de, 146, 167, 168, 174, 177
Hernández de Alfaro, Luis, 175, 176, 255n68
Hernandillo "el tuerto," 59
hidalgos, 26, 140
Hieronymites, xii, 78, 99, 100, 103, 104, 253n17; proposed reforms, 16, 67, 89
Higüey, 114, 142, 143, 150, 154, 189. See also Salvaleón de Higüey (Hispaniola)
hijos patrimoniales, 117
hogs, 33, 147, 150, 224n7
Hojacastro, Pedro de, 30
Holy Office. See Inquisition
Holy Sacrament, 63–64

INDEX

Honduras, 134, 193
hospitals, 45, 224n21; in Havana, 39; in San Juan, 25, 38; in Santiago, 39; in Santo Domingo, 39–40, 127–28, 202
hostages, 54, 56
House of Trade: San Juan, 24; Santo Domingo, 23, 24. See also *Casa de la Contratación* (Seville)
hurricanes, 35–36; in Hispaniola, 19, 111; in Puerto Rico, 48, 63–64
Hurtado, Lope de, 81–82, 96, 107, 108, 147, 155

Indians, 2, 3, 129; accused of murder, 88; children, 180; *cimarrones*, 59, 60, 62, 204, 229n107; communities of, 3, 17, 34, 46, 205; in Cuba, 109, 117; in *encomiendas*, 40, 49–50; enslaved, 8–9, 58, 81, 92–94, 105, 106, 124, 185, 194, 238n5, 256n81; as evangelizers, 103, 105–6; in experimental communities, 1, 2, 22, 33; freed, 13; impact of New Laws on, 93–95; and labor in construction, 23; in Puerto Rico, 47, 108–9, 113; recruited for expeditions, 33; in revolt, 173; sales of, 100; as servants, 39, 41, 85; treatment of, 96. See also *caciques*; Christianization; Enriquillo (Enrique); Indigenous people; labor; *naborías*; revolts
—women, 16, 22, 29, 42, 48, 54, 57, 68, 89, 92, 94, 100, 108, 119, 128, 158, 162, 168, 188–90, 202; in relationships with Spanish men, 181–86 (see also *cacicas*; marriages: between Spaniards and Indians)
Indigenous people, 1, 6, 7, 205; demography and mortality of, 4, 9, 12, 14, 17, 27, 34, 35, 43, 46–49, 68, 93, 109, 124, 130, 132, 169, 204, 218n35; migrations of, 215n1; in Puerto Rico, 48–49, 203–4; in slave trade, 32–33, 42, 46, 89–90, 150, 192, 193, 215n3, 222n104; testimony of, 2. See also Indians; population
Infante, Dr., 59
influenza, 36–37, 224n7
informaciones, 2, 167–69

ingenios, 31–32, 36, 51, 54, 136, 141–46, 192, 193, 199, 200; in Cuba, 145; in Hispaniola, 56, 77, 98, 114–15, 126, 143–44, 175, 178, 179, 230n183; in Jamaica, 145; loans for, 143–44; in Puerto Rico, 55, 63–64, 80, 105, 144, 152; water-powered mills for, 247n34
inns, 26, 83, 250n93
Inquisition, 45, 120, 122, 123, 140; staffing of, 243n117
interpreters: Indigenous, 35, 103, 108, 202; for Blacks, 53; Spanish, 134
Isabel (queen), 5, 8, 13, 15, 100, 198, 238n5
Italians, 11, 193. See also Genoese

Jardina, Inés de la, 163
Jews, 6, 28, 190
Jiménez de Cisneros, Cardinal, 5, 16, 231n5
judicial system, 76–77
just war, 8
Justiniano, Esteban, 51, 169

La Cartuja (Seville), 19, 241n86
La Isabela (Hispaniola), xi, 11–12, 21, 22, 207
La Margarita, 93, 94, 187
La Mejorada de Cotuy (Hispaniola), 22, 44, 59, 137–38, 140; gold mining in, 153–54
La Navidad (Hispaniola), xi, 11, 35
La Palma, 177, 197–98
La Yaguana (Hispaniola), 22, 26, 30, 53–55, 62, 117, 121, 195
labor: captive, 8; coerced, 33; for construction, 23, 52, 206; in gold mines, 36, 48, 67, 121, 153–54, 157–58; at hacienda de Toa, 48–49, 203–4; Indigenous, 15, 31, 33, 173; on sugar estates, 36, 104–5, 114, 142–43. See also Blacks; *encomiendas*; Indians; Indigenous people; *naborías*
labradores, 28, 114, 146, 147, 246n23
Lando, Francisco Manuel de, 29; as lieutenant governor of Puerto Rico, 79, 84; report on slaves and servants, 135
Lares de Guahaba, 22
Las Casas, Bartolomé de, 14, 15, 20, 92, 101, 102, 103

laws, affecting Black slaves, 95–97. *See also* Laws of Burgos; New Laws
Laws of Burgos, xii, 92, 102, 103, 105, 128, 160; amended, 92
Lebrón, Cristóbal, 119
Leeward Islands, 9
Lemba, Sebastián, 229n111
Lepe, Hernando de, 30–32, 152, 163–64, 202, 249n86
Lisbon, 10
Llerena, Alonso de, 86
López, Bachiller Diego, 43, 82, 105
López de Salcedo, Diego, 17, 18
Lovera, Juan de, 55
Lucayans, 8, 166, 180

Madeira, 10, 216n7
Maldonado, Juan, 157
Maldonado, Pedro Diez, 157
Manrique, doña Isabel de, 75, 187, 190
Manso, don Alonso, 105, 113, 114, 123, 133, 151, 243n117
Manzorro, doña Elvira, 42, 108, 184, 190, 257n91
Manzorro, Rodrigo, 42, 108, 217n17
Maraver, doña Isabel de, 164, 166–69, 187–88, 190
Marchena, Rodrigo de, 176, 256n70
Margarite, Mosen Pedro, 15
Marmolejo, Francisco, 184
Marques, Ana, 171
Marques, Antonio, 84, 120
marriages, 163, 171–80; between Spaniards and Indians, 67, 182–83, 202, 206
Martel, Diego, 201
Martín, Salvador, 164
Martinillo "el cristiano," 106
masons, 23, 24, 95, 168, 199
Matienzo, Juan Ortiz de, 19, 67, 90
Mayorga, Isabel de, 164, 173–79, 187
Mazariegos, Diego de, 94
Mazuelo, Pedro de, 44, 199
Medina, Diego de, 117

Medina, Leonor de, 96, 107, 108
Mejía, fray Pedro, 49
Meléndez, Abel, 177, 178
Méndez, Diego, 14, 217n26
Mendoza, don Antonio de, 135
Mendoza, Francisco de, 119
Mendoza, fray Antonio, 104
Mendoza, fray Domingo, 102
Mercedarians, 99, 103, 111–12, 137; church in Santo Domingo, 64, 73, 112; monastery in Santo Domingo, 112
merchants, 42, 51, 67, 75, 88, 90, 97, 155, 174, 176, 193, 198, 200–201, 219n41, 234n75, 255n63. *See also* Genoese; Germans; trade
Mesa, Francisco, 138
mestizas, 42, 108, 136, 168, 169, 170, 182, 184, 190, 191, 206, 245–46n14
mestizos, 53; children, 108, 182–87, 245n11; in Enrique's revolt, 58
Mexico, vii, xii, 5, 46, 132, 135, 170, 193, 197
migration, to the Caribbean, 27–29, 178, 222n91, 246n28. *See also under* women
military orders, 68. *See also* Alcántara, Order of; Santiago, Order of
militias, musters of: in San Juan, 56–57; in Santo Domingo, 56
Millán, Juan, 182–83, 190
miners, 134, 155–57, 158. *See also* copper; gold; salt
Mixton War, 135
Molina, Alonso de, 84, 249n86
Mona Island, 78, 105, 160, 239n33, 260n32
monasteries, 63. *See also* Dominicans; Franciscans; Mercedarians; regular orders
Montaño, Dr., 94
Montecristi, 62, 159, 246n24; Portuguese in, 199; settlement of, 138–40
Montesino, fray Antonio, xii, 102–3
Morales, Bachiller, 119
moriscos, 23, 190; affected by New Laws, 95; enslaved, 188, 193, 231n7, 258n111
Mosquera, Juan, 30, 50, 86, 90
Moya, Gonzalo de, 40, 118

INDEX   281

Moya, Luis de, 40, 118
Muriel, Diego, 47–48, 189, 203–4, 226n57
Muslims, 6, 28, 190

naborías, 1, 105–6, 167, 174, 183, 190, 194, 256n81
Narváez, Pánfilo de, xii, 20, 30, 32, 136, 137, 197
Native people. *See* Indigenous people
Navarra, 165
New Laws, 6; implementation in the Greater Antilles, 92–95, 120
New Spain, 93, 126, 133, 134, 135, 166, 172, 197. *See also* Mexico
Nicaragua, 112, 133, 134, 193
Niño, don Pedro, 156
Nombre de Dios (Panama), 133
notaries, 44, 77, 86–87, 235n87
Nuestra Señora de los Remedios (San Germán), 123
Nueva Galicia, 135
Nueva Sevilla (Jamaica), 23, 44, 115, 217n23
Núñez de Andrada, doña Isabel, 164–66, 167, 187
Núñez de Guzmán, Pedro, 81
nuns, 127–28

Ochoa, Pedro de, 41
Oribe, Juan, 147
Orihuela, Juan de, 78
Ovando, frey Nicolás de, xi, xii; fleet of 1502, 27, 30, 50, 101, 140, 167, 198, 217n21, 219n36; as governor, 13–18, 23, 28, 31, 39, 69, 89, 108, 129, 155, 173; military campaigns of, 58, 217n29
Ozama River, 17, 21, 44, 158, 216n13

Palacios Rubios, Juan de, 216n4
Palomo, Pedro, 119–21, 180, 235n78
Panama, xii, 20, 194, 195, 196
Pané, Ramón, 100–101
Pánuco, 150
Pasamonte, Esteban de, 85, 97, 173, 174, 176, 177, 256n72; *ingenio* of, 145

Pasamonte, Juana de, 32
Pasamonte, Miguel de, xi, 17, 97, 127,173, 202, 206, 219n46, 255nn60–61; as *encomendero*, 194–95; *ingenio* of, 145; as treasurer-general, 19, 32, 67, 78, 143, 167
patrols, 57–60, 173, 229n107
Paz, Pedro de, 78, 81, 172
pearls, 123, 132, 159, 194, 197; trade in, 42, 165, 197, 255n68, 256n70
Peña, Alonso de la, 95
Pérez Almazán, don Luis, 156
Pérez de Almazán, Hernán, 156
Pérez de Almazán, Pedro, 156
Pérez de Lugo, Luis, 80
Pérez Martel, Alonso, 79–80; *ingenio* of, 143, 144
personeros, 53, 72. See also *procuradores*
Peru, vii, 5, 30, 93, 113, 137, 173, 194, 195–96, 207
pesquisas, 207; of Columbus, 12, 15, 27, 217n17
pharmacists, 37, 38, 39, 40, 168
Philip II (prince), 5, 20, 94, 96
physicians, 37, 38, 39, 40, 224n21; salaries of, 224n15
pilots, 201, 257n83
Pimentel, doña Ana, 42
Pinzón, Vicente Yáñez, 15
Pizarro, Francisco, 17
Pizarro, Gonzalo, rebellion of, 30, 121, 196, 259n11
plants, medicinal, 10, 36, 40–41, 148–49, 197, 225n30. *See also* balsam; canafístula
Ponce, Juan, 80
Ponce de León, doña María, 84
Ponce de León, Hernán, 195
Ponce de León, Isabel, 195
Ponce de León, Juan, 23, 30, 44, 47, 123, 197, 200; children of, 234n61; death of, xii, 32, 194; made *adelantado* of Florida, 21; marriage of, 180–81
Ponce de León, Juan González, 197
Ponferrada, Hernando de, 177
population: depopulation, 132–34, 136–37, 145; figures, 135–38, 218n35; growth of

population (*continued*)
mixed populations, 136, 190, 205; growth of towns, 127–40; life expectancy for Europeans, 222n5; rural populations, 146. *See also* Indigenous people: demography and mortality
Porcallo de Figueroa, Vasco, 60–61, 74, 77, 87, 182
Portugal, 10, 145, 151, 199
Portuguese, 11, 193, 198–99; in Montecristi, 140, 199
procuradores, 72, 74, 80, 82, 90, 108, 113, 130, 155, 253n17
propios, municipal, 38, 77
Puerto del Príncipe (Cuba), 22, 60, 150, 181. *See also* Camagüey
Puerto Hermoso (Hispaniola), 159
Puerto Plata (Hispaniola), 32, 62, 222n104
Puerto Real (Hispaniola), 35

Quejo, Pedro de, 32
Quemado, Francisco, 126, 172, 224n8
Quesada, Bernaldino de, 25, 45 107, 183

Ramírez, don fray Miguel, 81, 111, 122, 125, 242n113
Ramírez de Fuenleal, Licenciado Sebastián, 99, 104, 123, 149, 154, 189
ranching, 151–52, 193; in Spain, 249nn82–83. *See also* cattle; *estancias*
Reconquista, 66, 161
reductions, 33, 46
regular orders, 16, 38, 100–102, 105, 110; education of Indigenous boys, 101, 102, 103. *See also* Dominicans; Franciscans; Hieronymites; Mercedarians; Trinitarians
Repartimiento of 1514, xii, 108, 166, 167, 218n33, 222n93, 255n61; *cacicas* in, 189; Spanish women in, 162
repartimientos, 15, 16, 17, 23, 28, 31, 33, 67, 133; in Jamaica, 240n52; reassignment of, 50, 81–82, 122, 218n32. See also *encomiendas*
Requirement (*Requerimiento*), 8–9

rescate, 218n32
residencias, 71, 75, 80, 88–89, 90, 91, 123, 188, 193, 207, 218n36; defined, 232n14
revolts: of Blacks in Hispaniola, 53, 58; Indigenous, 59–61, 195, 207; of Indigenous population in Puerto Rico, xii, 30, 57, 218n35. *See also* Enriquillo (Enrique)
Reyes Católicos, 27, 31, 89; conferral of title of, 100. *See also* Fernando (king); Isabel (queen)
Ribera, Ana de, 120
Río, Diego del, 115, 240n68, 241n84
Rojas, Juan de, 15
Rojas, Manuel de, 30, 60–61, 64, 71, 74, 76, 80–82, 110, 116, 133, 137, 150, 202; expenditures on patrols, 173; in Jamaica, 234n62; marriage and family of, 172–73; visit to Cuban towns, 181–82
Roldán, Bachiller Juan, 181
Romero, Pedro, 59
Ruano, Andrés, 106

Salamanca, University of, 123, 127
Salas, Beatriz de, 179–80
Salazar, Pedro de, 86–87
salt, 159, 200
Salvaleón de Higüey (Hispaniola), 20, 45, 114, 117, 137, 154, 162
Salvatierra de la Sabana (Hispaniola), 20, 30, 162
Sámano, Juan de, 125
Sámano, Licenciado Amador de, 125
San Germán (Puerto Rico), 22, 24, 38, 40, 49, 85, 88, 140, 149, 157, 184; French raids on, 64; *fundiciones* in, 155; *ingenios* near, 63–64, 144; parish in, 123; relocation of, 52
San Juan (Puerto Rico), 23, 24, 25, 26, 38, 39, 42, 47, 51, 76, 79–80, 140, 170, 171; establishment of, 44; *ingenios* near, 144; militia in, 56–57
San Juan de la Maguana (Hispaniola), 53, 57, 58, 62, 137, 159, 170, 190
San Martín, fray Tomás de, 119

INDEX

San Nicolás de Bari (hospital), 39, 40
San Pedro, Order of, 117
San Salvador (Cuba), 61. *See also* Bayamo
Sancti Spíritus (Cuba), 61, 87, 137, 147, 150, 182
Sanlúcar de Barrameda, Spain, 18, 87
Santa Bárbara (parish), 115
Santa Clara, Cristóbal de, 29, 89, 254n33
Santa María, xi, 11, 35, 207
Santa María del Puerto. *See* La Yaguana (Hispaniola)
Santa Marta, 134
Santa Olalla, Gonzalo de, 31, 51, 143–44
Santiago, Order of, 31, 126–27, 186, 202
Santiago (Cuba), 22, 26, 30, 38, 41, 43, 49, 61, 77, 82, 152, 157, 158; burning of, 64; conditions on *estancias* near, 96–97; copper mining near, 159; Franciscans in, 110; *fundiciones* in, 156
Santiago de los Caballeros (Hispaniola), 18, 120; earthquake in, 64
Santo Domingo, xi, 12, 13, 14, 18, 25, 26, 32, 38, 42, 85, 85–87, 93, 94, 127, 128, 130, 140, 160, 162, 169, 170, 175, 197, 201; founding of, 21, 22, 23; *fundición* in, 155; government in, 73–74, 97, 99–100; hospital in, 39–40; militia in, 56; moving of, 44; population of, 135–36
Santo Domingo, fray Bernardo de, 102
Sao Tomé, 10
Sarmiento, fray Diego, 110, 122
Sarmiento, Pedro, 51
schools, 125–28; in churches, 104; in convents, 104; for grammar (Latin), 104, 116, 118, 119, 126; in monasteries, 102–4; for theology, 119. *See also colegio*, in Santo Domingo; University of Santo Domingo
Seco, Sancho, 96, 106
Sedeño, Antonio, 184, 236n108
seminary. *See colegio*, in Santo Domingo
Sepúlveda, Licenciado, 177
Serrano, Licenciado, 50
Seville, Spain, 24, 28, 29, 41, 43, 78, 87, 97, 108, 119, 121, 139, 149, 159, 160, 170, 171, 172, 175, 175, 184, 197, 198; merchants of, 219n41

shrines, 129
slaves, 1, 41; branders (*marcadores*) of, 156 (see also *fundiciones*). *See also* Blacks: enslaved; Indians: enslaved; Indigenous people: slave trade in
smallpox, xii
Soria, Juan de, 186
Soto, Hernando de, 17, 32, 52, 61, 74, 81, 136, 195, 200
Sotomayor, don Cristóbal de, 30
South America, 7, 215n3
Spain, 5, 10, 12, 26, 28, 29, 31, 40, 42, 43, 82, 108, 201, 207, 208. *See also* Andalucía; Castile
Spaniards, 1, 2, 4, 6, 8, 23, 33, 37, 41–42, 66, 94, 108, 114, 129, 130, 132, 159, 182, 191, 205
stonecutters, 23, 24
Suárez, Bachiller, 101
Suárez, Catalina, 134–35, 245n8
Suárez de Deza, Pedro, 116, 120, 124
Suárez de Peralta, Juan, 29–30, 134–35, 245n8
sugar, 40, 130, 132, 141–42, 143–44, 145, 159, 197, 201; exported to Seville, 248n67. *See also ingenios*
suicide, among Indians, 36, 50
surgeons, 37–38, 40, 88
sweet potatoes. *See aje*

Taínos, 9, 216n5, 250n98
Tamayo, Andrés de, 163
Tamayo, Rodrigo de, 163
Tapia, Andrés de, 135
Tapia, Cristóbal de, 17
Tapia, Francisco de, 17, 40, 85, 201
Tarifeño, Juan, 75, 91, 124–25
Tastera, fray Jacobo de, 112
Tenochtitlan, 135
Tenorio, Rodrigo, 197
Tetzel, Johan, 158–59
Tiedra, Juan de, 170
Tiedra, Vasco de, 185
Tierra Firme, 20, 46, 84, 89–90, 103, 112, 117, 150, 184–85, 193, 194, 195, 197
Tisin, fray Juan de, 100–101

tithes, 39, 113, 115, 122, 139
Toa, hacienda de, 47–48, 105, 113, 189, 203–4, 226n54, 251n128; *ingenio* in, 143; Ribera de, 64
Toledo, doña María de, xi, 164, 169, 187, 206; arms presented, 56; arrival in Hispaniola, 18–19, 25, 27, 115; entourage of, 245n7
Toledo, Spain, 19, 31, 177, 222n105
Torre, Alonso de la, 90
Tostado, Francisco de, 145
trade, 2, 6, 26; factories, 10; transatlantic, 132, 159, 160, 174, 197, 207, 219n41. *See also* Africans; Blacks; Indigenous people; merchants
trapiches, 144
treasury, royal, 37, 38, 55, 89, 123, 134
Trejo, Francisco de, 86–87
Trinidad (Cuba), 41, 77, 133, 150; relocation of, 52, 61, 137, 182
Trinitarians, 104
Troche, Garcí, 64, 181, 234n61
Troche, Gaspar, 84
Troche, Vasco, 89

University of Santo Domingo, 127, 244n143

Vaca, Pedro, 42, 121–22
Vadillo, Licenciado Juan de, 41, 75, 80, 81, 88, 110, 190, 240n52
Vadillo, Pedro, 133, 134, 190
Valencia, Alonso de, 15
Valero, Juan, 117
Valladolid (Spain), xi, 14, 19, 20, 30
Vallejo, Luis de, 79–80
Vázquez, Licenciado Pero, 49
Vázquez de Ayllón, Lucas, xii, 19, 31–32, 50, 67, 79, 90, 165, 170, 202, 253n17; death of, 194; expedition to Florida, 32; participation in Indigenous slave trade, 222n104
Vázquez de Ayllón, Pero, 32; *información* of, 165

Velasco, Temiño de, 84
Velázquez, Ana, 163
Velázquez, Antonio, 107
Velázquez, Diego, 20, 80, 81, 82, 101, 134, 163, 194
Velázquez, Licenciado Sancho, 19, 88–89, 181, 188
Vélez de Mendoza, Alonso, 27–28
Venezuela, 11, 94, 159, 200
Veracruz, 172, 226n48
Verapaz, 3, 102
Verdejo, Cristóbal, 43, 172
Vidaguren, Pedro de, 56
Villalobos, doña Aldonza de, 187
Villalobos, Marcelo de, 19, 67, 75, 90, 187, 191
Villanueva, Asencio de, 140, 148, 157–58, 172
Villasante, Antonio de, 29, 50, 148–49, 202
Villasante, Blas de, 40, 47–48, 49, 55, 85, 157, 203–4
Villasante, doña Juana de, 40
Villasante, Juan de, 49
Villoria, Juan de, *ingenio* of, 142–43

white slaves. *See* Moriscos
Wolofs, 58, 63, 146, 247n47
women: rape of, 77, 82; Spanish, 75, 108, 119, 136, 156, 161–66, 180, 245–246n14; widows, 166–71, 188. *See also* Blacks: women; *cacicas*; Indians: women; marriage; *mestizas*

Xagua, bay of (Cuba), 160
Xaraguá, 13, 14, 23, 190; lake of, 159

Yaquimo (Hispaniola), 54
Yucatan, 85, 193
yucca, 9, 64, 96, 147, 196; grown commercially, 149, 160; processing of, 10, 48

Zuazo, Licenciado Alonso de, 58, 88, 89–90, 105, 133, 222n107

www.ingramcontent.com/pod-product-compliance
Lightning Source LLC
Chambersburg PA
CBHW021347300426
44114CB00012B/1115